ARTIFICIAL INTELLIGENCE PROGRAMMING

EUGENE CHARNIAK
Brown University

CHRISTOPHER K. RIESBECK
Yale University

DREW V. MCDERMOTT
Yale University

LEA LAWRENCE ERLBAUM ASSOCIATES, PUBLISHERS
1980 Hillsdale, New Jersey

Lawrence Erlbaum Associates, Inc., Publishers
365 Broadway
Hillsdale, New Jersey 07642

Library of Congress Cataloging in Publication Data

Charniak, Eugene.
Artificial intelligence programming.

Bibliography: p.
Includes indexes.
1. Artificial intelligence—Data processing.
2. LISP (Computer program language)
I. Riesbeck, Christopher K., joint author.
II. McDermott, Drew V., joint author.   III. Title.
Q336.C48   001.53'5'028542   79-22120
ISBN 0-89859-004-3

Printed in the United States of America

Contents

PART III: SAMPLE PROJECT

Preface

Artificial Intelligence (henceforth AI) is still a field where disagreement is more common than solid theory, and interesting ideas more common than polished programs. Yet there is slowly coming into being a small core of accepted (though not universally accepted) theory and practice. This book is an attempt to gather together the "practice" aspect of this "core" AI.

The practice of AI is, of course, the writing of programs. AI problems are usually ill-defined, and the theories proposed are often too complex and complicated to be verified by intuitive or formal arguments. Sometimes the only way to understand and evaluate a theory is to see what comes next. To find this out, and to check for obvious inconsistencies and contradictions, we write programs that are intended to reflect our theories. If these programs work, our theories are not proved, of course, but at least we gain some understanding of how they behave. When the programs don't work (or we find ourselves unable to program the theories at all), then we learn what we have yet to define or redefine.

With this emphasis on programming, it becomes important that an AI researcher have a wide library of programming tools available. This is particularly true because of the "level" problem; that is, your theory describes what to do at a fairly high level, but you need to tell the machine what to do at a low level. So a theory of, say, coherency in conversation will in all probability say nothing about pattern matching or efficient data retrieval. It is not that these topics are not worthy of their own theory. How people manage to retrieve knowledge efficiently under a wide variety of circumstances is a fascinating question; but if you are worried about conversation it is simply not your department.

The intent of this book is to give you a wide variety of commonly used tools for programming Artificial Intelligence theories: discrimination nets, agendas, deduction, data dependencies, backtracking, etc. By having these tools, we hope you will find that your programs better reflect your intentions.

Almost all the ideas that are described here are in common use, particularly at the larger Artificial Intelligence centers; but very few of them have ever been written down in one place. There are a number of books that introduce you to LISP (although none of them are completely satisfactory), and there are a number of books on theories and algorithms in Artificial Intelligence. Until now, however, there have been no books that fill in the middle ground and present the methods that all the old-timers know for getting from theory to practice. This is what this book is all about.

The major problem in writing a book such as this is that of selection. In some cases it is easy. It seems unlikely that anyone would seriously contest our inclusion of discrimination nets, pattern matching, or agendas. These techniques have been used by many researchers in the field and in a variety of problem areas—from natural language comprehension to problem solving to medical diagnosis. However, once one moves beyond this handful of topics, or even becomes specific about the type of pattern matching or agenda, then consensus is not so easy. So to some degree the selections made in this book are personal ones. Of course, to say they are personal is not to say they cannot be defended on scientific grounds but rather that the defense would take the form of an extended debate on the nature of AI and where it is going. For example, data dependencies receive a chapter to themselves here in spite of the fact that they are fairly new on the scene and hence relatively untested, at least compared to something like unification pattern matching. Naturally we try to show the usefulness of these ideas, but only to show how the ideas are motivated and not to defend particular approaches against competitors. Such a defense would be well worth having, but it would be out of place in a text such as this.

Selection also implies that some things are omitted, and there are at least two notable omissions from these chapters. One of these is inadvertent. The techniques discussed here all come from what might be thought of as "abstract" AI; that is, if we think of AI programs on a spectrum from "concrete" programs which must deal with the real world in terms of sound and light input (or sound and muscle output) to "abstract" programs which only deal with abstractions, the techniques described here fall most naturally toward the abstract end. This book does not have the space, and the authors do not have the expertise to do justice to the concrete end of things.

A second omission is quite deliberate. We have made no attempt to survey, much less teach, the many AI languages (CONNIVER, QA-4, KRL, etc.). This stems from our conviction that at present there is no commonly agreed-upon set of functions above the level of list processing, which everyone would agree is useful in a wide variety of AI settings. Experience has shown that each major project has found it necessary to build up its own tools, starting typically from LISP. We do not see this situation as likely to change in the foreseeable future; hence rather than covering the basics of the various languages we have tried instead to explain the techniques that typically lie behind these languages.

The book is divided into two parts. Since almost all serious programming in Artificial Intelligence is done in the language LISP, there are 10 chapters on how to improve your general abilities as a LISP programmer. Chapters 1 and 2 cover most of the basic LISP concepts needed for the rest of the book. We intend the introductory material to cover all the concepts of LISP needed later; but if you have never programmed in LISP before, we recommend that you spend some time writing simple LISP programs until you get a feel for the language.

The third through eighth chapters are concerned with the many features found (or implementable) in LISP that make the language an attractive one to use. Many of the ideas that pass under the rubric of "structured programming" are found here. Although LISP is almost as old as FORTRAN, it is surprisingly amenable to things like top-down programming and data types. Also, Chapters 3, 4, 5, and 9 define macros that are used throughout the rest of the book.

The first eight chapters of the second half of the book contain more advanced and complex techniques. Since this book is intended not just to be a description of ideas but also to give you a chance to learn the craft of Artificial Intelligence, we present actual LISP implementations of all the ideas discussed, along with exercises that modify and extend the code. These exercises are intended to make you familiar, in a practical hands-on way, with the techniques involved. We hope that the exercises will inspire you to experiment and learn on your own.

These chapters fall into several sequences. Chapters 11 and 14 deal with discrimination nets and data bases built with discrimination nets. Chapters 13 and 16 deal first with deduction and then with data dependencies used in deductive systems. Chapters 12, 17, and 18 deal with control structures of various sorts. In this last case, much of Chapter 18 may be read before Chapter 17. Only the last section of Chapter 18 uses the language SCHUM, defined in Chapter 17.

The last two chapters outline a programming project that, depending on how well we've succeeded, will lead you to use the methods we have described to develop a large, open-ended system. A reasonable start on the project should take about a month of work and is therefore suitable as a final term project in a one-semester course (a full-fledged version was a Ph.D. thesis).

This book is intended mainly for use as a textbook for an AI course in which programming is emphasized. This could be either an advanced or a fast elementary course. Any or all of the chapter sequences we described could be followed. The book might also be used as an auxiliary text for a systems course; for this purpose, the chapters on macros, structured programming, and alternative control structures would be most useful.

ACKNOWLEDGMENTS

This book is the outgrowth of a graduate course given by the authors for students in the Artificial Intelligence Project of the Yale Computer Science Department in the spring of 1978 at Yale University. We would like to acknowledge Roger Schank who originated the idea of the course. We'd also like to thank Dave Barstow and Walter Stutzman for their detailed comments on the complete manuscript, Laury Miller and Glen Edelson for their comments on the introductory chapters, and Jon Doyle for his comments on the chapter on data dependencies.

The Yale Artificial Intelligence Project is funded by the Advanced Research Projects Agency of the Department of Defense and the Office of Naval Research. During the writing of this book, Eugene Charniak and Christopher Riesbeck were supported by the Advanced Research Projects Agency monitored under the Office of Naval Research under contract N00014-75-C-1111.

EUGENE CHARNIAK
CHRISTOPHER K. RIESBECK
DREW V. MCDERMOTT

ADVANCED LISP
PROGRAMMING

1 LISP Review

LISP has jokingly been called "the most intelligent way to misuse a computer." I think that description is a great compliment because it transmits the full flavor of liberation: it has assisted a number of our most gifted fellow humans in thinking previously impossible thoughts [Dijkstra, 1972].

LISP was the world's first elegant language, in the sense that it provided a parsimonious base language with rich possibilities for extension. LISP has been applied mainly to problems of symbolic manipulation and artificial intelligence, partly because it is so easy to manipulate symbols in it and partly because AI programmers tend to be lazy and undisciplined, like pilots who refuse to file a flight plan before taking off: LISP's interactive structure allows you to get away with this.

The reader should note that LISP has not been standardized in the way that ALGOL and FORTRAN have been. In this book we use a dialect known as UCI-LISP (Meehan, 1978), which is an extended version of one of the most popular LISP dialects developed at Stanford University. We use very few features not found in all LISPS and point out the special cases that occur. Everything you need to know about LISP in general and about this dialect in particular is given in this and succeeding chapters.

1.1 DATA STRUCTURES

LISP data structures are called *S-expressions*. The S stands for *symbolic*. In this text, S-expression and expression will be used interchangeably. S-expressions are defined thus: An S-expression is

1. a NUMBER (e.g., 15)—a number consists of an optional plus or minus sign, followed by a digit, followed by zero or more digits.
2. a literal ATOM or SYMBOL (e.g., FOO)—a letter followed by zero or more letters or digits.
3. a STRING (e.g., "This is a string")—a double quote (") followed by zero or more characters, followed by another double quote.
4. a LIST of S-expressions (e.g., (A B) or (IS TALL (FATHER BILL))—a left parenthesis, followed by zero or more S-expressions, followed by a right parenthesis.

Unlike many other languages, parentheses are significant; that is, (A) is a list of one element that is the atom A. ((A)) is a list of one element which is in turn a list of one element which is the atom A. Notice also that the left and right parentheses must *balance;* that is, a well-formed S-expression will have a right parenthesis to close off each left parenthesis.

1.2 PROGRAM STRUCTURES

SYNTAX: The syntax of LISP is simple: *Every* S-expression is a *syntactically* legal program! That is, any given structure could be executed as a program. Most of them, however, will fail on semantic grounds.

SEMANTICS: The function that executes S-expressions (and hence defines the semantics of LISP) is called EVAL. EVAL takes one S-expression and returns another S-expression. The second expression is called the *value* of the first expression. We will notate this as "expression ⇒ value."

The rules for evaluation are fairly simple.

RULE 1: If the expression is a NUMBER, T, or NIL, then its value is itself. So 5 ⇒ 5.

RULE 2: If the expression is a LIST of the form

$$(function\ arg1 \ldots argK)$$

then the value is found by first evaluating each argument (*arg1* to *argK*) and then calling *function* with these values.

For example, the functions **PLUS** (for addition) and **TIMES** (for multiplication) are functions defined in LISP for doing arithmetic.

> (PLUS 15 2) ⇒ 17
> (TIMES 3 5) ⇒ 15
> (PLUS (TIMES 3 5) 2) ⇒ 17

Note that in order to evaluate the last expression, each argument had to be evaluated first. Since the first argument was a list (the one starting with **TIMES**), it had its own arguments to be evaluated (namely 3 and 5). The value of the **TIMES** was then added to 2, and the value of the addition was returned as the value of the **PLUS**.

RULE 3: If the expression is a LIST of the form

> *(reserved-word argl . . . argK)*

then the value depends completely on *reserved-word*. The arguments may or may not be evaluated.

A simple reserved word is **SETQ**. This is used for assigning values to atoms. (**SETQ** *atom expression*) causes *atom* to be "bound" (or "assigned") to the value of *expression*. The value of *expression* is returned as the value of the **SETQ**.
For example,

> (SETQ X (PLUS 15 1))

sets X to 16.

RULE 4: If the expression is an ATOM, then its value is the last value that has been assigned to it. If no value has been assigned, then an error results. So if X is bound to 16, X ⇒ 16.

STRINGs are treated like ATOMs, but they are rarely used in contexts where evaluation will occur. They are normally used only for printing, as we shall see later.
These four rules are employed by the LISP interpreter. The interpreter is a program that you run. You type an S-expression and it prints back another S-expression. This second S-expression is the value of the one you typed in. (If something goes wrong, an error message is printed instead of a value).
LISP programs are rarely compiled like ALGOL or FORTRAN programs; that is, you do not take a file of LISP text, convert it into internal machine code, and then run the machine code. Instead, you type LISP text to

the interpreter, which evaluates it and types the result back at you as more LISP text.

Although interpreting means that programs run slower, it also means that you always have your expressions available for inspection and modification during execution. LISP can support very powerful debugging and editing facilities for this reason.

The "top-level" loop of the LISP interpreter can be written in an ALGOL-like language as

```
BEGIN
LOOP: EXP : = READ ();
        VAL : = EVAL (EXP);
        PRINT (VAL);
        GO TO LOOP
    END;
```

This is usually referred to as the "READ-EVAL-PRINT" loop. All three functions are available to the user—that is, when you write a function using the LISP functions **READ**, **EVAL** or **PRINT**, you are calling the same machine code that the interpreter uses in the loop above.

The function **READ** reads one S-expression. It knows about balanced parentheses and that spaces terminate numbers and atoms.

The function **EVAL** applies the four rules of evaluation to the expression just read. It returns a new S-expression unless an error occurs, in which case an error message is printed.

The function **PRINT** prints one S-expression. Internally LISP stores everything as machine addresses, not as character strings. The functions **READ** and **PRINT** are responsible for converting from strings with letters, numbers, spaces, and parentheses into list structures and back again. This can be important.

For example, every time you type the name of a LISP function like **PLUS**, you want it to refer to the same internal machine code for doing addition. The function **READ** is responsible for taking the characters P, L, U, and S and converting them into a unique address reference. We will see shortly several other jobs that **READ** does.

The fact that the interpreter reads what you type and prints back its value explains why very few of the functions we will define will have any explicit input/output references. In LISP, almost everything is done by passing values between functions, including communication from the user to the interpreter and back.

Furthermore, in LISP, you do not define a "main program" with subroutines. Instead you define a set of functions. One of them may be the only one that you intend to call explicitly at the top level of LISP, but this does not rule out calling any of the others if you want. All functions are equal in the sight of the LISP interpreter.

Learning LISP is a matter of learning the reserved words and built-in functions, plus the appropriate programming techniques. A short list of the reserved words and functions needed for this book appears in the Appendix.

When we describe the various functions and reserved words, we need an informal notation for giving the syntax of the LISP expressions they are called with. The following conventions are used:

1. Any word in lowercase italics stands for an arbitrary LISP expression that can be substituted where the word appears. Usually the word will suggest what kind of expressions can be used (e.g., *atom* or *expression*).
2. Anything that begins and ends with a hyphen ("-") stands for zero or more occurrences of that thing, separated by spaces (e.g., *-atoms-*).
3. Anything else is exactly what should appear in the LISP expression.

Figure 1.1 contains an example of what a LISP expression looks like.

```
(PROG (SUM)
      (SETQ  SUM 0)
 LOOP (COND ((EQUAL N 0) (RETURN SUM))
            (T (SETQ SUM (PLUS SUM N))
               (SETQ N (DIFFERENCE N 1)))))
      (GO LOOP) )
```

FIG. 1.1. Sample LISP expression.

The LISP READ function ignores extra spaces and ends of lines. Therefore, you can (and should) break up expressions over several lines, with a great deal of indentation to set things off, in order to improve readability. Special printing functions exist that will do this for you automatically.

The expression in Fig. 1.1 adds up the integers from 1 to N. The reserved words used are PROG, SETQ, COND, RETURN, and GO. The functions used are EQUAL, PLUS, and DIFFERENCE.

PROG expressions are treated like BEGIN-END blocks in Algol. The first expression after the PROG symbol is a list of local variables. Local variables are assigned the atom NIL as their value when the PROG is entered. Their previous values are saved. When the evaluation of the PROG is finished, these previous values are restored and whatever values were assigned during the evaluation of the PROG are lost.

In this case, the only local variable is SUM. It will be set to NIL when the PROG is entered and unbound when it is exited.

The rest of the expressions in a PROG are statements or labels. If the expression is an atom, then it is a label for the next expression. Otherwise the expression is a statement. Only statements are executed in PROGs. Labels are never evaluated. In this case, the only label is LOOP. It labels the statement starting with (COND...).

After the local variables are bound, the statements of the PROG are evaluated in order. In this example, the SUM is first initialized to 0. Then there is a loop where SUM is augmented by N, and N is decreased by 1, until N is used up. This is brought about by using a conditional and a branching junction as in any other language.

The LISP conditional is a very elegant construct. Its format is given in Fig. 1.2. The *test1*s are evaluated in order until one evaluates to "true"; then the expressions following that test are evaluated. The value of the last is returned as the value of the whole COND. Thus, if *test1* returns true, then the expressions following it will be evaluated and the value of the last will be returned. If *test1* returns false, then *test2* will be evaluated, and so on.

> (COND (*test1* -*expressions*-)
> (*test2* -*expressions*-)
> ...
> (*testK* -*expressions*-))

FIG. 1.2.   Format of CONDITIONAL expressions.

"False" in LISP is represented by the literal atom NIL. "True" is represented in LISP by *anything* that is not NIL. Hence 1, FOO, and (A B C) are all instances of "true." The literal atom T is commonly used to represent "true" if no better expression is available. For example, (EQUAL N 0) returns T if N equals zero and NIL otherwise.

T and NIL are convenient to use because they are preassigned in LISP to have themselves as their values; that is, the value of T is T and the value of NIL is NIL. Since an expression is only evaluated once, no infinite loop results from having an expression evaluate to itself.

The last test in a COND is often just T. Since T is always "true" (non-NIL), this means that if the COND reaches the last branch, that branch will be taken. Thus the T serves the role of "else" in the conditional.

It may take awhile to become used to "true" being indicated by any non-NIL expression. Many predicates take advantage of this broad definition of "true" by returning something more useful than a mere T in the case where they succeed. See the definitions of MEMBER and SOME in the Appendix.

The other reserved words used in our example program are GO and RETURN.

> (GO *atom*)

causes control to pass to the statement of the current PROG that appears right after the label *atom*. LISP is very structured in its use of GO. You cannot jump into or out of a **PROG** form with a **GO**. **GO** can only be used to go back and forth within the current **PROG** body.

   (**RETURN** *expression*)

causes the evaluation of the **PROG** to finish, with the value of *expression* returned as the value of the **PROG**. If a **RETURN** were executed as the first expression of a **PROG**, then none of the other expressions in the **PROG** would ever be evaluated.

The only other way to leave a **PROG** besides using **RETURN** is to "fall off the end." Unless **GO** or **RETURN** is encountered, the interpreter evaluates the statements in a **PROG** in a sequential order. If it reaches the last one, then the **PROG** is finished and has the value **NIL**. (*Note:* In INTERLISP no value is defined for **PROG**s that fall off the end.)

You may have heard that LISP is a very strange language, but this example should demonstrate that it is fundamentally very conventional. Its syntax may take getting used to, but it has many advantages. By fully parenthesizing everything, we avoid having to write **BEGIN-END**s or **DO-OD**s. The tabular form of conditional means that there is no "dangling **ELSE**" problem and no need to insert clumsy **BEGIN**s and **END**s inside conditional clauses.

We have also seen that there are two ways to do a sequence of operations in LISP. We have just looked at the **PROG** that allows us to evaluate expressions in a linear sequence. Earlier we noted that because the evaluation procedure itself was recursive, evaluating the arguments of one function call could lead to evaluating other function calls.

For example, the normal LISP way of writing the **READ-EVAL-PRINT** loop of the LISP interpreter would be

```
(PROG ( )
   LOOP (PRINT (EVAL (READ)))
        (GO LOOP))
```

Notice that the evaluation is from outside to inside but that, in order to evaluate the **PRINT**, LISP first has to evaluate the **EVAL** and that, in order to evaluate the **EVAL**, LISP first has to evaluate the **READ**. Hence, the actual order of execution becomes **READ**, then **EVAL**, and finally **PRINT**.

1.3   PRIMITIVE OPERATIONS ON S-EXPRESSIONS

Our **PROG** example operated on numbers the way any other language would. LISP is, however, mainly for performing symbolic manipulations. Its most important functions are those that apply to symbolic expressions.

Two central functions are **CAR** and **CDR**. **CAR** takes a list and returns the first element of that list. **CDR** takes a list and returns the rest of the list minus the first element. In some other languages having list structures, CAR and CDR are called HEAD and TAIL, respectively.

With CAR and CDR we can reach *any* subpart of a list structure. For example, by taking the CDR of a list, followed by the CAR of the result, we obtain the second element of the original list. By taking two CDRs and then a CAR, we find the third element, and so on.

Assume we have the list (A B C). We immediately run into a problem if we try to apply CAR or CDR to this list. Suppose we try writing the following:

(CAR (A B C))

Compare this with the form

(PLUS (TIMES 3 5) 2)

Remember that in evaluating the PLUS expression, LISP first evaluated the TIMES subexpression. The same thing will happen with the CAR expression. LISP will first try to evaluate the subexpression (A B C). LISP assumes that any atom at the head of a list that is not known to be reserved word must be a function. Therefore, by Rule 2, it will try to apply the function A to the values of the atoms B and C. This is not what we want. We want (A B C) to be left alone.

To do this, we use the reserved word QUOTE. QUOTE returns its one argument unevaluated; that is,

(QUOTE *expression*) ⇒ *expression*

Since QUOTE turns out to be a very commonly needed function, most LISPs provide an abbreviation. An expression of the form '*exp* is transformed by the function READ into (QUOTE *exp*). Thus to obtain the list (A B C) we can use either

(QUOTE (A B C))

or

'(A B C)

To obtain pieces of this list, we write

(CAR (QUOTE (A B C))) ⇒ A
(CDR (QUOTE (A B C))) ⇒ (B C)
(CAR (CDR (QUOTE (A B C)))) ⇒ B

What happens if we take the CDR of a list of one element? Watch!

(CDR (QUOTE (A))) ⇒ ()

The CDR of a list that has one element is the empty list, which reasonably enough is written (). In LISP the empty list () is identified with the atom NIL. Thus NIL stands for the empty list as well as "false."

```
(PROG (SUM)
      (SETQ  SUM 0)
LOOP  (COND ((EQUAL L NIL) (RETURN SUM))
            (T
             (SETQ SUM (PLUS SUM (CAR L)))
             (SETQ L (CDR L))))
      (GO LOOP) )
```

FIG. 1.3. Expression to sum a list of numbers.

Given **CAR** and **CDR**, we can write a **PROG** expression, analogous to our first one, that sums up the numbers in a list L of numbers (see Fig. 1.3).

If L were assigned the value ' (1 2 3 4), then the expression above would return the value **10**.

So far we have seen how we can decompose a list using **CAR** and **CDR**. Of course, lists have to be built up as well as taken apart. To build them, we use the function **CONS**. (**CONS** *x 1*) creates a new list with *x* as the first element followed by the elements of *1*.

For example,

(CONS (QUOTE A) (QUOTE (B C))) ⇒ (A B C)
(CONS (QUOTE B) NIL) ⇒ (B)

What happens if we **CONS** an atom onto another atom (besides **NIL**, which represents the empty list)?

(CONS 'A 'B) ⇒ (A . B)

This is called a *dotted pair*. Dotted pairs are actually the fundamental data structures of LISP, but we will delay describing them until later, in Section 1.9, "Inside LISP".

Note that for any nonempty list *list,* the following identity holds

(CONS (CAR *list*) (CDR *list*)) = *list*

There are two other very handy functions for building lists: **APPEND** and **LIST**. APPEND takes two or more arguments, all of which should be lists, and returns a list built from the elements of each list. For example,

(APPEND '(A B) '(C D)) ⇒ (A B C D)
(APPEND '(A) '(B (C))) ⇒ (A B (C))
(APPEND '(A B) NIL) ⇒ (A B)

LIST takes one or more arguments and makes a list with them as elements. Thus

(LIST 'A 'B 'C 'D)   ⇒ (A B C D)
(LIST '(A B) '(C D))⇒ ((A B) (C D))
(LIST '(A B) NIL)   ⇒ ((A B) NIL)

1.4   TREE STRUCTURES

We now explore several common cases involving the decomposition and rebuilding of LISP data structures.

Consider the class of LISP arithmetic expressions:

1. A number is an arithmetic expression.
2. If *exp1* and *exp2* are arithmetic expressions, then (PLUS *exp1 exp2*) is an arithmetic expression.
3. If *exp1* and *exp2* are arithmetic expressions, then (TIMES *exp1 exp2*) is an arithmetic expression.

Now suppose we wanted a function that would compute the value of an arbitrary arithmetic expression. We define a new LISP function COMPUTE to do this. It will take a LISP arithmetic expression and compute its value. Obviously, COMPUTE is one part of the general EVAL function.

A definition of COMPUTE is given in Fig. 1.4. The LISP function NUMBERP returns T if and only if its one argument is a number.

```
(DE COMPUTE (AE)
  (COND ((NUMBERP AE) AE)
        ((EQUAL (CAR AE) 'PLUS)
          (PLUS (COMPUTE (CAR (CDR AE)))
                (COMPUTE  (CAR (CDR (CDR AE)))))))
        ((EQUAL(CAR AE) 'TIMES)
          (TIMES (COMPUTE (CAR (CDR AE)))
                 (COMPUTE (CAR (CDR (CDR AE)))))))))
```

FIG. 1.4.   Function to evaluate LISP arithmetic expressions.

The reserved word DE is used to define new functions. In this case, we are defining a function COMPUTE of one argument. The atom AE will be bound to that argument when the function is entered. The rest of the definition is an expression giving the value of COMPUTE. This expression is a COND.

In general the reserved word DE is written

(DE *function* (-*atoms-*) -*expressions-*)

which defines *function* as a function with the atoms as local (also called *formal*) variables and a function body made up of the expressions. The value of *function* when called with a set of arguments is found by binding the values of the arguments to the local variables, evaluating the expressions of the function body in order, and returning the value of the last expression evaluated.

In the definition of COMPUTE, notice that each clause of the COND mirrors exactly a clause of the recursive definition of "arithmetic expression."

The first clause tests whether AE is a number. If it is, then the value of the arithmetic expression is just that number.

The second clause checks the CAR of the expression to see if it is a PLUS. If it is, then the value of the whole expression is the sum of the values COMPUTEd for the two subexpressions: (CAR (CDR AE)), which is the second element of AE, and (CAR (CDR (CDR AE))), which is the third.

TIMES is handled like PLUS except that the two subexpression values are multiplied.

At this point it becomes relevant to introduce two more abbreviations. It is somewhat tiresome to have to write (CAR (CDR (CDR...))), so LISP allows you to abbreviate such expressions by just writing (CADDR ...). In general, C$xxxx$R may be used, where the x's are replaced with A's and D's. (In most implementations, at most four A's and D's may be written.)

Furthermore, as you can see, the number of parentheses left to close off at the end of an expression can become quite large (eight in this case). To simplify things, the LISP READ function treats a right square bracket (]) as a "super-parenthesis." That means that a right square bracket is converted by READ into as many right parentheses as there are unbalanced left parentheses. Many of our function definitions in this text are terminated with a right square bracket, indicating that the expression is finished. The use of square brackets is never required however. They are merely a convenience.

Notational matters aside, the real topic here is recursion. Many people have trouble grasping recursion at first. It helps to realize that most applications of it are to recursively defined data structures that are to be decomposed. If you can grasp the data-structure definition, the program to operate on it will be clear. (Consider trying to write COMPUTE without using recursion.)

This example is also a demonstration of how easy it is to write language interpreters in LISP. In this case, of course, the language being defined is a subset of LISP itself, but this need not always be the case. It is not uncommon in LISP to have programs that operate on other LISP programs, as we shall see.

1.5   LISTS

We can formally define the notion of a *list* as follows:

1. NIL is a list.
2. If *expression* is an expression and *list* is a list, then the result of (CONS *expression list*) is a list.

Since this is a recursive definition, it is natural to think of using recursion when doing operations on lists. For example, Fig. 1.5 defines the function

```
(DE SQUARE-LIST (L)
(COND   ((NULL L)   NIL)
        (T (CONS   (SQUARE (CAR L))
                   (SQUARE-LIST (CDR L))))   ))

(DE SQUARE (N) (TIMES N N)   )
```

FIG. 1.5.   Function to square a list of numbers.

SQUARE-LIST, which takes a list of numbers and returns a list of their squares. The function (NULL *expression*) is equivalent to (EQUAL *expression* NIL).

In order to SQUARE-LIST a list, the first element is squared and put on the front of the list obtained by applying SQUARE-LIST to the rest of the list. For example, (SQUARE-LIST '(2 3)) leads to the following chain of evaluation:

```
(SQUARE-LIST '(2 3))
= (CONS (SQUARE 2) (SQUARE-LIST '(3)))
= (CONS 4 (CONS (SQUARE 3) (SQUARE-LIST NIL)))
= (CONS 4 (CONS 9 NIL))
⇒ (4 9)
```

In the definition of SQUARE-LIST, there is one COND clause for each clause of the recursive definition of lists. If L is empty, then the list of its squares is empty, too. Otherwise, the list of squares is obtained by CONSing the square of the first element onto the squares of the rest of the elements.

The function SQUARE-LIST takes a list and transforms it into a list of equal length. It is just as easy to write a function that selects some elements and ignore others, thereby returning a list that is longer or shorter than the input list.

For example, Fig. 1.6 defines SORT-LIST, which takes a list of positive and negative numbers and returns a list of the square roots of the nonnegative elements of the list.

This function has one test for the empty list and three COND clauses for the recursive part of the list definition. If the CAR of L is less than zero, we skip

```
(DE SQRT-LIST (L)
(COND   ((NULL L) NIL)
        ((LESSP (CAR L) 0) (SQRT-LIST (CDR L)))
        ((EQUAL (CAR L) 0)
         (CONS 0   (SQRT-LIST (CDR L))))
        (T (CONS   (SQRT   (CAR L))
                   (CONS   (MINUS (SQRT (CAR L)))
                           (SQRT-LIST (CDR L))))))   ))
```

FIG. 1.6.   Function to square-root a list of numbers.

over it by just taking SQRT-LIST of the CDR. If it's zero exactly, we CONS a zero onto the remaining square roots. If it's positive, we have to include both the positive and negative roots. Thus one input list element can lead to zero, one, or two output elements. For example,

(SQRT-LIST ' (–9 0 4 –25)) ⇒ (0 2 –2)

As an example of another list-building function, we shall define the function REVERSE. (REVERSE *list*) returns a list of the elements of *list* backward. It already exists in LISP, but it is instructive to define it ourselves. One way of defining it is given in Fig. 1.7.

```
(DE REVERSE (L)
 (PROG (RESULT)
  LOOP (COND   ((NULL L) (RETURN RESULT))
              (T
               (SETQ RESULT (CONS (CAR L) RESULT))
               (SETQ L (CDR L)))   )
      (GO LOOP)   ))
```

FIG. 1.7.   Function to reverse a list.

Notice how in an iterative loop that the function CONS naturally builds a list backward.

Notice also that three ways of binding values to atoms are employed. First, L is the formal variable of the function and is bound to whatever list REVERSE is applied to. Second, RESULT is the local variable of the PROG and is bound to NIL initially. Third, during the loop both RESULT and L are explicitly assigned new values with the reserved word SETQ.

Both L and RESULT are local to the function REVERSE; that is, they are unaffected by and do not affect the values of L and RESULT in any other function or expression. It is a matter of good programming practice to make sure that all the variables used in a function are local, if at all possible, in order to avoid unexpected interferences between functions.

1.6   MAPPING FUNCTIONS

The control structure of SQUARE-LIST is so common that LISP provides facilities for doing it more directly. We do this with the function MAPCAR:

(DE SQUARE-LIST (L) (MAPCAR 'SQUARE L))

MAPCAR is a *mapping* function. It takes two arguments, a function and a list, and returns a new list consisting of the values of the function applied to the old elements.

```
(DE MAPCAR (F L)
(COND   ((NULL L) NIL)
         (T (CONS (APPLY F (LIST (CAR L)))
                  (MAPCAR F (CDR L))))   ))
```

FIG. 1.8.   Definition of MAPCAR.

MAPCAR could be defined as in Fig. 1.8.

Notice that the argument **SQUARE** to **MAPCAR** must be quoted. We are passing the name of a function for **MAPCAR** to use.

The function **APPLY** takes two arguments—a function and a list of expressions—and it evaluates the function with those arguments. We use the function **LIST** to make a list of expressions. **LIST** takes an arbitrary number of arguments and makes a list out of them. In this case we gave it one argument, so we obtain a one-element list in return.

For example,

```
(APPLY 'CONS (LIST 'A NIL))
     = (CONS 'A NIL)
     ⇒ (A)
```

In general

```
(APPLY for (LIST -expressions-))
= (value-of-fn -expressions-))
```

There are other mapping functions: **MAPC, MAPCAN, EVERY, SOME,** and **SUBSET**. See the Appendix for their definitions. In our LISP, **MAPCAR, MAPCAN,** and **MAPC** actually can take several list arguments, if their first argument is a function that can take more than one argument. In such cases, there must be as many lists as there are arguments to the function, and the function will be applied to tuples made up of corresponding elements from each list, until one of the lists is exhausted. For example,

```
(MAPCAR 'CONS '(A B) '(C D))
     ⇒ ((A . C)) (B . D))
```

1.7   LAMBDA EXPRESSIONS

Suppose we want to take a list of numbers and output a new list of the same length, consisting of the atoms **POS, NEG,** or **ZERO,** such that **POS** appears in the positions corresponding to positive numbers, **NEG** in those for negative numbers, and **ZERO** for the zeros. The code in Fig. 1.9 would do this.

The function **SYM-SIGN** will probably never be used anywhere else, however. It would be more reasonable if we could write the code for it directly

```
(DE SYM-SIGN (N)
    (COND  ((LESSP N 0) 'NEG)
           ((EQUAL N 0) 'ZERO)
           ((GREATERP N 0) 'POS)    ))
(MAPCAR 'SYM-SIGN L)
```

FIG. 1.9.   Example of mapping a function.

```
(MAPCAR '(LAMBDA (N)
            (COND  ((LESSP N 0) 'NEG)
                   ((EQUAL N 0) 'ZERO)
                   ((GREATERP N 0) 'POS)))
         L)
```

FIG. 1.10.   Example of mapping a LAMBDA body.

in the **MAPCAR** expression, without having to make up a name. In fact, we can do this, as shown in Fig. 1.10.

The general construct, called a *function constant* or *LAMBDA body* is

(LAMBDA (-*atoms-*) -*expressions-*)

It is a function without a name. When called, it is evaluated just like a function, by first binding the atoms (i.e., the local variables) to the arguments and then evaluating the expressions in the body of the **LAMBDA**.

Although most useful inside mapping functions, **LAMBDA** forms can be used anywhere a function can. So we could write

**((LAMBDA) (X) (PLUS X (QUOTIENT 1 X)))
(PLUS (SQUARE A) (SQUARE B)))**

which is equivalent to

**(PLUS (PLUS (SQUARE A) (SQUARE B))
       (QUOTIENT 1 (PLUS (SQUARE A) (SQUARE B))))**

except that we avoid computing A-squared plus B-squared twice by assigning it to the local variable X. Using LAMBDAs to obtain local variables to avoid extra calculations is a handy technique that will be discussed further in Chapter 3 on macros and read macros.

1.8   ATOMS

Numbers and literal atoms together are primitive in that for most purposes they have no internal structure such as lists do, and they each have their own particular set of basic operators.

With numbers there are the various arithmetic functions such as **PLUS** and **TIMES** and the ordering functions such as **GREATERP** and **LESSP**. With literal atoms there is a set of functions for attaching information to them. This is important and useful because literal atoms have one very useful property— each atom name that you type refers to one unique data structure. Once information is attached to an atom, you can find it easily by giving the atom's name. For example, once you have attached a function definition to the atom **SQUARE-LIST**, you can access and use that definition whenever you want just by using the name **SQUARE-LIST**.

Another thing we can attach to atoms is a value. There are two functions for doing this: **SETQ** and **SET**. We have already seen **SETQ** in use. For example, by saying (SETQ X 1) we attach the value 1 to the atom **X**. **SET** is like **SETQ** except that it is not a reserved word, so its first argument is evaluated. Thus

```
(SETQ X 'Y)  ⇒ Y
(SET X 1)    ⇒ 1
Y            ⇒ 1
```

That is, (SET X 1) changed the value of the atom that was the value of **X**. If **X** had not been set to an atom, an error would have occurred.

Besides values and function definitions, we can attach almost anything we desire to atoms. For example, suppose we wanted to store the fact that dogs have four legs. We could do this by writing

```
(PUTPROP 'DOG 4 'LEGS)
```

The atom **DOG** now has a *property* called **LEGS** with the *value* 4. This information can be retrieved whenever we want it by writing

```
(GET 'DOG 'LEGS) ⇒ 4
```

If we wanted to remove this property, we would write

```
(REMPROP 'DOG 'LEGS)
```

The reserved word **DEFPROP** is like **PUTPROP**, but you don't have to quote the arguments. Thus, to record the fact that dogs have four legs, we could have written

```
(DEFPROP DOG 4 LEGS)
```

The LISP interpreter itself has to keep information about various atoms available, such as the character string to use when reading or printing the atom, its value (if any), and its function definition (if any). Not surprisingly, many LISPs (including ours) use **GET** and **PUTPROP** to store this information. In our LISP, the print name is stored under the property **PNAME**. Compiled function definitions (which includes most of the built-in LISP functions) are stored under the **SUBR** indicator. Compiled reserved word definitions are stored under **FSUBR**.

Functions defined with **DE** are stored under **EXPR** as **LAMBDA** bodies. For example,

(DE SQUARE-LIST (L) (MAPCAR 'SQUARE L]

is equivalent to (but more convenient than)

(PUTPROP 'SQUARE-LIST
'(LAMBDA (L) (MAPCAR 'SQUARE L))
'EXPR)

One final note: In our LISP, the **CDR** of an atom is its property list (i.e., the list of all the properties that an atom has) and the values of those properties. The structure of an atom's property list is *STRANGE!*

(property-1 value-1 property-2 value-2...)

1.9 INSIDE LISP

Until now we have avoided saying anything about how LISP actually represents lists inside the machine. To some extent we never have to worry about how LISP really does it, but we need to describe an abstract data structure that is actually quite close to the real thing.

This abstract data structure is called a *dotted pair* or sometimes a *CONS cell*. A dotted pair is a pair of *pointers*. A pointer is either the null pointer (i.e., it is a pointer to **NIL**) or it is a "link" to another dotted pair or an atom. The first pointer is called the **CAR** of the pair and the second is called the **CDR**.

There are two ways commonly used to write a dotted pair. First there is a graphical notation. Graphically a dotted pair is written as a rectangle divided into a left and a right box. The null pointer is written as a diagonal slash in the appropriate box of the rectangle. An atom is written by putting its name in the appropriate box. A pointer is written by drawing an arrow from the appropriate box to the next dotted pair. A dotted pair whose **CAR** points to a dotted pair of the atoms **A** and **B** and whose **CDR** is the null pointer is drawn in Fig. 1.11.

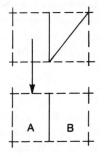

FIG. 1.11. Graphic notation for a dotted pair structure.

The LISP notation for dotted pairs is to write a left parenthesis, followed by the LISP notation for the data structure pointed to by the CAR, followed by a period, followed by the LISP notation for the data structure pointed to by the CDR, followed by a right parenthesis. The null pointer is written with NIL and atoms are written with their names.

Thus the graphical structure above is written as

((A . B) . NIL)

A list is a special case of dotted pair structure. A list is either

1. the null pointer or
2. a dotted pair whose CAR is an expression and whose CDR is a list.

Compare this data structure definition with the CONS procedure one given in Section 1.5, "Lists."

Thus the following are lists:

NIL
(A . NIL)
(NIL . NIL)
(A . (B . NIL))
((A . NIL) . NIL)
((A . NIL) . (B . NIL))

but the following are not:

A
(A . B)
(NIL . A)
(A . (B . C))
((A . NIL) . B)
((A . B) . (C . D))

Even though they are more restricted, lists are much more commonly used in LISP than nonlists. Almost anything that can be represented with dotted pairs can be represented with lists, although some extra space may be wasted, to hold the extra NILs. And many functions, such as the mapping functions, require that their arguments be lists. For example, the following expression will not work correctly because the second argument of the MAPCAR is not a list.

(MAPCAR 'PRINT '(A . B))

Since lists are commonly used but they look ugly in dot notation, LISP uses a different system, called *list notation,* which includes dot notation as a special case. It is the notation we have been using all along in this chapter.

The algorithm for writing a dotted pair structure in list notation is:

1. Set a pointer Q to the beginning of the dotted pair structure and write a left parenthesis.
2. Write the list notation for the data structure pointed to by the CAR of Q and reset Q to the CDR of Q.
3. If Q is now the null pointer, then write a right parenthesis; otherwise, write a space, and if Q is an atom, write a period, a space, Q's name, and a right parenthesis; otherwise write a space and go to step 2.

List notation in general is a lot easier to read than the equivalent dotted pair notation.

(A . NIL)	= (A)
(A . B)	= (A . B)
(NIL . NIL)	= (NIL)
(A . (B . NIL))	= (A B)
((A . NIL) . NIL)	= ((A))
((A . NIL) . (B . NIL))	= ((A) B)
(A . (B . C))	= (A B . C)

Exercise 1.1 Define the function DOT-PRINT that will take an arbitrary S-expression, and print it in dot notation. Use the expression (PRINC '"(") to print a left parenthesis, (PRINC ' " ") to print a space, (PRINC '".") to print a period, (PRINC '")") to print a right parenthesis, and (PRIN1 *atom*) to print the atomic expression *atom*. These functions will be described in Chapter 6.

Exercise 1.2 Define the function LIST-PRINT that will take a dotted pair and print it in standard LISP list notation. Use the same printing expressions as given for DOT-PRINT.

There exist two very basic LISP functions for altering the CARs and CDRs of a dotted pair. (RPLACA X Y) replaces the CAR of the dotted pair X with Y, whereas (RPLACD X Y) replaces the CDR of X with Y. For example,

    (RPLACA '(A . B) 'C)   ⇒ (C . B)
    (RPLACD '(A . B) 'C)   ⇒ (A . C)

These two functions, unlike the others we have described in this chapter, actually change internal pointers. This means that their effects are global and permanent. For example,

    (SETQ X '(A B))
    (SETQ Y X)
    (RPLACA X 'C)
    (CAR Y) ⇒ C

This is sometimes what you want and sometimes not. In any case, **RPLACA** and **RPLACD** should be used with care.

The function **CONS** in LISP could be defined in terms of **RPLACA** and **RPLACD** if we had available a function that would return a new, unused empty dotted pair cell whenever we wanted it. Suppose this function (which doesn't really exist) were called **NEW-CELL**. Then a definition of **CONS** would be

(DE CONS (X Y) (RPLACD (RPLACA (NEW-CELL) X) Y]

This is, we would obtain a new cell, replace the **CAR** of it with X, and replace the **CDR** of it with Y. The fact that **CONS** gets a new cell rather than reusing either X or Y can be important.

For example, suppose we defined the functions **INSERT-1** and **INSERT-2**, both taking an expression and a dotted pair and returning a dotted pair of the expression and the **CDR** of the original dotted pair. That is,

(INSERT-1 'A '(B . C)) ⇒ (A . C)
(INSERT-2 'A '(B . C)) ⇒ (A . C)

We define these functions as

(DE INSERT-1 (X L) (CONS X (CDR L)))
(DE INSERT-2 (X L) (RPLACA L X))

INSERT-1 builds a new dotted pair, whereas **INSERT-2** reuses the old one. With these definitions, the following sequence of evaluations would occur.

(SETQ X '(B . C))   ⇒ (B . C)
(INSERT-1 'A X)   ⇒ (A . C)
X   ⇒ (B . C)
(INSERT-2 'A X)   ⇒ (A . C)
X   ⇒ (A . C)

Notice that calling **INSERT-2** has changed the value of X! Furthermore, if we continued the sequence above with

(INSERT-2 X X)

we would create a circular list. The **CAR** of X would be X. Graphically this X would be set to the structure in Fig. 1.12.

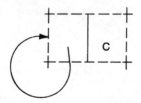

FIG. 1.12.   Graphic notation for a circular list.

Exercise 1.3 (Very difficult) Write the circular list X in LISP dotted pair notation.

One other function for changing the internal LISP structures is **NCONC**. **NCONC** is like **APPEND** in that it concatenates two lists together; however, **NCONC** physically alters the first list so that its final **CDR**, which used to point to **NIL**, now points to the second list.

Exercise 1.4 Define **NCONC** using **RPLACD**. What is the effect of (NCONC (SETQ X (LIST NIL)) X)?

1.10 EQUALITY

In Section 1.9 we noted that **CONS** uses fresh cells when it builds lists. That means that it is possible to build two lists which look the same but which are separate data structures.

For example,

```
(SETQ L1 (CONS 'A NIL))  ⇒ (A)
(SETQ L2 (CONS 'A NIL))  ⇒ (A)
(SETQ L3 L1)             ⇒ (A)
```

will generate two lists with the same form. Since each was built with a separate call to **CONS**, **L1** and **L2** will each occupy a different **CONS** cell; however, there was no call to **CONS** when **L3** was assigned the value of **L1**. Hence **L1** and **L3** will have the same **CONS** cell. Should LISP consider **L1** and **L2** to be equal or not? They are clearly not "as equal" as **L1** and **L3**.

To resolve this dilemma, LISP provides two equality functions, **EQUAL** and **EQ**. They both take two expressions and return **T** if they are equal (in some sense) and **NIL** otherwise.

(EQ *exp1 exp2*)

returns **T** if and only if *exp1* and *exp2* evaluate to the same atom or dotted pair cell. Hence

```
(EQ L1 L2)  ⇒ NIL
(EQ L1 L3)  ⇒ T
```

(EQUAL *exp1 exp2*)

returns **T** if and only if *exp1* and *exp2* look like the same list. **EQUAL** does not require that *exp1* and *exp2* be the same dotted pair cell. Hence

```
(EQUAL L1 L2)  ⇒ T
(EQUAL L1 L3)  ⇒ T
```

EQUAL is defined in terms of EQ. If *exp1* and *exp2* are atomic, then they are EQ and EQUAL only if they are the same atom. If they are both dotted pairs, then they are EQ if they are the same dotted pair, and they are EQUAL if the CAR of *exp1* is EQUAL to the CAR of *exp2* and the CDR of *exp1* is EQUAL to the CDR of *exp2*.

We would define EQUAL in LISP as shown in Fig. 1.13.

```
(DE EQUAL (X Y)
  (COND  ((EQ X Y) T)
         ((ATOM X) NIL)
         ((ATOM Y) NIL)
         ((EQUAL (CAR X) (CAR Y))
          (EQUAL (CDR X) (CDR Y]
```

FIG. 1.13.   Definition of EQUAL.

1.11   LOCAL VERSUS FREE VARIABLES

Consider the definition of WARNING in Fig. 1.14 that takes an expression, prints some warning message plus the expression, and returns either the expression that you type if your response is non-NIL, or else the original expression. The variables BAD-FORM and RESPONSE are *local* variables. RESPONSE is a PROG variable that is initially set to NIL when the PROG is entered and then set to whatever you type by the SETQ expression. BAD-FORM is a LAMBDA variable (remember that functions are really LAMBDA forms) that is set to whatever argument WARNING is called with.

```
(DE WARNING (BAD-FORM)
  (PROG  (RESPONSE)
         (PRINT (LIST *WARNING-MSG* BAD-FORM))
         (RETURN
           (COND ((SETQ RESPONSE (READ)) RESPONSE)
                 (T BAD-FORM]

(DE ATOM-WARNING (BAD-ATOM)
  ((LAMBDA (*WARNING-MSG*) (WARNING BAD-ATOM))
   'UNKNOWN-ATOM))
```

FIG. 1.14.   Example of local versus free variables.

The variable *WARNING-MSG* on the other hand is a *free* variable; that is, it is not a locally bound variable in any PROG or LAMBDA in which it occurs. It is impossible for BAD-FORM or RESPONSE to be unbound when WARNING is executed, but if we forget to give *WARNING-MSG* some value in advance, then an error will result.

Furthermore, the variables **BAD-FORM** and **RESPONSE** have a limited *scope*. By this we mean that **BAD-FORM** is only set to the argument of **WARNING**, and **RESPONSE** is only set to the result of the **READ** while the function **WARNING** is being executed. When **WARNING** is done, these values are forgotten. The function **WARNING** defines the scope of their values.

The value of ***WARNING-MSG*** on the other hand is not forgotten. For this reason, ***WARNING-MSG*** can also be called a *global* variable because its value is globally defined. Note, however, that a global variable can became temporarily local. For example, in the function **ATOM-WARNING**, which is also in Fig. 1.14, ***WARNING-MSG*** is a local **LAMBDA** variable that is set to **UNKNOWN-ATOM** for the duration of the execution of the function **ATOM-WARNING**. When **ATOM-WARNING** is done, ***WARNING-MSG*** is reset to its global value.

1.12 LISP STYLE

The functions defined in this book are written according to a number of general stylistic rules.

1.12.1 Indentation

Unindented LISP code is unreadable by anyone except the machine. Misleadingly indented code is even worse. This book contains lots of explicit examples of indentation. The general rule is to use spaces liberally—it takes LISP almost no time at all to ignore them. Lines should be short, with only one expression, unless there are several atoms in a row.

When you have to break an expression up into several lines, there are several standard options for where to start the second line. Figure 1.15 has two alternative indentations of the definition of **SQUARE-LIST**.

```
(DE SQUARE-LIST (L)
  (COND ((NULL L)  NIL)
        (T (CONS  (SQUARE (CAR L))
                  (SQUARE-LIST (CDR L))))    ))

(DE SQUARE-LIST (L)
  (COND ((NULL L)  NIL)
       (T  (CONS (SQUARE (CAR L))
               (SQUARE-LIST (CDR L))))    ))
```

FIG. 1.15. Two ways to indent an expression.

There are some special rules for indentation. Function definitions always have the DE, the function name, and the variable list on the same line. If the rest of the definition is too long, it is put on succeeding lines, indented at least one space. PROG expressions have the PROG and the variable list on the same line and the other expressions on succeeding lines, indented to line up with the variable list. Labels are indented to line up with the PROG. See the definition of REVERSE for an example.

Most LISPs have a function that prints expressions in an indented format. In our LISP the function is called SPRINT. Investigate what the function in your LISP does for different LISP constructs.

1.12.2 Naming

Choose variable and function names so that they suggest something (the right thing!) to the naive reader. Don't call a function to embed a graph in a plane FEGP—call it GRAPH-EMBED; but don't expect names to replace comments. Good names can only remind the reader of what is happening.

Set up some conventions for naming things consistently. For example, have some standard way of naming special variables (these are described in the chapter on compiling). In this book, we use the convention that all special variables have asterisks ("*") as the first and last characters.

If some of your functions are clearly predicates (i.e., it is only important whether they return NIL or not), then give them names like FOOP (P for predicate) or IS-FOO. Variables used as switches (i.e., it is only important whether they are set to NIL or not) should be given names like FOO-SW (SW for switch) or FOO-FLAG.

1.12.3 Comments

In our LISP, comments are signaled by a tilde ("~"). When READ sees a tilde, it starts ignoring characters until a line feed is read. Thus you can write anything you want on a line after a tilde. In Chapter 3, we will show you how to define a comment character.

Programs in LISP require as much commenting as in any other language. Try to have a structure to your comments, such as specifying in a fixed order, for each function; what its input variables represent; what kinds of values it is expected they will have; what special variables the function uses; and what kind of value the function returns.

Be sure to keep your comments up to date. If you are changing your code a lot, remove the comments until things settle down. A misleading comment can be worse than no comment at all.

1.12.4 Function Size

Functions should be small, certainly never more than 20 lines. If things start to nest deeply (i.e., you have 10 levels of parentheses), then start breaking up the subexpressions into subfunctions, in order to give the poor reader a rest.

Beware of indiscriminate breakup, however. If you have to use several special variables or more than three or four arguments to the subfunctions or have trouble coming up with better names than FOO1, FOO2, and so on, then you are probably breaking things up the wrong way.

1.12.5 Cleverness

Avoid it. Clever tricks are those that depend on how a particular LISP is implemented. For example, our LISP implements atoms as lists, but not all LISPs do this and hence any code using this fact will not be transportable. As another example, in our LISP, MAPC always returns NIL, but in MACLISP it returns the value of the second expression evaluated. Thus, in our LISP the following code would do the MAPC then BAZ, but in MACLISP it would do the MAPC and then FOO:

```
(COND   ((MAPC 'TEST '(A B C))
         (FOO))
        (T (BAZ)))
```

To paraphrase Samuel Johnson, we advise you to look over your code very carefully, and whenever you find a part that you think is particularly fine, strike it out.

2

FEXPRs and LEXPRs

In Chapter 1 we described the function **DE** that is used to define normal LISP functions. Almost every function that you need to define in LISP can be, and should be, defined using **DE**.

The functions that **DE** creates are called (in our LISP) EXPRs. When an EXPR function is executed, all its arguments are evaluated and bound in a one-to-one correspondence with the function's formal local variables. That means that an EXPR always takes the same number of arguments. If too many or too few are given, an error results.

Reserved words in LISP do not have these properties. First, not all the arguments to a reserved word may be evaluated. For example, the second argument to **SETQ** is evaluated but the first is not. Second, reserved words may take an arbitrary number of arguments. For example, there can be as many or as few statements in a **PROG** as we wish.

2.1   DEFINING RESERVED WORDS

In our LISP you can define your own reserved words, using the reserved word **DF**, which is very similar to **DE**. Reserved word functions are called FEXPRs (pronounced either "fex-purs" or "eff-expurs") and differ from EXPRs in the following ways:

1. A FEXPR takes exactly one formal local variable.
2. When a FEXPR is called, its formal variable is bound to the list of arguments as they appeared, *not* to their values.

DF is used thus:

(DF *function* (*atom*) -*expressions*-)

which defines *function* to be a FEXPR with the formal variable *atom* and a function body containing the expressions given. The value of *function* when called is the value of the last expression evaluated.

Let us define QUOTE-LIST as a FEXPR that just returns the binding of the formal variable.

(DF QUOTE-LIST (L) L)

The following input/output would occur when QUOTE-LIST is called:

(QUOTE-LIST A) ⇒ (A)
(QUOTE-LIST A B C) ⇒ (A B C)
(QUOTE-LIST) ⇒ ( )

Notice that L is always bound to a (perhaps empty) list. Notice also that none of the arguments are evaluated. Notice finally QUOTE-LIST can take an arbitrary number of arguments.

Many of the reserved words we have already seen could be defined as FEXPRs. For example,

(DF QUOTE (L) (CAR L]
(DF SETQ (L) (SET (CAR L) (EVAL (CADR L]
(DF DEFPROP (L) (PUTPROP (CAR L) (CADR L) (CADDR L]

These functions need to be FEXPRs because they have arguments that must not be evaluated. QUOTE is a necessity in LISP because we have to have some way of preventing evaluation. The functions SETQ and DEFPROP are a convenience. They could always be replaced with SET and PUTPROP, using the function QUOTE, but SETQ and DEFPROP allow us to write things without the extra baggage of quoting.

Sometimes we need FEXPRs in order to be able to have an arbitrary number of arguments. For example, suppose we wanted to define the function LIST (but we'll call it CONS-LIST to avoid confusing the interpreter) that CONSes together an arbitrary number of expressions; that is,

(CONS-LIST 'A 'B 'C) = (CONS 'A (CONS 'B (CONS 'C NIL)))
⇒ (A B C)

CONS-LIST could be defined as in Fig. 2.1. Note that we have to reverse the list at the end to keep things in the right order. This CONS-LIST will do what we want.

(CONS-LIST) ⇒ NIL
(CONS-LIST 'A) ⇒ (A)
(CONS-LIST 'A 'B) ⇒ (A B)

```
(DF CONS-LIST (L)
  (PROG (RESULT)
  LOOP (COND   ((NULL L) (RETURN (REVERSE RESULT)))
              (T (SETQ RESULT (CONS (EVAL (CAR L)) RESULT))
                 (SETQ L (CDR L))
                 (GO LOOP]
```

FIG. 2.1.   FEXPR version of CONS-LIST.

Exercise 2.1   In CONS-LIST we explicitly call the function EVAL on each argument. What would have happened if we didn't?

2.2   DEFINING FUNCTIONS WITH AN INDETERMINATE NUMBER OF ARGUMENTS

CONS-LIST is not a good example of when to use a FEXPR. What we needed was a way to have an arbitrary number of arguments, but we wanted all those arguments evaluated. Since arguments are left alone in FEXPRs, we were forced to call the function EVAL ourselves.

Another way to define CONS-LIST is to define it as a LEXPR. A LEXPR is like an EXPR in that all the arguments are evaluated first and then the LEXPR is applied. A LEXPR is like a FEXPR in that any number of arguments can be given.

A LEXPR is defined using DE, but instead of giving a list of formal variables, an atom is given instead; that is, the format for using DE to define a LEXPR is

(DE *function atom -expressions-*)

This defines *function* to be a LEXPR, with the special formal variable *atom* and a function body containing the expressions given. The value of *function* when called is the value of the last expression evaluated.

When a LEXPR is called, the arguments are evaluated and saved temporarily by the LISP system. The formal variable is bound to *the number of arguments in the call;* that is, if we called a LEXPR with three arguments, then its formal variable would be set to 3. If we called that same function again with no agruments, the formal variable would be set to 0.

To illustrate, we define the LEXPR ARG-COUNT, which (just like QUOTE-LIST) does nothing more than return the value of its formal variable.

(DE ARG-COUNT N N)

ARG-COUNT behaves in the following way:

(ARG-COUNT) ⇒ 0
(ARG-COUNT 'A) ⇒ 1
(ARG-COUNT 'A 'B 'C) ⇒ 3

When a LEXPR is called, its formal variable tells how many arguments there are. In order to obtain an argument, we use the function ARG. (ARG *n*) returns the *n*th argument of the current LEXPR. An error occurs if no LEXPR is being evaluated or if the LEXPR has fewer than *n* arguments.

A LEXPR version of CONS-LIST could be defined as in Fig. 2.2. This definition is almost the same as the FEXPR one. Notice the correspondences between N and L, between ARG and EVAL, and between SUB1 and CDR. Notice also that since we are picking up the arguments from last to first, we do not have to reverse the list at the end.

```
(DE CONS-LIST N
 (PROG (RESULT)
  LOOP (COND   ((EQUAL N 0) (RETURN RESULT))
               (T (SETQ RESULT (CONS (ARG N) RESULT))
               (SETQ N (SUB1 N))
               (GO LOOP]
```

FIG. 2.2.   LEXPR version of CONS-LIST.

Exercise 2.2   LISP has three functions for grouping expressions together: PROG1, PROG2 and PROGN. They each take an indeterminate number of arguments and evaluate them. PROG1 always returns the value of the first argument, PROG2 always returns the value of the second argument and PROGN always returns the value of the last argument. All three functions can be defined very simply using LEXPRs. Define them.

2.3   PROBLEMS WITH FEXPRS

Both FEXPRs and LEXPRs have their uses. In general it is best to reserve FEXPRs for those situations where you want to prevent evaluation from occurring. There are two usual reasons for wanting this:

1. Conditional evaluation—for example, using COND, AND could be defined as a FEXPR, where each argument is evaluated until either a NIL is found or the list of arguments is exhausted. Since AND is supposed to stop evaluating arguments once a NIL is found, it is a FEXPR. But a still better solution involves macros, which will be described in Chapter 3.

2. Avoiding excessive quoting—when defining functions or initializing a data base, everything that is written is explicit and constant; that is, we say to LISP "Define a function with this particular name and this particular set of

local variables and this particular function body." Rather than quoting all these constants, we create the FEXPRs DE and DEFPROP, which automatically quote everything.

> *Exercise 2.3* Define AND and OR and DE. Remember that DE defines functions by storing LAMBDA bodies under the property EXPR. See Section 1.8.

Unfortunately, FEXPRs tend to be somewhat intractable. In making it easy to have constant arguments, they make it hard to pass variable ones. For example, there is a handy function in LISP for printing function definitions in a highly indented, readable format. The function is called PP (for pretty-print) and for convenience PP is a FEXPR. To pretty-print the definitions of the functions FOO, BAZ, and FOOBAZ, you write

> (PP FOO BAZ FOOBAZ)

Suppose however that you have a function that generates a list of functions and you want to pretty-print the functions in the list. For example, suppose the function PROG-CALLERS returned all the functions known to the interpreter that have a PROG form as their function body. It would be nice if we could just write

> (PP (PROG-CALLERS))

but this will just give PP the form (PROG-CALLERS), and PP will give an error message because it is expecting the names of functions, not S-expressions.

The normal solution to this problem is to write

> (EVAL (CONS 'PP (PROG-CALLERS)))

that is, first we call PROG-CALLERS to obtain the list, then we make the form (PP *fn1 fn2* ...), and then we execute this form with EVAL.

FEXPRs present a similar problem for APPLY and the mapping functions. In order to be able to handle FEXPRs uniformly, APPLY and the mapping functions have to build the necessary S-expression to evaluate first, often adding QUOTEs to prevent premature evaluation of arguments.

Some implementers of LISP feel this is more work than it is worth, so, in some LISPS, by fiat, you cannot use FEXPRs with APPLY or the mapping functions. In other LISPs, special actions are taken by APPLY and the mapping functions to handle FEXPRs as well. You are better off not depending on this facility and using FEXPRs only when absolutely necessary.

> *Exercise 2.4* Assume we have the two functions F1 and F2, defined as

```
(DE F1 (X) X)
(DF F2 (L) (EVAL (CAR L)))
```

F1 and F2 normally return the same value for the same arguments. Change the definition of MAPCAR given in Chapter 1 so that when it maps F1 and F2 across the same list, the same result is returned. After doing this, try using your MAPCAR on QUOTE-LIST.

When you need to define a function taking an indefinite number of arguments, you have two options. First, you can use LEXPRs. LEXPRs can be used with APPLY and the mapping functions without problem, because the arguments to LEXPRs are evaluated before the LEXPR is applied, just as is done with EXPRs. Second, you can use MACROs. These will be discussed in Chapter 3.

When you have to define a FEXPR, because you want to avoid argument evaluation, you should consider defining two functions—a FEXPR for function calling purposes and an EXPR to do the work. For example, suppose we wanted a function UNDEFINE that would remove user-created function definitions; that is,

```
(UNDEFINE FOO BAZ FOOBAZ)
```

would remove any EXPR definitions that FOO, BAZ, and FOOBAZ might possess.

One way to define UNDEFINE would be

```
(DF UNDEFINE (L)
  (MAPC '(LAMBDA (X) (REMPROP X 'EXPR)) L]
```

but a better way would be

```
(DF UNDEFINE (L) (UNDEFINE-LIST L]
(DE UNDEFINE-LIST (L)
  (MAPC '(LAMBDA (X) (REMPROP X 'EXPR)) L]
```

In both cases, UNDEFINE does what we want, allowing us to specify easily a list of function names (without quoting) for undefining. However, the second form of definition gives us another function that takes a constructed list of function names. If we wanted to, we could easily undefine all the functions that PROG-CALLERS finds by writing

```
(UNDEFINE-LIST (PROG-CALLERS))
```

No matter how confident you may be that you will never want an EXPR version of a FEXPR function that you are defining, we recommend that you define both at the same time. If the function is really useful, eventually you will want to use it in ways you didn't expect.

2.4   FEXPRS IN INTERLISP

INTERLISP has a much more sophisticated system of function types, allowing the user the ability to control independently how many arguments a function takes and whether or not those arguments are evaluated.

First, there are two types of LAMBDA forms: regular LAMBDAs and NLAMBDAs. When a LAMBDA is applied, its arguments are evaluated. When an NLAMBDA is applied, its arguments are not evaluated.

Second, there are two types of argument lists for both kinds of LAMBDA. If the argument list is a list or NIL, then the LAMBDA takes a fixed number of arguments, which are assigned values in the normal way. This is called a *spreading* LAMBDA. If the argument list is an atom other than NIL, then the LAMBDA takes an indefinite number of arguments. If a LAMBDA has an atomic argument list, then the atom is bound to the number of arguments. If an NLAMBDA has an atomic argument list, then the atom is bound to the list of the unevaluated arguments. In either case, this is called a *nospreading* LAMBDA.

Some examples of different types of LAMBDA expressions and their results are

((LAMBDA (X) X)	(ADD1 2))	⇒ 3
((NLAMBDA (X) X)	(ADD1 2))	⇒ (ADD1 2)
((LAMBDA X X)	(ADD1 2))	⇒ 1
((NLAMBDA X X)	(ADD1 2))	⇒ ((ADD1 2))

EXPRs in our LISP are implemented as spreading LAMBDAs, FEXPRs as nospreading NLAMBDAs, and LEXPRs as nospreading NLAMBDAs. There is no direct equivalent to INTERLISP's spreading NLAMBDA in our LISP.

3 Macros and Read Macros

If there is one group of features that is consistently underutilized by beginning LISP users, it is macros and read macros. Not only do they allow you to abbreviate commonly used pieces of code, but by the judicious use of these features you can build yourself a new language on top of LISP—a language more convenient for the problems you are facing than LISP itself. (There are, however, limits on the degree to which this new language can differ from LISP. See Chapter 17.)

Most, but not all, LISPs support macros. If yours does not, at the end of this chapter we give a way to simulate them using FEXPRs.

3.1 MACROS

Macros are a special type of LISP function. They differ from others in that they go through not one but two rounds of evaluation. The first is called *macro expansion*. During macro expansion the macro is evaluated and is expected to produce (expand into) more LISP code. This code is then in turn evaluated as if it were in place of the original call to the macro, and the value it returns is the value of the macro as far as any further processing is concerned.

To understand this better, let us consider the macro POP that we will define shortly. POP takes one argument, the name of a variable that has previously been bound to a list. POP resets this variable to its CDR and returns the item removed from the list (i.e., the original list's CAR). Thus if A is set to the list (1 2 3), (POP A) returns 1 and sets A to (2 3). Executing (POP A) again returns 2 and sets A to (3).

Macros are defined with the function **DM** (Define Macro), which has the same syntax as **DF** (i.e., a name, a one-element variable list, and one or more expressions). Macros are similar to FEXPRs in that their arguments are not evaluated, but they differ from FEXPRs in that their single variable is bound to the entire function call. For example, if **FOO** is a macro with the formal variable **BODY**, then if we call (**FOO A B C**), **BODY** will be bound to (**FOO A B C**).

The definition for **POP** is

```
(DM POP (BODY)
     (LIST   'PROG1
          (LIST 'CAR (CADR BODY))
          (LIST 'SETQ  (CADR BODY)
                    (LIST 'CDR (CADR BODY]
```

When LISP evaluates the function call (**POP A**) in the situation above, it first expands **POP** with **BODY** set to (**POP A**). The result of this expansion will be the code

```
(PROG1 (CAR A)
       (SETQ A (CDR A)))
```

(As mentioned in Chapter 2, **PROG1** evaluates all the expressions it is given, returning as its value the value of the first expression.) Now the **PROG1** will be evaluated. It will return as its value the **CAR** of the list (**1 2 3**) (i.e., **1**), and then **A** will be set to (**CDR A**), as desired.

Exercise 3.1 Write the macro **PUSH** (a companion to **POP**). (**PUSH** *exp var*) will have the effect of (**SETQ** *var* (**CONS** *exp var*)), but will return the value of *exp* as its value. For example,

```
*(SETQ NAMES '(FRED BILL GEORGE))
(FRED BILL GEORGE)
*(SETQ SENTENCE '(IS A PERSON))
(IS A PERSON)
*(PUSH (CAR NAMES) SENTENCE)
FRED
*SENTENCE
(FRED IS A PERSON)
```

(*Note:* Be careful that your implementation does not cause the first argument of PUSH to be evaluated twice. Explain how this mistake would cause bugs in the evaluation of (**PUSH (POP A) B**).)

Now given the earlier comparison made with FEXPRs it is instructive to ask whether the same thing could have been done with them. The answer is yes and no. A FEXPR definition of **POP** would be

```
(DF  POP (BODY)
    (PROG1(CAR (EVAL (CAR BODY)))
        (SET (CAR BODY) (CDR (EVAL (CAR BODY]
```

This code goes through the same motions as the macro version, and 99.99% of the time it will have the same results, but there are differences. One is efficiency. Later we show how macro expansions can be directly inserted into the code so that macro expansion need only occur once. If this is done, the macro version will be more efficient that the FEXPR version, since we will have eliminated a function call (the call to POP).

But there is a more serious difference between the two versions of POP, leading to different results in certain cases. For example,

```
*(SETQ BODY '(A B C))
(A B C)
*(POP BODY)
BODY
*BODY
(A B C)
```

Clearly POP is not working correctly. The problem is a conflict in variable names. To see the effect of this, let us step through POP on this example. The argument to POP is BODY, so the variable BODY (in POP) is bound to (BODY). We first evaluate (CAR (EVAL (CAR BODY))).

BODY	⇒	(BODY)
(CAR BODY)	⇒	BODY
(EVAL (CAR BODY))	⇒	(BODY)
(CAR (EVAL (CAR BODY)))	⇒	BODY

That explains why the function returned the same value. As for why it had no effect on BODY, it is because it SET BODY in the FEXPR; but when we left the FEXPR, this version of the variable BODY "went away" leaving the top-level variable untouched.

The FEXPR version goes through the same motions as the macro version but in a different environment. In particular it is going through the motions in an environment where BODY has a new value. Besides showing the utility of macros, this example also shows that it is a bad idea to use FEXPRs in situations in which some of the arguments are to be evaluated. But if it must be done, be sure to give the variables in the FEXPR odd names.

Efficiency and environment differences are two reasons for using macros. In later chapters we will see more.

Exercise 3.2 Suppose you wanted to define a function called MY-RETURN, which is only to be used in PROGS. This function will first call a cleanup function to undo some global effects the program might have made, and then it returns from the PROG. Explain why this must be implemented as a macro.

Another use of macros has to do with the creation of temporary variables. Figure 3.1a gives a typical case where they are needed. It would clearly be better to save the value of (A-COMPLEX-FUNCTION INPUT-VAR) than to compute it twice. Chapter 1 introduced two ways to create local variables in our program. One of these is PROG. The use of PROG in this case is illustrated in Fig. 3.1b.

PROG will work fine, but in some respects it is not optimal. For one thing, PROG is usually used in conjunction with GOs and loops. Since this is not required here, anyone reading the code will be slightly misled, not knowing that there are no loops and that no RETURN will be executed that would prevent the evaluation of the second computation. Furthermore, the RETURN at the end involves a bit of extra typing.

The second method for the creation of temporary variables is the use of LAMBDA expressions. Figure 3.1c uses LAMBDA on our example. In some respects it is better. We no longer mislead the reader by the use of PROG, and the RETURN is not needed. But overall, the separation of TEMP and the expression we set it to do make this harder to read.

```
(DE COMPUT-THINGS (INPUT-VAR)
 (FIRST-COMPUTATION (A-COMPLEX-FUNCTION INPUT-VAR))
 (SECOND-COMPUTATION (A-COMPLEX-FUNCTION INPUT-VAR) INPUT-VAR))
```

FIG. 3.1a.   The temporary variable problem—no variable.

```
(DE COMPUTE-THINGS (INPUT-VAR)
 (PROG  (TEMP)
        (SETQ TEMP (A-COMPLEX-FUNCTION INPUT-VAR))
        (FIRST-COMPUTATION TEMP INPUT-VAR)
        (RETURN (SECOND-COMPUTATION TEMP)))
```

FIG. 3.1b.   The temporary variable problem—using PROG.

```
(DE COMPUTE-THINGS (INPUT-VAR)
 ((LAMBDA (TEMP)
          (FIRST-COMPUTATION TEMP)
          (SECOND-COMPUTATION TEMP INPUT-VAR))
  (A-COMPLEX-FUNCTION INPUT-VAR]
```

FIG. 3.1.c   The temporary variable problem—using LAMBDA.

```
(DE COMPUTE-THINGS (INPUT-VAR)
 (LET   (TEMP (A-COMPLEX-FUNCTION INPUT-VAR))
        (FIRST-COMPUTATION TEMP)
        (SECOND-COMPUTATION TEMP INPUT-VAR]
```

FIG. 3.1d.   The temporary variable problem—using LET.

```
(LET    (var-1 val-1 ... var-n val-n)
        exp-1
        ...
        exp-n)
```

will expand to

```
((LAMBDA  (var-1 ... var-n)
          exp-1
          ...
          exp-n)
  val-1 ... val-n)
```

FIG. 3.2. The expansion of the LET macro.

The solution to the temporary variable problem is provided by a macro that will be used constantly throughout the rest of this book: the LET macros illustrated in Fig. 3.2. Figure 3.1c gives COMPUTE-THINGS using LET. The code for LET is in Fig. 3.3.

```
(DM LET  (BODY)
   (PROG  (VARS-N-VALS VARS VALS)
          (POP BODY)
          (SETQ VARS-N-VALS (REVERSE (POP BODY)))
    LOOP  (COND  ((NULL VARS-N-VALS)
                  (RETURN (CONS (APPEND (LIST 'LAMBDA VARS) BODY)
                                VALS))))
          (PUSH (POP VARS-N-VALS) VALS)
          (PUSH (POP VARS-N-VALS) VARS)
          (GO LOOP]
```

FIG. 3.3. Code for the LET macro.

Before going on we might note how INTERLISP handles macros, to obtain some feel for how LISPs differ on this point. In fact, there is nothing in INTERLISP that exactly corresponds to macros as presented here. The closest you can come is compiler macros. These are definitions which can take several different forms which can produce code to be substituted into the code in which the macro finds itself. The difference is that this is only done during compilation (see Chapter 8 for more on compilation). Hence these macros differ in two important ways from the macros described above. First, assuming you want to run the code interpretively, you must have two definitions of the function: one to be used during interpretation and one for compilation. This can lead, of course, to inadvertent differences. Second, as we have pointed out, macros are also useful in interpreted code (where efficiency is not a factor). There is no way to use INTERLISP macros in this way. If you care enough, however, you can get around this limitation by using the INTERLISP error correction facility. Basically this involves telling the error corrector what to do in the case it comes across an error like finding an undefined function **LET**. You tell it, in effect, to replace the code with some new code. But while this has the same effect, the process is not as convenient.

3.2 READ MACROS

As we have already noted, the top level of LISP is a **READ-EVAL-PRINT** loop. LISP reads something in, evaluates it, and prints out the results. Normal macros are expanded during the evaluation phase. There is a second kind of macro in LISP that is expanded during the reading phase and hence is called a *read macro*. Read macros are always single characters. When the reader comes across a character defined as a read macro, the macro is executed and the resulting code is inserted in the place where the read macro character would have gone.

We have already come across one read macro, the single quote mark that is used to replace **QUOTE**. Single quote is defined as follows:

(DRM /' (LAMBDA ( ) (LIST (QUOTE QUOTE) (READ]

This says that when a single quote is read, LISP should replace it with a list consisting of **QUOTE** and the next S-expression in the input (obtained by an explicit call to the function **READ**). The / in front of the quote mark above tells LISP to ignore any special properties this character might have. We put it there just in case single quote already has a read macro. You can find more on the use of / in Chapter 6 (I/O in LISP).

This example illustrates several features of the read macro. First, because defining a character as a read macro makes it difficult, if not impossible, to use the character in a normal manner, read macros should not be letters or numbers. Second, in our LISP, the defining function **DRM** (Define Read Macro) requires that the **LAMBDA** be explicitly included. More generally, a read macro is a function of no arguments, since as soon as the macro character is seen, the macro code is executed. Usually, as with single quote, more information will be required—in this case the expression to be quoted. To obtain this information the read macro must explicitly call an input function such as **READ** (see Chapter 6) to read in more of the input. Normally anything read will not be reread when the macro is done. This allows us to take over control of reading.

Exercise 3.3 Write a read macro that will pretty-print all the properties of the atom following the macro character, except the print name. As mentioned in Chapter 1, in many LISPs the property list of an atom is the **CDR** of the atom, making it easy to get at. If this is not the case for your LISP, extra effort may be required, or you might just have to give up on this exercise entirely. Most LISPs have a pretty-printer these days. In our LISP you type

(SPRINT *var col*)

to obtain the pretty-printed version of *var* starting in column *col*.

The read macro as we have described it places the expanded macro in the place where the macro character stood. Sometimes however this is not exactly what you want. Suppose you wanted to define a comment character ; that would cause the rest of the line on which it appears to be considered as comment (i.e., the LISP reader should be instructed to ignore it completely). As a first approximation we could write

```
(DRM /; (LAMBDA ( )  (PROG ( )
                LOOP (AND (EQ (READCH) CR)
                (RETURN NIL)) (GO LOOP]
```

READCH is a function that reads in a single character. In this case we want to know when we reach the end of the line. In our LISP, CR is bound to the character for carriage return. So this read macro says that when LISP sees a ;, it should continue reading until encountering a carriage return and then return NIL.

The problem here is that we do not want this function to return anything, not even NIL. For example, suppose our input looked like

```
(COND((AND  (HUMAN X)    ;If X is both human and female, then ...
          (FEMALE X))
      ...)
```

This will come out looking like

```
(COND ((AND (HUMAN X) NIL (FEMALE X)) ...)
```

This is obviously not what we wanted.

The solution to this and similar problems is the *splice macro*. The splice macro is just like the read macro (and, in fact, the term *read macro* is commonly used for both), but the splice macro must return a list that is then spliced into the read stream. For example, if the splice macro % returns the list (A B C), then the input (1 2 % 3 4) will be read as (1 2 A B C 3 4).

To define a splice macro we use the function DSM (Define Splice Macro). If we define ; with DSM rather than DRM, the above code for our macro will be fine. NIL will still be returned, but it will now be spliced into the read stream leaving no trace.

It might be noted that splice macros are not used very often. Most of the time we want the nonsplice variety. Furthermore, in those cases where we use a splice macro, most of the time it is to enable the macro to produce no output at all (i.e., we will be splicing in a NIL). For one exception to this generalization, however, see Exercise 8.1.

3.3 THE |" READ MACRO

One problem that frequently occurs in LISP programs is the creation of complex list structures. For example, suppose we wanted to create something like the following pattern.

```
(PROG vars
      LOOP -expressions-
           (GO LOOP))
```

Using the typical LISP functions we will be forced into something like

```
(CONS 'PROG
      (CONS  VARS
      (CONS  'LOOP
            (APPEND EXPRESSIONS
                  '((GO LOOP]
```

Although we have indented to make the correspondence as close as possible, the second expression is difficult to read and requires a fair amount of thought to create, since the decisions whether to use CONS, LIST, or APPEND require skipping around the structure being built rather than simply starting at the top and working down.

To do this busy work for us we will create the |" read macro. (Actually, the bar is the read macro. It looks at the next character to decide on the proper expansion.) |" (or *quasi-quote*) can be thought of as an extension of QUOTE. Using this macro the expression above will be written

```
|"(PROG  @VARS
         LOOP |@EXPRESSIONS
         (GO LOOP))
```

Here @ says to evaluate the following expression to find out what goes here (i.e., *unquote*), whereas |@ says to do the same but to splice in the results (*splice-unquote*). The basic code for the macro is given in Fig. 3.4.

The expansion of the |" macro will be provided by QUASI-QUOTE. SKEL will be bound to the expression following the |" (see Exercise 3.4). How QUASI-QUOTE works may seem a bit mysterious, so let us work through the example above. The program consists of QUASI-QUOTE, which states how to handle the basic units, and COMBINE-SKELS, which tells us how to put the units together. Let us start by ignoring the latter and only looking at what will happen to each of the individual elements, PROG, @VARS, |@EXPRESSIONS, GO, and LOOP. This is illustrated in Fig. 3.5. LISP first calls QUASI-QUOTE with SKEL = (PROG...), which decides that SKEL is not NIL, (QUOTE...), (*UNQUOTE*...), or (*SPLICE-

```
(DE  QUASI-QUOTE (SKEL)
    (COND  ((NULL SKEL) NIL)
           ((ATOM SKEL) (LIST 'QUOTE SKEL))
           ((EQ (CAR SKEL) '*UNQUOTE*) (CADR SKEL))
           ((AND (CONSP (CAR SKEL)) (EQ (CAAR SKEL) '*SPLICE-UNQUOTE*))
           (LIST 'APPEND (CADAR SKEL) (QUASI-QUOTE (CDR SKEL))))
           ((COMBINE-SKELS   (QUASI-QUOTE (CAR SKEL))
                             (QUASI-QUOTE (CDR SKEL))
                             SKEL]

(DE COMBINE-SKELS (LFT RGT SKEL)
    (COND  ((AND (ISCONST LFT) (ISCONST RGT)) (LIST 'QUOTE SKEL))
           ((NULL RGT) (LIST 'LIST LFT))
           ((AND (CONSP RGT) (EQ (CAR RGT) 'LIST))
           (CONS 'LIST (CONS LFT (CDR RGT))))
           ((LIST 'CONS LFT RGT]

(DE ISCONST (X) (OR (NULL X) (EQ X T) (NUMBERP X)
                    (AND (CONSP X) (EQ (CAR X) 'QUOTE]
```

FIG. 3.4.   The basic code for the |" macro.

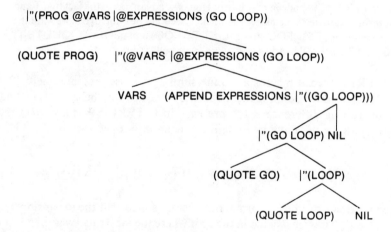

FIG. 3.5.   A trace of QUASI-QUOTE.

UNQUOTE* ...). So it must compute |"PROG and |"(@VARS ...). As Fig. 3.5 indicates, |"PROG returns (QUOTE PROG), and |"(@VARS ...) leads to |"@VARS and |"(@EXPRESSIONS ...). This goes on and eventually we will have computed everything shown in Fig. 3.5. Then we will enter **COMBINE-SKELS** and start combining the values, working from the bottom up. Note that (QUOTE LOOP) and NIL combine into (QUOTE (LOOP)). Figure 3.6 gives a table of these combinations and which **COND** clause of **COMBINE-SKELS** is responsible.

LFT	and RGT	combine into	because of COND clause
'LOOP	NIL	'(LOOP)	2
'GO	'(LOOP)	'(GO LOOP)	1
'(GO LOOP)	NIL	'((GO LOOP))	1
VARS	(APPEND...)	(CON VARS (APPEND...))	4
'PROG	(CONS VARS...)	(CONS 'PROG (CONS...))	4

FIG. 3.6. Combining portions to obtain the whole.

Exercise 3.4 To make this work we need two read macros. One is @, which should expand into (*UNQUOTE* *variable-name*). The other is |. This macro should read in the next character from the read string (use READCH to read in a single character). Then the expansion should depend on what the next character is. If it is an "at" sign, then the expansion is (*SPLICE-UNQUOTE* *variable-name*). If it is a double quote mark, then the expansion is found by calling (QUASI-QUOTE (READ)). Write these read macros. Note that there will be a problem in the | macro in writing the code for testing what the next character is since double quote is a special character indicating a string in many LISPs. This can be avoided using the aforementioned /.

Exercise 3.5 The code in Fig. 3.4 does not take advantage of the fact that T and numbers evaluate to themselves and hence need not be quoted [i.e., we want the expansion of (T 5 @FOO) to be (LIST T 5 FOO) and not (LIST (QUOTE T) (QUOTE 5) FOO)]. Add code to make this change.

INTERLISP read macros are quite similar to those presented here. The actual functions for defining them differ, but the way they behave is the same. One interesting difference is the presence in INTERLISP of an *infix* read macro. This would allow us to define + as an infix operator, as in A+B.

3.4 MACRO EXPANSION IN INTERPRETED CODE

When we first introduced normal macros, we stated that the expansion was evaluated *as if* it were located in the spot where the macro call was found. We have stressed the "as if" since the macro expansion will not in fact replace the macro call if you are running interpreted code, which is the usual situation. What this means then is that unless you make some special effort, all normal macros will be expanded every time they are encountered. (This is not true for read macros, which are only expanded at read time.)

It is very costly (in term of time) to expand macros repeatedly. This is because macro expansion requires CONSing, which leads to *garbage collection*. After LISP has built up the expansion, it is executed and thrown away. LISP has something called a *garbage collector* to reclaim such garbage, and it takes a fair amount of time. To give some approximate figures (the figures you obtain will depend on your machine as well as the amount of free storage and total storage you are using): A garbage collection takes about 1 CPU second, and it will reclaim, say, 10,000 free cells (a *free cell* is one available for use by a future CONS). This works out to about 100 microseconds per free cell. This may not seem very much, but compare this to about 20 microseconds for a function call. And this is for *each* CONS. Even the smallest of our macros uses two or three CONSes, and many take 10 times that.

This is all by way of explaining how you may do the expansion once and have it substituted into the code. There are two basic ways to do this. One is to have each macro be in charge of making sure that its expansion is physically put into the code, the other is for each function to ensure that all the macros in it are expanded and the expansions substituted in. We demonstrate both ways. You may choose the one you like best.

To give a macro the ability to insert its expansion into the code, we define it using the function MACLOBBER:

   (MACLOBBER *old-code new-code*)

For example, we might define LET as

   (DM LET (OLD-CODE)
      (MACLOBBER OLD-CODE (LET-EXPANDER OLD-CODE)))

Here LET-EXPANDER is the code we defined earlier, except now it will be an EXPR. MACLOBBER will take this new code and put it in where the old code was previously. MACLOBBER is defined in Fig. 3.7. To understand how it works, you should think of OLD-CODE as a pointer to the first cell of a list that represents the old code. MACLOBBER replaces both the CAR and the CDR of this cell with the CAR and CDR of the first cell of the new code. (Drawing this out using the box notation introduced in Chapter 1 should help.)

```
(DE MACLOBBER (OLD NEW)
   (COND   ((AND *MACLOBSW* (CONSP NEW))
            (RPLACA OLD (CAR NEW))
            (RPLACD OLD (CDR NEW))
            OLD)
           (NEW)   ))
```

FIG. 3.7.   Code for MACLOBBER.

Exercise 3.6   Why does MACLOBBER return OLD rather than NEW in the case that it is successful in making the change? (*Hint:* Consider the case where the macro expands into a second macro.)

The other way of handling macro expansion is to expand them at function definition time. To do this we define new function definition functions that

```
(DM DEX (BODY) (CONS 'DE (EXPANDMACROS (CDR BODY]

(DE EXPANDMACROS (L)
 (COND    ((OR (ATOM L) (EQ (CAR L) 'QUOTE)) L)
             ~We do not expand anything quoted.
           ((ISMARCRO (CAR L))
             ~If L is a macro call, apply the macro body to L.
             (EXPANDMACROS ((ISMACRO (CAR L)) L)))
           (T (EXPANDREST L]

(DE EXPANDREST (L)
 (COND    ((ATOM L) L)
           (T (CONS (EXPANDMACROS (CAR L)) (EXPANDREST (CDR L]

(DE ISMACRO (A) (AND (ATOM A) (NOT (NUMBERP A)) (GET A 'MACRO]
```

FIG. 3.8.   The code for DEX.

first go through the function body expanding any macros, and then define the
function to be the code so produced. The code for the new EXPR defining
function, DEX, is given in Fig. 3.8. The generalization to the other defining
functions should be obvious.

3.5   SIMULATING MACROS WITH FEXPRS

If your LISP does not support macros but has FEXPRs (or the equivalent
NLAMBDAs), you may write your own macro handling facilities. The code is
given in Fig. 3.9.

```
(DF DM (L)
     (PUTPROP (CAR L)   (LIST 'LAMDBA '($$$L)
                              (LIST 'MACHAC (LIST 'QUOTE (CAR L)) '$$$L))
                        'FEXPR)
     (PUTPROP (CAR L) (CONS 'LAMBDA (CDR L)) 'MACRO)
     (CAR L]

(DE MACHAC ($$$FN $$$L) (EVAL ((ISMACRO $$$FN) (CONS $$$FN $$$L]
```

FIG. 3.9.   Simulating macros with FEXPRs.

Should you wish to expand macros in place, you can do it using the macro
expansion facility provided in DEX. It is not possible to use MACLOBBER,
however.

Exercise 3.7 Explains why MACLOBBER will not properly expand the
macros defined using the definition of DM given in Fig. 3.9.

4

Data Type
Definition

When LISP was first invented, no one had ever heard of "Structured Programming," the recent movement among programmers to discipline themselves (and each other) to write cleaner, more modular code (Dahl et al., 1972). Many LISP programs continue to be written as if the valuable insights from this movement had never been gained, and the impression has caught on that LISP is reactionary. Actually, LISP is so extensible that it is easy for the user to add his own features to make his code cleaner. In this chapter, we will show how to implement modular data types, and in chapter 5 we will show how to implement the clean control structures that have become so popular.

A *data type* is a class of data structures, instances of which are built and used throughout a program. All programs manipulate data types, but not always, as we shall recommend, explicitly.

We will demonstrate the need for explicit data types with an example. Say you have a program for understanding stories, and one kind of data structure it manages is called a *goal node*. A goal node is to consist of three *slots:* a character, a state of affairs he wants to bring about, and a list of the plans he might try. The obvious way to represent a goal node is with a list of the form

   (*character state -plans-*)

For example, we might have (MACBETH (= MACBETH KING) (MURDER...) (TREASON ...) ...). To construct a goal node from a

47

given character, state, and list of plans, you could just CONS the three things together. To extract the plans from a node, you just use CDDR. And so on.

This is obvious; but it's wrong, if you want your program to be writable, readable, and changeable.

A program is *writable* to the extent that its complexity does not inhibit its development. (This point has been stressed by the structured programmers.) While writing a complex program, you have better things to do than to worry about the details of data structures. You should be able to write (CHAR:GOALNODE X), and not think about whether GOALNODEs will be implemented as lists, arrays, or symbol property lists. Besides, the most efficient implementation can only be chosen after it is known how these objects will be used. Making a decision too early can put unnecessary constraints on the program.

Readability is important later, for you and for colleagues who read your code. Reading others' code and having them read yours are important. You can learn more about good LISP programming practice by reading a good programmer's code than by reading a book like this. You can learn even more by having a good programmer criticize your code. (Computer science is different from poetry and engineering in that it is all too easy to avoid ever having any audience for your work—except the machine, which tells no tales.)

Changeability is the most important property. Continuing our example, let's say you decide to add another slot to goal nodes. For instance, you might want to add a list of plans that tried and failed, or you may decide to change the implementation of a data structure, for efficiency, pretty-printing, or some other reason. To make such changes, you must find and revise every piece of code that builds or accesses a goal node. This is tedious and error-prone, since you have to inspect every CONS and CDR. Worse, a D buried in a CADADR might be a CDR that needs changing.

We fully expect you to ignore our advice in this chapter, until you have written and tried to maintain a large, relatively permanent program. One of us (DVM) learned his lesson as a result of taking part in the development of the Conniver programming language (Sussman & McDermott, 1972). His responsibility was writing the data base code. This code does some fairly elaborate things to some fairly complex data structures. The code was sprinkled with CDADRs that really meant "the context markers of the status field of." (At least, we *think* that's what they meant. No one knows any more.) Several times in the life of this code, nice changes were proposed whose implementation was just too frightening to contemplate.

This code eventually died a natural death (hastened by the aforementioned atherosclerosis). Its author learned his lesson, and the next AI language he implemented obeyed the discipline we will now describe.

4.2 THE CONSERVATIVE APPROACH TO TYPE DEFINITION

There are different degrees to which you can commit yourself to explicit data type definition. You should at least do this: When you need a data type, define in one place in the program what the format of that type is, and give mnemonic names to the functions that construct structures of that type, access and set their slots, test whether something is of that type, etc. Do not allow code anywhere else in the program to manipulate a list of that type with any other function but one of these standard ones.

Following this discipline makes program changes simpler. Many changes in a data type are confined to the place in the program where the type is defined. Others (such as a change in the number of arguments to the type constructor) are easy to perform because a text editor can be told to search for the names of the functions whose calls are being changed.

As a result of writing his program this way, DVM's new code is much easier to change. For example, a certain data type was intended to represent CAR-CDR chains for use in representing the positions of atoms in formulas. This was originally implemented as bit strings, where 10110 might represent CADDAR. For efficiency (given our LISP's regrettable clumsiness with numbers), this data type was changed completely, and implemented as a tree structure of atoms. Once the new data type had been invented, plugging it into the program took a few minutes. If all code had been allowed to manipulate objects of this type as integers, it would have been necessary to inspect every arithmetic operation in the program, a tedious and unreliable process.

What we have been outlining is the "conservative" approach to data type definition. Before we describe more radical ways of using these ideas, let us give you an example of how GOALNODEs might be defined. This is shown in Fig. 4.1. We have defined four functions: one to construct GOALNODEs and three to access their slots. Here, and throughout this book, a function to access slot s of an object of type t is named $s:t$. We have defined the three access functions three different ways, to show the possibilities. The first method, used for CHAR:GOALNODE, is the most straightforward, but a little inefficient. It seems unfair that the conscientious programmer should have to pay for an extra subroutine call. The other two methods remedy this. The second just makes STATE:GOALNODE a synonym of CADR. The

```
(DE GOALNODE (C S P) (CONS C (CONS S P))    )
(DE CHAR:GOALNODE (GN) (CAR GN)    )
(PUTPROP 'STATE:GOALNODE (GET 'CADR 'SUBR) 'SUBR)
(DM PLANS:GOALNODE (L) (LIST 'CDDR (CADR L))    )
```

FIG. 4.1. A type definition (conservative approach).

third defines a macro that causes (PLANS:GOALNODE...) to expand into
(CDDR...). The main advantage of the macro method is that it can lead to
very efficient compiled code. (We discussed in Chapter 3 how to avoid the
overhead of macro expansion in interpreted code.) The main disadvantage of
the macro method is that MAP functions don't handle macros, so we can't say
(MAPCAR 'PLANS:GOALNODE GNLIST).

> *Exercise 4.1*   Add three functions,
>
> CHAR:GOALNODE:SET, STATE:GOALNODE:SET, PLANS:GOALNODE:SET,
>
> each with two arguments, which assign values to the corresponding slots. For
> example,
>
> (PLANS:GOALNODE:SET GN1
>   (CONS NEWPLAN (PLANS:GOALNODE GN1)))
>
> should add a new plan to the plans of GN1. Try defining these functions in the
> three ways we defined the slot-accessing functions.

Using CARs and CDRs more sparingly has the nice side effect that CAR
and CDR get back some of their meaning. CAR should always mean *first
element of a list,* or *function.* CDR should always mean *rest of the elements,*
or *arguments.* You should almost never use CAR-CDR compositions outside
of data-type definitions.

There is one apparent exception. In macro definitions, you will need CAR-
CDR chains to extract pieces of the macro form. It is pointless to define a data
type "call to macro FOO," which is used only in the definition of FOO. This is
only an apparent exception, because, of course, the macro definition may
itself be thought of as defining a data type. Changes in the syntax of a macro
require changing just the definition and the places where the macro is called.

> *Exercise 4.2*   A more troublesome exception is the use of CDR in some LISPs
> to obtain the property list of a symbol. Show how to eliminate this problem by
> defining a type SYMBOL with slot PLIST. There is no particular need for a
> constructor of symbols, but you might also want a function IS-SYMBOL for
> testing whether something is a nonnumeric atom.

4.3   THE LIBERAL APPROACH

It may have occurred to you that defining all these functions can become
tedious. Why not let the computer do it? We should be able to say something
like

(RECORD-TYPE GOALNODE (CHAR STATE . PLANS))

that is, give a "picture" of what a typical GOALNODE looks like, and have all the right functions defined automatically.

The second argument to RECORD-TYPE is a structure of slot names. The intent is that each GOALNODE have the appropriate contents in the corresponding place; for example, the PLANS are kept in the CDDR. (A data structure with fixed named slots is called a *record*.) This we will call the "liberal" approach to type definition. RECORD-TYPE is defined in Fig. 4.2. A call to the RECORD-TYPE macro expands into a call to DE that defines the type constructor. By convention, the name of the type is the name of the constructor; in our example, GOALNODE will be defined as a function of three arguments that CONSes them together into a new goal node. The two functions SLOT-FUNS-EXTRACT and STRUC-CONS-FORM build the argument list and the body of the constructor, respectively. The former just makes a list of the atomic symbols in the "picture" of the type; as a side effect, it defines macros for accessing the slots. It does this by creating calls to DM and evaluating them. Notice that the symbols for the new function being defined and its corresponding CAR-CDR composition must be put together out of characters; this is done with READLIST and EXPLODE. EXPLODE takes an atom and returns a list of its characters. READLIST takes a list of characters and returns the corresponding atom.

```
(DECLARE (SPECIAL *TYPE*))

(DM RECORD-TYPE (L)
    (LET (*TYPE* (CADR L) SLOTS (CADDR L))
      (LIST 'DE *TYPE* (SLOT-FUNS-EXTRACT SLOTS NIL)
        (STRUC-CONS-FORM SLOTS)    )))

(DE SLOT-FUNS-EXTRACT (SLOTS PATH)
    (COND  ((NULL SLOTS) NIL)
           ((ATOM SLOTS)
            (EVAL  |"(DM @(READLIST  |"( |@(EXPLODE SLOTS) :|@(EXPLODE *TYPE*)))
                   (L)
                   (LIST
                     '@(READLIST  |"(C |@PATH R))
                     (CADR L))))
            (LIST SLOTS))
           ((NCONC(SLOT-FUNS-EXTRACT (CAR SLOTS) (CONS 'A PATH))
                  (SLOT-FUNS-EXTRACT (CDR SLOTS) (CONS 'D PATH))))  )  )

(DE STRUC-CONS-FORM (STRUC)
    (COND  ((NULL STRUC) NIL)
           ((ATOM STRUC) STRUC)
           ((LIST 'CONS
                  (STRUC-CONS-FORM (CAR STRUC))
                  (STRUC-CONS-FORM (CDR STRUC))))    ))
```

FIG. 4.2. Macro for automatic type definition.

Exercise 4.3   Modify RECORD-TYPE to take an optional flag argument that identifies every record. So

   (RECORD-TYPE GOALNODE $GN (CHAR STATE . PLANS))

would define goal nodes to look like

   ($GN *character state -plans-*)

Further, specifying a flag causes the function IS-GOALNODE to be defined, which tests whether something is a goal node. If the flag is NIL, there is to be no flag, and consequently IS-*type* will not be defined. If the flag is omitted, it defaults to the name of the type. This is the version of RECORD-TYPE that we will assume in subsequent chapters.

Exercise 4.4   Modify RECORD-TYPE to define a slot-setting macro for each slot.

Exercise 4.5   Modify RECORD-TYPE to define slot accessing and setting functions by the PUTPROP trick of Fig. 4.1.

Exercise 4.6   Not all data types are implemented as records. Write a macro (ATOM-TYPE *type* [*flag*] (-*slots*)) that defines its type to be implemented as a generated symbol; its slots are to be represented as properties, accessed and set with GET and PUTPROP. If the flag is non-NIL, it means that T is to be put under the indicator *flag* on data of this type, for use by the function IS-*type*, which your macro should define. If the flag is absent, it is the same as the type name. (If the flag is non-NIL, the name of the generated symbol should be derived from the flag.)

Exercise 4.7   Both RECORD-TYPE and ATOM-TYPE can be modified to define a constructor with a "keyword" syntax. (This is done in INTERLISP; see Teitelman, 1975.) In this notation, a goal node might be constructed by writing

   (GOALNODE CHAR 'MACBETH STATE '(=MACBETH KING))

where the plans have been left unspecified. This notation allows you to omit any initial slot value. This only makes sense if there is a way to specify default values for omitted slots. One way is to allow (OPTIONAL *slot default*) instead of a slot in the data-type definition. We can make the default plans be NIL by defining GOALNODE thus:

   (RECORD-TYPE KEYWORD GOALNODE
          (CHAR STATE . (OPTIONAL PLANS NIL)))

(The symbol KEYWORD indicates the type of constructor desired.) Implement this scheme. Make sure a keyword-syntax constructor treats it as an error to omit a nonoptional slot.

4.4   THE RADICAL APPROACH

In this book, we will follow the liberal track, and use RECORD-TYPE often. You can go even further if you like. The goal of the "radical" approach to type definition is to automate all type-dependent code generation. For example, say we have a list GNL of goal nodes and a variable GN bound to some particular goal node, and we wish to know if GN is in GNL. Do we use MEMBER, which looks for an EQUAL, or MEMQ, which insists on EQ-ness? (See Appendix.) It might appear obvious that MEMBER is what we want, but not necessarily. If goal nodes are indexed (see Chapter 11) so that a new one is never CONSed together if an old EQUAL one may be used instead, then MEMQ is more appropriate. In this case, using the inappropriate membership function can be inefficient or incorrect. The worst case would be a change to the program that made GOALNODEs possibly circular, so that MEMBER would loop forever. So we're back to the old problem of finding every place in a program where an out-of-date notation is used.

The solution is to introduce a macro MEM, called thus: (MEM GOALNODE GN GNL). MEM uses information about the type GOALNODE to pick MEMBER or MEMQ.

Exercise 4.8 Write the macro (MEM *type element list*). It should look to see if there is a function MEM:*type* defined; if so, it should expand into a call to it. Otherwise, it should look on the property list of type for the indicator EQUAL-TEST. If this is EQ, MEM expands into a call to MEMQ, else MEMBER. Write a macro (EQU *type x y*) that expands into EQUAL:*type,* EQUAL, or EQ, depending on analogous circumstances.

There are several other functions that are ambiguous with respect to equality. These include ASSOC, REMOVE, UNION, INTERSECTION, and ENTER. They can all receive the same treatment.

At about this point the returns from explicit type definition begin to diminish. The problem of finding all occurrences of MEMBER and changing them tends not to be as horrifying as finding all CDRs. We will let you decide how radical to be.

5

Flow of Control Functions

In this chapter we are concerned with developing two macro functions to simplify the writing of iterative loops in LISP. Although these functions are handy and can make heavily iterative code much cleaner, the reader should be aware that part of what this chapter is doing is designing another language on top of LISP.

LISP after all is based on the simple principle of the functional application of LAMBDA forms to argument lists. The macros we shall present try to hide this aspect of LISP. For those people familiar with other languages these macros will probably be much more intuitive that the built-in LISP functions such as MAPC.

The died-in-the-wool LISP hacker should also be aware of the alternatives presented here. An important consideration in coding in any language is knowing who will be trying to read, modify, and/or learn from your program afterward. Changing the surface of the language with the judicious use of well-designed macros can be an important factor in the usability of a system.

5.1 ITERATION

Most high-level languages have one or more mechanisms available for writing iterative loops. Since LISP has recursion, such loops are not essential, but often they are more practical. For example, any operation that is done to each element in a list that is 1000 elements long should be done iteratively, if the user wants to avoid stack overflow.

LISP provides several means for implementing iteration. First, there are the mapping functions. Mapping functions take a function and a list and apply the function to every element in the list. There are many different such functions, and they will be described in Section 5.6, "Mapping functions and the FOR macro."

Second, there is the PROG form. A PROG form is the LISP version of ALGOL's BEGIN-END block; that is, a PROG form allows the programmer to define an environment containing a set of local variable assignments and gives him some control over the flow of control. The general format of a PROG form, as you should already know, is

(PROG (-*atoms*-) -*exps*-)

If an expression is an atom then it is considered to be a label for the expression that follows it.

Two examples of PROGs are given in Fig. 5.1. The first is the expression given in Chapter 1, which calculates the sum of the integers between 1 and N. The second is the expression used to define the ";" comment read macro in Chapter 3, which reads characters until the end of the line is found.

```
(LAMBDA ( ) (PROG ( )
            (LOOP   (AND (EQ (READCH) CR) (RETURN NIL))
                    (GO LOOP]

(PROG   (SUM)
        (SETQ SUM 0)
  LOOP  (COND   ((EQUAL N 0) (RETURN SUM))
                (T (SETQ SUM (PLUS SUM N)))
                (SETQ N (DIFFERENCE N 1))))
        (GO LOOP)    )
```

FIG. 5.1.   Examples of PROG loops.

The PROG form is very general—in fact, it is too general. When you see a PROG, you have to read it very carefully to see what is going to happen. Many of the evils that the proponents of "structured programming" hoped to eliminate arose from the unrestricted use of labels and GO's.

Fortunately, the LISP macro facility allows us to define more limited (though not limiting) forms for doing iteration.

5.2   THE BASIC LOOP MACRO

The more structured languages such as ALGOL and PASCAL have an iterative form called the *WHILE loop*. For example,

WHILE X < Y DO X := X + FOO(X)

This says that the predicate X < Y should be tested. If it is true, then set X to the sum of X and FOO(X). Then repeat the loop.

Sometimes, it turns out to be more reasonable to have a loop that does an action and then tests to see if it should stop or not. These are *UNTIL loops.* For example,

DO X : = X + FOO(X) UNTIL X≥Y

will add FOO(X) to X first, then compare X against Y, and stop when X is greater than or equal to Y. Note that UNTIL stops the loop when its predicate is true and that WHILE stops the loop when its predicate is false.

We are going to define a macro called LOOP that will combine both WHILE and UNTIL loops into one, as well as allowing us to set up local variables for use only in the loop.

Using LOOP we would define the two loops in Fig. 5.1 as shown in Fig. 5.2. As can be seen, the subexpressions in the code are now labeled with what they do. We can see which expressions determine when the loop terminates and which ones (if any) determine what value the loop returns.

```
(LAMBDA ( ) (LOOP (UNTIL (EQ (READCH) CR]

(LOOP   (INITIAL SUM 0)
        (UNTIL (EQUAL N 0))
        (NEXT SUM (PLUS SUM N)
             N (DIFFERENCE N 1))
        (RESULT SUM]
```

FIG. 5.2. Examples of LOOP loops.

5.3 SYNTAX AND SEMANTICS OF LOOP

We are going to define LOOP as a macro that will expand into a PROG form. LOOP will take an arbitrary number of arguments, each of which is a list of the form (*keyword -exps-*). The keywords forms are

(INITIAL -*var exp*-)
(WHILE *exp*)
(DO -*exps*-)
(NEXT -*var exp*-)
(UNTIL *exp*)
(RESULT *exp*)

The *vars* are variables and the *exps* are expressions. The meaning of these forms are:

1. (INITIAL -*var exp*-)—initialize each *var* to *exp*, the expression following. For example,

   (INITIAL X 1 Y (PLUS X X))

would set X to 1 and Y to 2.

2. (WHILE *exp*)—stop the loop if the expression evaluates to false (NIL).

3. (DO -*exps*-)—evaluate the expressions from left to right.

4. (NEXT -*var exp*-)—reset each *var* to *exp*, the expression following.

5. (UNTIL *exp*)—stop the loop if the expression evaluates to true (non-NIL).

6. (RESULT *exp*)—return the value of the expression when the loop stops.

We can define the WHILE and UNTIL forms of other languages in terms of LOOP quite easily.

   WHILE *exp1* DO *exp2*

is equivalent to

   (LOOP (WHILE *exp1*) (DO *exp2*))

and

   DO *exp1* UNTIL *exp2*

is equivalent to

   (LOOP (DO *exp1*)(UNTIL *exp2*))

Furthermore, the WHILE and UNTIL keywords specify when the loop should *stop*. This means that infinite loops (such as are sometimes needed in input situations) can be written simply as

   (LOOP (DO *exp*))

rather than (as in ALGOL-like languages)

   WHILE TRUE DO *exp*

Finally since the WHILE, UNTIL, NEXT, and DO clauses can appear in any order, we can have expressions like

   (LOOP (UNTIL *exp1*) (DO *exp2*))

which means the *exp1* should be tested first, and *exp 2* should be done only if *exp1* is NIL. Likewise we could put WHILE after DO rather than before or have an UNTIL-WHILE loop.

5.4   DEFINING LOOP

LOOP will expand into a PROG form, with local variables and SETQs for
the INITIAL clauses, with conditionals for the WHILE and/or UNTIL
clauses, with SETQs for the NEXT clauses, and with a RETURN expression
for the RESULT clause. There are many slightly different forms that the
desired PROG could take. Figure 5.3 shows one of the simplest. The actual
order of the WHILE, DO, NEXT, and UNTIL clauses of course depends on
the particular LOOP form being expanded.

```
(PROG      (-vars-)                 from INITIAL
           -(SETQ var exp)-         from INITIAL
 LOOP      (OR exp (GO EXIT))       from WHILE
           -exps-                   from DO
           -(SETQ var exp)-         from NEXT
           (AND exp (GO EXIT))      from UNTIL
           (GO LOOP)
 EXIT      (RETURN exp))            from RESULT
```

FIG. 5.3.   Format of LOOP expansion.

Looking at the figure, we can see that LOOP generates a frame of the form

   (PROG (. . .) . . . LOOP . . . (GO LOOP) EXIT (RETURN . . .))

where the ellipses represent zero or more expressions.

Figure 5.4 shows the code for the LOOP macro. It involves the main
function LOOP plus several subfunctions.

The main function LOOP uses the |" read macro from Section 3.3 to build
the PROG form, primarily by splicing together translations of each LOOP
clause. We splice things together using APPLY and MAPCAR.

The DO, NEXT, WHILE, and UNTIL clauses are translated by DO-
CLAUSE. The INITIAL and RESULT clauses are treated separately by the
LOOP macro because only one of each is supposed to occur and their
translations always go in the same place (INITIAL at the beginning and
RESULT at the end). The function GET-KEYWORD is used to access these
two clauses.

The INITIAL clause contains both the PROG variables and their initial
values, in the format

   (INITIAL -var exp-)

The variables and expressions are first grouped into the more tractable form.

   (-(var exp)-)

using the function PAIR-UP. Then the function VAR-LIST gets the variables
and SETQ-VARS builds the initializing SETQs.

```
(DM LOOP (L)
|" (PROG  @(VAR-LIST    (GET-KEYWORD 'INITIAL L))
          |@(SUBSET     'CADDR
                        (SETQ-VARS (GET-KEYWORD 'INITIAL L)))
  LOOP    |@(APPLY 'APPEND (MAPCAR 'DO-CLAUSE (CDR L)))
          (GO LOOP)
  EXIT    (RETURN  |@(GET-KEYWORD 'RESULT L]

(DE GET-KEYWORD (KEYWORD CLAUSES)
  (LET (ITEM (ASSOC KEYWORD CLAUSES))
   (COND (ITEM (CDR ITEM]

(DE DO-CLAUSE (CLAUSE)
  (SELECTQ   (CAR CLAUSE)
             ((INITIAL RESULT) NIL)
             (WHILE  |"((OR  @ (CADR CLAUSE) (GO EXIT))))
             (DO (APPEND (CDR CLAUSE) NIL))
             (UNTIL  |"((AND @(CADR CLAUSE) (GO EXIT))))
             (ERROR '"unknown LOOP keyword"]

(DE PAIR-UP (L)
  (COND ((NULL L) NIL)
        ((NULL (CDR L))
         (ERROR '"Odd number of INITIAL elements"))
        ((CONS (LIST (CAR L) (CADR L)) (PAIR-UP (CDDR L]

(DE VAR-LIST (L) (MAPCAR 'CAR (PAIR-UP L]

(DE SETQ-VARS (L)
  (MAPCAR '(LAMBDA (PAIR) (CONS 'SETQ PAIR))
          (PAIR-UP L]
```

FIG. 5.4. Definition of the LOOP macro.

Exercise 5.1 SETQ-VARS builds a SETQ for every variable-expression pair. However PROG initializes local variables to NIL, so SETQ of variables to NIL can be omitted. Change the call to SETQ-VARS in LOOP to avoid setting variables to NIL. Do not change SETQ-VARS since you will want it in the next exercise.

DO-CLAUSE uses the built-in function SELECTQ to translate a clause based on the CAR of that clause. SELECTQ is a reserved word that takes the following format:

(SELECTQ *exp* -(*test* -*exps*)- *expl*)

SELECTQ evaluates *exp* and then looks at each *test*. If a test is an atom and *exp* is equal to it or if a test is a list and *exp* is a member of it, then, as in COND, the remaining expressions in the clause containing the test are evaluated, and the value of the last is returned. If no test can be found for *exp,* then *expl* is evaluated and returned.

Thus, in Fig. 5.4, DO-CLAUSE takes a clause and returns a (possibly empty) list of expressions. If the clause is an INITIAL or a RESULT, DO-CLAUSE returns NIL because the LOOP itself has already generated code for these clauses.

If the clause is (WHILE *exp*), then DO-CLAUSE returns a list of (OR *exp* (GO EXIT)). EXIT is the label for the RETURN expression of the expanded PROG form. Hence this form says "either the WHILE expression is non-NIL or else exit the loop."

If the clause is (DO -*exps*-), then DO-CLAUSE returns just the list of expressions.

If the clause is (UNTIL *exp*), then DO-CLAUSE returns a list of (AND *exp* (GO EXIT)). This form says "if the UNTIL expression is non-NIL, then exit the loop."

Exercise 5.2   The definition of DO-CLAUSE given in Fig. 5.4 does not handle NEXT clauses. Redefine DO-CLAUSE to generate the necessary SETQs.

5.5   A LOOP EXAMPLE

LINEREAD is a function of no arguments that reads in a line of one or more expressions and makes a list of them; that is,

```
(LINEREAD)A B C D        returns (A B C D)
(LINEREAD)A              returns (A)
(LINEREAD)A (B
C)                       returns (A (B C))
```

Furthermore, if the last expression is followed by a space or a comma, reading continues on the next line, thus:

```
(LINEREAD)A B,
C                        returns (A B C)
```

The definition of LINEREAD is quite simple, if we use LOOP and the PEEKC function. PEEKC returns the ASCII value of the next character waiting to be read. LINEREAD will read an expression; then use PEEKC to see if the next character is a carriage return (ASCII value 13). If it is, LINEREAD quits; otherwise it reads another expression.

Space and comma prevent LINEREAD from seeing a carriage return, but both are ignored by the function READ.

```
(DE LINEREAD ( )
  (LOOP (INITIAL PTR NIL)
        (NEXT PTR (NCONC1 PTR (READ)))
        (UNTIL (EQ (PEEKC) 13))
        (RESULT PTR)))
```

Exercise 5.3   The definition of LINEREAD just given always reads at least one expression. If the line is empty, another line is read. Fix LINEREAD so that it returns NIL when it reads an empty line. This requires only one very simple change.

Exercise 5.4   While comma makes a reasonable character for continuing a line, space does not. Fix LINEREAD so that it skips over all spaces at the end of a line. This requires a simple LOOP within the main loop. Avoid using flags to pass information from one loop to the other.

5.6 MAPPING FUNCTIONS AND THE FOR MACRO

You should be familiar with the four basic mapping functions: MAP, MAPC, MAPLIST, and MAPCAR. They each take a function (e.g., a LAMBDA expression) and a list and apply the function repetitively to the list. MAP and MAPLIST both apply the function to successive tails of the list. MAPC and MAPCAR both apply the function to successive elements of the list. In our LISP, MAP and MAPC both return NIL. MAPLIST and MAPCAR both return a list of the values returned by the application of the function. Figure 5.5 shows what happens for each MAP function when we apply PRINT to the list (A B C).

To this basic set of function, several others have been added. MAPCON and MAPCAN are like MAPLIST and MAPCAR, respectively, except that

Map function	Printed output	Returned value
MAP	(A B C)	NIL
	(B C)	
	(C)	
MAPC	A	NIL
	B	
	C	
MAPLIST	(A B C)	((A B C) (B C) (C))
	(B C)	
	(C)	
MAPCAR	A	(A B C)
	B	
	C	

FIG. 5.5.   Mapping PRINT across the list (A B C).

NCONC is applied to the final list. This means that the function applied should always return NIL or a list. In the final result, all the NILs are removed by the NCONC.

For example, if we wanted to apply the function FOO to the list L and save all the non-NIL results, we would write

```
(MAPCAN '(LAMBDA (X)
            (LET (Y (FOO X)) (COND (Y (LIST Y)))))
         L)
```

The function SUBSET applies a function to every element in the list and returns all the *elements* of the list for which the function returns a non-NIL value. Thus, if instead of the value of FOO we wanted to save the elements of L for which FOO was non-NIL, we would write

```
(SUBSET 'FOO L)
```

An additional extension to the mapping functions in our LISP is the ability to map functions of more than one argument (this does not apply to SUBSET). As a simple example, the following

```
(MAPCAR 'CONS '(A B C) '(1 2 3))
 ⇒ ((A . 1) (B . 2) (C . 3))
```

One of the most striking things about the mapping functions is how unmnemonic their names are. The conceptual links between MAPC and MAPCAR or MAPCAN and MAPCON are not reflected at all. The most reasonable names are MAP, MAPLIST, and MAPCON. MAPLIST lists the answers produced by MAP and MAPCON concatenates them. Unfortunately, these are the three least useful functions! Most commonly we want to apply a function to the elements of a list, not the tails.

It is also the case that one has to learn various idioms for getting all the power from the mapping functions that is available. The example of MAPCAN given above is a common idiom used to collect non-NIL values.

The FOR macro is designed to bring some order to the chaos of the mapping functions and to make it easy to write the common idioms. Thus, the MAPCAN example becomes

```
(FOR (X IN L) (FILTER (FOO X)))
```

and the SUBSET example becomes

```
(FOR (X IN L) (WHEN (FOO X)) (SAVE X))
```

The general format of the FOR macro is

```
(FOR -(variable IN list)-
     (WHEN exp1)
     (DO | SAVE | FILTER | SPLICE exp2))
```

The **WHEN** clause is optional. If absent, *expl* is assumed to be **T**. The **FOR** macro expands into a mapping function with the *variables* as the **LAMBDA** variables and the *lists* as arguments. The **LAMBDA** body is such that whenever *expl* evaluates to non-**NIL** for some setting of the **LAMBDA** variables, then *exp2* is evaluated. **DO** means that no results are saved. **SAVE** means that a list of all the results is returned. **FILTER** means that a list of all the non-**NIL** results is returned. **SPLICE** means that the list formed by applying **NCONC** to all the results is returned.

5.7 EXAMPLES OF THE FOR MACRO

Figure 5.6 shows what various **FOR** forms translate into.

As can be seen, sometimes the mapping form is simpler and sometimes (particularly "**WHEN**" or "**FILTER**" are involved) the **FOR** form is simpler.

```
(FOR (X IN L) (DO (FOO X)))
(MAPC 'FOO L)

(FOR (X IN L) (SAVE (FOO X)))
(MAPCAR 'FOO L)

(FOR (X IN L) (SPLICE (FOO X)))
(MAPCAN 'FOO L)

(FOR (X IN L) (FILTER (FOO X)))
(MAPCAN  '(LAMBDA (X)
              (LET (X (FOO X)) (COND (X (LIST X)))))
         L)

(FOR (X IN L) (WHEN (FOO X)) (DO (BAZ X)))
(MAPC '(LAMBDA (X) (COND ((FOO X) (BAZ X)))) L)

(FOR (X IN L) (WHEN (FOO X)) (SAVE X))
(SUBSET 'FOO L)

(FOR (X IN L) (WHEN (FOO X)) (SAVE (BAZ X)))
(MAPCAN '(LAMBDA (X) (COND ((FOO X) (LIST (BAZ X))))) L)

(FOR (X IN L) (WHEN (FOO X)) (SPLICE (BAZ X)))
(MAPCAN '(LAMBDA (X) (COND ((FOO X) (BAZ X )))) L)

(FOR (X IN L) (WHEN (FOO X)) (FILTER (BAZ X)))
(MAPCAN  '(LAMBDA (X)
              (COND ((FOO X)
                     (LET (X (BAZ X)) (COND (X (LIST X)))))))
         L)
```

FIG. 5.6. Mapping equivalents of different FOR loops.

5.8   DEFINING THE FOR MACRO

In order to build the appropriate mapping structure, the FOR macro has to decide on two things:

1. the mapping function;
2. the LAMBDA expression.

Four pieces of information turn out to be required:

1. the LAMBDA variable(s) in the IN clause(s);
2. whether or not there is a WHEN clause;
3. whether a DO, SAVE, SPLICE, or FILTER is being done—we'll call this the *type* of the FOR loop;
4. what the expression in the DO, SAVE, SPLICE, or FILTER looks like—we'll call this the *body* of the FOR loop.

We therefore need functions to obtain each of these pieces. These functions look through all the arguments of the FOR loop for the things they need. This will mean the keyword clauses can appear in any order in the FOR loop. This can be considered either a feature or a bug. It's a matter of taste.

A set of functions for the FOR macro are given in Fig. 5.7. As with LOOP, FOR puts together the expressions generated by a number of subexpressions.

```
(DM FOR (L)
 (LET  (VARS   (VARS:FOR L)
        ARGS   (ARGS:FOR L)          <exercise 5.5>
        TEST   (TEST:FOR L)
        TYPE   (TYPE:FOR L)
        BODY   (BODY:FOR L))         <exercise 5.6>
  (CONS (MAKE-MAPFN VARS TEST TYPE BODY)
   (CONS (LIST 'QUOTE
               (MAKE-LAMBDA VARS
                   (ADD-TEST TEST
                       (MAKE-BODY VARS TEST TYPE BODY))))
         ARGS]

(DE VARS:FOR (L)
 (MAPCAN  '(LAMBDA (X)
               (COND ((IS-VAR-FORM X) (LIST (VAR:VAR-FORM X))))
          L]

(DE IS-VAR-FORM (X) (AND (EQ (LENGTH X) 3) (EQ (CADR X) 'IN]

(DE VAR:VAR-FORM (X) (CAR X]
```

FIG. 5.7.   Definition of the FOR macro.

```
(DE TEST:FOR (L)
 (LET (ITEM (ITEM:FOR '(WHEN) L))
  (COND (ITEM (CADR ITEM]

(DE TYPE:FOR (L)
 (LET (ITEM (ITEM:FOR '(DO SAVE SPLICE FILTER) L))
  (COND (ITEM (CAR ITEM))
         ((ERROR '"No body in FOR loop"]

(DE ITEM:FOR (KEYWORDS L)
 (LET (ITEM NIL)
  (SOME '(LAMBDA (KEY) (SETQ ITEM (ASSOC KEY (CDR L))))
        KEYWORDS)
 ITEM]

(DE MAKE-MAPFN (VARS TEST TYPE BODY)
 (COND   ((EQUAL TYPE 'DO) 'MAPC)
          ((NOT (EQUAL TYPE 'SAVE)) 'MAPCAN)
          ((NULL TEST) 'MAPCAR)
          ((SUBSET-TEST VARS BODY) ' SUBSET)
          ('MAPCAN]

(DE SUBSET-TEST (VARS BODY)
 (AND (EQUAL (LENGTH VARS ) 1) (EQUAL (CAR VARS) BODY]

(DE MAKE-BODY (VARS TEST TYPE BODY)
 (COND ((EQUAL TYPE 'FILTER)
         (LIST 'LET (LIST 'X BODY) '(COND (X (LIST X)))))
        ((OR (NOT (EQUAL TYPE 'SAVE)) (NULL TEST))
         BODY)
        ((SUBSET-TEST VARS BODY) NIL)
        ((LIST 'LIST BODY]

(DE ADD-TEST (TEST BODY)
 (COND ((NULL TEST) BODY)
        ((NULL BODY) TEST)
        (T (LIST 'COND (LIST TEST BODY]

(DE MAKE-LAMBDA (VARS BODY) (LIST 'LAMBDA VARS BODY]
```

FIG. 5.7. Definition of the FOR macro.

In keeping with record package conventions, functions that extract arguments from FOR loops end with :FOR. These functions are the only ones that depend on the particular syntax we have specified for FOR loops. If we changed the syntax of FOR, only these functions would have to be modified.

The function VARS:FOR gets the LAMBDA variables from the "(*variable* IN *list*)" clause(s).

Exercise 5.5 Define the function ARGS:FOR, which is just like VARS:FOR except that it returns the list(s) to which the mapping function is to be applied.

The function TEST:FOR gets the WHEN clause, if any. TYPE:FOR gets the type of the FOR loop. This can be DO, SAVE, SPLICE, or FILTER.

Exercise 5.6 Define the function BODY:FOR, which is just like TYPE:FOR except that it returns the expression that is the body of the FOR loop.

The function MAKE-MAPFN is responsible for choosing whether to use MAPC, MAPCAR, MAPCAN, or SUBSET. The decision is based on the following rules:

1. If the type of the FOR is DO, then use MAPC.
2. If the type of the FOR is FILTER or SPLICE, then use MAPCAN.
3. If the type of the FOR is SAVE and there is no WHEN clause, then use MAPCAR.
4. If the type of the FOR is SAVE, there is a WHEN clause, and the only thing being saved is the LAMBDA variable, then use SUBSET.
5. Otherwise use MAPCAN.

The function MAKE-BODY is responsible for building the expression that is to be evaluated and perhaps saved. There are four choices: no expression, the body given in the FOR loop, LIST applied to the body given in the FOR loop, or a filtering form that returns only non-NIL values.
The decision is based on the following rules:

1. If the type is FILTER, then build a form that returns LIST of non-NIL values of the FOR body.
2. If the type is not SAVE or there is no WHEN clause, then use the FOR body directly.
3. If the only thing being saved is the LAMBDA variable (i.e., we can use SUBSET), then use NIL.
4. Otherwise, build the form that returns LIST of the FOR body.

After MAKE-BODY has built an expression, ADD-TEST is called to insert a conditional around that expression, if there is a WHEN clause. A conditional is not needed if there is no WHEN clause test, or if there is no expression (which happens when SUBSET is used).
Finally the function MAKE-LAMBDA takes the variable list and the expression returned by ADD-TEST and builds a normal LAMBDA form.

Exercise 5.7 **MAKE-LAMBDA** could be smarter. For example,

(MAKE-LAMBDA '(X Y) '(CONS X Y))

returns

(LAMBDA (X Y) (CONS X Y))

when **CONS** alone is sufficient. Redefine **MAKE-LAMBDA** to take this optimization into account.

Exercise 5.8 The only mapping functions not taken into account with the **FOR** macro are **EVERY** and **SOME** (see the appendix). Define the macro **FOR-ALL** so that

(FOR-ALL (*var* IN *list*) -*exps*-)

expands into

(EVERY '(LAMBDA (*var*) -*exps*-) *list*)

Likewise, define a **THERE-EXISTS** macro so that

(THERE-EXISTS (*var* IN *list*) -*exps*)

expands into

(SOME '(LAMBDA (*var*) -*exps*-) *list*)

Exercise 5.9 Fix the definition of **FOR** so that more than one expression can appear in the DO, FILTER, SAVE, SPLICE, and WHEN clauses. In the simplest solution, **FOR** would put a **PROGN** around every sequence of more than one expression. The better solution would check to see if the sequence of expressions can be used without the **PROGN**. For example, the **PROGN** is not needed in either of the following two cases:

(LAMBDA (-*vars*-) (PROGN *exps*-))
(COND (*exp* (PROGN -*exps*-)))

5.9 CONCLUSION

Two macros have been presented in this chapter: the **LOOP** macro based on the **PROG** form and the **FOR** macro based on the mapping functions. The **LOOP** macro is more restricted than a **PROG**, whereas the **FOR** macro is more general than any one mapping function. Both are an attempt to induce a uniform structure to iteration in LISP. In particular, a keyword syntax has been used instead of the normal positional one.

The keyword approach has several advantages: It allows for optional arguments, it allows freedom in the ordering of arguments, and it forces a labeling of the function of expression. It also has its disadvantages: Expressions are longer, some legal orderings of arguments can be very misleading (e.g., putting a test after an expression that it will actually be evaluated before), and sometimes expressions will be in a keyword clause that do not really perform the function intended for that keyword.

The macro facility in LISP allows the programmer to use the keyword syntax when he wants to. Used judiciously, it can be a powerful tool for the construction of readable programs. The option is there. Experience is the best teacher of when to use it.

6

I/O in LISP

Functions for doing input and output are often given short shrift in high-level programming languages. The best known example is ALGOL-60, which considered input/output to be part of the system implementation, not of the language proper.

In LISP, input and output tends to be less important because the LISP interpreter takes care of the most important input (namely, reading in the initial expression) and the most important output (namely, writing out the final value). Once evaluation starts, functions communicate by passing values and no input or output is needed.

There are certainly many tasks, however, where user interaction is needed or where information needs to be displayed and/or saved for later use. LISP has accumulated a large number of functions for input and output. Like the mapping functions, there is little rhyme or reason to the naming conventions. Fortunately only a few functions are really necessary for most uses. Unfortunately, these functions are very implementation dependent.

I/O functions in LISP can be divided into two classes. First, there are the functions that actually perform an input or output operation. For example, READ causes one S-expression to be read. Second, there are the functions that affect where the input or output is directed. For example, there is the function INC that does no input itself but causes future inputs to come from a file. We describe these classes separately.

6.1 CHARACTER STRINGS AND S-EXPRESSIONS

The crucial thing to remember in doing I/O in LISP is that internally LISP is dealing with those dotted pair data structures described in Chapter 1. Externally LISP is typing and reading sequences of characters; that is, you and the LISP interpreter talk about LISP's internal data structures by typing and reading strings of characters. Some internal structures cannot be represented as characters strings (e.g., circular lists) and some character strings do not represent any internal structure [e.g., (A . B C))]. You should always keep in mind that there is a difference between what you see and what you get.

There are several functions in our LISP for converting from expressions to character strings and back. The function EXPLODE takes an expression and returns a list of the characters that are used to write the external character string representation of that expression. Some examples of EXPLODE's behavior are

    (EXPLODE 'ABC) ⇒ (A B C)
    (EXPLODE 12) ⇒ (1 2)
    (EXPLODE '(A B C)) ⇒ (/(A / B / C /))

The first two examples show that atoms (including numbers) are split up into the characters needed to print them. The third example shows that a list is likewise split up. The result of EXPLODEing the list (A B C) is a list of seven elements: a left parenthesis, and A, a space, a B, another space, a C, and a right parenthesis. These are exactly the characters LISP would type if you printed the list (A B C). Keep in mind the fact that EXPLODE takes an *S-expression* as input; that is,

    (EXPLODE '(A   B C)) = (EXPLODE '(A B C))

because the internal S-expressions build by READ for the two lists look the same.

The reason for the slashes in the third EXPLODE is a bit complicated. Certain characters in LISP are special in that READ does special things when it sees them. For example, a left parenthesis tells READ that a list is starting, a right parenthesis says that a list is ended, and a space terminates an identifier but is otherwise ignored. When LISP has to PRINT the *character* for a space or a parenthesis, it has to put slashes (/) in front of the parentheses and spaces. A slash tells both the user and READ that the very next character is to be taken as is and not treated like a special character. Suppose that PRINT did not do this. Then the third EXPLODE example would be printed.

    (EXPLODE '(A B C)) ⇒ ((A B C))

which looks like the list ((A B C)).

Using the slash, we can put any character we want in an atom. Thus A/ B is an atom, consisting of an A, followed by a space, followed by a B. Why you would want such an atom is your own problem.

One important thing to remember is that the very next character after the slash is the character that is taken. The end of a line in most systems is signaled by some character (in ASCII-based systems, line breaks are often signaled with carriage returns, which are controls-Ms). If you put a slash at the end of the line, then the line break character will be taken as a regular character, not a line break.

Since slashes are somewhat ugly, it is wise initially to assign all the special characters to global variables like ATSIGN (@), DBQUOTE ("), and BLANK. Then when we need to use one of these characters, we can just use the mnemonic name for it. To set the three variables just mentioned we would write

```
(SETQ ATSIGN ' /@)
(SETQ DBQUOTE ' /")
(SETQ BLANK ' /)
```

The inverse function of EXPLODE is READLIST. This converts a list of characters, such as EXPLODE produces, into an S-expression. A set of characters that does not produce a legitimate expression (e.g., there is an unbalanced set of parentheses) causes an error.

Thus:

```
(READLIST '(A B C)) ⇒ ABC
(READLIST '(1 2)) ⇒ 12
(READLIST '(/( A / B / C /))) ⇒ (A B C)
```

Exercise 6.1   Define the function CONCATENATE, which takes two atoms and makes a new atom by concatenating them together; that is,

```
(CONCATENATE 'AB 'CD) ⇒ ABCD
```

6.2   READING IN LISP

Input in LISP is done primarily with the LISP function READ. This function takes a sequence of characters and builds an S-expression. This expression is the value of the READ function.

READ starts by setting a level counter to zero and scanning for a nonblank character (line breaks such as carriage return and line feed are considered blanks). If a left parenthesis is read, the level counter is incremented by one. If a right parenthesis is read, the level counter is decremented by one. Whenever a right parenthesis, blank, or line break is read, the level counter is checked. If it is not greater than zero, reading stops, and a list of all the characters read is passed to READLIST, which turns the string into the S-expression which is returned by READ.

Although we usually want to read a whole expression, there are times when we only want to read one character. There are two functions available to do this: READCH and TYI. READCH reads and returns one character; that is, READCH returns an *atom* whose print name is one character long.

TYI is based on the idea of character codes. Characters are stored internally as numbers. Different machines have different coding schemes. Two common ones are ASCII and EBCDIC. The TYI function reads one character and returns the numeric code for that character. Since character coding schemes are usually systematic, certain general facts can be deduced about a character from its numeric code. For example, in ASCII, all the control (nonprinting) characters have a numeric code less than 32 and the codes for the lowercase characters are exactly 32 more than their uppercase equivalents.

To show how READCH and TYI work, we will place the character read immediately after the function call and before the ⇒ value.

> (READCH)A ⇒ A
> (TYI)A ⇒ 65 (on ASCII systems)
> (READCH)
⇒ <line break character>
> (TYI)
⇒ <numeric code for line break>

6.3 WRITING IN LISP

LISP has a confusing array of printing functions, even though conceptually printing is easier. These have accumulated over the years as people wanted more control over how their output looked. LISP never distinguished the print function from the idea of print formats. Instead, different printing functions were developed that wrote expressions in different ways. We first describe a few of the available functions and then define a general output function.

The basic output function is PRINT. PRINT does not worry at all about formatting things for readability. For example, suppose we printed the definition of the FEXPR CONS-LIST described in Chapter 2.

```
(PRINT (GET 'CONS-LIST 'FEXPR))
(LAMBDA (L) (PROG (RESULT) LOOP (COND ((NULL L) (R~
ETURN RESULT)) (T (SETQ RESULT (NCONC1 RESULT (EVA~
L (CAR L)))) (SETQ L (CDR L)) (GO LOOP)))))
```

[The tilde (~) comment character at the end of some lines is used by LISP to continue an identifier (like RETURN and EVAL in this case) across a line break.]

The form above is readable to LISP, and if no one else was going to look at the function definition, this would be good enough. However the above is certainly not readable for humans. Therefore when we want to print a big S-expression so that people can read it, we can use a function called **SPRINT**.

(**SPRINT** *expression number*)

will print *expression* in an indented format that people can read. *Number* specifies the left margin. Normally we will use 1 for this, meaning that the printing of the expression starts in column 1.

For example, we could print **CONS-LIST**'s **FEXPR** definition by typing

(**SPRINT** (**GET** '**CONS-LIST** '**FEXPR**) 1)

which would lead to the form in Fig. 6.1.

```
(LAMBDA (L)
 (PROG  (RESULT)
 LOOP  (COND ((NULL L) (RETURN RESULT))
             (T (SETQ RESULT (NCONC1 RESULT (EVAL (CAR L))))
             (SETQ L (CDR L))
             (GO LOOP]
```

FIG. 6.1.   Example of pretty-printing.

The **SPRINT** function in our LISP is fairly smart. It has special indentation rules for functions, for reserved words, for labels, and so on. It also uses balanced pairs of left and right square brackets to demarcate the clauses of conditionals. Other LISPs have similar "pretty-printing" functions. You should make yourself familiar with the one you have. If your LISP doesn't have one, you should try writing one.

Sometimes the **PRINT** function is not satisfactory because of another feature that it has: **PRINT** is the inverse of **READ**. This means that (**PRINT** *exp*) produces a character string *string* such that **READ** *string* will produce the S-expression *exp*. Believe it or not, this is not always what we want!

For example, a string in our LISP is a sequence of characters starting and ending with a double quote mark ("). Therefore, when we **PRINT** a string, these double quotes must be included if **READ** is to be able to recognize the output as a string later. For example,

(**PRINT** '"This is a string")

causes the printout

"This is a string"

Notice that since the string is treated like a literal atom by **EVAL**, we had to quote (') it.

Normally, though, we print a string to obtain the characters inside it. We don't want the quote marks. To do this, we use the function **PRINTSTR**.

PRINTSTR takes an S-expression and prints it, just like PRINT, but PRINTSTR omits the double quotes that delimit strings. Thus,

(PRINTSTR '"This is a string")

causes the printout

This is a string

Both PRINT and PRINTSTR have one side effect that we might not want: They always put the expression printed on a new line. (PRINT in some LISPs prints the expression first and then starts a new line.)

In our LISP, PRINT and PRINTSTR are defined in terms of several more basic functions: TERPRI, PRIN1, and PRINC. (PRIN1 exp) causes exp to be printed in LISP rereadable form, that is, string quotes and all. (PRINC exp) causes exp to be printed without any string quotes that it might have. Both PRIN1 and PRINC return exp and neither cause a new line to be printed (unless the expression is so long that it requires several lines to print). (TERPRI exp) causes a line break and returns exp. It is often put around the argument of a printing function to force a new line.

The definitions in our LISP of PRINT and PRINTSTR are

```
(DE PRINT (X)
 (PROG1 (PRIN1 (TERPRI X)) (PRINC '" ")]
(DE PRINTSTR (X)
 (PROG1 (PRINC (TERPRI X)) (PRINC '" ")]
```

The function PROG1 evaluates its arguments and returns the value of the first. Thus PRINT and PRINTSTR both return the expression printed as their value.

All the printing functions described so far can print whole S-expressions. There is one function that can only print one character. It is TYO, the inverse function of TYI. (TYO exp) takes a number and prints the character that has that number as its internal numeric code. TYO returns exp. The primary use of TYO is to print control characters.

Exercise 6.2 Define the function SHIFT-UP, which reads characters until it sees a period and then prints out the characters read, with all the lowercase characters shifted to uppercase. This will require knowing what encoding system your machine uses.

6.4 THE WRITE MACRO

The printing functions in our LISP are confusingly named and not very well organized. Furthermore each LISP has developed a slightly different set, usually with names that are just as bad. So we define a macro WRITE that will be useful for doing almost all the printing that we need, without requiring us to remember whether we want a PRINT, PRINTSTR, TERPRI, PRINC, or PRIN1.

Our WRITE macro will take an arbitrary number of arguments. Some of these arguments will be printing instructions and others will be expressions to be printed. For example,

(WRITE T "The value of " FOO " is " (TAB 40) (EVAL FOO))

will start a new line (the T does this), print the string "The value of" without string quotes, print the value of FOO, print the string " is" (again without quotes), move to the fortieth column on the line (the TAB does this), and print the result of (EVAL FOO). WRITE will then return the value of (EVAL FOO). If FOO evaluates to the atom BAZ and BAZ evaluates to 25, then the expression above will type

The value of BAZ is   25

The WRITE expression above expands into the code in Fig. 6.2. Notice that with explicit strings, PRINC is used and its argument is quoted but that with other expressions PRIN1 is used and its argument is evaluated.

```
(PROGN  (TERPRI NIL)
        (PRINC '"The value of")
        (PRIN1 FOO)
        (PRINC '"is")
        (TAB 40)
        (PRIN1 (EVAL FOO)))
```

FIG. 6.2. Expansion of WRITE macro.

The function TAB is our LISP is used for columnarization. (TAB *exp*) prints enough spaces so that the next character printed will start in column *exp*. Two related functions that we will use are SPACES and LINES. (SPACES *exp*) causes *exp* spaces to be printed. (LINES *exp*) causes *exp* new lines to be printed; that is, (LINES 1) is equivalent to one TERPRI, (LINES 2) to two TERPRIs, and so on.

Exercise 6.3 Define the functions SPACES, LINES, and TAB, using PRINC and TERPRI to print spaces and new lines. For TAB you will also need the function CURRCOL, which returns the current printing column. In some LISPs CURRCOL itself has to be defined using the functions LINELENGTH and CHARCT. (LINELENGTH NIL) in our LISP returns the maximum number of characters that can be put in an output line. (CHARCT) returns the number of characters left in the current line.

Our WRITE macro will allow the following arguments:

1. The character T starts a new line.

2. The forms (LINES *exp*), (SPACES *exp*), and (TAB *exp*) are executed directly.
3. Any other form is printed using PRIN1. Note that this means that if a variable or expression in a WRITE returns a string value, it will be printed using PRIN1; that is, the string quotes will appear.

In order to recognize explicit strings we need the function STRINGP. In our LISP, (STRINGP *exp*) returns T if and only if *exp* is a string (i.e., it is an atom that begins and ends with a double quote).

Exercise 6.4   Define STRINGP. (*Hint:* use EXPLODE).

Our definition of WRITE appears in Fig. 6.3. This code builds a PROGN expression, where each argument of the WRITE macro (found in the CDR of L) is converted into the appropriate print expression, and the conversions are collected into a list.

```
(DM WRITE (L)
 (CONS 'PROGN
  (FOR   (X IN (CDR L))
       (SAVE (COND ((STRINGP X)
                    (LIST 'PRINC (LIST 'QUOTE X)))
                   ((EQ X 'T) '(TERPRI NIL))
                   ((AND  (CONSP X)
                          (MEMQ (CAR X) '(LINES SPACES TAB)))
                    X)
                   (T (LIST 'PRIN1 X]
```

FIG. 6.3.   Definition of WRITE macro.

Exercise 6.5   Add the following facility to WRITE: If the form (CODE *exp*) is seen, then the character with the numeric code *exp* is printed.

6.5   FILES IN LISP

File handling in any language is extremely machine and/or operating system dependent. LISP is no exception, but fortunately it is possible to define more general functions that allow you to keep your functions free of file considerations.

6.6   FILE INPUT IN OUR LISP

Before we can present the more useful functions, we have to describe the set of file primitives available in our particular operating system. We actually present very simplified versions of the functions available.

There are four functions of note: INPUT, OUTPUT, INC, and OUTC. The first two tell LISP that a file exists. The last two tell LISP to direct future reading or writing to that file.

Before we can read anything from a file, we must call the function INPUT. It is a reserved word and is called thus:

(INPUT *channel file*)

Neither argument is evaluated. *File* is the name of the file you want to read. It must already exist in your file directory area. *Channel* can be any literal atom that isn't already being used a as channel. By convention, an implicit

(INPUT NIL <your teletype>)

is always in effect, so don't use NIL. INPUT makes *channel* the name of a line of communication to be used between LISP and the file. *Channel* is returned as the value of INPUT.

LISP associates three things with a channel name: the file name, whether the channel is for input or output, and where in the file the next input (or output) should be. INPUT initially sets the channel name to point to the first character in the file. When READ or any other LISP input function reads characters from that channel, the pointer is updated to point to the next unread character.

For example, to make the file FOO available for future input we could write

(INPUT FILE-CHAN FOO)

This makes the atom FILE-CHAN the channel name for input from the file FOO. In LISP jargon, we have *opened* the file FOO for input.

Note that more than one channel can be associated with the same file. Although it is not good practice to do so, you could have one channel for input from the file and one for output to the file (assigning output channels is described in the next section). Or you could have two input channels, each one differing only in where they say the last input from that file occurred.

INPUT has two things wrong with it. First, we don't really care what symbol we use for the channel name, but we do need to make sure that it is unique. It would be handier to define a function that opens a channel for input that creates a unique, new channel name every time it is called. Second, since INPUT is a FEXPR, if we want to open a file stored in a variable (which is the common situation), we first have to build an expression and then evaluate. For example, if X is set to a file name, we would have to type

(EVAL (LIST 'INPUT 'FILE-CHAN X))

in order to open it for input.

In order to define a better function, we first need a subfunction that can create new atoms. In Fig. 6.4, the function NEWSYM is defined to do this,

```
(DE NEWSYM (SYM)
  (COND ((OR (CONSP SYM) (NUMBERP SYM))
          (ERROR '"NEWSYM only takes literal atoms"))
        (T (LET (COUNT (ADD1 (OR (GET SYM 'SYM-COUNT) 0)))
             (PUTPROP SYM COUNT 'SYM-COUNT)
             (READLIST (APPEND (EXPLODE SYM) (EXPLODE COUNT]
```

FIG. 6.4.   Definition of NEWSYM.

using the functions **READLIST** and **EXPLODE** given earlier. The first time you apply **NEWSYM** to an atom, it returns that atom concatenated with the number 1. The second time it is applied to that atom it concatenates 2, and so on. It does this by keeping a counter for each atom under the property **SYM-COUNT**. Each time **NEWSYM** is called, it updates the counter, explodes both the atom and the counter, appends the results together, and returns the atom formed from the merged lists.

With **NEWSYM** defined, we can then define the function **INCHAN** to be an EXPR that takes a file name, generates a new channel name, opens the file for input on that channel, and returns the channel name.

```
(DE INCHAN (FILE)
  (EVAL (LIST 'INPUT (NEWSYM 'INP) FILE]
```

Opening an input file does not have any immediate effect on reading. In order to tell LISP that the next read operation should take its characters from an opened file, we use the function **INC**.

```
(INC channel flag)
```

INC is a function; that means that both arguments are evaluated. *Channel* must be an atom previously associated with a file with **INPUT**. *Flag* can be either **T** or **NIL**. When **INC** is called, it tells LISP that the source of future input characters will come from the file associated with *channel*. **INC** returns the previous channel (i.e., the channel you just switched away from).

Flag tells LISP what to do with the previous input channel. If *flag* is **T**, then LISP will *close* the file. This means that the previous channel and file are dissociated, which means that you can no longer ask for further input from it. If *flag* is NIL, then the previous channel is left open. You can't *close* the terminal (the NIL channel), but as a matter of good programming your initial call to **INC** should always have *flag* equal to NIL, which will leave open the input channel that was in effect before your function started.

For example, suppose we had a function that did the following sequence of operations:

```
(SETQ CHAN-1 (INCHAN 'FILE-1))
(SETQ CHAN-2 (INCHAN 'FILE-2))
(INC CHAN-1 NIL)
```

```
(READ)
(INC CHAN-2 T)
(READ)
```

The first INC would switch from the terminal to FILE-1. The READ function would read the first expression from FILE-1. The next INC would then switch to FILE-2, so that the next READ would read the first expression in FILE-2. The T flag in the INC expression means that CHAN-1 and FILE-1 are no longer associated. If the function later tried to execute

```
(INC CHAN-1 T)
```

an error would result.

Suppose that our function continued with the following:

```
(SETQ CHAN-1 (INCHAN 'FILE-1))
(INC CHAN-1 NIL)
(READ)
(INC CHAN-2 NIL)
(READ)
```

The INPUT reopens FILE-1. The next INC redirects input to FILE-1. Notice that the flag is NIL, so FILE-2 is not closed. Because FILE-1 has been reopened, the next READ will get the first expression of FILE-1 once again. The following INC switches input back to FILE-2. Because FILE-2 was not closed and reopened, the following READ will get the second expression on FILE-2.

In other words, when a file is opened, reading starts at the beginning of the file. Successive readings get successive expressions from the file until it is closed. After a file is closed, it has to be reopened before it can be used for input again. When it is reopened, reading starts from the beginning again.

What happens when you try to read something and there is no more in the file? This causes an error. If our function wants to do things after reaching the end of a file, we need some way of detecting the error and taking care of the problem ourselves.

The reserved word ERRSET in our LISP allows us to catch and deal with such errors.

```
(ERRSET expression T)
```

evaluates *expression* and returns either an atom (usually NIL) if an error occurred or a *list* of the result of the evaluation if no error occurred. (The second argument is included for completeness. It is used to determine whether or not our LISP's error package is called. We are not going to deal with the error package in this text.

For example, if ADD1 receives a nonnumeric argument, then an error occurs. We can evaluate the ADD1 inside an ERRSET and find

(ERRSET (ADD1 1) T) ⇒ (2)
(ERRSET (ADD1 T) T) ⇒ NIL

By using **ERRSET**, therefore, one expression can evaluate another and check afterward to see if an error occurred.

The loop in Fig. 6.5 is typical of file input. This loop just reads and prints every expression in the file **FILE-1**, but obviously any action could replace the **DO** clause. The important points to note are passing the result of the **INPUT** directly to **INC**, detecting the end of the file with **ERRSET**, closing **CHAN-1** at the end, and taking the **CAR** of **EXP** because **ERRSET** makes a list of the value returned by the **READ**.

```
(LOOP   (INITIAL EXP NIL
                 OLD-INPUT (INC (INCHAN FILE-1) NIL))
        (NEXT EXP (ERRSET (READ) T))
        (WHILE (CONSP EXP))
        (DO (PRINT (CAR EXP)))
        (RESULT (INC OLD-INPUT T]
```

FIG. 6.5.   Example of file input loop.

6.7   FILE OUTPUT IN LISP

Output files in LISP are treated in a manner similar to input files; that is, we first have to open a file for output by writing

(OUTPUT *channel file*)

which associates *channel* with the file *file*. **OUTPUT** is a reserved word and neither argument is evaluated. *Channel* can be any atom except **NIL** (the terminal) or one that is already associated with a file for either input or output.

As with **INPUT**, the **OUTPUT** only declares the existence of a file. To direct writing to that file, you have to use **OUTC**.

(OUTC *channel flag*)

where *channel* must be an atom previously associated with a file by **OUTPUT**. *Flag* can be either **T** or **NIL**. Since **OUTC** is a function, both arguments are evaluated. The previous output channel is returned.

If *flag* is equal to **NIL**, then the previous output file is left open. That means that if that channel is switched back to later with another **OUTC**, then the next expression written will follow the last expression written to that file. If *flag* is equal to **T**, then the previous output file is closed. That means that the file and the channel are dissociated and you can no longer switch to that channel with **OUTC**.

Furthermore whenever you open or reopen a file with OUTPUT and then switch to it with OUTC, the file is emptied and writing starts from the beginning. Whatever used to be in the file is lost. This means that you should not close a file until you are definitely finished with it.

You must close the file, however, before anyone else (including your own LISP functions) can read the new information. If you open a file for output and write characters on it but never close the file, everything written is forgotten, and the old version of the file stays in effect.

The following expression shows how output can be sent to a file. Note that output means explicit printing by a function. If the expressions below do not print anything, it does not matter that it returns some value—nothing will have been written on the file, which will therefore be empty.

```
(LET (OLD-OUTPUT
        (OUTC (OUTPUT CHAN-1 FILE-1) NIL))
    -expressions-
    (OUTC OLD-OUTPUT T]
```

Exercise 6.6 Define OUTCHAN to do the same thing for OUTPUT that INCHAN did for INPUT.

6.8 SEPARATING I/O FROM YOUR FUNCTIONS

In a well-modularized set of functions, the issue of where the input and output should go is very separate from what the functions do; that is, the purpose of most functions is to take one expression and transform it into another. The fact that the expressions are coming from and/or going to a file rather than a terminal is not really important. In fact, for many functions the issue of reading and writing is not relevant; these functions take arguments and return values.

This is not only a theoretical point, it is a practical one as well. Some of the hardest functions to debug are those that contain explicit code for reading or writing to files. In order to debug a function that reads from a file, we have to create and/or edit some test file first. In order to debug a function that writes a file, we have to run it and then edit the output file if any. We cannot easily take advantage of the interactive nature of LISP and of its well-developed debugging facilities.

All is not lost, however, for we can define several functions that will allow us to separate I/O behavior from function behavior. First we define the function FILEIN. FILEIN takes two arguments: a file and a function. FILEIN opens the file for input, applies the function to every expression in the file, and then closes the input file.

For example, if we wanted to print out every expression in the file FOO, we would write

(FILEIN 'FOO 'PRINT]

The function FILEIN can be defined fairly easily (see Fig. 6.6). It is essentially the same loop that we wrote earlier in the section on file input. FILEIN takes a file name and a function of one argument. FILEIN takes care of the file opening, reading, checking for end of file, and closing. FILEIN also is written such that the previous input channel is remembered and returned to when FILEIN is done. This means that FILEIN can be called within FILEIN without problems.

```
(DE FILEIN (FILE FN)
  (LOOP  (INITIAL EXP NIL
                  OLD-INPUT (INC (INCHAN FILE) NIL))
         (NEXT EXP (ERRSET (READ) T))
         (WHILE (CONSP EXP))
         (DO (APPLY FN EXP))
         (RESULT (INC OLD-INPUT T]
```

FIG. 6.6.   Definition of FILEIN.

One common function available in our LISP and others is DSKIN. DSKIN is the standard function for reading in a file of function definitions. DSKIN takes a list of files and reads and evaluates the expressions in all of them. To read in function definitions from FOO and BAZ, we would write

(DSKIN FOO BAZ)

DSKIN can be nicely defined using FILEIN (see Fig. 6.7).

```
(DF DSKIN (FILE-LIST)
  (FOR    (FILE IN FILE-LIST)
          (DO (FILEIN FILE 'EVAL]
```

FIG. 6.7.   Definition of DSKIN.

The output function we define is FILEOUT. It takes two arguments: a file name and a list of expressions. FILEOUT opens the file named for output, evaluates the expressions, and then closes the file. FILEOUT itself does no explicit writing.

The definition of FILEOUT is simple and essentially like the expression given in Section 6.7 (see Fig. 6.8). FILEOUT takes care of opening and closing the output file and returning output to the previous channel when it is done. This means that FILEOUTs can be called within FILEOUTs without problems.

```
(DE FILEOUT (FILE EXP-LIST)
  (LET (OLD-OUTPUT (OUTC (OUTCHAN FILE) NIL))
    (FOR (X IN EXP-LIST) (DO (EVAL X)))
    (OUTC OLD-OUTPUT T]
```

FIG. 6.8. Definition of FILEOUT.

A standard LISP reserved word is **DSKOUT**, which takes a file name followed by a sequence of S-expressions. These expressions are evaluated and their output is sent to the file named. For example, if we wanted to pretty-print the functions **FOO** and **BAZ**, saving the output on the file **DEFS**, we would write

```
(DSKOUT DEFS (PP FOO BAZ))
```

We can easily define **DSKOUT** in terms of **FILEOUT**.

```
(DF DSKOUT (L) (FILEOUT (CAR L) (CDR L]
```

FILEIN and **FILEOUT** make it very easy to do "file transduction." File transduction is the process of converting data in one file in one format into data in another file in another format.

For example, suppose we wanted a function that would take two files, one containing a number of LISP macro definitions and the other containing function definitions using the macros, and would produce a third file containing the same functions present in the second file but with all the macros expanded into normal LISP code. This is a common way of preparing files for transfer to other LISP systems.

The function first has to define the macros, by reading and evaluating the definitions in the first file; then it has to print on the new file the result of applying the function **EXPANDMACROS** to each expression in the second file (see Fig. 6.9). Notice how modular this is. We can debug **PRINTEX** on simple expressions first without any file I/O at all. Then we could debug the application of **PRINTEX** to the expressions in **DEF-FILE** by just executing the two **FILEIN** expressions. Finally, when we were sure we had what we wanted, we would embed the **FILEINs** in the **FILEOUT**, saving the output on **EXP-FILE**.

```
(DE CONVERT (MACRO-FILE DEF-FILE EXP-FILE)
  (FILEOUT  EXP-FILE
            (FILEIN MACRO-FILE 'EVAL)
            (FILEIN DEF-FILE 'PRINTEX]

(DE PRINTEX (X) (PRINT (EXPANDMACROS X]
```

FIG. 6.9. Example of file transduction.

7

Editing LISP Expressions

In the introduction to LISP, we said that one of the advantages of interpreting LISP code rather than compiling it is that we still had the LISP expressions to play with when running our functions. In this chapter we discuss how to take advantage of this.

7.1 IN-CORE EDITING

Most of us who have worked with an interactive system of any kind are familiar with editors. The most common is the operating system's "file editor." The file editor is used to create and update files kept on a fast long-term storage medium such as a disk.

With interactive languages like LISP and APL, the important conduits for information exchange are the function definitions and the data base. Under both LISP and APL lies the concept of a "workspace" that is the currently active set of function definitions and global variable values. In some LISP systems the workspace is called the "core image," but workspace is a much better name for it.

Since the functions you define are rarely right the first time, you will need to edit their definitions to fix the problems. To do this you have two options. First, your functions are most likely stored on a system file. Hence when one of your functions fails to execute properly while you are running the interpreter, you can leave the interpreter, edit the file with the system's file editor, run the interpreter again, and reload the file with the corrections.

If your operating system supports a good file editor, then this cycle of "run LISP, load file, execute, leave LISP, edit file, reload file" is often the best way to go. On many systems, however, the file editor is not that good, and furthermore there may be a high price to pay in terms of time for constantly leaving, reentering LISP, and restoring the state of the computation.

If this is the case, then a second option for function editing is to use a workspace LISP editor. Such an editor is a set of functions that make it easy for you to display and modify the S-expressions present in the workspace. If your LISP does not have one (or you don't like the one it has), this chapter tells you how to go about writing one of your own. Such editors are fairly easy to write because LISP function definitions are just LISP data structures. And such editors have one big advantage over file editors: A simple LISP editor will not let you unbalance parentheses!

The editor we describe here is a very simple one. It has neither the complexity nor the power of the editor that can be found in INTERLISP, for example. On the other hand, it is small (taking up less than 600 CONS-cells of storage if macros are not expanded) so that it does not burden small LISP systems, it allows the user to change those things that most often need changing, and it is fairly extendible. Finally, it shows what kinds of things need to be kept in mind in designing your own editor.

7.2   A SAMPLE EDIT SESSION

The editor we present is a set of LISP functions that make it easy to modify an S-expression. Some of the functions move an *edit pointer* to subexpressions with the main expression, and others modify the subexpression pointed to.

Although we talk primarily about editing an atom's function definition, our editor will actually operate on the entire property list of an atom. In this way, we do not restrict our editor to changing function definitions only. If your LISP does not let you get at the entire property list (or if the property list does not include function definitions), then you should redefine the function EDIT (in Fig. 7.3) accordingly.

We start editing an atom by typing (EDIT*atom*). EDIT is defined as a reserved word to avoid the need for quoting. Calling EDIT initializes some special variables, the most important one being the internal edit pointer. The purpose of the edit pointer is to make it easy to specify where a change should be made (e.g., "Insert the expression A right here!" where "here" is the location of the edit pointer).

For example, suppose that SQUARE was defined as follows:

```
(DE SQUARE (N) (TIMES N N))
```

For some reason, we happen to try to execute (SQUARE NIL) and get an error because N is not a number. We realize that SQUARE should test to make sure that N is a number before trying to square it. Using the editor, we could fix SQUARE without leaving our workspace. Figure 7.1 contains an annotated trace of an actual edit run. Some further notes should be made. In our LISP, property lists have the form

(-*property value-*)

You should ignore the property PNAME. We are only interested in the EXPR property, which is the function definition for SQUARE.

```
*(EDIT SQUARE)    [the asterisk is the LISP prompt for an expression]
                  [we tell LISP to edit the property list of SQUARE]
EXPR              [the edit pointer is at EXPR, which is the first item]
(# (LAMBDA (N) TIMES N N)) PNAME ( . . . )) [on the property list]
NIL               [—note how # marks EXPR's position]

*(R)              [now we move the edit pointer to one expression to the]
                  [right—now the pointer is at the LAMBDA form]
(LAMBDA (N) (TIMES N N))
(EXPR # PNAME ( . . . ))    [note where the # is now]
NIL

*(F TIMES)        [now we move the edit pointer to the first occurrence]
                  [of the atom TIMES]

TIMES
(# N N)
NIL

*(U)              [now we move the edit pointer up to the list that]
                  [contains TIMES (i.e., to (TIMES N N))]

(TIMES N N)
(LAMBDA (N) #)
NIL

*(S (AND NUMBERP N) #))  [we embed (TIMES NN) inside the AND]
                  [—the # stands for the (TIMES N N)]
(AND (NUMBERP N) (TIMES N N))
(LAMBDA (N) #)
NIL

*(T)              [now we move back to the top of the expression]
                  [to see what we've done]

EXPR
(# (LAMBDA (N) (AND [NUMBERP N] [TIMES N N])) PNAME ( . . . ))
NIL
                  [SQUARE has been fixed]
```

FIG. 7.1.   Sample editor run.

(EDIT SQUARE) initialized the editor for the entire property list of SQUARE, and the edit pointer is initially set to the start of the property list. To tell us this, the editor printed out the element pointed to by the edit pointer, plus the list containing that element, with a number sign (#) used to indicate where in the list the element appears.

When we typed (F TIMES), the editor went through the S-expression being edited, starting at the edit position, until it found a subexpression EQUAL to TIMES. If one had not been found, the edit pointer would not have changed. Since the search was successful, the edit pointer was moved to the atom TIMES. Again, the edit pointer position was printed.

When we typed (S (AND (NUMBERP N) #)), the editor substituted the expression (AND (NUMBERP N) (TIMES N N)) for the expression pointed to by the edit pointer [i.e., (TIMES N N)]. The number sign in the argument to S stood for the expression pointed to by the edit pointer.

The function S permanently changed the workspace definition of SQUARE. Now if we evaluate (SQUARE NIL), NIL will be returned. Note that there is no concept of "leaving" the editor.

Exercise 7.1 The fix to SQUARE could have been done with just two edit function calls (not counting the initial call to EDIT). What are they?

7.3 THE EDITOR COMMAND FUNCTIONS

There are nine editor command functions. Six of them are used to move the edit pointer. They are:

1. (R): Right—move the edit pointer right one expression. If the pointer is at the end of the list, nothing happens.

2. (L): Left—move the edit pointer left one expression. If the pointer is at the start of the list, nothing happens.

3. (D): Down—move the edit pointer down (i.e., move it to the first element of the expression currently being pointed to). If the pointer is at an atom, nothing happens.

4. (U): Up—move the edit pointer up (i.e., move it to the list containing the expression currently being pointed to). If the pointer is at the top level of the edited expression, nothing happens.

5. (T): Top—move the edit pointer back to the first element of the edited expression.

6. (F *expression*): Find—move the edit pointer to the first occurrence of *expression*. If *expression* is omitted, then the last expression searched for is assumed. If *expression* is not found, then the edit pointer is not moved. See the comments below.

There are two functions for modifying the expression pointed to by the edit pointer:

7. (S *-exps-*): Substitute—splice the list (*-exps-*) in place of the edit pointer expression. Any occurrence of a number sign in the expressions is replaced with the edit pointer expression. Note that (S) will delete the edit pointer expression. See the comments below.

8. (G *number*): Group—if *number* is greater than zero, then the next *number* expressions, starting with the edit pointer expression, are collected into a list. If *number* is zero or less, then nothing happens.

There is one function for displaying the edit pointer position:

9. (W *number*): Where—prints the edit pointer expression, then prints the list containing it, then the list containing that list, and so on, until *number* higher lists have been printed (or there are no more higher lists). If *number* is omitted, then 1 is assumed.

The Find (F) function starts searching at the edit pointer and goes "to the right." For example, in the expression (1 (2 (3 4) 5) 6), the expressions to the right of 1 are (2 (3 4) 5) and 6; the expressions to the right of 2 are (3 4), 5, and 6; the expressions to the right of 3 are 4, 5 and 6; and so on.

Substitute (S) is a very general and powerful function. Suppose that the edit pointer is pointing at the (2 3) in the list (1 (2 3) 4). Then

(S A) would change (1 (2 3) 4) to (1 A 4)
(S A B) would change (1 (2 3) 4) to (1 A B 4)
(S # A) would change (1 (2 3) 4) to (1 (2 3) A 4)
(S A #) would change (1 (2 3) 4) to (1 A (2 3) 4)
(S # #) would change (1 (2 3) 4) to (1 (2 3) (2 3) 4)
(S) would change (1 (2 3) 4) to (1 4)
(S . #) would change (1 (2 3) 4) to (1 2 3 4)
(S #)) would change (1 (2 3) 4) to (1 ((2 3)) 4)

The last three examples are particularly interesting. The third last example shows how to delete an expression. The second last example shows how to ungroup (i.e., remove parentheses from) an expression. The last example shows how to add parentheses to an expression.

Substitution is not powerful enough, however, to allow us to add parentheses around more than one expression. To do this, we need the Grouping (G) function. Assuming again that the edit pointer is pointing at the (2 3) in the list (1 (2 3) 4), then

(G 1) would change (1 (2 3) 4) to (1 ((2 3)) 4)
(G 2) would change (1 (2 3) 4) to (1 ((2 3) 4))
(G 3) would change (1 (2 3) 4) to (1 ((2 3) 4))

Note that (G 1) has the same effect as (S (#)).

7.4 INTERNAL FUNCTION DEFINITIONS

The internal editor functions are defined in Fig. 7.2. The command functions that the user calls are defined in terms of these internal functions.

The editor uses the following special variables:

1. *EDIT-EXP*—this is the whole form being edited. Its value is initialized to the atom's property list by EDIT and is never reset.

2. *EDIT-PTR*—this is the edit pointer. When we talk about "the expression being pointed to" or "the current edit pointer," we are referring the expression that is the CAR of *EDIT-PTR*. At the start, *EDIT-PTR* is initialized to *EDIT-EXP*.

3. *EDIT-LINE*—this is the list containing the edit pointer. *EDIT-PTR* is either *EDIT-LINE* or some tail of *EDIT-LINE*. *EDIT-LINE* is used when moving the edit pointer left. *EDIT-LINE* is initialized to *EDIT-EXP*.

4. *STACK*—this is a list of the edit positions "above" the current one. The Down (D) function puts the current values of *EDIT-PTR* and *EDIT-LINE* on the front of *STACK*. The Up (U) function resets *EDIT-PTR* and *EDIT-LINE* to the values saved on the front of *STACK* and resets *STACK* to the CDDR of itself. *STACK* is initially NIL, when the edit pointer is at the top level of the expression being edited.

The internal functions for moving the pointer around are ED-RIGHT, ED-LEFT, ED-UP, and ED-DOWN. They take no arguments. They return NIL if no move occurred. ED-RIGHT sets *EDIT-PTR* to the CDR of *EDIT-PTR*. ED-LEFT resets *EDIT-PTR* one expression to the left in *EDIT-LINE* by figuring out how many CDRs of *EDIT-LINE* *EDIT-PTR* currently is and making it one less (SUFLIST is described shortly).

ED-DOWN does three things: It pushes *EDIT-LINE* onto *STACK*, it pushes *EDIT-PTR* onto *STACK*, and it resets *EDIT-PTR* and *EDIT-LINE* to the CAR of *EDIT-PTR*. ED-UP undoes an ED-DOWN by resetting *EDIT-PTR* and *EDIT-LINE* to the top two elements of *STACK* and removing those elements from *STACK*.

ED-RESET takes three arguments and assigns them to *EDIT-PTR*, *EDIT-LINE*, and *STACK*, respectively. Commonly ED-RESET is used

```
(DE SHOW (N)
 (WRITE T (CAR *EDIT-PTR*))
 (LOOP  (INITIAL S (CONS *EDIT-PTR* (CONS *EDIT-LINE* *STACK*)))
        (WHILE S)
        (DO (WRITE T (MARK-POS (POP S) (POP S)))))
        (UNTIL (ZEROP (SETQ N (SUB1 N]

(DE MARK-POS (P L)
 (COND ((ATOM L) P)
       ((EQ P L) (CONS '# (CDR L)))
       (T (CONS (CAR L) (MARK-POS P (CDR L]

(DE ED-FIND ( )
 (LOOP  (INITIAL SAVE (LIST *EDIT-PTR* *EDIT-LINE* *STACK*)
                 FOUND NIL)
        (WHILE (OR (ED-DOWN) (ED-RIGHT) (ED-NEXT)))
        (UNTIL (SETQ FOUND (EQUAL *KEY* (CAR *EDIT-PTR*))))
        (RESULT (COND ((NOT FOUND)
                       (APPLY 'ED-RESET SAVE)
                       (WRITE "not found"]

(DE ED-RESET (X Y Z)
 (SETQ *EDIT-PTR* X) (SETQ *EDIT-LINE* Y) (SETQ *STACK* Z]

(DE ED-UP ( )
 (AND *STACK* (ED-RESET (CAR *STACK*) (CADR *STACK*) (CDDR *STACK*]

(DE ED-DOWN ( )
 (AND  (CONSP (CAR *EDIT-PTR*))
       (ED-RESET (CAR *EDIT-PTR*) (CAR *EDIT-PTR*)
                 (CONS *EDIT-PTR* (CONS *EDIT-LINE* *STACK*]

(DE ED-LEFT ( )
 (AND  (NOT (EQ *EDIT-PTR* *EDIT-LINE*))
       (SETQ *EDIT-PTR*
             (SUFLIST *EDIT-LINE*
                      (SUB1 (DIFFERENCE (LENGTH *EDIT-LINE*)
                                        (LENGTH *EDIT-PTR*]

(DE ED-RIGHT ( )
 (AND  (CONSP (CDR *EDIT-PTR*))
       (SETQ *EDIT-PTR* (CDR *EDIT-PTR*]

(DE ED-NEXT ( )
 (PROG NIL
  LOOP (COND ((NULL (ED-UP)) (RETURN NIL))
             ((ED-RIGHT) (RETURN T))
             (T (GO LOOP]

(DE INPLACE (A D) (RPLACA *EDIT-PTR* A) (RPLACD *EDIT-PTR* D]
```

FIG. 7.2. Editor functions.

to get back to the top of the edited expression by calling (ED-RESET *EDIT-EXP* *EDIT-EXP* NIL). It is also used by ED-FIND to recover from a search failure.

Searching is done with the internal functional ED-FIND, which looks through *EDIT-EXP* for an expression EQUAL to *KEY*. ED-FIND first saves the current values of *EDIT-PTR*, *EDIT-LINE*, and *STACK*, in case the search fails. Then ED-FIND moves around in *EDIT-EXP* using the pointer positioning functions.

Using the pointer positioning functions has two advantages. First, if the search is successful, *EDIT-PTR*, *EDIT-LINE*, and *STACK* will already be set to the desired new values. Second, ED-FIND can be defined relatively straightforwardly, because the recursion is handled implicitly by the positioning functions and *STACK*.

ED-FIND uses the function ED-NEXT to implement going "to the right" of an expression. When ED-RIGHT returns NIL (i.e., we can't go right any more), ED-FIND calls ED-NEXT, which does an ED-UP until an ED-RIGHT becomes possible again.

The function SHOW takes one number N as an argument. It prints the current edit pointer expression and then prints the top N *EDIT-LINE* lists on the stack.

SHOW calls the function MARK-POS, which takes two lists, P and L, where P is some tail of L. MARK-POS prints L, with a number sign being printed in place of the first element of P, thus marking where P starts in L. SHOW applies MARK-POS to pairs of elements from *STACK*, which is a list of the form

   (-pos list-)

where the first pos-list pair has the most recently saved values of EDIT-PTR* and *EDIT-LINE*, the second pair has the next most recent, and so on.

In order to modify internal LISP pointers, it becomes handy to define the function INPLACE, which changes both the CAR and the CDR of *EDIT-PTR*. Its definition is straightforward.

7.5 COMMAND FUNCTION DEFINITIONS

The editor command functions are defined in Fig. 7.3.

EDIT is a FEXPR that takes an atomic argument. It checks to make sure that the atom has a nonatomic property list. If so, it initializes the special editor variables and prints the current edit pointer position.

The macro DEF-CMD defines editor command functions so that they are all FEXPRs with the argument EXPS and they all call the internal function

```
(DF EDIT    (FN)
   (COND   ((CONSP (CDAR FN))
              (SETQ *EDIT-EXP* (CDAR FN))
              (SETQ *KEY* NIL)
              (ED-RESET *EDIT-EXP* *EDIT-EXP* NIL)
              (SHOW 1))
            (T (WRITE T "can't edit" FN]

(DM DEF-CMD (L)
 |" (DF @(CADR L) (EXPS) |@(CDDR L) (SHOW 1]

(DEF-CMD D (ED-DOWN]

(DEF-CMD F (COND (EXPS (SETQ *KEY* (CAR EXPS)))) (ED-FIND]

(DEF-CMD G
 (LET (N (CAR EXPS))
  (COND   ((NOT (NUMBERP N))
             (WRITE "Group needs a number"))
           ((*GREAT N 0)
             (INPLACE (PRELIST *EDIT-PTR* N)
                      (SUFLIST *EDIT-PTR* N]

(DEF-CMD L (ED-LEFT))

(DEF-CMD R (ED-RIGHT))

(DEF-CMD S
 (LET (L    (SUBST (CAR *EDIT-PTR*) '# EXPS))
   (COND   (L   (NCONC L (CDR *EDIT-PTR*))
                (INPLACE   (CAR L) (CDR L)))
            ((CONSP (CDR *EDIT-PTR*))
             (INPLACE (CADR *EDIT-PTR*) (CDDR *EDIT-PTR*)))
            ((ED-LEFT) (RPLACD *EDIT-PTR* (CDDR *EDIT-PTR*)))
            ((ED-UP) (RPLACA *EDIT-PTR* NIL))
            (T (WRITE "can't delete that"]

(DEF-CMD T (ED-RESET *EDIT-EXP* *EDIT-EXP* NIL))

(DEF-CMD U (ED-UP))

(DF W (EXPS) (SHOW (COND (EXPS (CAR EXPS)) (T 1]
```

FIG. 7.3.   Editor command functions.

SHOW at the end. By making them FEXPRs, the editor functions don't need quoting and can have optional arguments. By adding a (SHOW 1) to each definition, all the editor functions will tell the user what happened. Note that the printing function, W, is not defined with DEF-CMD, since we don't want a printout after it is done.

The substitution function first takes its argument and replaces any occurrences of the atom # with the edit pointer expression. Then it checks to see if the result is NIL or not. If it isn't, then there is a list of expressions to be spliced into the CAR of *EDIT-PTR*. Three LISP pointers have to be changed: the end of the list just built and the CAR and CDR of the current edit pointer.

Graphically the transitions involve going from Fig. 7.4a, to b and finally to c.

EDIT POINTER

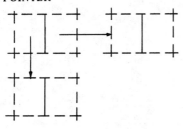

L

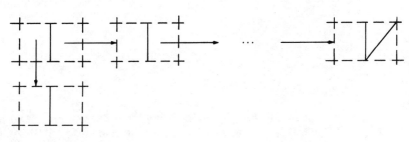

FIG. 7.4.a   Initial lists.

EDIT POINTER

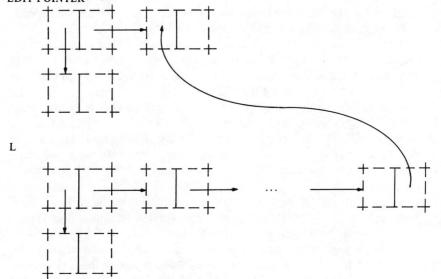

FIG. 7.4b.   After splicing the lists together.

EDIT POINTER

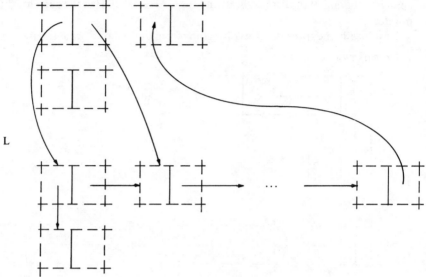

L

FIG. 7.4c. After changing the CAR and CDR of the edit pointer.

The first transition is done by NCONCing the list of expressions with the CDR of *EDIT-PTR*. The second transition is done by INPLACEing the*EDIT-PTR*'s CONS-cell with the new list.

If Substitute has a NIL argument, then we need to delete the CAR of *EDIT-PTR*. Deletion is a little tricky, since we have to do things differently when deleting the last, or only, element of a list.

One way to delete a CONS-cell from a list is to overwrite it with the CAR and CDR of the next CONS-cell. Graphically, we are going from Fig. 7.5a to b. Assuming that the next position is a CONS-cell with a CAR and CDR, we can do this with a simple INPLACE.

If we are deleting the last element of a list, then the next position is an atom (usually NIL). There is no CONS-cell to copy. In this situation, we have to change the CDR of the element in front of it. Graphically we go from Fig. 7.6a to b. This can be implemented by moving the edit pointer to the left with ED-LEFT and then replace the CDR of the new position with the CDR of the cell we are deleting.

We are still not home free, however. Suppose that the edit pointer is pointing to the only element in a list with one element. This means that there is no CONS-cell to the right and we can't move left either.

Fortunately all is not lost. Since the result of the deletion would be the empty list, NIL, we can try going up one level and replacing the list itself with NIL; that is, if the edit pointer was at B in (A (B) C) and (S) was typed, then

EDIT POINTER

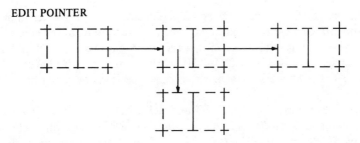

FIG. 7.5a. Initial lists.

EDIT POINTER

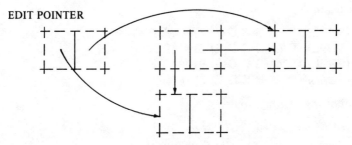

FIG. 7.5b. After deleting the edit pointer.

EDIT POINTER

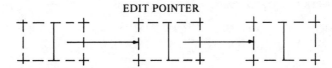

FIG. 7.6a. Initial lists.

EDIT POINTER

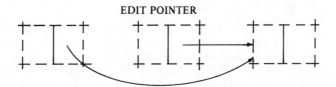

FIG. 7.6b. After going left and deleting the edit pointer.

the editor could delete B by going up one level and replacing (B) with NIL, yielding (A NIL B).

If the editor is at the top level of the expression being edited, this approach will fail. You cannot delete the only element in the list you are editing. If you try, the editor will print an error message.

The complete code for deletion appears as part of the definition of the function S in Fig. 7.3.

The group (G) function, given an argument N that is greater than zero, groups into one list the next N expressions, starting from the edit pointer. This means we have to make a list of the first N expressions of *EDIT-PTR* and replace the CAR of *EDIT-PTR* with this list. We also have to change the CDR of *EDIT-PTR* to get rid of the expressions we have just put in the CAR.

The built-in functions PRELIST and SUFLIST make this easy. Both take two arguments: a list *list* and a number *number*. PRELIST returns a list of the first *number* elements of *list* (or *list* itself if *list* is less than *number* elements long). SUFLIST returns everything but the first *number* elements of *list*. For example,

> (PRELIST '(A B C D E) 3) ⇒ (A B C)
> (SUFLIST '(A B C D E) 3) ⇒ (D E)
> (PRELIST '(A B C D E) 6) ⇒ (A B C D E)
> (SUFLIST '(A B C D E) 6) ⇒ NIL

The following identity holds.

> (APPEND (PRELIST *list number*)
>   (SUFLIST *list number*))
> = *list*

All G with the argument *number* has to do is

> (INPLACE (PRELIST *EDIT-PTR* *number*)
>   (SUFLIST *EDIT-PTR* *number*))

Exercise 7.2 If your LISP does not have PRELIST and SUFLIST, then define them. Watch out for the cases where the number is less than one or greater than the length of the list.

Exercise 7.3 Define more editor command functions. In particular, define a function to pretty-print the edit pointer expression. Define a pair of functions so that you can pick up a copy of the edit pointer expression at one place and put it down in another place. Define a function that repeats other functions [e.g., (RPT 3 (F FOO)) would do three searches]. Define a help function that will print a short description of the available commands.

Exercise 7.4 Change the editor so that it operates on a copy of the edit expression. This way you are protected if you make a mistake. Define the function CLOSE, taking no arguments, which replaces the original expression with the edited copy.

Exercise 7.5 Define a command interpreter for the editor. When this function is called, it starts reading single characters and looks them up in a command table. This table associates characters with edit expressions. For example, the table might associate the character > with the function (ED-RIGHT) and < with (ED-LEFT). One special command will be needed—say Q—for leaving the interpreter, which does not call any editor function. If your LISP allows you to go into an "instant response" mode (which means that every character you type is sent immediately to your program without waiting for the end of a line), then the interpreter should use this mode.

7.6 FINAL NOTES ON WORKSPACE EDITING

The editor we have constructed is very primitive. There are several reasons for this. First, we wanted to give you the flavor of writing an editor without bogging down in details. Second, we wanted to allow you the freedom to extend the editor in as many possible directions as possible. Finally, we were really designing an editor for making simple patches only. Serious rewriting of LISP code (which should not be done as a sideline to debugging anyway) would be done on the source file.

You could, of course, build a very powerful workspace editor, capable of making virtually any changes to an expression that you could want. The problem with using any such editor, however, is that any changes you make do not affect the file containing the original LISP code. Whenever you use a workspace editor, you should be careful to note all the changes you've made, so that you can incorporate them into the source file later.

In INTERLISP they have tried to make it easy for you to do this updating automatically without leaving LISP. They created a set of functions to make it easy for you to save your definitions and data on an external file for later reloading. The idea is that with a convenient LISP editor and an easy way to save what you've done it should never be necessary for you to leave LISP at all during a programming session.

8 Compilation

8.1 WHY COMPILE?

As we note near the beginning of Chapter 1, LISP programs are usually interpreted rather than compiled. There are many advantages to this, all stemming from the fact that in the interpretive process we still have the original code around. This is especially useful in the debugging process, where we might like to change this code as we are executing it (see Section 7.1). But you pay a price for using an interpreter, mostly in speed of execution, so completely debugged code that will be executed often should be compiled. Not only will this result in faster execution, but compiled code takes about three-quarters the space of interpreted. Also, since compiled code is put in a special *binary program space*, the garbage collector never has to look at it.

There are difficulties associated with compilation, however. One is the quality of LISP compilers. There is many a LISP implementation with a respectable interpreter but a compiler full of bugs. This has had the unfortunate effect of giving LISP compilation a bad press. On the other hand the number of reliable compilers is increasing, so let us assume that we have a decent compiler and go on from there.

Even with a good compiler, however, there will be some programs that work when interpreted but not when compiled. In this section we look at the compilation process so that you will understand why this is the case. In the course of doing so we will see that one can write compilable programs by simply avoiding a few of LISP's features. Furthermore, we will argue that most of these features should be avoided anyway (on grounds of good programming practice) and hence will suggest that the discipline of writing

98

compilable programs is a good one whether or not one actually intends to compile one's code.

8.2 WHAT THE COMPILER DOES

The LISP compiler is just another LISP function. It involves a lot of code, however, so in most implementations it is not available in the LISP one uses for day-to-day debugging. [An exception here is INTERLISP (Teitelman 1975). INTERLISP handles compilation quite differently from most implementations, so we will often comment on how this well-known dialect differs from what we describe here.] Rather than always including the compiler, most implementations have a second version of LISP that is only used when one wants to compile.

Conceptually the compiler comes in two parts. One part is just a file transducer like those in Chapter 6. The other part, the compiler "proper," takes LISP functions and turns them into their compiled form. We first talk about the compiler "proper" and then the file transduction aspects of the compilation process.

Compilation turns LISP functions into LAP (Lisp Assembly Program) code. LAP code looks like machine language, except that every instruction is a legal S-expression. The most obvious manifestation of this is the parentheses around each command. (More modern LISPs compile into machine code. INTERLISP, for example, makes two passes. The first goes into LAP; the second, machine code. However, only the second is saved.)

It is instructive to see exactly what this machine language looks like. For example, the program

(DE DIV (X Y) (QUOTIENT Y X))

might become the code in Fig. 8.1. To understand what is going on we must know that the registers of the machine are used to pass arguments to call functions, and the push-down stack (named P) is used to remember arguments both within a function, and in the case that subfunctions are called. PUSH P,1 says to push the contents of register 1 onto the stack. So the

```
PUSH    P,1          ;Put the first argument on stack P
PUSH    P,2          ;Same for second
MOVE    1,0(P)       ;Put first arguments of QUOTIENT in register 1
MOVE    2, -1(P)     ;Put second in register 2
PUSHJ   P,QUOTIENT   ;Go to QUOTIENT saving return loc on stack
POP     P            ;Remove arguments from stack
POP     P
POPJ    P            ;Go to location on top of stack
```

FIG. 8.1. Machine code for a simple function.

first two lines tell us to take the arguments from the registers where they were put by the function that called DIV and put them on the stack. Next, we MOVE QUOTIENT's arguments to the registers in preparation for calling it. We go to QUOTIENT using PUSHJ, which puts the address of the next machine location on the top of the stack. When QUOTIENT returns, it will do so by going to that address. It will also leave its value in register 1. When we return to DIV, we remove DIV's arguments from the stack (using POP) and then go to the address on the top of the stack (which was left there just as DIV left an address before going to QUOTIENT). This is done with the POPJ.

As mentioned above, the compiler acts as a file transducer. It takes the name of a file and creates a second file of LAP or machine language functions. To use the compiled functions you simply read this new file into your LISP just as you would read a normal LISP file. The net result of "LAPing" in compiled code is that each function name will now have a SUBR (or FSUBR or LSUBR) property, just like the primitive LISP functions.

Actually, the above is an oversimplified version of what goes on. To be more precise, the action taken by the compiler during transduction will fall into one of four categories depending on what it is that we have in the input file.

(DE...) or (DF...)	The function is compiled as illustrated above and put in the output file. The function will *not* be defined in the LISP in which the compiler is embedded.
(DM...)	The macro will be defined (as with interpreted code). It will typically *not* be included in the output file.
(DECLARE *exp-1*...)	We discuss the use of DECLARE later. DECLARE is a no-op to the interpreter, so it is used to tell things to the compiler that are of no significance to the interpreter. The expressions inside will simply be EVALed in the normal LISP fashion.
Anything else	It will simply be passed unchanged to the output file.

The compiler also expands all macros, provided that the macro definition appears before the macro is used. This makes macros especially efficient when used in code that is going to be compiled. Note that macros will even be expanded if they appear at the top level.

8.3 VARIABLES IN COMPILED CODE

The actual code shown in Section 8.2 is not particularly important. What is important here is the observation that the machine code no longer contains any references to X and Y, the names of the variables in the EXPR version of

DIV. X and Y have been replaced, in effect, by locations on the stack P. This is fine provided that all references to X and Y appear in DIV (which is the case here). But suppose we wanted to refer to X or Y in a subfunction. For example, the code for RECORD-TYPE (Chapter 4) binds the variable *TYPE* to the name of the record being defined. This variable is not only used in RECORD-TYPE but also in SLOT-FUNS-EXTRACT, which is called by RECORD-TYPE. Put yourself now in the place of the compiler trying to compile SLOT-FUNS-EXTRACT. How do you create code to find the value of *TYPE*? Given what we have said so far about how variables are replaced by stack locations, you cannot generate code that refers to *TYPE* by name, because the name *TYPE* will have gone away just as X and Y went away in DIV. Instead you would have to say "pull out the value stored in some location of the stack." But which location? There is no way to know, since in general this will depend on who called whom and the number of arguments in intervening functions.

To get around this problem the compiler must be told about any such variables before you give the compiler the function in which the variable is defined. Even better, tell the compiler about the variable before it appears anywhere. To do this, just before the definition of RECORD-TYPE we include the following:

   (DECLARE (SPECIAL *TYPE*))

We say we have declared the variable *special,* and any variable that is used free in a function is said to be a *special variable.* The special declaration tells the compiler that the current value of *TYPE* should always be kept in its value cell. The *value cell* of a variable is attached to the name of the variable, so that given its symbolic name the value can be retrieved. Typically this attachment is accomplished by putting the property VALUE on the property list of the atom serving as the variable. In almost all LISPs the value of a variable is stored in such a fixed value cell. Interpreted LISP always uses values cells to store current values.

The fact that special variables use value cells means that binding a special variable requires more work than binding an ordinary one. Its old value must be stored on a stack since we are going to change the value cell. For various reasons, this can be expensive. On the other hand, referring to a special variable's value is cheap, since the value cell is always in the same place.

One may also declare the variable UNSPECIAL after you are done with it. In this way, should you later use the same name for a nonspecial variable, the compiler will not continue to think that the variable is special; however, it is probably a bad idea to use the same name for both a special and nonspecial variable.

Again, INTERLISP is different. In this version of LISP there are essentially two kinds of compilation. One, *block compiling,* roughly corresponds to what we have described here; however, the standard method of compilation keeps the names of all variables around, making them all special, in effect. This means that one need not worry about the use of special variables. Of course, this mode is less efficient.

There is a real question as to whether one wants to ease the use of special variables however. We believe that they should be avoided. As already noted, they are less efficient than regular variables but, more important, special variables tend to make for bad code.

For one thing special variables make code harder to debug. If a variable is local, we know that its value cannot change between one use and the next inside a function unless the function changes it. With special variables this is not true. If we call a subfunction, it may, either accidentally or deliberately, change the value of a special variable. Special variables also make code harder to read since one cannot ascertain the significance of a special variable by looking at the immediately surrounding code. So special variables should always be given mnemonic, visually striking names (such as prefix and postfix asterisks), and they should be set apart in the code. Declaring them special at the start of your code is a good way of doing the latter.

8.4   THE EFFECT OF COMPILATION ON EVAL AND SET

The treatment of variables under compilation has another effect. Certain programming practices that work fine in interpreted code will not work in compiled code. In particular, explicit calls to **EVAL** and **SET** will not work smoothly because these functions refer to variables via their symbolic names that will be lost unless we happen to declare them all special beforehand. For example, in Chapter 3 (macros) we contrasted two definitions for the function **POP**. (POP X), as you may remember, **SETQ**s X to its **CDR** and returns the item removed from the list. Figure 8.2 repeats both definitions.

Now suppose we compile the FEXPR version. When we execute (POP X), we will have to execute (**EVAL** (CAR BODY)), which in turn means doing an **EVAL** of X. But there will be no way to find the value of X because we are no longer in the function in which it was defined. We are in **POP** (assuming of course we have not declared X special).

```
(DM POP (BODY)
    (LIST  'PROG1
        (LIST 'CAR (CADR BODY))
        (LIST 'SETQ (CADR BODY) (LIST 'CDR (CADR BODY]

(DF POP (BODY)
    (PROG1 (CAR (EVAL (CAR BODY)))
        (SET (CAR BODY) (CDR (EVAL (CAR BODY]
```

FIG. 8.2.   Two definitions of **POP**.

With the macro version this is not a problem since, as we have already noted, the macro will be expanded at compile time and inserted into the code. Hence X will be a local variable if we use the macro version. In general it is a good practice to replace FEXPRs with calls to EVAL by MACROs (or sometimes by LEXPRs). (Again, INTERLISP, by keeping variable names around, removes these problems.)

Of course, a call to EVAL is all right if its argument evaluates to something that does not contain any variables. When this in turn is evaluated, there will be no special variables to give us trouble. (Remember, the argument to EVAL is evaluated twice.) The call to EVAL in SLOT-FUNS-EXTRACT (Chapter 4) has this property.

8.5 COMPILING NON-EXPRS

In Section 8.1 we noted how the compiler treats different inputs (e.g., EXPR and MACRO definitions). In this section we look closely at some of the problems that may arise due to ramifications of these rules. One problem is that when the compiler is working on a function call, it has to decide then and there how to handle the arguments. If the compiler does not know what kind of function it is looking at, it assumes it's an EXPR. Hence anything else (i.e., LEXPRs, FEXPRs, and MACROs) must be either defined prior to its appearance in any function to be compiled or declared in a DECLARE. Doing the latter is similar to declaring a variable special. The format in our LISP is

(DECLARE (*FEXPR -function-names-))

Since a human reader trying to understand your code will need the same information, it is a good idea in general to declare or define special function types prior to their use. (INTERLISP has essentially the same restriction.)

A second problem is specific to macros. Suppose a macro uses an auxiliary function (other than another macro). The auxiliary function will be compiled but not defined at compile time. When the compiler tries to expand a call to the macro, there will be an error when the auxiliary function is called. There are several ways around this, but the easiest is to have any such functions not only compiled but also read into the compiler LISP (with DSKIN or its equivalent). In this way they will be defined and the macro can use them. (In INTERLISP one can operate the compiler in several different modes. One of these is similar to what we just described. It will not save EXPR code in the compiler LISP; however, there is also a mode where all function definitions will be not only compiled but also executed. In this mode one need not worry about this problem with MACROs.)

The fact that macros are not passed along to the output file can sometimes cause problems. For example, one might be compiling a file of utility functions that are to be used in conjunction with other functions in other files. Usually compilers will have switches that cause the macro definitions to appear in the output file as well.

8.6 CONCLUSION

We have noted various ways in which interpreted code will fail to work properly when compiled and we have given four recommendations for avoiding these problems.

1. Declare all special variables SPECIAL.
2. Avoid using SET and explicit calls to EVAL or, at least, be extra careful should you use them.
3. Define non-EXPRs before they appear elsewhere in the code.
4. Any auxiliary functions used by macros should be read into the compiler LISP as well as compiled.

Note that only the first three will have any direct effect on the code one writes. Of these three we have already noted that the first and third make sense even if compilation is not intended. Concerning the second, SET is rarely used anyway. So the real price of always writing compilable code is the extra care taken with EVAL. But even here the problem with EVAL is the problem of special variables, and in most cases where the use of EVAL is justified, any variables it uses ought to be declared special on the general grounds of readability. Hence it is our opinion that one should strive to write compilable code whether or not one actually intends to compile it.

Exercise 8.1 There is a problem associated with the compilation of files which use RECORD-TYPE or any other function which itself defines further functions. In particular, we will often want these subsequent functions to be compiled (if they are EXPRs, FEXPRs, or LEXPRs) or passed to the output file (if they are MACROs). First note that the definer function (e.g., RECORD-TYPE) must itself be a macro, or else calls to it will simply be passed to the output file without any processing taking place. If the macro expands to (DE . . .), then the one function will be compiled. But suppose the definer function defines several functions (as does RECORD-TYPE). How can we have all of them compiled or passed along? To solve this problem, define a splice macro (name it, say, %), which when preceding a macro call will cause the output of the macro to be spliced into the input stream. Explain how this will do the trick.

9 Data-Driven Programming

9.1 INTRODUCTION

In Chapter 3, one exercise involved defining a read macro, |, which was used, in effect, to extend read macros to more than one character. So |" was a macro for creating list structure, whereas |@ had a different use. A typical form for the bar macro would be

```
(SETQ CHARACTER (READCH))
(COND  ((EQ CHARACTER '/") something-to-do)
       ((EQ CHARACTER '/@) something-else-to-do)  )
```

We need one COND clause for each of the next characters that would have a particular meaning when preceded by a bar.

It would be really handy to be able to keep adding things to the bar macro. For example, we might define |L to expand to LAMBDA. The trouble is, each time we want a new use for bar, we must redefine the bar macro by adding a new COND clause.

There is, however, a way to circumvent this problem. Suppose we replace the code above with the following:

```
(SETQ CHARACTER (READCH))
(COND((GET CHARACTER 'MACRO-PROGRAM)
       (APPLY (GET CHARACTER 'MACRO-PROGRAM)
              NIL))
     ((ERROR "ILLEGAL USE OF | - BAR-MACRO")))
```

Here we are associating with each possible next character the name of a function (of no arguments) that will tell us what to do if this particular character follows a bar. Then on the property list of double quote, atsign, etc., we would have the appropriate programs. In the case of atsign, for example, we would have

```
(DEFPROP /@ BAR-ATSIGN-MACRO MACRO-PROGRAM)
(DE BAR-ATSIGN-MACRO ( ) (LIST '*ATSIGN* (READ)))
```

This method of attaching programs to data and deciding what to do next by retrieving the programs associated with the incoming data is a very useful programming trick. Indeed, it is so useful that it has been raised from the level of a trick and has become a technique. It has also been given a name, *data-driven programming*. In this chapter we discuss a few examples of data-driven programming.

9.2   THE := MACRO

A useful construct that employs this technique is the := macro, which has the following format.

(:= *left-side right-side*)

This expands into code that makes the left-hand side equal to the right-hand side. So, for example,

(:= X 3)	expands to	(SETQ X 3)
(:= (CAR X) 3)		(RPLACA X 3)
(:= (CDR X) (FOO 'A))		(RPLACD X (FOO 'A))
(:= (GET X 'AGE) 13)		(PUTPROP X 13 'AGE)

Clearly this macro must work by examining the code that appears on the left-hand side and using it to decide on the correct expansion. Now it would be possible to code this with a large COND, as follows:

```
(DM := (EXPRESSION)
    (LET(LFT (CADR EXPRESSION) RGT (CADDR EXPRESSION))
        (COND((ATOM LFT)  |"(SETQ @LFT @RGT))
            ((EQ (CAR LFT) 'CAR)  |"(RPLACA @LFT @RGT))
            ...]
```

As should be clear, we are in exactly the same situation we were in with the bar macro. If we use the above coding method, each time we wish to expand the applicability of := we will need to redefine it. If we use data-driven programming, we obtain the code of Fig. 9.1.

```
(DM := (EXPRESSION)
    (LET (LFT (CADR EXPRESSION) RGT (CADDR EXPRESSION))
        (COND ((ATOM LFT) |"(SETQ @LFT @RGT))
            ((GET (CAR LFT) 'SET-PROGRAM)
                (CONS (GET (CAR LFT) 'SET-PROGRAM)
                    (APPEND (CDR LFT) (LIST RGT]

(DEFPROP CAR RPLACA SET-PROGRAM)
(DEFPROP CDR RPLACD SET-PROGRAM)
(DEFPROP GET GET-SET-PROGRAM SET-PROGRAM)

(DE GET-SET-PROGRAM (ATM PROP VAL) (PUTPROP ATM VAL PROP]
```

FIG. 9.1. The := macro.

Exercise 9.1 Extend := so it can handle (:= (CADR X) . . .). Since we will need it later, define the SET-PROGRAM of CADR to be RPLACAD:

(RPLACAD *exp1 exp2*)

This does the same thing as

(RPLACA (CDR *exp1*) *exp2*)

Exercise 9.2 Quite frequently the left-hand expression is repeated in the right-hand expression as well. For example, if the SUB-PARTS property of BIRD has the value (WINGS EYES), and we want to add SKIN, we would say

(:= (GET 'BIRD 'SUB-PART)
    (CONS 'WING (GET 'BIRD ' SUB-PART)))

Redefine := to recognize the special symbol *—* on the right-hand side of the expression as representing the expression on the left-hand side. So the above could be written

(:= (GET 'BIRD 'SUB-PART) (CONS 'WING *—*]

One final feature would be useful in our := macro. In Chapter 4 we introduced a function which automatically produced macros of the form STATE: GOALNODE which in this example returns the STATE slot from a data structure called a GOALNODE. Exercise 4.4 modified the data type definition package to also define functions like GOAL:GOALNODE:SET that would be used to set the value of the goal slot of the goal node. Given our := macro, it would be nice to do away with these and replace them with expressions like

(:= (GOAL:GOALNODE GOAL-NODE-2)
    '(HAVE MACBETH KNIFE))

This would replace

(GOAL:GOALNODE:SET GOAL-NODE-2
                    '(HAVE MACBETH KNIFE))

There are several reasons for doing it this way: It would make our programming style more consistent, we would reduce the number of functions needed to define a data type, and it is trivial to do. The basic idea is this. GOAL:GOALNODE is a macro and hence will be expanded to a function, like CADR. Rather than worry about how to reset the GOAL:GOALNODE, we tell our program how to reset CADR. But we have already done this in Exercise 9.1. That is to say, this is something we would want our LISP to be able to do whether or not we ever thought of GOALNODEs.

So all we need to do is modify := to check if the left-hand side function is a macro. If so it should expand the macro (but not evaluate it) and then call := on the result; that is, we would have the following stages:

```
(:= (GOAL:GOALNODE GOAL-NODE-2)
    '(HAVE MACBETH KNIFE))
(:= (CADR GOAL-NODE-2) '(HAVE MACBETH KNIFE))
(RPLACAD GOAL-NODE-2 '(HAVE MACBETH KNIFE))
```

(The function RPLACAD is defined in Exercise 9.1.)

Exercise 9.3   Redefine := to accommodate the functions defined by the record package. The only thing at all tricky here is how you expand the macro on the left-hand side. Note that you cannot simply evaluate it, since that will both expand it and evaluate the resulting code.

Exercise 9.4   All LISPs today have a pretty-print function (one that prints out LISP S-expressions in indented format) and many of these function have what are called *print macros*. These allow the user to define functions that tell the program how to print out certain constructs. The pretty-printer looks to see if the CAR of the list is an atom with a PRINT-MACRO property. If it is, it will APPLY this function to the list and print out what the function returns. If your LISP has such a facility, learn how to use it. Then, (1) write a print macro to convert (QUOTE X) to 'X if the pretty-printer does not do this already; (2) write a pretty-print macro to tell the program to print out (LET (FUNCTION-1-VAL (FUNCTION-1 ARGUMENT) FUNCTION-2-VAL (FUNCTION-2 ARGUMENT))...) as

```
(LET (FUNCTION-1-VAL (FUNCTION-1 ARGUMENT)
      (FUNCTION-2-VAL (FUNCTION-2 ARGUMENT))
      ...)
```

9.3   DATA-DRIVEN PROGRAMMING
AS AN ORGANIZATIONAL DEVICE

So far we have been looking at examples where data-driven programming was used at a "low level" in the definition of utility functions, such as the bar macro. However, the technique can also be used as a global organization device. In such cases the top-level program will be a little executive program that dispatches on incoming data to the various subprograms. Consider a system that maintains bibliographies (cf. Sandewall 1975). It might be designed in the following way. A bibliographic entry would be defined as an atom with various properties on its property list, each corresponding to a field of the entry: AUTHOR, TITLE, PUBLISHER, etc. Attached to each of these field names would be programs for printing out the field for different types of entries: book, article, etc. Thus

(GET FIELD ENTRY-TYPE)

would tell us how to print out FIELD (e.g., TITLE) if the entry is ENTRY-TYPE (e.g., ARTICLE). For example, the title of books might be underlined, whereas the titles of articles would be in quotes.

We could go even further. Perhaps we want our program to have more than one way of doing bibliographies. In such a case our program would have to know that titles of articles in American Psychological Association format do not have quote marks around them, and only the first letter of the first word is capitalized. On the other hand, Turabian, an authority on such matters, uses quote marks, and capitalizes nonfunction words. We could extend our system to handle this by doing something like

(GET (GET FIELD ENTRY-TYPE) BIB-STYLE)

The general idea here should be clear. The resulting program would be, in fact, a system of small programs distributed on the property lists of the data coming in. There would be an executive program that combined everything in the correct order, but it would be quite small and uninteresting (Fig. 9.2).

```
(DE DO-BIB (ENTRIES BIB-STYLE)
    (FOR (ENTRY IN ENTRIES)
        (DO (LET (ENTRY-TYPE (GET ENTRY 'TYPE))
            (FOR (FIELD IN (GET BIB-STYLE 'FIELD-ORDER))
                (DO (an appropriate-print-command
                    (APPLY(GET (GET FIELD ENTRY-TYPE) BIB-STYLE)
                    (LIST (GET ENTRY FIELD]
```

FIG. 9.2.   The top level of a bibliography program.

Exercise 9.5 If your LISP has good string manipulating facilities, you might try to write this program. There are many complexities we did not discuss above. For example, what about multiple authors? Different schemes treat them differently. Or again, the field order will probably be influenced by the entry type. Assume that the output of this program will be fed to a second program that formats typing on a page, so that one does not have to worry about where to put line feeds, etc. This is hardly a short exercise. On the other hand, when combined with a good text editing system and computerized bibliographic data, it could be a useful one.

10 Miscellaneous Programming Techniques

In the second half of the book, we will discuss more advanced, specialized AI programs. Before that, we would like to tidy up our survey of low-level programming by giving brief descriptions of a few simple techniques that improve the efficiency or elegance of LISP programs. That is the purpose of this chapter.

10.1 SET OPERATIONS ON LISTS

Many LISPs provide a built-in function for intersecting lists. This function is defined essentially as

```
(DE INTERSECT (L1 L2)
    (SUBSET '(LAMBDA (X) (MEMBER X L1)    ) L2))
```

This algorithm works fine for short lists, but for large lists it takes time proportional to the product of the lengths of the two lists. Many people are under the impression that this is an inherent bound on the complexity of taking intersections, but, in many cases, it isn't.

The most important such case is intersecting two long lists of symbols. In such a case, it is more efficient to mark the symbols in one list, then collect the marked symbols in the other list. The marking is accomplished by putting a property on a symbol's property list. The scheme works because an occurrence of a marked symbol on the second list points to the very same properties. The code is shown in Fig. 10.1. Notice that the program must clean up the marks after collecting the intersection. (This program is sensitive to

```
(DE SYMS-INTERSECT (L1 L2)
  (FOR (S IN L1) (DO (:= (GET S 'MARK) T))  )
  (PROG1 (SUBSET '(LAMBDA (S) (GET S 'MARK)  ) L2)
         (FOR (S IN L1) (DO (REMPROP S 'MARK))  ))  )
```

FIG. 10.1. Marking technique for symbol-list intersection.

being interrupted in midstream. It might be better to do the REMPROPs before the marking, or to use a new symbol each time instead of MARK.) The overhead of property-list marking and searching makes SYMS-INTERSECT less efficient for small lists. But for large lists, it takes time proportional to the sum of the lengths of the two lists rather than the product. [Actually, it takes time proportional to 2(length of L1) + length of L2. It might be worth it to check the lengths first and mark the shorter of the two lists.]

This same technique can be used to implement other set operations, such as union and complement. For example, to do a union, mark one list and append it to the unmarked elements of the other list.

Exercise 10.1 Write the following three programs to manipulate lists of symbols using the mark technique: SYMS-UNION unions two lists of symbols; SYMS-DIFFERENCE takes the set difference of two such lists (i.e., the symbols in the first list and not in the second); SYMS-NODUPLS takes one list of symbols and returns a new list with the same symbols, with duplicates removed.

This idea works particularly well with symbols, but it can be made to work for other data types as well. For a user-defined data type, it often pays to include a mark field for use in set operations on lists of elements of that type. (We will use this technique in later chapters.)

If the lists involved contain integers from 1 to 50 (or some other small upper bound), we can create an array MARK, letting (MARK i) = T if i is marked. If the integers cover too large a range to make this practical, we could instead use a binary tree (Knuth 1973b). Each node of this tree would contain a test number and two subtrees. The left subtree would contain numbers less than the test number; the right subtree, numbers greater. Then searching for a number would involve hunting down the tree in the obvious way. Marking a number means adding it to this tree, by growing a new subtree at the appropriate point.

Exercise 10.2 Implement a function NUMS-INTERSECT that uses this scheme.

This approach is worse than linear, since in general the time to search the tree depends on the logarithm of its size. But it is still better than the naive method.

If the lists contain general S-expressions, it might appear that we are stuck with the inefficient algorithm. However, if the lists being manipulated are large enough, it may be worthwhile to build a special data structure for storing S-expressions, analogous to the binary tree for numbers, that can be searched in faster than linear time. In Chapter 11, we will look at such a data structure, called a *discrimination tree*. As with the large-number case, this structure can be used to perform intersections in time proportional to $N1 + (N2 \log N2)$, where $N1$ and $N2$ are the lengths of the two lists.

For both numbers and list structures, we can also use a hash table for efficient set operations, as described in Exercise 10.5.

10.2   HEADED LISTS AND QUEUES

Many iterative LISP programs build lists. The most straightforward way to do this is to initialize the target list to NIL and execute

(:= L (CONS *new-element* L))

as each new element is generated. One feature of this scheme is that the elements of the resulting list appear in the opposite order of their generation. Sometimes this is irrelevant, but sometimes it is a nuisance.

The wrong way to get around this problem is to change the CONS statement to (:= L (APPEND L (LIST *new-element*))). Each APPEND copies the entire list, so this does a lot of needless CONSing. It is slightly better to write (:= L (NCONC L (LIST *new-element*))), but this still takes time proportional to the square of the length of the final list, so it is only advisable for short lists, constructed in loops whose speed is not critical.

There are several right ways to get around the problem. The best, when applicable, is to find a MAP function (or FOR loop) to build the list. This works only when the target list is generated from the elements of some other lists in a sequential way. When you can't do this, the best approach is usually to CONS the elements together backward and then REVERSE the result at the end. This is such a common construction that no one will have trouble seeing what the code is doing, and it only takes time proportional to the length of the target list.

However, this method will work only if the program builds the entire list before using any of it. Sometimes this isn't true. For example, a breadth-first search of a tree will have a main loop of the form

```
(LOOP (INITIAL NODES NIL CURRENT-NODE top-node-of-tree)
      (DO sprout-some-nodes-from-CURRENT-NODE
          add-them-to-end-of-NODES)
      (UNTIL (NULL NODES))
      (NEXT CURRENT-NODE pop-next-node-off-NODES))
```

Here we interleave pulling nodes off the list with tacking them on. The NCONC method we mentioned will work in this case [e.g., *"add-them-to-end"* would be implemented as (:= NODES (NCONC NODES *new-nodes*))], but it has the same inefficiency as before. None of the other methods will work at all.

A data structure like NODES is called a *queue*. In order to implement it efficiently, we must keep, in addition to NODES itself, a variable LAST-CELL that is set to the last cell of the NODES list. This allows us to implement *"add-them-to-end"* as

> (:= (CDR LAST-CELL) *new-nodes*)
> (:= LAST-CELL (LAST *—*))

Unfortunately, this suffers from bugs. Whenever the queue is empty (e.g., the first time through the loop), it will have no last cell. The solution is to force it to have a last cell, by giving NODES a dummy or "header" cell that comes before the real elements. With this amendment, the code is shown in Fig. 10.2. Notice that there is one slightly inelegant case; when the last cell is the only cell, the program must reset LAST-CELL when it pops the front of the queue.

```
(LOOP (INITIAL NODES (LIST '$DUMMY$)
             LAST-CELL NODES
             CURRENT-NODE top-node-of-tree)
      (DO sprout-some-nodes-from-CURRENT-NODE
             (:= (CDR LAST-CELL) new-nodes)
             (:= LAST-CELL (LAST *—*)))
      (UNTIL (NULL (CDR NODES)))
      (NEXT LAST-CELL (COND ((EQ (CDR NODES) LAST-CELL) NODES)
                            (T LAST-CELL)  )
            CURRENT-NODE (CADR NODES)
            (CDR NODES) (CDDR NODES)))
```

FIG. 10.2.   Keeping track of the last cell of a list.

Of course, there is a major style problem with the code of Fig. 10.2: It reveals too many details of the implementation of queues. We would do better to define queues with

> (RECORD-TYPE QUEUE NIL (LAST-CELL . ELEMENTS))

and provide functions for adding and removing elements from a queue.

Exercise 10.3.   Implement this data type and the functions ENQUEUE and DEQUEUE. (ENQUEUE *q l*) adds the elements of *l* to the end of the queue *q*. (DEQUEUE *q*) removes and returns the first element of *q*. The constructor for queues, (QUEUE, *l*) takes just one argument (the initial ELEMENTS), finds its last cell, and CONSes it on. Notice that the call to RECORD-TYPE is not really doing very much for us, since it doesn't define the right constructor, and it defines a useless slot function, LAST-CELL:QUEUE. It might be worthwhile, however, to keep it around for its documentation value.

Header cells are useful for other purposes. Lists used as long-term data structures are often subject to continual additions and deletions of elements. In some cases, it is fine to use CONS and REMOVE for these purposes. One problem with REMOVE is that it copies its argument, so a long permanent list may be copied many times. The solution to this problem is to use DREMOVE, which actually alters its argument without doing any copying.

Unfortunately, this doesn't solve another problem. The same list may be pointed to from more than one place. It may be the value of two variables, or it may occur as a sublist of another data structure. For example, say L1 = (A B C) is being used as a data structure, and there are two other data structures L2 = (L1...) and L3 = ...L1...); that is, L1 occurs as the CAR of L2, but occurs somewhere else in L3. Executing (DREMOVE 'B L1) will change L1 to be (A C) and hence correctly update L2 and L3. Unfortunately, this will not work for removing A, because DREMOVE only alters the CDRs of a list. You can get around this problem for L2 by writing

(:= (CAR L2) (DREMOVE 'A L1))

but this doesn't take care of L3 or any other lists and variables that may point to L1.

Giving each data list a header solves this problem, since it makes all the data elements come after the front of the list. [The programming language IPL-V (Newell et al., 1964) provided a header for every list, partly for this reason.] Rather than using CDR to find the elements of a list with a header, define

(RECORD-TYPE HEADED-LIST ELEMENTS)

The format of a headed list will be (HEADED-LIST -elements-). If L2 is kept as a headed list, an element can be removed by executing

(:= (ELEMENTS:HEADED-LIST L2) (DREMOVE element *—*))

no matter where it occurs.

One more use of headed lists is worth describing. Sometimes a program must go through a long list removing some elements; usually this should be done with SUBSET, but in critical loops the resulting CONSes could be too expensive. One solution is to loop through the list, keeping a variable PREV pointing at the cell just before the one containing the element being examined. If the element is to be deleted, it can be done by executing

(:= (CDR PREV) (CDR *—*))

Of course, this only works if there is always a previous cell. To be sure there is, the program must make its argument into a headed list.

10.3 HASH TABLES

LISP allows you to attach properties to symbols using GET and PUTPROP. Sometimes it is desirable to attach properties to other structures. The orthodox way to do this is to define a property-list slot for these structures. (Curiously enough, IPL-V used the header slot of each list as a property list.) However, this solution can be ugly. Sometimes the list structure is to be used for other purposes in which an extra slot is inappropriate; for example, a recursively defined data structure would have to have such a slot at every level. Further, you will pay for the slot even if it is empty. What you really want is a way of attaching properties to an arbitrary list cell without forethought. One way to do this is with hash tables.

A *hash table* is an array for storing aribtrary key-value associations, such that the average time for a random access to the table does not depend on the number of associations. The basic mechanism is to store an association in the array slot whose subscript is given by a "hash function" applied to the key. To retrieve the value corresponding to a key, you apply the hash function to get the subscript back (Knuth 1973b). More formally, to store the association <K, V>, you set (ARRAY (HASHFUN K)) to V. To retrieve the value for K, you just evaluate (ARRAY (HASHFUN K)).

This simple scheme suffers from an obvious problem: The hash function can give the same subscript for two different keys. (In the usual jargon, the two keys "hash to the same value.") This must happen sometimes, since the set of keys is never small enough, and orderly enough, for HASHFUN to be one-to-one. One solution is to make the entry for array entry *i* be an association list ((*K1 V1*) (*K2 V2*) ...) of associations whose keys *K1, K2, ...* hashed to *i*. On retrieval, the computer must look down this list for the appropriate entry. Such a list is called a *bucket*.

One way to look at this is to compare it with the straightforward a-list implementation of a table; we have replaced the required long a-list with an array of short a-lists and swapped a long linear search for a search down a short bucket. Of course, nothing guarantees that a bucket will be short. This depends on the hash function and the set of keys that gets used. In some applications, many of the keys will be similar, so it is desirable that similar keys be hashed to very different subscripts. (This is why it is called a "hash" function; it makes hash of any patterns in the keys.)

We will use hash tables to generalize PUTPROP and GET to allow an arbitrary S-expression as first argument. With the restriction to symbols dropped, we can see these functions as associating a value with an arbitrary ordered pair of keys, corresponding to the symbol and indicator in PUTPROP and GET. So our associations look like

(RECORD-TYPE ASSN NIL (LKEY RKEY VAL))

The complete code is shown in Fig. 10.3. The array **HARRAY** contains the buckets of associations. (This is one of the few places we use LISP arrays. [We have nothing against arrays, but applications for them just don't come up very often in the problems we look at in this book.] Different LISPs define and access arrays in different ways. In ours, (**ARRAY** *name type size*) defines an

```
(DECLARE (SPECIAL *TABLE-SIZE*))
~The size of the hash array. (47 is actually rather small.)

(:= *TABLE-SIZE* 47)

~HARRAY is an array of buckets of associations
(ARRAY HARRAY T 47)

~An association is a relation between two keys and a value.
~(Generalizes normal LISP relation between a symbol,
~an indicator, and a value.)
(RECORD-TYPE ASSN NIL (LKEY RKEY VAL))

~Make an association
(DE PPUT (K1 K2 V)
    (LET (I (PHASH K1 K2) A NIL)
      (:= A (PASSN I K1 K2))
      (COND (A (:= (VAL:ASSN A) V))
            (T (STORE (HARRAY I) (CONS (ASSN K1 K2 V) (HARRAY I))))  )))

~Retrieve an association
(DE PGET (K1 K2)
   (LET (A (PASSN (PHASH K1 K2) K1 K2))
      (COND (A (VAL:ASSN A))  )))

~Remove an association
(DE PREM (K1 K2)
    (LET (I (PHASH K1 K2) A NIL)
      (:= A (PASSN I K1 K2))
      (COND (A (STORE (HARRAY I) (DREMOVE A (HARRAY I))))  )))

~Given two objects, generates table subscript of bucket to
~look in. MAKNUM is a built-in function that returns a fixnum
~equal to the address of its argument. E.g., (MAKNUM NIL) = 0.
(DE PHASH (K1 K2)
    (REMAINDER (+ (MAKNUM K1) (MAKNUM K2)) *TABLE-SIZE*)  )

~Given a table subscript I and two keys, returns the association
~in bucket I with those two keys, or NIL if there isn't one.
(DE PASSN (I K1 K2)
    (CAR (SOME '(LAMBDA (A) (AND (EQ (LKEY:ASSN A) K1)
                                (EQ (RKEY:ASSN A) K2))  )
           (HARRAY I)))  )
```

FIG. 10.3.   Hash table for arbitrary S-expressions.

array; *type* = T means an array of S-expressions. Once defined, the *n*th slot of the array may be accessed by evaluating (*name n*). It may be set with the reserved word (STORE (*name n*) *value*).)

We define three functions for manipulating properties. (PPUT *k1 k2 v*) associates the key pair <*k1, k2*> with the value *v*. (PGET *k1 k2*) retrieves the value for *k1* and *k2,* or NIL if there isn't one. (PREM *k1 k2*) removes an association. These functions are straightforward implementations of the hashing scheme, except for the slightly unorthodox use of two keys as the arguments to the hashing function PHASH and the bucket search.

The function PHASH is somewhat "hackish." It is intended to deliver a subscript given an object. It uses the function MAKNUM, which, in our implementation, returns a number equal to the machine address of the representation of its argument. [For example, (MAKNUM NIL) = 0.] This function, or something like it, is found in most LISPs. The resulting numbers for the two keys are scrambled by adding them modulo the size of the hash array. (This ensures that the result is a legal subscript.)

It can be shown that if the number of entries in a hash table is small (e.g., about half the buckets are empty), then the average retrieval time for the table is a small constant that doesn't depend on the number of entries at all! This makes the hash table a potent data-structuring device, which deserves more use.

Unfortunately, there are some drawbacks:

1. Hashing costs the overhead of allocating an array. This array must be big enough so that it never becomes full. So it is not usually economical to define lots of hash tables for short-term use; instead, you must define a big array and use it in lots of places. [This is one reason for using two keys. If one-shot tables were cheap, it would sometimes be cleaner to solve a problem using a special table with one key per entry rather than introducing a distinguishing second key. This is done in SNOBOL (Griswold et al., 1971). See Exercise 10.5.]

2. In some LISPs, the garbage collector relocates list cells. This means that every garbage collection will wreck a hash table based on MAKNUM. (Some of these LISPs supply built-in hash tables that the garbage collector maintains when necessary.)

3. Using our PHASH means that you cannot retrieve a value using a key that is merely EQUAL to the one it was stored under; that is, if X = (A), doing (PPUT 'IND X 'VAL) will cause (PGET 'IND X) to be VAL, but (PGET 'IND '(A)) will be NIL. In fact, our functions are really hanging properties off arbitrary memory locations, not S-expressions as such. For example, changing the CAR of a list in memory will not change the properties attached to it.

An alternative scheme is to use a hash function that returns the same value for **EQUAL** keys. This will only work on noncircular list structures and will not be tolerant of side effects on keys, but it can be useful.

Exercise 10.4. Implement such a hashing function. (*Hint:* You need an atom-hasher and a way of combining the hash values for the **CAR** and **CDR** of an expression.)

Exercise 10.5. Using an **EQUAL**-invariant hash function like that of Exercise 10.4, implement an efficient function for intersecting two lists of S-expressions. (*Hint:* store the expressions of one list in a hash table. You can use **PPUT** and company or a special-purpose table containing only "keys.")

II

AI PROGRAMMING
TECHNIQUES

11

Simple
Discrimination Nets

11.1 THE GENERAL DISCRIMINATION NET

A frequent programming problem is the classification of information on the basis of some of its properties. In the simple case where the classification can be made on the basis of single tests then we need nothing more than the function **COND**, that is, we would have something like

(COND ((*test-1* **TO-BE-CLASSIFIED**) *result-1*)
((*test-n* **TO-BE-CLASSIFIED**) *result-n*))

However, suppose the classification in general requires that a large number of tests be applied to **TO-BE-CLASSIFIED**. Conceptually we can think of this as forming a net or tree, as in Fig. 11.1. Such structures are called *discrimination nets* (or discrimination *trees* if, as is the case in Fig. 11.1, they form a tree).

To make this a bit more concrete, let us consider an actual application. This is taken in a much simplified form from the BABEL program of Goldman (1975). The problem he confronted was how to decide on the best English word to describe a situation where the situation is initially described in a semantic representation [in his case, Conceptual Dependency (Schank 1975)]. So, for example, if the input were "ingest a medicine," then the best word would be "take" as in "*take* a pill." On the other hand if we were given "ingest food," we would use the word "eat." A discrimination net is a convenient representation for these tests, as shown in Fig. 11.2.

Now given such a net we could, in fact, encode it as embedded **COND**s. However, the resulting code would be somewhat obscure, and furthermore

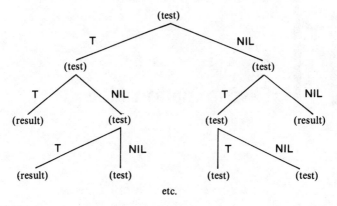

FIG. 11.1. A general discrimination net.

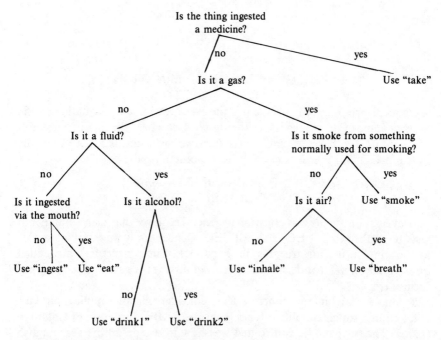

FIG. 11.2. Discrimination net from BABEL.

there are situations where embedded CONDs will not work. This would occur if instead of the tree in Fig. 11.2 we had a real net (i.e., where there are two different nodes that can go to the same next node). This is a situation that occurs in BABEL.

So instead of trying to make do with primitive LISP functions, let us develop the functions we need for handling discrimination nets. We will eventually have to define data types for terminal and nonterminal nodes, which we shall call **TERMINAL** and **NODE**, respectively. **TERMINAL**s will consist of a **RESULT** slot, whereas **NODES** will have a **TEST** slot and a **NEXT-NODES** slot. Assuming we define our data types with the data definition package of Chapter 4 we will have the following functions at our disposal.

(RESULT:TERMINAL *terminal-node*)
(TEST:NODE *non-terminal-node*)
(IS-TERMINAL *node*)

Given these we need only one more data-dependent function: one to select the next node to visit, given the results of the test and the current node.

(NEXT-NODE *test-result current-node*)

With these we can now define a function that handles our discrimination net.

```
(DE DISCRIMINATE (ITEM NODE)
    (COND   ((NULL NODE) NIL)
            ((IS-TERMINAL NODE) (RESULT:TERMINAL NODE))
            ((DISCRIMINATE ITEM
                (NEXT-NODE ((TEST:NODE NODE) ITEM)
                    NODE]
```

Exercise 11.1   The function above makes no real use of recursion. Write an iterative version using the **LOOP** macro.

In order to write **NEXT-NODE** we must select an implementation. One possibility would be to represent nonterminal nodes as lists with the first element the test and the rest being an a-list of (TEST-RESULT . NEXT-NODE) pairs.

Of course, if we know that the test only returns **T** and **NIL** results, we can make use of this fact and make **NODE** of the form (TEST NODE-IF-T NODE-IF-NIL). Since this is the case for the BABEL example, let us do it this way.

```
(RECORD-TYPE TERMINAL (RESULT))
(RECORD-TYPE NODE NIL (TEST NODE-IF-T NODE-IF-NIL))

(DE NEXT-NODE (TEST-RESULT NODE)
    (COND(TEST-RESULT (NODE—IF-T:NODE NODE))
        ((NODE-IF-NIL:NODE NODE]
```

Exercise 11.2   Suppose we represent the input to the BABEL discrimination net as (INGEST *agent object instrument portal*), and we handle the testing by writing a function that takes the test to perform and asks the user if the test is true or not. Write the functions needed to do all this and, using them, encode the BABEL net given earlier.

11.2 DATA BASE DISCRIMINATION NETS—LISTS OF ATOMS

A different kind of discrimination net, and one that will come up again in later chapters, is the discrimination net that classifies expressions according to their syntactic form. Such a net would classify two expressions as the same if and only if they are **EQUAL**. One can think of such a net being used as a data base where we will be asking if some fact is stored in the data base, and we need an efficient way to find out.

We will start out by restricting the expressions to lists of atoms. So, for example, the net to discriminate among (A), (A B), (B A), (B B), and (B C) is shown in Fig. 11.3. If the discrimination net search ends in a node written as

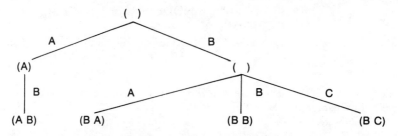

FIG. 11.3. Sample discrimination net of lists of atoms.

( ), then the desired list is not part of the data base. If the list is part of the data base, it will end with a filled in node [e.g., (A B)]. Note that it is also possible that the search will end early because there is no link with the proper label leading from the current node. For example, the search for the list (A C A) will terminate after reaching the node labeled (A) since there is no C link leading from this node. Code to implement this kind of discrimination net appears in Fig. 11.4.

The basic idea behind the program is that we **CDR** down **ITEM** until we reach the end of the list. However, this may be halted by a failure to find a next node (the first **COND** pair). If we do reach the end of the list, **ITEM** is in the data base if and only if **ITEM** is stored on the node we have reached. So, for example, consider how **FETCH-LIST-OF-ATOMS** will work on the tree given above and the input (A B). Neither **NODE** nor **ITEM** is **NIL** so we call **FETCH-LIST-OF-ATOMS** with **ITEM** = (B) and **NODE** = the node represented above as (A). Again neither **NODE** nor **ITEM** is **NIL** so we call it

```
(RECORD-TYPE NODE NIL (ITEM . A-LIST))
     ~An A-LIST consists of a list of LINKs.

(RECORD-TYPE LINK NIL (KEY . NODE))
       ~A LINK specifies the key which should cause us to follow the
       ~link and the node at the other end of the link.

(DE FETCH-LIST-OF-ATOMS (ITEM NODE)
     (COND ((NULL NODE) NIL)
           ((NULL ITEM) (ITEM:NODE NODE))
           ((FETCH-LIST-OF-ATOMS  (CDR ITEM)
                                  (NEXT-NODE (CAR ITEM) NODE]
(DE NEXT-NODE (KEY NODE)
     (LET  (LINK (ASSOC KEY (A-LIST:NODE NODE)))
           (COND (LINK (NODE:LINK LINK]
```

FIG. 11.4.   Code for fetching a list of atoms.

again, this time with **ITEM** = **NIL** and **NODE** = the node represented above as **(A B)**. This time we will return the item stored at this node, or **(A B)**.

But, as should be clear from the fact that we want to use this discrimination net for a data base, we also need a function to add items to the data base. The function **INDEX-LIST-OF-ATOMS** in Fig. 11.5 should do the job. Note that **ESTABLISH-NODES** corresponds to **FETCH-LIST-OF-ATOMS** except that it does not check for failure to find the next node, since this will not be allowed to happen. **ESTABLISH-NODE** corresponds to **NEXT-NODE**, except, if there is no next node, one is created, and a link is added to the **A-LIST** of the current node. **INDEX-LIST-OF-ATOMS** simply adds **ITEM** to

```
(DM ADD-TO-A-LIST (EXP) (CONS 'CONS (CDR EXP]

(DE INDEX-LIST-OF-ATOMS (ITEM NODE)
     (LET (FINAL-NODE (ESTABLISH-NODES ITEM NODE))
          (COND   ((ITEM:NODE FINAL-NODE))
                  (T (:= (ITEM:NODE FINAL-NODE) ITEM) ITEM]

(DE ESTABLISH-NODES (ITEM NODE)
     (COND   ((NULL ITEM) NODE)
             ((ESTABLISH-NODES  (CDR ITEM)
                                (ESTABLISH-NODE (CAR ITEM) NODE]

(DE ESTABLISH-NODE (KEY NODE)
     (LET (LINK (ASSOC KEY (A-LIST:NODE NODE)))
          (COND   (LINK (NODE:LINK LINK))
                  ((LET (NEXT-NODE (NODE NIL NIL))
                   (:= (A-LIST:NODE NODE)
                       (ADD-TO-A-LIST (LINK KEY NEXT-NODE) *—*))
                  NEXT-NODE]
```

FIG. 11.5.   Code for indexing a list of atoms in discrimination net.

the final node provided by **ESTABLISH-NODES** in the case that it is not there already.

11.3   DATA BASE DISCRIMINATION NETS—GENERAL S-EXPRESSIONS

Now let us consider the same problem we tackled in Section 11.2 except now we want to handle arbitrary expressions rather than just lists of atoms. The first problem we must confront is how to express the structure of an expression in terms of a linear string of keys; that is, in the discrimination net for lists of atoms at each node we needed a key to take us to the next node. This key was, of course, the atom at the front of the yet undiscriminated portion of the list. The list itself served then as the string of keys, telling us which key should be used to take us to the next node. Things are not so simple unfortunately when we consider arbitrary expressions. For example, we now need to distinguish between **(A B)** and **(A . B)**. Of course, the way we write expressions on a page is itself a linear encoding for expressions, but unfortunately it is not a unique encoding; for example,

$$(A . (B . NIL)) = (A . (B)) = (A B).$$

Exercise 11.3   Why do we need a unique encoding?

Exercise 11.4   Suppose we build a discrimination net to handle lists of arbitrary expressions; that is, the top level must be a list, but each element may be any expression. Why is the code for **FETCH-LIST-OF-ATOMS** limited to lists of atoms? What small change will make it work for lists of expressions? How efficient will this code be if for some reason every item in the data base is of the form **((A B))**, that is, when every item is a list containing one sublist?

In fact, there are many ways to encode an expression uniquely in a linear format. The one we will use here stems from the observation that given any expression there is exactly one way to build it up using only the function **CONS**. So we obtain ((A . B) C D) from

(CONS (CONS 'A 'B) (CONS 'C (CONS 'D NIL)))

Furthermore, since **CONS** always takes two arguments, the parentheses may be deleted, giving us

CONS CONS A B CONS C CONS D NIL

This is the linear string of keys we need. In our functions we will not be concerned with building an expression by using **CONS**, but rather we will want to get the **CONS** formulation by looking at the expression.

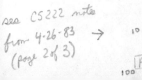

Exercise 11.5   Write a function CONS-EXP, which given an arbitrary expression produces the unparenthesized CONS expression which would build it.

With the CONS-EXP function from Exercise 11.4 we can trivially build the general expression discrimination net by feeding the results of CONS-EXP to FETCH-LIST-OF-ATOMS. This would require actually building the list to hand to FETCH-LIST-OF-ATOMS, however, and CONSes, as we have already noted, are expensive. What follows is a version that avoids them by integrating CONS-EXP and FETCH-LIST-OF-ATOMS into one. It also economizes on the size of the discrimination net by taking advantage of the fact that with the new scheme for linearizing expressions a single node cannot have both an item stored on it and an a-list pointing to further nodes; that is, we once again have a distinction between terminal and nonterminal nodes. Note that the basic construct used in these functions is the link rather than the node. Exercise 11.7 gives a hint as to why this is the case. The only tricky part of the program in Fig. 11.6 is the double recursion that occurs in

```
(RECORD-TYPE LINK NIL (KEY . A-LIST))
(RECORD-TYPE TERMINAL NIL (KEY . ITEM))
(DM ADD-TO-A-LIST (EXP) (CONS 'CONS (CDR EXP]

(DE INDEX (ITEM LINK)
    (LET (TERMINAL-LINK (ESTABLISH-LINKS ITEM LINK))
        (COND  ((ITEM:TERMINAL TERMINAL-LINK))
               (T (:= (ITEM:TERMINAL TERMINAL-LINK) ITEM) ITEM]

(DE ESTABLISH-LINKS (ITEM LINK)
    (COND  ((ATOM ITEM) (ESTABLISH—LINK ITEM LINK))
           ((ESTABLISH-LINKS
             (CDR ITEM)
             (ESTABLISH-LINKS  (CAR ITEM)
                               (ESTABLISH-LINK '*CONS* LINK]

(DE ESTABLISH-LINK (KEY LINK)
    (COND  ((ASSOC KEY LINK))
           ((LET (NEW-LINK (LINK KEY NIL))
             (:= (A-LIST:LINK LINK) (ADD-TO-A-LIST NEW-LINK *—*))
             NEW-LINK]

(DE FETCH (ITEM LINK)
    (LET (TERMINAL-LINK (TRAVERSE-LINKS ITEM LINK))
        (COND (TERMINAL-LINK (ITEM:TERMINAL TERMINAL-LINK]

(DE TRAVERSE-LINKS (ITEM LINK)
    (COND  ((NULL LINK) NIL)
           ((ATOM ITEM) (TRAVERSE-LINK ITEM LINK))
           ((TRAVERSE-LINKS
             (CDR ITEM)
             (TRAVERSE-LINKS (CAR ITEM) (TRAVERSE-LINK '*CONS* LINK]

(DE TRAVERSE-LINK (KEY LINK) (ASSOC KEY (A-LIST:LINK LINK]
```

FIG. 11.6.   INDEX and FETCH for arbitrary S-expressions.

TRAVERSE-LINKS and **ESTABLISH-LINKS.** These two functions are essentially identical except, of course, that **ESTABLISH-LINKS** will add new links if none are there. In both cases then the double recursion serves the same purpose, and we will just consider **TRAVERSE-LINKS.**

Suppose we wish to determine if **(HUMAN JACK)** is in the data base of Fig. 11.7. (The numbers in quotations are for ease of reference only.) **FETCH** will immediately hand **(HUMAN JACK)** off to **TRAVERSE-LINKS.**

(TRAVERSE-LINKS '(HUMAN JACK) *DATA-BASE*)

Here ***DATA-BASE*** is bound to the discrimination net. To make things compatible, it will have the form of a link; that is,

(*TOP* . *a-list*)

Upon entering **TRAVERSE-LINKS** we note that **ITEM** (=**(HUMAN JACK)**) is not an atom, so we do the double recursion.

(TRAVERSE-LINKS '(JACK)
     (TRAVERSE-LINKS 'HUMAN
          (TRAVERSE-LINK '*CONS* *DATA-BASE*)))

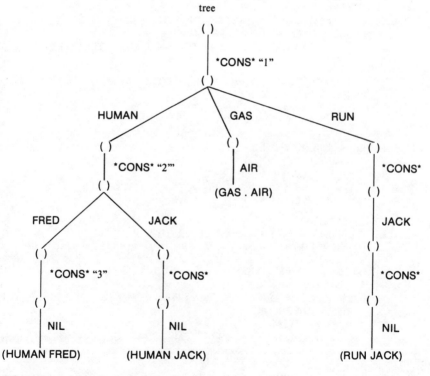

FIG. 11.7.   Sample discrimination net of arbitrary S-expressions.

In effect we are saying here that since ITEM is not an atom, we must first follow the path for *CONS* since that must be the first thing in our representation of the expression. We achieve this with the call

(TRAVERSE-LINK '*CONS* LINK)

and this will return the link with the key *CONS*. To distinguish links from atoms in this discussion we will use lowercase for the links and add on any numerical differentiater. So we are currently at link *cons*-1, leaving us now to evaluate

(TRAVERSE-LINKS '(JACK)
 (TRAVERSE-LINKS 'HUMAN *cons*-1))

This says that starting from *cons*-1 we must first traverse the tree according to the links provided by the CAR of ITEM (i.e., 'HUMAN), and from the point where that leaves us off we must traverse the tree according to the CDR. In evaluating

(TRAVERSE-LINKS 'HUMAN *cons*-1)

since ITEM (= 'HUMAN) is atomic, we will simply call TRAVERSE-LINK and return the link "human". With this done the expression above reduces to

(TRAVERSE-LINKS '(JACK) human)

In much the same way, this call will lead us down the rest of the path to (HUMAN JACK).

Exercise 11.6 Why is it the case that a node will never have both an item and an a-list? Note that this reestablishes the distinction between terminals and nonterminals. However, we do not indicate on a node whether a node is terminal or not but rather can infer this on the basis of the computation to date. Explain why we can get away with this.

Exercise 11.7 Note that the functions take the LINK as the fundamental unit rather than the node (where a node would be an a-list for nonterminals and an item for terminals. Explain what would go wrong with ESTABLISH-LINK if we used nodes as the basic unit and tried to rewrite the function as ESTABLISH-NODE.

Exercise 11.8 Write a very short function UNINDEX that removes an ITEM from the discrimination net. It should rely on TRAVERSE-LINKS to do the real work.

So far we have been thinking of this discrimination net as a mechanism for handling a data base. As such it is clearly deficient, since we cannot handle situations where we need to know, say, how old Jack is; that is, we cannot ask

(AGE JACK-1 ?X)

Here ?X is a variable, and we have no mechanism for variables. This is covered in Chapter 14.

This is not to say that the program developed in this last section is useless. Such a discrimination net allows one to "uniquify" expressions. In LISP, there is only one atom with a given print name; that is, unless one really works at it, the JACK-1 we type now will refer to the same atom as the JACK-1 we typed earlier, and in particular anything we put on JACK-1's property list will be available the second time. This is not true for lists. If we type in (FATHER JACK-1), it will not be the same piece of list structure as an earlier (FATHER JACK-1). For this reason, even if list structures could have property lists in LISP, they would not be all that useful. One can implement such a facility however with a "uniquifier." This is nothing more than our INDEX function, since if the expression is a new one, it adds it; and if it is an old one, it returns a pointer to the one already stored in the net, hence establishing a canonical version of the expression. Although we have not included a place for a property list, it would be easy to do.

Exercise 11.9 Write the functions E-PUT and E—GET that will use PUTPROP and GET, for atomic expressions and a uniquifier otherwise. Compare with Exercise 10.4.

12

Agenda Control
Structures

In this chapter we describe a somewhat amorphous collection of techniques, called by names like *agenda-based control, queue-based control, streams, coroutines,* and *possibilities lists.* What they all have in common is the use of a very simple kind of data-driven programming to represent states of a suspended process.

12.1 BEST-FIRST TREE SEARCH

We begin with an example. We wish to write a program for doing heuristic search in order to solve a simple puzzle. The kind of puzzle we have in mind is one with some kind of board, with pieces that can move in various ways. From each board position, there will be a finite number of successor positions reachable by one move. The object is to find a sequence of moves that gets the board into a winning position (cf. Nilsson, 1971). This way of looking at the problem defines a *search space* through the set of all board positions reachable from some initial position. There are various classical ways to search such a tree; the one we will look at is called *best-first* search. We assume that there is some way of estimating how close a position is to being a winning position; that is, that there is an *evaluation function* that maps positions into estimates. A best-first search proceeds by generating moves, and hence new positions, from the most promising board position that has been reached so far. This process is called *sprouting*, since iterating it gives rise to a tree of board positions.

You might think that implementing this algorithm would require representing the portion of the tree searched so far, but this is often unnecessary. All we really need in many cases is a representation of the "growing edge" of the tree, the nodes whose descendants have not yet been sprouted (Fig. 12.1). Each element of the list represents a scored board position. The main search loop of the program will then look like

```
(LOOP  [WHILE (AND NODELIST (NOT (IS-WINNER (CAR NODELIST)]
        (DO (:= NODELIST
                (MERGE (CDR NODELIST) (SORT (SPROUT (CAR NODELIST)]
```

where **SPROUT** takes a node and returns a list of its descendants. **MERGE** and **SORT** sort board positions in descending order by their estimated values. (Whether these values are recomputed each time or stored when the position is first created is a low-level implementation decision that need not concern us.)

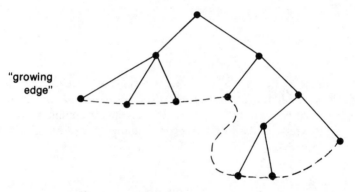

"growing edge"

FIG. 12.1. Search tree for a simple puzzle.

Exercise 12.1 Write a program to color connected planar maps with four colors using the given loop. The program is given some representation of a planar map. (The map representation must specify for each country what other countries are connected to it and what its color is; initially all countries are uncolored.) A winner is completely colored. Sprouting a given map means picking an uncolored country adjacent to a colored country and coloring it all possible ways that don't cause it to be the same color as a neighbor. Experiment with different evaluation functions. For example, you might use "number of colored countries" as an evaluation or you might try "number of colored countries — number of colors used" or some more sophisticated measure.

Now let's modify the example a bit, by considering puzzles in which more than one kind of move is possible. One such puzzle is the "Missionaries and Cannibals" puzzle, in which there are three missionaries and three cannibals trying to cross a river in a boat that will hold two people. If the cannibals ever outnumber the missionaries on either side of the river, they will eat them. (If the missionaries outnumber the cannibals, the cannibals will be converted to some religion they might not like, but at least they will be alive.) The problem is to find a sequence of river crossings that will get everyone across the river.

Now board positions will specify how many representatives of each culture are on each side of the river and where the boat is. If the boat is on the left side, sprouting new board positions means making all legal moves of people to the right side; similarly, if the boat is on the right, legal moves move people back the other way.

We could just hide this structure in the sprout function, but it is instructive to make it more visible. Then the central loop becomes

```
(LOOP   [WHILE (AND NODELIST (NOT (IS-WINNER (CAR NODELIST]
        (DO (:=NODELIST
                (MERGE (CDR NODELIST)
                    (SORT (COND ((IS-LEFT-NODE (CAR NODELIST))
                                (LEFT-SPROUT (CAR NODELIST)))
                                ((RIGHT-SPROUT (CAR NODELIST]
```

It should be clear that this can be generalized. We can think of our search tree as a growing crowd of competing processes, each generating an alternative line of attack. A process can run for a while and then suspend itself until the main loop decides to try it again. The map-coloring processes suspended themselves just before generating another partial coloring. The missionaries-and-cannibals processes can suspend themselves in one of two places: before generating a left-to-right move or before generating a right-to-left move. We could generalize this for more complicated puzzles to allow any number of possible suspensions, one for each place where evaluation was possible. The code would start to look like Fig. 12.2. This is getting clumsy.

```
(LOOP   [WHILE (AND NODELIST (NOT (IS-WINNER (CAR NODELIST]
        (DO (:= NODELIST
                (MERGE (CDR NODELIST)
                    (SORT (SELECTQ (TYPE:NODE (CAR NODELIST))
                        (LEFT
                         (LEFT-SPROUT (CAR NODELIST)))
                        (RIGHT
                         (RIGHT-SPROUT (CAR NODELIST)))
                        (UP...)
                        (DOWN...)
                        (SIDEWAYS...)
                        ...]
```

FIG. 12.2.   Allowing several suspension points.

We've seen this pattern before (Chapter 9), and it's an obvious sign that data-driven programming is called for. We could attach LEFT-SPROUT to LEFT under the SPROUT indicator, but there is no reason to do this, since then LEFT would be serving no purpose except to hold this association. Instead, we just put the function **LEFT-SPROUT** itself in the node, and the code becomes

```
(LOOP  [WHILE (AND NODELIST (NOT (IS-WINNER (CAR NODELIST]
            (DO (:=NODELIST
                 (MERGE (CDR NODELIST]
                        (SORT  ((FUN:NODE (CAR NODELIST))
                               (BOARD-POSITION:NODE (CAR NODELIST]
```

Now **LEFT-SPROUT** is the **FUN:NODE** of half the nodes; **RIGHT-SPROUT** is the **FUN:NODE** of the others. It is the responsibility of **LEFT-SPROUT** to make **RIGHT-SPROUT** the **FUN:NODE** of the nodes it creates, and vice versa. In a sense, each node represents a suspended process, which may be run, in which case it does a little computation and returns a list of created processes. Each process is represented by two things: a function, which is like a program counter (it tells where to go to resume the process); and a data structure, which is like a saved process state (it provides the data the process will work on).

> *Exercise 12.2* Write a program to solve the missionaries-and-cannibals problem using the code given. A board position will be a data structure representing who is on which bank of the river; it will also have a slot **PATH:BOARD-POS** that tells how the position was arrived at. This is necessary because the solution we are interested in is the path, not the final state, which is always the same. If you write this program correctly, it will have two parts: a general puzzle solver (initialization, the loop given above, and **MERGE** and **SORT**) and the sprout functions and data types for the missionaries-and-cannibals problem.

12.2 COROUTINES AND AGENDAS

We can make one further generalization. So far we have assumed that a board position was kept at all nodes. This is too restrictive, since it means board positions must be defined to be general enough to contain all the information any sprout function could want. This can be a nuisance, since some processes might want to suspend themselves in states with quite different saved data structures from the states of other processes. For example, in the map problem, we might want to generate alternative map extensions one at a time; the saved state for "generate first extension" would need slightly different state information from "generate next extension." There is no reason for the main loop to deal with these differences. In fact, the main loop needs to know only three things about a process: the "program-counter function," the saved state, and the score. So we arrive at a definition like

(RECORD-TYPE NODE NIL (SCORE FUN ARGS))

We call **FUN** a "program counter," because, like the program counter of an interrupted machine-language process, it tells where to resume execution of it. (The term *coroutine* is also used for members of a set of processes, all but one of which are suspended at any given time.)

A node list managed in this way is called an *agenda*. There are many variations on this theme. The node list could be made a special variable, and **FUN:NODE**'s could be called for their side effects, one of which might be to add to the list. Another variation is the technique [used in KRL (Bobrow & Winograd, 1977) and AMORD (de Kleer et al., 1977a)] of letting the node list be a set of buckets of nodes; high-priority buckets run before low-priority ones, but there is no sorting within a bucket, and no score slot is needed in a **NODE**. A **FUN:NODE** might do some computation; then set

```
(:= (BUCKET 3)
    (CONS (NODE 'CONTINUE (LIST FOO 5)) *—*))
```

In all the examples so far, a process stays suspended only because more attractive-looking processes are available to run. It is just as easy to have coroutines suspended for other reasons (e.g., because some other process must be completed before they can go). There are several ways to arrange for this. The simplest is to hide the **NODE** for process A as the value of a saved state variable of process B; B's last action could be to put A's node back on the node list. A more formal technique is also possible. In addition to the node list of processes ready to run, we could have a list of processes that are not ready. These blocked processes could be checked periodically or when some enabling event occurs to see which of them could be moved to the ready list (see Barstow, 1979).

All these techniques suffer from one drawback: since LISP doesn't have a natural notation for operations that suspend one coroutine and start another, the user is forced to resort to the clumsy language of packaging up one function and calling another to simulate what he wants. For example, in the last code fragment we gave, the user probably wanted to write something like

```
...
(do some stuff)
(SUSPEND 3)              ˜specify agenda priority level
(continue with more stuff)   ˜return when
...                          ˜higher priorities satisfied
```

Instead, he had to express the actions after resumption in an asymmetric and unrevealing way. One way out of this problem is to use LISP to implement a language with more powerful control structures built in; we will do this in Chapter 17. Another approach is given in the following exercise.

Exercise 12.3 (Very difficult) Write a macro (**PROC** *vars -body-*) whose syntax is like **PROG**, but having the following semantics. The *vars* are state variables of the process being defined. **SUSPEND** may occur at the top level of the **PROC**, or at the top level of **COND**s appearing at the top level of the **PROC**. **PROC** must actually expand into several function definitions (**DE's**), roughly one per label and **SUSPEND**. For example, the code in Fig. 12.3 is to be expanded into the code of Fig. 12.4.

```
(DE FOO (X)
  (PROG (Y)
    (PROC (X Y)
LOOP  (BAR X)
      (SUSPEND 3)
      (:= X (BLECH Y))
      (GO LOOP)  ]
```

FIG. 12.3.   A function that creates a process.

```
(DE FOO (X)
  (PROG (Y) (PROC1 X Y)  ))

(DE PROC1 (X Y) (PROC2 X Y)  )

(DE PROC2 (X Y)
    (BAR X)
    (:= (BUCKET 3) (CONS (NODE 'PROC3 (LIST X Y)) *—*))  )

(DE PROC3 (X Y)
    (:= X (BLECH Y))
    (PROC2 X Y)  )
```

FIG. 12.4.   Interpretation of function FOO.

12.3   STREAMS

An especially nice version of the agenda idea is the *stream*. The node lists we have looked at so far include only process nodes. A stream is a mixed list, consisting of arbitrary objects and process nodes called *generators*. A stream is supposed to behave like a list of the objects that are there, plus potential objects that will be generated when they are needed. This is useful for examining only a small part of infinite or very long lists.

For example, the following function returns a stream of all the integers starting with **K**.

```
(DE GINTS (K)
    (LIST K (GENERATOR 'GINTS (LIST (+ K 1)))))]
```

Generators are defined by

```
(RECORD-TYPE GENERATOR $GEN (FUN . ARGS))
```

So (GINTS 0) returns

(0 ($GEN GINTS 1))

a list with one item (the 0) and one generator.

Streams are processed using **SAR** and **SDR**, which are like **CAR** and **CDR** except for their handling of generators. Applying **SAR** to the stream above gives 0. If you call **SDR**, it will notice the generator and return the value of

(APPLY 'GINTS '(1))

which is

(1 ($GEN GINTS 2))

The empty stream represented by **NIL**. A stream that starts with a generator gives us trouble, because we will have to call it twice to get the **SAR** and the **SDR** and because it isn't obvious whether the stream is empty. (A stream consisting only of generators is functionally empty if none of them generate anything.) So we usually insist on working with *normalized* streams, which don't start with a generator. We can define **SAR** and **SDR** thus:

```
(DE SAR (S) (CAR (NORMALIZE S))   )
(DE SDR (S) (NORMALIZE (CDR (NORMALIZE S)))   )
```

where **NORMALIZE** is as shown in Fig. 12.5

```
(DECLARE (SPECIAL *REST*))

(DE NORMALIZE (S)
    (COND  ((OR (NULL S) (NOT (IS-GENERATOR (CAR S))))
            S)
           ((LOOP (INITIAL *REST* NIL)
                  (NEXT *REST* (CDR S))
                  S (APPEND
                       (APPLY  (FUN:GENERATOR (CAR S))
                               (ARGS:GENERATOR (CAR S)))
                       *REST*)))
           (WHILE (AND S (IS-GENERATOR (CAR S))))
           (RESULT S]
```

FIG. 12.5. Definition of **NORMALIZE**.

The use of the special variable ***REST*** is an extra feature. It is a free variable that generators can access and set to manipulate the contents of the stream. For example, we could do the puzzle search example easily with the code shown in Fig. 12.6. In this figure, **MERGE** and **SORT** are assumed to know how to sort generator calls to **PUZZ**. Then

(NORMALIZE (LIST (GENERATOR 'PUZZ (LIST INITIAL]

returns a stream of winning board positions.

```
(DE PUZZ (BOARD)
    (COND   ((IS-WINNER BOARD) (LIST BOARD))
            (T
            [:= *REST*
                (MERGE *REST*
                        (SORT (FOR (B IN (SPROUT BOARD))
                            (SAVE
                              (GENERATOR
                                'PUZZ (LIST B)))   ]
        NIL]
```

FIG. 12.6.   Puzzle solver using streams.

One further example. The following function takes two streams and interleaves them:

```
(DE INTERLEAVE (S1 S2)
    (COND((NULL S1) S2)
        ((LIST (SAR S1)
            (GENERATOR 'INTERLEAVE
                (LIST S2 (SDR S1]
```

Exercise 12.4   Notice that INTERLEAVE always SDRs S1, whether or not the caller will ever use the SAR of the result. Modify the definition to eliminate this problem. (*Hint:* There is a solution with no auxiliary functions. It involves an explicit call to NORMALIZE.)

Exercise 12.5   Generalize INTERLEAVE to take a single argument, which is a stream of streams. Make sure that every element of every stream will ultimately be generated, even if some of the streams are infinite.

Exercise 12.6   Define a FEXPR called FTRANS such that (FTRANS *filespec*) will return a stream of objects read from a file.

Exercise 12.7   Change FTRANS so that it expands top-level macro calls that it finds in a file. Further, if a macro expands into a list of the form

($SPLICE$ *x1 . . . xN*)

the elements *x1, . . ., xN* are to appear in the stream instead of this list. [Be sure that your solution correctly handles a macro that turns into a ($SPLICE$) alone.]

Streams may be thought of as a communication device for structures of "semicoroutines" (Dahl et al., 1972). These are coroutines which exist in a subordinate relation to a "master" routine which keeps asking them for more information. The generators in a stream represent the suspended "slave" coroutines; the objects are the information being sent back to the master. For example, we may think of GINTS as sending back integers to its master. As with ordinary coroutines, we are forced to be more clumsy than we would like. Although GINTS is simple enough to be transparent, even this simple function could more revealingly be written

```
(DE GINTS (K)
    (LOOP (DO (YIELD K) (:= K (+ K 1]
```

where (YIELD x) sends x to the master coroutine and suspends the slave coroutine until the master wants more data. Writing the coroutine this way shows clearly its (harmless) infinite loop structure. As with our original coroutines, we must either put up with our inability to write functions this way, or implement a more powerful language in LISP, or write a complex macro.

> *Exercise 12.8* Modify the definition of PROC (Exercise 12.3) so that it handles YIELD instead of SUSPEND.

If the same stream is SDR'ed down twice, you may or may not get the same results the second time. If you do always get the same objects out, the stream is called *memoryless*. For example, (GINTS 0) is a memoryless stream, because it always generates the same objects (the natural numbers). With (FTRANS FILE1), you will not, because each SDR has a side effect in some I/O channel. A stream of random numbers must also have some memory.

If a memoryless stream is used more than once, you will repeat some work each time. Using a memoried stream twice can be perilous. With a stream of random numbers, you probably want different users of the stream to see different values; with a file stream, two users will see mutually exclusive subsets of the file, which is probably not what you want.

One way to impose some order on all this is to provide a variant of SDR that actually changes the CDR of a (normalized) stream to be the SDR when the SDR is computed. Then the next program that does a SDR of the same stream will find the value already generated. Streams used in this way are called *pipes*. [They are called "possibilities lists" in Conniver (Sussman & McDermott, 1972).]

> *Exercise 12.9* Implement pipes; that is, implement two functions PAR and PDR that get the first element and remaining elements of a pipe. A pipe has the property that (PAR (PDR S)) is always the same object. Be sure your code does the right thing with an unnormalized pipe.

13 Deductive Information Retrieval

Many AI programs solve problems in a domain by using lots of knowledge about it. Of course, any program, in AI or not, can be said to embody knowledge of a domain. The distinguishing characteristic of many AI programs is that their knowledge is stored explicitly in a data base of some kind. In this and subsequent chapters, we will explore the programming techniques required to maintain such a data base. There are two main issues in writing programs this way: how facts are to be represented and how they are to be accessed.

13.1 PREDICATE CALCULUS

Almost all representation schemes are based on a predicate-argument notation. In this notation, facts are represented as *formulas* of the form

(*pred -args-*)

One such formula might be (COLOR BLOCK2 MAROON). The semantics of this expression are the same as for the corresponding LISP form: Its value is "true" if and only if BLOCK2 really is MAROON colored. The difference is that in LISP the predicate (here, COLOR) must be associated with a program that actually returns T or NIL for any pair of arguments. In a representation system, such a program does not usually exist, so we must fall back on weaker, more general algorithms for inferring the colors of objects. This means that in addition to notations for known facts, a representation system requires algorithms that make inferences of new facts.

One of the simplest systems is predicate calculus (PC). In addition to predicates and arguments, PC supplies *connectives* and *quantifiers*. Connectives combine simple formulas into more complex ones. For example, we may wish to say, "BLOCK2 is either MAROON or CHARTREUSE." This would be expressed as

(OR (COLOR BLOCK2 MAROON)
    (COLOR BLOCK2 CHARTREUSE))

One of the most useful connectives is IMPLIES. (IMPLIES p q) is true if p is false or q is true. It is called IMPLIES because it allows us to infer q if p is known to be true. For example, we could say

(IMPLIES (MATERIAL BLOCK2 IRON) (HEAVY BLOCK2))

to mean, "If BLOCK2 is made of iron, then it is heavy."

The two quantifiers, FORALL and EXISTS, give PC its inferential power. They enable us to talk about all objects or some unknown object. Quantifiers are used in conjunction with bound variables. If p is an expression containing the variable X, then

(FORALL (X) p)

is true if and only if p is true no matter what value of X is substituted into p. For example,

(FORALL (X) (IMPLIES (IN X BOX1) (COLOR X
CHARTREUSE)))

means, "If anything is in BOX1, it is chartreuse," or, "Everything in BOX1 is chartreuse."

(EXISTS (X) p) means that *some* value of X makes p true. For example,

(EXISTS (X) (AND (IN X BOX1) (COLOR X CHARTREUSE)))

means, "Something in BOX1 is chartreuse."

For reasons that will become clear, quantifiers are not explicitly represented in computer programs that manipulate PC formulas. Instead, we adopt the convention that all variables are universally quantified. Thus, "Everything in BOX1 is chartreuse" would be expressed as

(IMPLIES (IN ?X BOX1) (COLOR ?X CHARTREUSE))

We now must prefix variables with ? in order to distinguish them from predicates and constants. Existential quantifiers are handled quite differently. Since an EXISTS asserts that there is an unknown object with a property, we can state the same thing by just giving the unknown object a name. So "Something in BOX1 is chartreuse" would be written

(AND (IN THING59 BOX1) (COLOR THING59 CHARTREUSE))

This will not work for all existential quantifiers, but only those that do not occur inside a universal. There is a generalization of this trick, called "Skolemization," which will work on any formula. See Nilsson (1971) for details. In any case, complicated uses of existentials will not come up in our applications.

Predicate calculus provides only the skeleton of a representation scheme. To put meat on the bones, there are three further things you must do:

1. You must invent a vocabulary that allows you to say everything you need to say in your domain. PC provides only the connectives, IMPLIES, OR, AND, NOT, etc. Symbols like COLOR and IN are supplied by you.

2. You must supply an internal representation of each formula (i.e., a data structure).

3. There must be inference algorithms for manipulating the data structures.

The choice of vocabulary is a deep problem about which we will have little to say. There is a substantial literature on vocabularies for various applications (e.g., Schank, 1975), but there is no universal vocabulary on which all agree.

For the other two design issues, there is also no one best approach, but there is an obvious approach that works well in many cases. This is to let the internal data structures just be list structures isomorphic to the predicate-argument notation, and to let the algorithm for manipulating it be a search for chains of inferences on these list structures. In this chapter, we will explain this algorithm, which is called "deductive information retrieval." In Chapter 14, we will explain how to maintain a data base of such list structures with reasonable efficiency. In Chapter 15, we will discuss an alternative internal representation.

The term *theorem prover* is often used to refer to the kind of program we will be examining (Nilsson, 1971; Robinson, 1965). These programs are somewhat in disrepute in AI, partly because they have been overadvertised, but they can provide a useful mechanism for doing deductive information retrieval and a useful framework for thinking about it. Because the applications for which such programs actually work well are not as grandiose as the name *theorem prover* would imply, we will usually use the more descriptive term *deductive retriever*. In many applications, you can get away with programs less powerful than the ones we will describe, but it helps to know what the real versions look like.

13.2 DEDUCTIVE RETRIEVAL

Deductive retrievers operate by *chaining* through IMPLIES formulas to deduce the answers to *requests*. For example, say a program knows that "BLOCK2 is CHARTREUSE." All we mean by *"knows"* is that this fact is stored in our data base, as the list structure:

(COLOR BLOCK2 CHARTREUSE)

We use the term *assertion* to mean a formula in the data base (since adding a formula to the data base is something like asserting it to be true).

The deductive retriever is used by giving it a *request pattern*, with the intent that it deduce from what it knows all the formulas that fit the pattern. For example, we might give the retriever the request pattern (COLOR BLOCK2 ?WHAT), meaning, "Find the color of BLOCK2." The question mark before WHAT indicates that WHAT is a variable. As we said, in an assertion a variable is interpreted as universally quantified; in a request, a variable behaves as a slot to be filled.

Given a request, the deductive retriever looks through its data base of formulas until it finds an assertion that *unifies* with the request. (This search can be made more efficient than it sounds. See Chapter 14.) Two formulas are unified by finding values for their variables such that substituting values for variables in each formula gives the same instance formula. In our example, the unifying substitution of

(COLOR BLOCK2 ?WHAT)

and

(COLOR BLOCK2 CHARTREUSE)

is

| request variables: | {WHAT = CHARTREUSE} |
| assertion variables: | { } |

because substituting the variables as shown gives the common instance (COLOR BLOCK2 CHARTREUSE). The result of the unification is interpreted as an answer to the request: BLOCK2 is chartreuse.

In some applications, this sort of one-step retrieval is all you need. In general, however, deductive retrievers must use assertions to deduce formulas that are not immediately available. For example, let's assume the retriever did not know BLOCK2's color after all but did know "Everything in BOX1 is CHARTREUSE." This is just the formula

(IMPLIES (IN ?X BOX1) (COLOR ?X CHARTREUSE))

According to logic theory, this implication may be used, in conjunction with the assertion **(IN BLOCK2 BOX1)**, to derive an answer to the original request. This requires two steps. In the first, we plug **BLOCK2** into the implication to obtain

> (IMPLIES (IN BLOCK1 BOX1)
> (COLOR BLOCK2 CHARTREUSE))

(This is the rule of *universal instantiation*.) Then we can deduce (**COLOR BLOCK2 CHARTREUSE**) by a rule (called *modus ponens*) that allows the inference of Q from P and (**IMPLIES** P Q).

We could use inference rules like this directly, and try making all possible inferences from a set of assertions until we deduced a formula that answered the given request. This is obviously too inefficient. Instead, deductive retrievers use the more directed "backward chaining" technique. They do not actually use an implication until a request is made that unifies with the implication's right-hand side. When such a request is made, the unification is performed, and the resulting bindings are used in the left-hand side to generate a new request for the deductive retriever. (Of course, there may be more than one applicable implication. Most deductive retrievers try them all, until success is attained.) This approach combines universal instantiation and modus ponens into one rule. In our example, the unification would be

> Request: (COLOR BLOCK2 ?WHAT)

with

> RHS: (COLOR ?X CHARTREUSE)

giving the result:

> request variables: {WHAT = CHARTREUSE}
> assertion variables: {X = BLOCK2}

We then generate a *subrequest*, by substituting into the left-hand side of the implication the variable values as shown, to get (**IN BLOCK2 BOX**).

The request-variable bindings come into play later. If the assertion (**IN BLOCK2 BOX**) is in the data base, we are done; the subrequest succeeds immediately (with empty variable bindings on each side). We can retrieve the answer to the original request by tracing back up the chain of unified implications, collecting request-variable values.

For a more complex example, consider answering the request (**LOVES ?X ?Y**), using the implication

> (IMPLIES (NOT (ORPHAN ?X))
> (LOVES (FATHER ?X) MOTHER ?X)))

In this case, the result of the unification is

request variables: {X = (FATHER ?X)*, Y = (MOTHER ?X)*}
assertion variables: { }

The variables in the request are bound to patterns that are only partially filled in. An asterisk flagging a pattern indicates that its variables are from the other side of the unification. (Otherwise, we would have X bound to its own FATHER. Notice that we have changed the ground rules that we started with, since the result of unification is no longer a set of variable bindings that will literally generate a common instance of two patterns. A variable's value may itself contain variables to be replaced, and we must keep track of which pattern a variable comes from. It should be clear, however, that these changes are purely for convenience. By making up new variable names and making all the specified substitutions, we could derive a unifying set of bindings.)

The subrequest in this case is just (NOT (ORPHAN ?X)), since the ?X from the implication was not bound to anything. Now say (NOT (ORPHAN FRED)) is in the data base. The subrequest unifies with this assertion giving

request variables: {X = FRED}
assertion variables: { }

as the substitution. We retrieve the answer to the original request by using {X = FRED} instead of { } in the first substitution. This gives a new substitution

request variables: {X = (FATHER ?X)*, Y = (MOTHER ?X)*}
subanswer variables: {X = FRED}

Now we can get rid of the asterisks by using the value of X in the subanswer bindings. This gives {X = (FATHER FRED), Y = (MOTHER FRED)} as the answer to our original request (i.e., "Fred's father loves Fred's mother"). If the original request was actually a subrequest of something else, we could repeat the process by using these bindings to get rid of asterisks in earlier unifications.

Now suppose the assertion

(IMPLIES (AND (ALIVE (FATHER ?Z))
              (ALIVE (MOTHER ?Z)))
         (NOT (ORPHAN?Z)))

is in the data base. Now the request (LOVES ?X ?Y) will retrieve the same answer as before, but we have the potential to generate additional answers by using the new assertion on the subrequest (NOT (ORPHAN ?X)). This will unify with (NOT (ORPHAN ?Z)) to give the substitution

request variables: {X = ?Z*}
assertion variables: { }

and the subrequest (AND (ALIVE (FATHER ?Z)) (ALIVE (MOTHER ?Z))).
This is an example of a *conjunctive request*, a request to retrieve instances
of a conjunction. A deductive retriever will handle this by calling itself
recursively to generate answers (i.e., variable bindings) for the first conjunct,
and select the answers that also satisfy the second conjunct. For example, if
the data base contains

> (ALIVE (FATHER MARTHA)) (ALIVE (FATHER FRITZ))
> (ALIVE (FATHER DICK))
> (ALIVE (MOTHER FRITZ)) (ALIVE (MOTHER SAM))
> (ALIVE (MOTHER MARTHA))

the answers {Z = MARTHA}, {Z = FRITZ}, and {Z = DICK} will be obtained
for the first conjunct, but only the first two of these give satisfiable requests
when plugged into the second conjunct. These answers will be passed back up
the implication chain as before, ultimately giving answers {X = (FATHER
MARTHA), Y = (MOTHER MARTHA)} and {X = (FATHER FRITZ),
Y = (MOTHER FRITZ)}.

This concludes our description of deductive retrieval. For more
information, consult Nilsson (1971), Chang and Lee (1973), and Moore
(1975). In the rest of this chapter, we will explain how to implement a simple
deductive retriever. Most of the complexity lies in the unification algorithm,
so let's look at that first.

13.3   A UNIFICATION ALGORITHM

So far we have characterized unification purely in terms of its results, which
are sets of bindings that make patterns equal. It might appear that this would
require a complex algorithm, which guesses bindings and later revises them.
This turns out not to be necessary, because the only revision a binding
requires is to further instantiate the variables that appear in it, and this
happens automatically in the course of the unification, when it's done right.

The best way to understand all this is to compare unification with testing
for EQUALity. EQUAL is a built-in LISP function, which might have been
defined as

```
(DE EQUAL (X Y)
   (COND  ((ATOM X) (EQ X Y))
          ((ATOM Y) NIL)
          ((EQUAL (CAR X) (CAR Y))
           (EQUAL (CDR X) (CDR Y)))  ))
```

UNIFY is a generalization of EQUAL, which can fail for the same reasons (e.g., two un-EQ atoms in corresponding positions) but can succeed where EQUAL doesn't, namely, when a variable is unified with something. When this happens, it tells us what the binding of that variable must be in the final result of the unification. As unification proceeds, we must remember the bindings that accumulate, so later manipulations will be consistent.

Figure 13.1 presents a simple uniticiation algorithm, which unifies two patterns which have no variables in common.

```
~The internal representation of predicate-calculus variable ?x is (*VAR* x)
(RECORD-TYPE PCVAR *VAR* (SYM))
(DRM /? (LAMBDA ( ) (LIST '*VAR* (READ))   ))


~A substitution is implemented as a list of bindings
(RECORD-TYPE BDG NIL (SYM VAL))


(DE SYM-LOOKUP (SYM SUB) (ASSOC SYM SUB))
(DE SUBCONS (BDG SUB) (CONS BDG SUB))


(DE UNIFY (PAT1 PAT2) (UNIFY1 PAT1 PAT2 NIL)   )


(DE UNIFY1 (PAT1 PAT2 SUBST-SO-FAR)
    (COND ((IS-PCVAR PAT1)
            (VAR-UNIFY PAT1 PAT2 SUBST-SO-FAR))
          ((IS-PCVAR PAT2)
            (VAR-UNIFY PAT2 PAT1 SUBST-SO-FAR))
          ((ATOM PAT1) (AND (EQ PAT1 PAT2) (LIST SUBST-SO-FAR)))
          ((ATOM PAT2) NIL)
          ((FOR (SUBST-FROM-CAR IN
                  (UNIFY1 (CAR PAT1) (CAR PAT2) SUBST-SO-FAR))
              (SPLICE (UNIFY1 (CDR PAT1) (CDR PAT2) SUBST-FROM-CAR]


(DE VAR-UNIFY (V P SUB)
    (LET (BDG (SYM-LOOKUP (SYM:PCVAR V) SUB))
        (COND (BDG (UNIFY1 (VAL:BDG BDG) P SUB))
              ((LIST (SUBCONS (BDG (SYM: PCVAR V) P) SUB)))   )))
```

FIG. 13.1.   Simple version of UNIFY (with bugs).

UNIFY returns NIL if the two patterns cannot be unified. It returns a list of one element, a substitution, if the patterns can be unified. This one substitution will hold bindings for variables from both patterns. The function UNIFY1 does all the work. It has an extra argument, SUBST-SO-FAR, which is the substitution it has derived so far; if UNIFY1 succeeds, it will return a list containing (a possibly augmented version of) SUBST-SO-FAR; if UNIFY1 fails to find a unifying substitution, it returns NIL.

UNIFY1 works as follows. If both arguments are atomic, they must be EQ. If neither argument is a variable, they must be lists whose respective CARs and CDRs can be unified by the same substitution. Otherwise, one is a variable, and the function VAR-UNIFY is called. Its object is to update the substitution SUB to include a binding of the variable V to the pattern P. If V has no binding in SUB already, VAR-UNIFY returns SUB augmented with a new binding of V to P. If V is bound in SUB, VAR-UNIFY verifies that P is compatible with the old value by calling UNIFY1. This can create new variable bindings. For example, in unifying (P ?X ?X) and (P (F ?Y) (F A)), the second call to VAR-UNIFY will try to bind ?X to (F A) and find ?X already bound to (F ?Y). The resulting call to UNIFY1 will cause ?Y to be bound to A.

Unfortunately, this simple algorithm doesn't quite cover all the cases. If we unify (P ?X ?X) with (P ?X A), the first call to VAR-UNIFY sets ?X to itself. Then the next call to VAR-UNIFY will find ?X as its own value and get into an infinite loop. Another kind of circularity is exemplified by the unification of (P ?X ?X) and (P ?Y (F ?Y)). In this example, ?X will first be set to ?Y. So the unification of ?X with (F ?Y) requires unifying ?Y with (F ?Y), and ?Y will be bound to a term containing itself. This is simply incorrect, since Y = (F ?Y) does not really define a substitution [unless you assign a meaning to an infinite term like (F (F (F...))).]

So we must change the last clause of VAR-UNIFY to check for circularities, as shown in Fig. 13.2, and we need the auxiliary function OCCURS-IN.

```
(DE VAR-UNIFY (V P SUB)
    (LET (BDG (SYM-LOOKUP (SYM:PCVAR V) SUB))
        (COND  (BDG (UNIFY1 (VAL:BDG BDG) P SUB))
               ~Don't bother to bind V to itself--
               ((EQUAL V P) (LIST SUB))
               ~Don't bind V to anything containing V--
               ((NOT (OCCURS-IN V P SUB))
                (LIST (SUBCONS (BDG (SYM:PCVAR V) P) SUB)))  )))


(DE OCCURS-IN (V P SUB)
    (COND  ((ATOM P) NIL)
           ((IS-PCVAR P)
            (OR (EQUAL V P)
                (LET (B (SYM-LOOKUP (SYM:PCVAR P) SUB))
                    (AND B (OCCURS-IN V (VAL:BDG B) SUB))  )))
           ((SOME '(LAMBDA (Y) (OCCURS-IN V Y SUB))
                  P))  ))
```

FIG. 13.2. Patch to simple version of UNIFY.

Checking for circularities slows unification down. Since every part of PAT1 and PAT2 is either traversed by UNIFY1 or assigned to a variable, both patterns must be examined in their entirety. In pathological cases, the same piece of pattern may be looked at over and over, so that the simple unification algorithm is exponential in the size of its arguments. If you have an application that does not require full-blown unification, this check is the first thing to try to eliminate. [Patterson and Wegman (1976) give an algorithm that checks each piece of pattern exactly once, so its running time is linear.]

Our algorithm is still not perfect. Its main problem is that it doesn't distinguish two variables that happen to have the same name but come from different arguments of UNIFY. (We required this in some of our examples of deductive retrieval.) There are two possible responses to this problem. Most deductive retrievers rename all the variables in one pattern (with newly generated symbols) before unifying, and then use the simple algorithm. Besides incurring the overhead of having to copy one of the patterns (creating a lot of new symbols along the way), this response makes it difficult to associate what you wrote with what is used. This makes debugging awkward (and makes it hard to interface LISP code to the retriever. See below.) The alternative is to accept the burden of maintaining two separate substitutions during a unification. To keep things simple, we will proceed using the first alternative, but we would recommend the second in general. (See Exercises 13.1, 13.11, and 13.12.)

Exercise 13.1   Write a version of UNIFY that distinguishes two variables of the same name if one occurs in PAT1 and the other in PAT2. This requires simulating renaming as the unification proceeds. This is done by carrying around an extra argument for each pattern argument to UNIFY1, VAR-UNIFY, and OCCURS-IN. For example, UNIFY1 will have arguments (PAT1 SIDE1 PAT2 SIDE2 SUB). The substitution will have to consist of two a-lists, one for each side. (We will call these *double substitutions*.) SYM-LOOKUP must be told which side to use. Furthermore, you will have to implement some version of the asterisk notation we used earlier, to indicate when a variable is bound to an expression with variables from the other a-list.

13.4   A DEDUCTIVE RETRIEVER

Figure 13.3 shows a simple deductive retriever. It assumes that all the assertions are kept in a special data structure *DATA-BASE* of type DB. INDEX adds an assertion to this data structure. FETCH finds assertions that could unify with a given pattern. (In the current version, it does this by finding *all* the assertions! In Chapter 14, we will show how to be much more selective, using a discrimination tree as an index.)

If RETRIEVE is given a nonconjunctive request, it looks first for immediate answers and then possible backward chains. That is, it searches the assertions twice, once for formulas unifying with the request immediately and then again for formulas of the form (← *request* ?SUBREQ), for use in generating subrequests. ["(← *q p*)" means "*q* is implied by *p*"; we write it

```
(DECLARE (SPECIAL *DATA-BASE*))

~The assertions are kept in a data base, which, until
~the next chapter, is just a list.
(RECORD-TYPE DB (ASSERTIONS))

(:= *DATA-BASE* (DB NIL))

~Adds an assertion to the data base
(DE INDEX (FORMULA)
   (:= (ASSERTIONS:DB *DATA-BASE*) (CONS FORMULA *—*))  )

~Finds assertions in *DATA-BASE* which could unify with PATTERN
~(This version is not very selective!)
(DE FETCH (PATTERN) (ASSERTIONS:DB *DATA-BASE*)  )

~Given a request pattern, RETRIEVE returns a list of substitutions
(DE RETRIEVE (REQUEST)
   (COND   ((EQ (CAR REQUEST) 'AND)
            (CONJ-RETRIEVE (CDR REQUEST) NIL))
           ((NCONC
               (FOR (A IN (FETCH REQUEST))
                    (SPLICE (UNIFY REQUEST (VARS-RENAME A)))  )
               (LET (IMPLPAT ¦"(← @REQUEST ?SUBREQ))
                    (FOR (A IN (FETCH IMPLPAT))
                         (SPLICE (CHAIN IMPLPAT A))  ))))  ))

~If assertion A unifies with IMPLPAT = (← original-request ?SUBREQ),
~try subrequest
(DE CHAIN (IMPLPAT A)
   (FOR (SUB IN (UNIFY IMPLPAT (VARS-RENAME A)))
        (SPLICE
            (FOR (ANSWER IN (RETRIEVE (PCVAR-VAL '?SUBREQ SUB)))
                 (SAVE (APPEND ANSWER SUB))  ))  ))

~Conjunctive requests are handled by generating answers
~to the first conjunct and substituting them into the remaining
~conjuncts for further processing
(DE CONJ-RETRIEVE (CONJUNCTS ANSWER-SO-FAR)
   (COND   ((NULL CONJUNCTS) (LIST ANSWER-SO-FAR))
           ((FOR (ANSWER IN (RETRIEVE (VARSUBST (CAR CONJUNCTS)
                                                ANSWER-SO-FAR)))
                 (SPLICE
                    (CONJ-RETRIEVE
                        (CDR CONJUNCTS)
                        (APPEND ANSWER ANSWER-SO-FAR)))  ))  ))

(DE PCVAR-VAL (PCVAR SUB)
   (LET (BDG (SYM-LOOKUP (SYM:PCVAR PCVAR) SUB))
        (COND   (BDG (VARSUBST (VAL:BDG BDG) SUB))
                (T PCVAR)  )))
```

FIG. 13.3.   A simple deductive retriever.

150

backward for reasons to be discussed in Section 13.5.] Since **RETRIEVE** uses the simple unifier we gave, it must rename variables in assertions.

Exercise 13.2 Write the function **VARS-RENAME**. Be sure that it replaces every occurrence of a variable with the same "**NEWSYM**'ed" variable. (See Chapter 6.)

The function **CHAIN** creates and tries subrequests. A subrequest is obtained by looking up **SUBREQ** in the bindings obtained in the unification of (← *original-request* ?SUBREQ) with the assertion A. Its value may have variables with known values in it, so the function **PCVAR-VAL** uses **VARSUBST** to get rid of them. (**VARSUBST** *pat substitution*) returns a new version of *pat* with all possible variables replaced with their values from *substitution,* including variables that occur in the values of variables. For example,

```
(VARSUBST '(P ?X)
          '((X (F ?Y ?Z)) (Y A)))
⇒
(P (F A ?Z)).
```

Notice that **PCVAR-VAL** returns the variable it was given, if it has no binding in the given substitution. This reflects a difference between PC variables and ordinary programming-language variables. PC variables start off unassigned and gradually become "more assigned," as their values approach being constants. So it is inappropriate to give an error message when there is no binding of **PCVAR** (and even more inappropriate to return **NIL**); instead, we just return the variable itself, to reflect the fact that its value is completely unconstrained. In the current usage, this should never happen, but it will be important later.

Exercise 13.3 Write the function **VARSUBST**.

When we have an answer to a subrequest, we must **APPEND** the original substitution to be sure of including all relevant variables. This is how answers are transmitted back up the implication chain.

Conjunctive requests are handled by **CONJ-RETRIEVE**. This function generates answers to the first conjunct and **VARSUBST**s them into the other conjuncts before working on those conjuncts. The variable bindings returned by **CONJ-RETRIEVE** are accumulated in the variable **ANSWER-SO-FAR**, which is augmented by the bindings discovered at each step. When there are no more conjuncts, this substitution is returned.

Exercise 13.4 Because of the way answers are passed, they keep growing. The final answer will contain many bindings of variables that originated in subrequests and are meaningless at the calling level. Sometimes the same variable will have more than one binding (all but one hidden) in a substitution produced by RETRIEVE. For example, in processing the request

  (AND (MALE ?X) (NURSE ?X))

in the presence of the assertions

  (MALE (FATHER ?X))   (NURSE (FATHER FRED))

CONJ-RETRIEVE will produce the binding X = (FATHER ?G0059) and then hide it by adding a binding X = (FATHER FRED) to the final answer of the original conjunctive request. The first binding is still there but never accessed.

This crude deductive retriever does not bother to get rid of all these irrelevant bindings, on the theory that the caller will not look at them anyway. However, they do slow down variable look-ups. Write a version of RETRIEVE that returns a cleaned-up substitution without this problem.

Exercise 13.5 As written, RETRIEVE returns only variable bindings. Change it so that it returns in addition the proof that the bindings are based on. (A proof need only be a list of assertions used in arriving at an answer.)

Exercise 13.6 (Difficult) RETRIEVE currently returns all the answers it can find, even if the caller is only interested in one (or a few) of them. This is especially a problem if there are an infinite number of answers. Fix these problems by making RETRIEVE's value be a stream of answers. This will require breaking most of the loops and mapping functions in the retriever, replacing them with sets of generator functions (as explained in Chapter 12). Make sure that every answer will ultimately be generated, even if some subrequest or conjunct has an infinite number of answers (cf. Exercise 12.5).

Exercise 13.7 A disjunctive request is of the form (OR *req1 ... reqN*). It will be satisfied by an answer to any of the disjuncts. Add code to RETRIEVE to handle such requests. (If you use the stream version, make sure all answers are found, even if a disjunct has an infinite number of answers.) Rather than adding a clause to RETRIEVE, you should probably make it data-driven.

13.5 OTHER TOPICS

13.5.1 Forward Chaining

In explaining deductive retrieval, we argued that backward chaining was superior to unguided deduction, because it concentrates on implications that have a chance of being relevant to requests. In some cases, however, it is advisable to perform some deductions before requests are known. An example due to Moore (1975) illustrates this. Let us give a program the facts that all dogs are mammals, all cats are mammals, all dolphins are mammals, etc. Further, let us tell it that mammals are warm-blooded, have hair, etc. If we represent these facts by implications to be used in backward chaining, then in answering the request (BLOOD-TEMP FIDO ?WHAT), we will generate subrequests (IS FIDO DOLPHIN), (IS FIDO CAT), (IS FIDO DOG), etc. It could take a while to search through all these subrequests until we found one that was satisfied.

A better approach is to add (IS FIDO MAMMAL) to the data base when (IS FIDO DOG) is added and avoid backward chaining in this case; that is, we will express each implication in one of two ways:

($\rightarrow p\ q$) is to be used to deduce q when p is added to the data base.

($\leftarrow q\ p$) is to be used to generate subrequest p from request q.

As with backward chaining, we combine universal instantiation and modus ponens in a single inference rule, the rule of *forward chaining:* When r is added to the data base, if ($\rightarrow p\ q$) is in the data base, and p unifies with r, then substitute into q the variable bindings from the unifying substitution, and add the result to the data base.

For example, if the data base contains

($\rightarrow$ (IS ?X DOG) (IS ?X MAMMAL))

and (IS FIDO DOG) is added, then the binding X = FIDO is substituted into the right-hand side, to give (IS FIDO MAMMAL), which is also added.

Figure 13.4 shows the code for the function ADD, which performs forward chaining. It adds a new assertion to *DATA-BASE* and then calls itself recursively to add consequences derived from chaining.

```
(DE ADD (PAT)
   (INDEX PAT)
   (LET IMPLPAT  |"(→@ PAT ?RIGHT))
      (FOR (A IN (FETCH IMPLPAT))
         (DO (FOR (SUB IN (UNIFY IMPLPAT A))
               (DO (ADD (PCVAR-VAL '?RIGHT SUB)))  )))))
```

FIG. 13.4.   Function to add assertions.

Exercise 13.8   One thing ADD doesn't do is check to see if its argument is already in the data base. Rewrite it so it does this checking and, if the assertion is already there, leaves the data base as it finds it. Notice that it is not sufficient to check for an EQUAL assertion, since assertions with variables are "the same" if they differ only in the names they give to their variables, for example,

(← (MORTAL ?X) (IS ?X MAN)) and
(← (MORTAL ?G0059) (IS ?G0059 MAN))

both express the idea, "All men are mortal." Two formulas that are the same except for variable renaming are called *variants*. Write a function VARIANTS that tests for this, and use it in your revised ADD.

13.5.2 Retrieving Implications

Our deductive retriever is not "complete," in the sense that these are theorems that are derivable by the rules of logic that RETRIEVE will never find. This is not necessarily a drawback, since special-purpose deductive retrievers tend to run faster than complete ones when they succeed at all. However, there are some cases when you need a more nearly complete algorithm.

Most of the incompleteness of RETRIEVE stems from its neglect of interactions among parts of a request. For example, let us say that we wished to prove, "If Fred is a professor, then he is poor." Further, assume that the data base contains the implications

    (→ (OCCUPATION ?X PROFESSOR) (PAY ?X LOW))
    (← (POOR ?X) (PAY ?X LOW))

The request will be phrased as (IMPLIES (OCCUPATION FRED PROFESSOR) (POOR FRED)). It should be clear that the request is deducible from the assertions; how can we make RETRIEVE do it?

This particular case could be handled by a special assertion of the form

    (← (IMPLIES ?P ?Q)
        (AND (→ ?P ?R) (← ?Q ?R)))

but this is too specific. There may be several ways of getting from professorhood to poverty, and it will be impossible to list all the possible ways. (Forward chaining will not help at all.)

What we need to do is temporarily add (OCCUPATION FRED PROFESSOR) to the data base and try to deduce (POOR FRED). If we succeed, we will have succeeded in proving the implication. The code for doing this is shown in Fig. 13.5. We are assuming that RETRIEVE has been made data-driven (as suggested in Exercise 13.7); forms beginning with atoms with RETRIEVER properties are handled by the functions under those properties. The function IMPL-RETRIEVE rebinds *DATA-BASE* so that the forward deductions it does will be invisible when it returns. Then it ADDs the left-hand side of the implication and tries to deduce the right-hand side. The answers so generated are answers to the original request.

```
(DE IMPL-RETRIEVE (PAT)
    (LET  (LEFT (CADR PAT) RIGHT (CADDR PAT)
          *DATA-BASE* (DB (ASSERTIONS:DB *DATA-BASE*)))
        (ADD LEFT)
        (RETRIEVE RIGHT)  ))

(DEFPROP IMPLIES IMPL-RETRIEVE RETRIEVER)
```

FIG. 13.5.   Implication handler.

13.5.3 AI Languages

We have at several points added special-purpose code to the deductive retriever. We even made it data-driven in order to facilitate this. But this is not as convenient as we might want, since the user will have to know a lot about the internals of the program in order to write new special-purpose hacks. For example, let us say we wish to include the rule, "Two things are presumed unequal if they can't be unified." (This isn't always correct, but it usually is.) We could write

```
(DE NOT-EQUAL-RETRIEVE (PAT)
            ~PAT is of form (NOT (= ...))
    (COND((NOT (UNIFY (CADADR PAT) (CADDR (CADR PAT))))
          (LIST NIL))  ))
```

but this is a bit mystifying. (Also, we need a more complex data-driven scheme, since the CAR of PAT is just NOT.)

It would be nicer to be able to write something like this:

```
(ADD '(← (NOT ( = ?X ?Y))
         (LISP (COND ((NOT (UNIFY ?X ?Y))
                      (SUCCEED))   ))))
```

where we can refer to ?X and ?Y by name and have a more attractive communication convention. The flag LISP is supposed to tell the deductive retriever to evaluate what follows rather than use it as a subrequest. Within this evaluation, question-marked variables are to evaluate to the values established during the initial unification.

This is accomplished by the code shown in Fig. 13.6. We have redefined CHAIN to check for the LISP flag. If it finds it, it binds *PCVARBDGS* to the current substitution and EVALs the given code. The way this is done is somewhat ugly. We have to be unusually careful about variable names because we use a simple-minded unifier. (See Exercises 13.11 and 13.12.) The first ugliness this entails is that CHAIN must call VARS-RENAME to edit the LISP code. Even worse, we cannot EVAL (CADR (PCVAR-VAL '?SUBREQ SUB)); instead, we must EVAL (CADR (CADDR A)). [Remember that A is of the form (← p (LISP ...)).] The reason is that PCVAR-VAL would do a VARSUBST on the code, replacing variables with their values, which would then not evaluate properly. We avoid this problem by using un-VARSUBSTed LISP code and having PC variables evaluate to their values in *PCVARBDGS*; this is accomplished by defining *VAR* as the appropriate FEXPR.

Exercise 13.9 Write the SET-function for *VAR*, so that we can say (:= ?X ...) inside LISP expressions.

```
(DE CHAIN (IMPLPAT A)
  (:= A (VARS-RENAME A))
  (FOR (SUB IN (UNIFY IMPLPAT A))
    (SPLICE
      (FOR (ANSWER IN
            (LET (SUBREQ (PCVAR-VAL '?SUBREQ SUB))
              (COND  ((EQ (CAR SUBREQ) 'LISP)
                ~In doing LISP calls, we must use *PCVARBDGS*
                ~as variable bindings rather than using PCVAR-VAL
                (LET (*PCVARBDGS* SUB)
                  (EVAL (CADR (CADDR A)) )))
              (T (RETRIEVE (PCVAR-VAL '?SUBREQ SUB))) )))
        (SAVE (APPEND ANSWER SUB)) )) ))

~Within the evaluation, pcvars evaluate to their values in *PCVARBDGS*
(DF *VAR* (L) (PCVAR-VAL (PCVAR (CAR L)) *PCVARBDGS*) )

~Success means the *PCVARBDGS* work, so return them
(DE SUCCEED ( ) (LIST *PCVARBDGS*) )
```

FIG. 13.6. Interface to LISP code from RETRIEVE.

One thing we would like to be able to do is call the deductive retriever from inside a LISP expression. One way to do this is have a macro (FOR-EACH-ANSWER *request -body-*), which calls RETRIEVE recursively on the given *request,* and, for each answer found, evaluates *body.* For example, we could express, "All four-legged animals with lots of hair are lovable," as

```
(ADD '(← (LOVABLE ?X)
      (LISP (FOR-EACH-ANSWER (IS ?X ANIMAL)
        (FOR-EACH-ANSWER (FUZZY ?X)
          (COND ((AND (ATOM ?X)
                (EQUAL (GET ?X 'LEGS) 4))
            (NOTE)) )))) )
```

The function NOTE is like SUCCEED but merely saves the current answer until the evaluation is finished.

Exercise 13.10 Write FOR-EACH-ANSWER and NOTE. The only tricky part of this is getting the bindings right. This requires having FOR-EACH-ANSWER use the current *PCVARBDGS* for the variables in its pattern and then rebind *PCVARBDGS* before evaluating the body. (*Note:* Making NOTE work will require a change to CHAIN.)

Exercise 13.11 Write a function (SUB-UNZIP *sub side*) that takes a double substitution *sub* (see Exercise 13.1) and returns an equivalent double substitution with no "asterisks" on the given *side.* For example, the substitution

```
LEFT   {X = (FOO ?X)*, Y = (BAR ?Z)}
RIGHT  {X = (BLECH), Z = (ZAP ?Y)*}
```

can be "unzipped to the left" to give

LEFT {X = (FOO (BLECH)), Y = (BAR ?Z)}
RIGHT {X = (BLECH), Z = (ZAP ?Y)*}

and "unzipped to the right" to give

LEFT {X = (FOO ?X)*, Y = (BAR ?Z), Z = ?G0054*}
RIGHT {X = (BLECH), Z = (ZAP (BAR ?G0054))}

This function is necessary to extract asterisk-free a-lists from substitutions, as we will see in Exercise 13.12.

Exercise 13.12 Rewrite **RETRIEVE** so that it uses the unifier of Exercise 13.1 and the unzipper of Exercise 13.11 to avoid having to use **VARS-RENAME**. The main function this will affect is **CHAIN**. Rather than APPENDing each returned substitution and the original one, it will have to carry out steps like these: (a) get a double substitution from **UNIFY**; (b) unzip it to the assertion side to give two a-lists, **TOP-AL** and **SUB-AL**; (c) use the (asterisk-free) bindings in **SUB-AL** for the subrequest; (d) for each a-list **ANS-AL** returned by **RETRIEVE**, create a new double substitution with **TOP-AL** and **ANS-AL**; (e) unzip this to the **TOP-AL** side to get (finally!) an asterisk-free answer a-list. For example, given the assertions (← (LOVES ?X (DOG ?X)) (IS ?X BOY)) and (IS (SON ?Y) BOY), the request (LOVES ?X ?Y) will generate the subrequest (IS ?X BOY) via the substitution

TOP-AL {X = ?X*, Y = (DOG ?X)*}
SUB-AL   { }

The subrequest will return answer {X = (SON ?Y)}; plugging this in for SUB-AL and "unzipping" turns TOP-AL into {X = (SON ?G0055), Y = (DOG (SON ?G0055))} (i.e., one answer to the question, "Who loves what?" is, "Everyone's son loves his dog."). This scheme postpones renaming as long as possible, but can't avoid it entirely.

With this new binding scheme, LISP code called during backward chaining can retain its original variable names, which is helpful during debugging. (This scheme is used in DUCK. McDermott 1977b)

We can also allow calls to LISP code during forward chaining. For example, we might want to write

```
(ADD '(→ (QUADRUPED ?X)
         (LISP (COND     ((ATOM ?X)
                          (:= (GET ?X 'LEGS) 4))  ))))
```

The LISP code is not restricted to making forward inferences. This mechanism can be used to implement software interrupts of the data base, programs that wait for some result and then take some action. These programs are often called *demons* (Charniak, 1972).

Exercise 13.13 Change **ADD** to call LISP code when appropriate. This is simpler than for the backward-chaining case, since there is nothing to be returned.

When a deductive retriever is augmented with this code-calling mechanism, plus fancy control structures like those we will describe in Chapter 17, it is called an "AI Language" (purely for historical reasons, since languages without such features are also used in AI). The original AI language was PLANNER (Hewitt, 1971). See Bobrow and Raphael, 1974, for an overview.

13.5.4 Pattern Matching

Many AI programs operate by attempting to find a match between one structure and another, that is, to find the ways parts of one might correspond to parts of another. If "finding correspondences" seems like a vague characterization of pattern matching, that's because it is. Many rather different things go by the name "pattern matching." They tend to fall into two broad classes:

1. "Macro-matching," in which two "large" structures are compared for similarities and differences. [The classic example of this is the GPS program (Ernst & Newell, 1969), which looked for differences in order to try to get rid of them.]
2. "Micro-matching," in which two "small" structures, each containing variables, are compared in an effort to find a common instance. Unification is an elegant example of micro-matching.

Micro-matching is well understood. Its output is clear, and algorithms for doing it have been studied thoroughly (Boyer & Moore, 1972; Patterson & Wegman 1976). Not so much is known about macro-matching. Very general macro-matching problems are known to require expensive algorithms, and interesting special cases are as yet unknown. (For some speculation, see Bobrow and Winograd, 1977; and Hayes–Roth, 1978). We will discuss one form of macro-matching in Chapter 15.

Often micro-matching is used as a component of a macro-matcher. For example, Cullingford's (1978) SAM program understands stories by matching them against a "script," which is (to oversimplify) a list of expected events. This macro-matching is implemented by micro-matching each piece of the story against pieces of the script until a matching element is found.

Another example is the problem solver STRIPS (Fikes & Nilsson 1971). This program was given a conjunction describing the desired state of the world, and a data base describing the current state of the world. Just like GPS, it looked for differences between the two in order to try to get rid of them. It matched the conjunction against the data base by trying to retrieve it. If it succeeded, the conjunction was true in the current world, and the problem was solved; otherwise, some subrequest would fail to unify with anything. Such unsatisfiable subrequests were then noted as differences to be eliminated.

Exercise 13.14 Write a program (MATCH *conjunction database*) that does STRIPS-style matching. MATCH will look a lot like RETRIEVE, except that it will tolerate failed subrequests ("gaps"). It will return a list of answers, each consisting of variable bindings plus subrequests that failed. These may be thought of as capturing "similarities" and "differences" between the two arguments to MATCH. MATCH must return a list of answers, because in general there will be more than one match. For example, if (COLOR BLOCK1 RED) and (SIZE BLOCK2 LARGE) are in the data base, the conjunction

   (AND (COLOR ?X RED) (SIZE ?X LARGE))

has two matches:

   X = BLOCK1 but missing (SIZE BLOCK1 LARGE)

and

   X = BLOCK2 but missing (COLOR BLOCK2 RED)

You may want to distinguish between two kinds of gaps: those due to a subrequest simply failing and those for which MATCH was able to prove that the subrequest is actually false (i.e., its negation is true).

This implementation of macro-matching can be a useful "off-the-shelf" algorithm for any application in which one of the structures being matched may be thought of as a conjunction and the other as a data base of facts. For example, Winston's (1975) learning program did this kind of matching between a visual concept it was debugging (a conjunction) and the current scene (the data base). In some cases, it is not as efficient as a more specialized algorithm. See (Hayes-Roth, 1978) for discussion.

13.6 THE PROS AND CONS OF DEDUCTIVE INFORMATION RETRIEVAL

"Theorem proving" is a controversial technique. After an initial enthusiastic reception by the AI community (Nilsson, 1971), it came under strong criticism by researchers who found it too inefficient (Winograd, 1972). Despite this criticism, the technique continues to be used. There are two reasons for this: (1) Nowadays it is used only with indexing techniques (see Chapter 14) and AI language features that ameliorate the inefficiency. (2) It is used only when it works. In this section, we will briefly discuss the sources of inefficiency in deductive retrieval and when these inefficiencies are really bad.

The principal source of inefficiency in deductive retrieval is the way it handles conjunctive requests. Given a request of the form (AND p q), a retriever finds answers (variable bindings) for the request p and discards those answers that don't work when substituted into q. For example, consider the request

    (AND (IS ?X IRISH) (SOBER ?X))

RETRIEVE will handle this by finding all the IRISH persons it can and testing whether each of them is SOBER. If the program doing the retrieval is acquainted with 100 Irishmen, it will check the sobriety of each of them. This will take a while and may have a very small return.

This approach is an instance of the AI technique known as "generate and test," in which the only response to an inadequacy in a tentative problem solution is to generate another tentative solution, without using any information about the kind of inadequacy that was found. There is nothing inherently wrong with this method. If the data base just has a lot of assertions about Irish persons and sober persons, there is no better way to proceed than to loop through the Irish people, checking their sobriety. Indeed, this is just a special case of the intersection problem we discussed in Chapter 10. With the proper index, the deductive retrieval method may be thought of as an implementation of the mark-and-test method of doing intersections. (One possible improvement on the basic algorithm is to estimate the sizes of the two answer sets and to try sweeping through the smaller. A reasonable estimator is the number of the candidates returned by FETCH, but this is obviously worthless without an index of the kind we will describe in Chapter 14.)

Unfortunately for "generate and test," there are many applications where it is worthless. For example, a problem-solving program generates plans for bringing about states of affairs. Consider how it might find a plan for bringing about (AND (DRESSED FRED) (AT FRED OFFICE)). (Fred would need such a plan for getting going in the morning.) One way is to generate plans for getting dressed and throw away those that don't happen to achieve (AT FRED OFFICE). For example, we could generate the list of plans

    BEGIN put clothes on END
    BEGIN put clothes on; go to supermarket END
    BEGIN eat supper; put clothes on END
    BEGIN put clothes on; take clothes off; put clothes on END
    ...
    BEGIN put clothes on; buy a canary; go to office END

Eventually we will find a plan that happens to land Fred at the office, but it could take a long time, and the resulting plan could be absurd.

Deductive retrievers were actually tried on problem solving of this kind. Needless to say, the results were not encouraging. Plainly, the plan generator needs feedback from the plan tester. It needs to be able to use the fact that the original plan ("put clothes on") didn't achieve the other goal in order to alter it so it will.

A strong clue that the deductive retriever is going to hit an explosion like this is the presence of "recursive" backward-chaining rules for generating new answers to a conjunct. A recursive set of rules is one which generates subrequests which themselves trigger rules in the set. For example, in plan generation, there could be rules like

```
(← (PLAN-FOR (DRESSED) (PROG ?PLAN (BUY ?SOMETHING)))
   (PLAN-FOR (DRESSED) ?PLAN))
```

which generates a subrequest which unifies with this rule itself. When rules like this are present, they can generate an infinite sequence of answers to a conjunct, which come out in no particular order.

In spite of its limitations, deductive retrieval can be useful, when combined with indexing, forward chaining, and judicious calls to LISP code during deductions. In this form, it has been used to retrieve possible explanations of disease symptoms (Shortliffe, 1976), simple plans for a problem solver (McDermott, 1978), facts about the state of the problem solution (Fikes & Nilsson, 1971; Sacerdoti, 1977), and voltage and current values of electronic circuits (Stallman & Sussman, 1977).

14 Discrimination Nets With Variables

14.1 PLAN RETRIEVAL

At the end of Chapter 11 we developed a discrimination net capable of efficiently deciding whether or not a particular S-expression had been entered in a data base. There are many situations, however, in which the machinery developed is not sufficient for our needs. An obvious example is the retrieval mechanism needed for the deductive system given in Chapter 13, where we needed to retrieve information using patterns with variables and where the facts in the data base also could have variables. In this chapter we show how to upgrade our discrimination nets to handle these cases. We start, however, with a much simpler situation.

Suppose we have a data base containing plans for accomplishing various goals. For instance, we might have a plan of the following form:

```
(PLAN TALK-PLAN                      ˜The name of the plan
   (INFORM ?PERSON-1 ?PERSON-2 ?FACT)  ˜For one person to inform a
                                       ˜second of some fact-
   (ACHIEVE (AT ?PERSON-1 ?PERSON-2))  ˜have the two at the same place
   (SAY ?PERSON-1 ?FACT) )             ˜and then say the information.
```

(As in Chapter 13, items preceded by ? are variables.) One of the things we would want the system to do is take a specific goal and find ways in which it might be accomplished. Let us suppose we have a data base consisting of TALK-PLAN plus the plans given in Fig. 14.1. Now, suppose we were presented with the goal:

   (INFORM GELLER FRIEND (SHOW DICE 6))

```
(PLAN ESP-PLAN
    (INFORM GELLER ?PERSON ?FACT)                    ˜GELLER may inform by
    (MENTALLY-TRANSFER GELLER ?PERSON ?FACT))    ˜direct mental connection.

(PLAN THINK-PLAN
    (INFORM ?PERSON GELLER ?FACT)                    ˜To inform GELLER
    (THINK ?PERSON ?FACT))                           ˜just think the fact.

(PLAN REMEMBER-PLAN
    (INFORM ?PERSON-1 ?PERSON—1 ?FACT)               ˜To inform yourself of some-
    (REMEMBER ?PERSON-1 ?FACT))                      ˜thing, just remember it.
```

FIG. 14.1.   A data base of plans.

To see how **GELLER** might accomplish this we look in the data base for ways of **INFORM**ing people of things. With appropriate extensions we can use discrimination nets to help in this process.

To do this we will have had to enter the plans of Fig. 14.1 into our discrimination net. We do this by using the goal of the plan [e.g., (**INFORM GELLER ?PERSON ?FACT**)] as the key for discrimination. This requires that our discrimination net be able to handle variables in the data base, but we may assume there are no variables in the input. Figure 14.2 shows such a net with all the plans above. When given a specific goal, we feed it to the discrimination net that returns any plan with a matching pattern.

Note that in Fig. 14.1 all variables "look alike" in that they are only indicated by ***VAR***. This means that we have broken the retrieval into two parts. We first use the discrimination net to find potential plans and then use a matcher to see whether there is, in fact, a match between the goal and the plan key. This becomes apparent in **REMEMBER-PLAN**. Suppose we are trying to find plans to accomplish

(INFORM GELLER FRIEND (SHOW DICE 6))

The initial retrieval will give us **REMEMBER-PLAN** since at that point it does not "know" that in **REMEMBER-PLAN** the two variables are in fact the same and hence must be bound to the same thing. It will, however, be eliminated at the matching stage.

This separation between the two phases is not inevitable, and at least one worker (Rieger, 1977) uses a discrimination net in which the two phases are combined. The only time the combination can remove possibilities early, however, is when there are repeated variables. It is our experience that this occurs infrequently enough that it is not worth the extra space and effort to give different variables distinct paths through the net.

The code for fetching from a data base with variables (called **FETCH1**, as it is the first in a series of fetch functions) is illustrated in Fig. 14.3. It is instructive to compare it to the code for the case without variables (see Fig. 11.6). The major difference is that the new **TRAVERSE-LINKS** returns a list

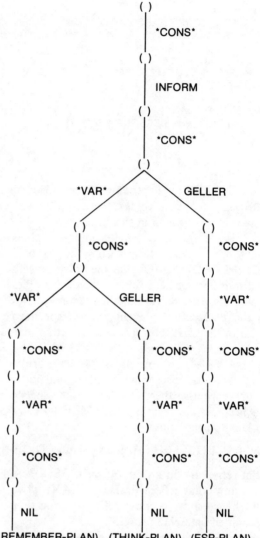

FIG. 14.2.   Discrimination net with variables in the data.

of links rather than a single link, since there may also be links reached by following a *VAR* link. To keep things compatible, TRAVERSE-LINK also returns a list, even though it can only reach a single link. Also note that we allow a terminal node to have more than a single item attached to it. For example, REMEMBER-PLAN and TALK-PLAN will be found on the same terminal.

```
(RECORD-TYPE LINK NIL (KEY . A-LIST))
(RECORD-TYPE TERMINAL NIL (KEY . PLANS))

(DRM /? (LAMBDA ( ) (LIST '*VAR* (READ]
(RECORD-TYPE MVAR *VAR* (SYM]
```

˜FETCH1 makes a single list containing each element of the sublist
˜in the list return by TRAVERSE-LINKS1.
```
(DE FETCH1 (PATTERN LINK)
    (FOR(TERMINAL IN (TRAVERSE-LINKS1 PATTERN LINK))
        (SPLICE (COPY (CDR TERMINAL]
```
˜The "FOR-SPLICE" combination expands to a MAPCAN, which uses NCONC to
˜splice things together. Since we do not want to change our terminals,
˜we COPY them before handing them to the splicer.

```
(DE TRAVERSE-LINKS1 (PATTERN LINK)
    (NCONC
     (COND ((ATOM PATTERN) (TRAVERSE-LINK PATTERN LINK))
           ((FOR (SUB-SUB IN
                  (FOR (SUB-LINK IN (TRAVERSE-LINK '*CONS* LINK))
                       (SPLICE (TRAVERSE-LINKS1 (CAR PATTERN)
                                                SUB-LINK))))
                 (SPLICE (TRAVERSE-LINKS1 (CDR PATTERN) SUB-SUB)))))
     (TRAVERSE-LINK '*VAR* LINK]

(DE TRAVERSE-LINK (KEY LINK)
    (LET  (A-LIST (ASSOC KEY (A-LIST:LINK LINK)))
          (COND (A-LIST (LIST A-LIST]
```

FIG. 14.3. The code for a plan fetcher.

Exercise 14.1 The comparison between the variable and no-variable cases will also reveal that the latter is missing a check to see if LINK is NIL. Why wasn't this needed?

Exercise 14.2 Write an INDEX1 function to go along with FETCH1. It will take three arguments: a plan, the discrimination key, and the topmost link of the net. We give it both the plan and the discrimination key (which happens to be the goal pattern of the plan) so that INDEX1 will be independent of the structure of plans.

14.2 FETCHING FACTS

As in Chapter 13, allowing variables in the data base is only half the story. We must also handle variables in the input. For example, suppose we wanted to identify at least one of Jack's parents. Using the RETRIEVE function from Chapter 13, we would have

(RETRIEVE (SON JACK ?X))

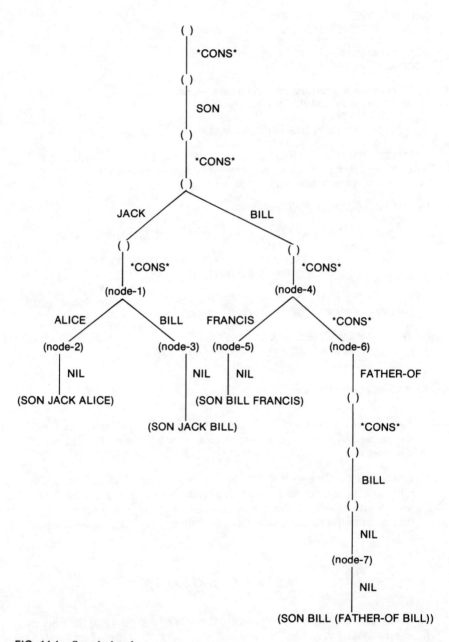

FIG. 14.4. Sample data base.

To retrieve such information efficiently we could use our discrimination net, provided it can accept variables in the input.

To see what has to be done to handle input variables, let us consider the request above with the data base illustrated in Fig. 14.4. Suppose we have traversed the tree as far as (SON JACK . . .), so we must now handle the input variable ?X. We will now be at the node labeled "node-1". (For reasons alluded to in Exercise 11.7 the programs pass links to each other, not nodes. Hence at this point TRAVERSE-LINKS would be looking at the link just above node-1. Except when actually tracing the workings of the program, however, it is easier to think, and talk, in terms of nodes. Just remember that in each case the appropriate link is the one just above the node mentioned.) Since we have a variable in the input, we want to go down one expression in the discrimination net for all possible expressions. In this case, the expressions to skip are ALICE and BILL. This will leave us at nodes node-2 and node-3. Hence we need to revise our code so that if it sees a variable in the input, it calls a new function SKIP-EXP to "skip over" one expression in the discrimination net. This is what is done by the code in Fig. 14.5. Note that after the check to see if PATTERN is an MVAR, the rest of TRAVERSE-LINKS2 is virtually identical to TRAVERSE-LINKS1.

Going from node-1 to nodes 2 and 3 (Fig. 14.4) is a simplified case, however, because all the expressions to be skipped over were atoms. When we

```
(DE FETCH2 (PATTERN LINK)
      (FOR (TERMINAL IN (TRAVERSE-LINKS2 PATTERN LINK))
            (SPLICE (COPY (CDR TERMINAL]

(DE TRAVERSE-LINKS2 (PATTERN LINK)
  (COND    ((IS-MVAR PATTERN) (SKIP-EXP LINK))
            ((NCONC
              (COND ((ATOM PATTERN) (TRAVERSE-LINK PATTERN LINK))
                    ((FOR
                      (SUB-SUB IN
                        (FOR (SUB-LINK IN (TRAVERSE-LINK '*CONS* LINK))
                              (SPLICE (TRAVERSE-LINKS2 (CAR PATTERN)
                                                        SUB-LINK))))
                      (SPLICE (TRAVERSE-LINKS2 (CDR PATTERN) SUB-SUB)))))
              (TRAVERSE-LINK '*VAR* LINK]

(DE SKIP-EXP (LINK)
  (FOR (LOWER-LINK IN (A-LIST: LINK LINK))
    (SPLICE
      (COND ((NOT (EQ (KEY:LINK LOWER-LINK) '*CONS*)) (LIST LOWER-LINK))
            (this is where the code requested in Exercise 14.3 goes)
      ]
```

FIG. 14.5.   The code for the general TRAVERSE-LINKS.

allow them to be general S-expressions, the situation becomes more difficult. So consider what will happen if we ask

(FETCH2 (SON BILL ?X) *DATA-BASE*)

Again when we come to the variable, we want to skip over one expression in the data base paths, but now the expression is **FRANCIS** in one case and **(FATHER-OF BILL)** in the other. In this situation we will be starting at node-4 and we want to end up at nodes node-5 and node-7, since node-7, not node-6, corresponds to skipping over **(FATHER-OF BILL)**. Clearly this situation is more complex since we cannot just go down one node in the tree as we did when we were only looking at atoms. Now the depth we must travel will be dependent on the depth of the S-expression over which we are skipping. Or to put this slightly differently, if **SKIP-EXP** is required to skip over an expression starting with ***CONS***, it must "count out" the nodes to make sure that it ends up at the right depth in the tree.

Although this sounds very complicated, the code to do this is quite short—one line in fact. This is one of those cases where the problem is exactly fitted to the language.

Exercise 14.3 The required code to skip over one expression in the discrimination net fits in the one line reserved for it in **SKIP-EXP**, Fig. 14.5. Fill in this line.

Exercise 14.4 It is frequently useful to allow fetches from the data base where one does not know the exact length of the data item. In such cases one would like to have a variable at the end of the pattern that matches everything left in the data base entries, for example,

(RETRIEVE (PROG ?VARS . ?EXPS))

Variables that match several S-expressions are called *segment variables*. Segment variables that match everything left in an S-expression are called *terminal* segment variables. Make any modifications needed so that **TRAVERSE-LINKS** can handle terminal segment variables.

Exercise 14.5 Write a function **FETCH** (using **FETCH2**) and **INDEX** (using **INDEX1** from Exercise 14.2) that will serve as the retrieval and indexing components for the deductive retrieval system of Chapter 13. FETCH will be a function of one argument, **ITEM**, which will have one of the forms

(→ *pat consequent*)	e.g., (→ (YOUNG ?X) (HAPPY ?X))
(← *pat antecedent*)	e.g., (← (HAPPY ?X) (YOUNG ?X))
pat	e.g., (SON ?X (FATHER-OF ?X))

FETCH will keep three data bases, one for each type of input and will hand *pat* and the appropriate data base off to FETCH2. Index will work analogously.

Exercise 14.6 Exercise 13.8 asks the reader to write a function VARIANTS, which given an item decided if there was a variant of it in the data base (equal up to renaming of variables). Write a function **FETCH-VARIANTS** that finds variant candidates using the discrimination nets built by **INDEX** (designed in Exercise 14.5). (*Hint:* **FETCH** will do the job but returns too many formulas, in general).

So far we have pretty much ignored the question of removing things from our data base, except as a problem at the end of Chapter 11. This asked for a function, **UNINDEX**, which used **TRAVERSE-LINKS** to find the thing to erase and then just removed it. Note however that this is hardly optimal. For example, suppose we want to erase

(SON BILL (FATHER-OF BILL))

from Fig. 14.4. The method described leaves a lot of "dead" branches; that is, there is a lot of the tree that leads to nothing at all. It would clearly be better to remove these dead branches, unless we do not do much erasing. What we must do is to keep track of the last point in the tree where there was a "live" branch coming off from the path leading to the item to be erased. Everything above that point remains alive; everything below it is dead and should be removed.

Exercise 14.7 Write this **UNINDEX** function. If you are like most people, you will need one or more free variables to do it. There is a version which is, in general, less efficient but which does not use free variables. Can you find it? (Don't worry if you can't.)

14.3 VARIATIONS ON THE DISCRIMINATION NET THEME

With the completion of the exercises above you will have a complete, and reasonably general, data base facility. However, it is by no means the only way in which discrimination nets can be used to build data bases. In this section we look at eight design decisions involved in the creation of a discrimination net data base. Since they are for the most part orthogonal, the program we created is only one of about 256 possibilities.

1. Are variables allowed in the input patterns?
2. Are variables allowed in the data patterns?

In our final version, of course, we allowed both. There are applications however for the other three possibilities. Rieger (1977) only allows variables in the data patterns since he was building a "demon" facility; that is, he wanted to be able to assert new facts about the world and have them set off "demons." So, if we are told that *A* is *B*'s father, a demon might be set off that will add the new fact, "*A* is older than *B*" (cf. forward chaining in Chapter 13). In this situation there may very well be no need for variables in the input. We also mention in Chapter 11 that the no-variable case can be used to "uniquify" lists.

   3. Does one keep track of variable bindings during fetching?

We commented on this in Section 14.1 and recommended against doing so.

   4. Should one return a list or a stream of the possibilities?

At the start of this chapter we assumed without thinking that our program would return a list. However, it is certainly possible to have the program return one possibility and a program for finding the rest. The early AMORD discrimination net (de Kleer et al., 1977b) did this. In a more recent version of AMORD (de Kleer et al., 1978), however, the fetch function returns a list of possibilities. Unless one envisions having very large numbers of possibilities, and frequently finding what one wants early on, it is doubtful that it is worth the extra work to use streams.

   5. Should one use CAR or CAR-CDR indexing?

When we look for a way to represent S-expressions as a linear string of atoms, we require that it be capable of handling arbitrary S-expressions. To do this requires that our net discriminate on both the CAR and the CDR of every subexpression in the pattern. Almost all the time, however, this generality is not needed, since the items in the data base are all list structures in which no atom but NIL ever occurs in a CDR. In such cases, discriminating on the CDR's of expressions is of no help at all, since they are always *CONS* or NIL. Instead one could use only the CARs. We could use the atom *LIST* to indicate the start of a list and *END-LIST* for the end. For example;

Original	*Representation*
BILL	BILL
(HUMAN JACK)	*LIST* HUMAN JACK *END-LIST*
(NUM (AGE ?X))	*LIST* NUM *LIST* AGE *VAR*
	END-LIST *END-LIST*

The advantage of the CAR-CDR indexing used here is that it is completely general, and, as anyone who does Exercise 14.4 discovers, one receives terminal segment matching at no cost. Positional indexing, on the other hand, is more parsimonious in the amount of storage needed for the net since it is

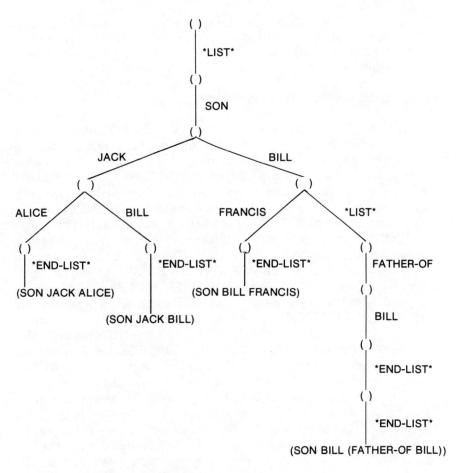

FIG. 14.6. CAR indexing for the data base of Fig. 14.3.

not indexing on the CDR's of the list, just the CARs. Compare, for example, Fig. 14.4 and 14.6. The latter gives the CAR indexing version of the former. Rieger (1977) and McDermott (1977b) use CAR indexing.

The CAR-CDR indexing in this chapter has been based on the unique way an expression can be built up from CONS. de Kleer et al. (1977b) use a different and somewhat more space-efficient form of CAR-CDR indexing. It is based on the fact that S-expressions have a unique representation of the form:

> *an atom   OR*
> (*expression-1 . . . expression-n-minus-1 . expression-n*)

Exercise 14.8   We did not use this form of **CAR-CDR** indexing because the functions that manipulate it are somewhat more complex than the ones needed for ***CONS*** indexing. Now that you are experts, however, write the appropriate functions.

6. Should one uniquify subexpressions?

Frequently in the data the subexpressions correspond to unique objects, like (**FATHER BILL**)—Bill's father. One can reflect this correspondence in the data base implementation by uniquifying all subexpressions. Suppose, for example, we want to fetch (**SON ?X (FATHER BILL)**). In the system designed in this chapter, after skipping over the expression that is to match the **?X** we would continue down the tree looking for (**FATHER BILL**); that is, we would look first for a ***CONS***, followed by the atom **FATHER**, followed by ***CONS***, etc. In a system that uniquifies subexpressions this would look somewhat different. When we reached (**FATHER BILL**), we would temporarily halt work on (**SON ?X (FATHER BILL)**), return to the top of the discrimination net, and discriminate on (**FATHER BILL**). By doing this we would obtain a unique version of (**FATHER BILL**); that is, we would have a pointer (call it **POINTER**) to our canonical (**FATHER BILL**). We can now use this pointer in our discrimination of (**SON ?X (FATHER BILL)**), which we can now treat as (**SON ?X POINTER**). **POINTER** can be discriminated on as if it were an atom since it is the unique representation of (**FATHER BILL**). By doing this we can save space since (**FATHER BILL**) only appears once in the data base, no matter how many statements contain it, as all the statements will use **POINTER** instead. This allows us to attach properties to (**FATHER BILL**) as mentioned in the discussion of uniquify in Chapter 11.

Under some circumstances these benefits will be paid for in time. For example, suppose we want to know if Fran married somebody's father.

(**FETCH (MARRY FRAN (FATHER ?X)) *DATA-BASE***)

Now suppose we have 50 terms of the form (**FATHER** *someone*), but the only statement that will match the above is (**MARRY FRAN (FATHER GEORGE**)). When we uniquify (**FATHER ?X**), we find the 50 fathers and then we have to look through the 50 possibilities for the last place of (**MARRY FRAN** . . .). Needless to say, in this case it will be much faster if one does not uniquify subexpressions. It may be, however, that these circumstances are not that common in practice. Offhand it is hard to say whether the space saved is worth the time it might cost.

Of current systems, most do not uniquify subexpressions. An exception is (de Kleer et al., 1977b).

7. Should one completely discriminate the data?

This chapter's discrimination net creates a discrimination path that represents every aspect of the incoming pattern. One can also have a system that only discriminates the pattern enough to distinguish it from what is already in the data base. The advantage of this is that it can save space. The disadvantage is that it can cost time. To see how partial discrimination works, let us consider an example. We start with an empty data base and add (SON JACK BILL). Since there is nothing from which it must be distinguished, we do nothing and obtain a net with a single node, the top one, containing our single item (Fig. 14.7a). When we add (AGE JACK 5), however, we distinguish it from what is already there. Both start with *CONS*, so that is not sufficient, but the CAR of the list will do it, so that is where the discrimination stops (Fig. 14.7b).

    (SON JACK BILL)

FIG. 14.7a.   Partially discriminating data base with one element.

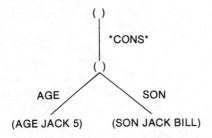

FIG. 14.7b.   Partially discriminating data base with two elements.

This scheme will take longer to fetch an item than one using complete discrimination. For example, suppose we now request

    (FETCH (SON ?X JACK) *DATA-BASE*)

If we completely discriminate, we will find out that there are no possibilities in the course of going through the data base. The partial discrimination method will retrieve (SON JACK BILL) and hand it off to the pattern matcher, a more expensive way to decide that it will not do.

On the other hand, there are situations where the savings in space can more than compensate. These are situations where the size of the patterns in the data base become very large. For example, at the start of this chapter we considered a system for fetching plans from a plan data base. Originally we only discriminated the items on the basis of the goal of the plan, not on the entire plan itself. Although this was fine for our stated purpose (finding ways to accomplish a goal) suppose we also wanted to do plan recognition. In such a task we are given actions (Jack walked over to Bill), and we want to infer motives (Jack wanted to communicate with Bill). To do this we must also locate plans on the basis of their subacts, and hence we would want the entire plan schema indexed. With patterns of such a length, having the discrimination net represent every feature of the pattern becomes very expensive, and partial discrimination becomes proportionally more attractive. (The "large pattern" problem is also behind the separation in Exercise 14.5 of the deductive information retriever data base into three data bases. With a partial discrimination technique this would not have been necessary.)

8. Should one use multiple indexing?

But partial discrimination by itself can be quite inefficient unless we also have multiple indexing. To understand multiple indexing, let us first consider it in the more familiar context of our standard discrimination net data base.

To discriminate an S-expression we need a linear string of atoms to key upon. (As we noted above in the discussion of unique subexpression, strictly speaking they need not be atoms but simply unique pointers.) We assumed without any discussion that the order of these atoms would be the same left-to-right order used for printing. We could have done it some other way, or, and this is the important point, we could have done it in more than one way at the same time. For example, any time we see a *CONS*, we could create two subnets—the usual one, plus a second in which we first discriminate on the CDR and then on the CAR.

Admittedly, this is rather farfetched, but when we move back to our consideration of partially discriminated data bases, it becomes much more plausible. Suppose, for example, we add to our partially discriminated data base of Fig. 14.7 the following statements:

(SON BILL ALICE) (SON FRED ANN)

The result is given in Fig. 14.8.

Now this will work quite well if we ask, say, "who is Bill the son of". We will be handing to the net the pattern

(SON BILL ?X)

By the time we discriminate on BILL we will be down to a desired item. But suppose instead we ask for Ann's sons; i.e.,

(SON ?X ANN)

This will not work very well at all. When we come to ?X, there will still be 3 possible items in the data base. Of course, this could just as well be 30 items, if we knew about 30 different sons. We then discriminate on ?X, but this only tells us to skip down a level, which brings us to the bottom of the tree, and there are still 3 (or 30) potential items and we will have to use pattern

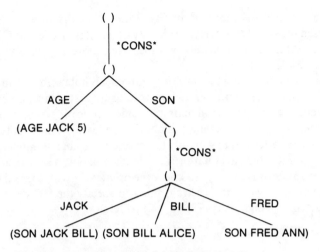

FIG. 14.8.   Problems with partial discrimination.

matching to decide among them. The problem is that the net discriminated on the son (or CADR position), whereas to handle our question efficiently we need to discriminate on the parent (or CADDR position). In a complete discrimination net we would have discriminated on both, so the problem is not so bad. But if we have a situation in which complete discrimination is not feasible, then we must somehow overcome this problem.

The solution is multiple indexing. We write our FETCH routine such that when it comes upon such situations it reindexes so as to discriminate on the crucial item. So, in the case at hand, it would note that the next nonvariable is in the CADDR position, and it would index on that as well—leaving two subnets below the SON node in the net. This is illustrated in Fig. 14.9.

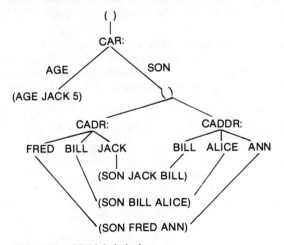

FIG. 14.9.   Multiple indexing.

Note the use of CAR indexing in Fig. 14.9 rather than the CAR-CDR indexing used previously. As we have already noted, it is rare for the CDR's to help us in discriminating, and this becomes even more apparent when one moves to multiple indexing.

We commented in passing that multiple indexing is not useful in completely discriminated nets. Furthermore, such restructuring costs space, which is one of the benefits of the partial indexing scheme. Hence it would seem that partial discrimination and its required multiple indexing is only useful if one anticipates large patterns that will only be accessed in a small number of ways. It is our experience that most patterns are fetched in only a small number of ways. For example, it is rare not to know the predicate involved, and usually at least one of the arguments is always there to specify the fact desired. For example, out of the eight ways (2 * 2 * 2) to fetch

>   (AGE FRED 5)

only two are remotely plausible.

>   (AGE FRED ?X)

and perhaps

>   (AGE ?X 5)

Hence the "small number of ways to access" restriction is probably not as serious as might first appear. As for the usefulness of large patterns, since they do cause problems with the most obvious retrieval schemes, people have avoided them. [One exception here is McDermott (1977a), and hence it is not surprising that the only program at present that incorporates partial discrimination and multiple indexing is DUCK (McDermott 1977b).] Whether the prejudice against large patterns is justified or not is hard to say; however, the possibility of using them certainly deserves to be kept in mind.

Exercise 14.9 Write a data base facility that uses partial discrimination and multiple indexing. (Difficult) [*Hint:* You need a way of referring to the positions being discriminated on (e.g., the CDADDADR) and a way of suspending the discrimination process so that it can be resumed (see Chapter 12).]

15

Slot and Filler
Data Bases

15.1 EXPANDING PROPERTY LIST FACILITIES

In Chapter 1 we saw that LISP has facilities for attaching S-expressions to symbols via their property lists. We could, for example, attach to CANARY, under the property COLOR, the value YELLOW. Although property lists are a convenient way to store facts about the world, so far we have not used them for this purpose. In Chapter 14 we were concerned with the implementation of data bases, but rather than property lists we used a discrimination net technique. In this chapter we examine an alternative approach that starts with the property list as its basic idea but extends its usefulness by adding more machinery on top of it.

We could also approach this topic from a more theoretical point of view. Minsky (1975) published an influential article arguing for a data structure (called a *frame*) that he described as follows:

> We can think of a frame as a network of nodes and relations. The "top levels" of a frame are fixed, and represent things that are always true about the supposed situation. The lower levels have many *terminals*—"slots" that must be filled by specific instances or data. Each terminal can specify conditions its assignments must meet. [Minsky, 1975, p. 212]

There have been a number of attempts to realize such structures. Many have been specialized to particular areas—for example, the frames of Charniak (1977) and the *scripts* of Schank and Abelson (1977) are aimed at problems in language comprehension. There have also been attempts to

177

design a more general knowledge structure based upon this idea: KRL (Knowledge Representation Language) of Bobrow and Winograd (1977), and FRL (Frame Representation Language) of Roberts and Goldstein (1977).

Under Minsky's description a frame could be considered an extended property list structure—a frame is an atom, the slots are property indicators, and the slot fillers are the values of the properties. This has pretty much been the approach taken by those aiming at structures that are not tailored to a particular problem, and it is this approach we describe here, albeit in a much reduced version. Our version takes ideas from both KRL and FRL. Any commonality of implementation is purely coincidental, however, since we have not seen the code behind either of the aforementioned papers.

15.2   AN INTRODUCTION TO XRL

We call our representation XRL (Unknown Representation Language). The basic unit of knowledge is called a FORM and is implemented as an atom with properties and values. To some degree, however, we hide this close affinity to property lists behind a new syntax designed to emphasize the major difference between XRL structures and their property list cousins. This is the emphasis in XRL on the ISA hierarchy; that is, we design our representation to take advantage of the fact that many properties of an item, such as the number of legs on a particular cow, may be inferred from the superclasses (as indicated by ISA relationships) to which the item belongs: cow, mammal, and animal.

To become familiar with the new notation, as well as the use of ISA links, let us start on a sample problem that illustrates XRL. We will look at the problem of representing knowledge about houses and apartments to rent. A user would consult our program about possible places to rent, giving his requirements and preferences, and the program would select an appropriate apartment (or house) to rent.

Each dwelling would be represented as an individual FORM. Using our usual property list notation we could define a new apartment as in Fig. 15.1a. Here we have created APT1, an apartment at 100 York Street with three rooms, white walls, and wood floors, In XRL this would become Fig. 15.1b.

FORM is our function for creating a FORM. It is similar to DEFPROP. FORM is a FEXPR, and it is given some "buzz" words like "AN" and "WITH" which makes things easier to read but which have no effect on processing. The ordering of the properties following the WITH is not significant; that is, we would have the same FORM if we specified the wall color before the street name. (Henceforth we refer to the properties as the *slots* of the FORM.)

Now suppose it turns out that all of the apartments at 100 York Street have white walls and wood floor surfaces. It would be helpful to state this once and for all, so we need not keep repeating it over and over for each apartment

```
(DEFPROP APT1 YORK STREET-NAME)
(DEFPROP APT1 100 STREET-NUM)
(DEFPROP APT1 3 NO-OF-ROOMS)
(DEFPROP APT1 WHITE WALL-COLOR)
(DEFPROP APT1 WOOD FLOOR-SURFACE)
(DEFPROP APT1 APARTMENT ISA)
```

FIG. 15.1a. Property list definition of a FORM.

```
(FORM APT-1
      AN APARTMENT
      WITH  [STREET-NAME = YORK]
            [STREET-NUM = 100]
            [NO-OF-ROOMS = 3]
            [WALL-COLOR = WHITE]
            [FLOOR-SURFACE = WOOD])
```

FIG. 15.1b. XRL definition of a FORM.

there. What we want to do, in other words, is to define a new FORM, called APT-AT-100-YORK, which will have these properties, and then define APT1 as an instance of this new FORM. This is done in Fig. 15.2.

In using this representation we should be careful about exactly what it is supposed to mean. This will become clearer when we give the code, but it is never a bad idea to try to state clearly the significance of a representation independently of the code that manipulates it. Here, when we add a property to to a superclass, it is assumed to be true of the subclass unless we are explicitly told otherwise. One consequence of this definition is that whenever we attach a property such as [WALL-COLOR = WHITE] to a superclass, we are not stating a requirement on all APT-AT-100-YORK's; that is, it does not mean that the WALL-COLOR property of all subclasses must be WHITE— only that WHITE is assumed unless otherwise specified. We say that the lower nodes *inherit* the *defaults* of the upper nodes.

Suppose someone comes into our rental agency requesting a dwelling with low street noise. We may have been lucky enough to put this as a property on each dwelling, but the odds are that we lacked the foresight to anticipate all

```
(FORM APT-AT-100-YORK
      AN APARTMENT
      WITH  [STREET-NAME = YORK]
            [STREET-NUM = 100]
            [WALL-COLOR = WHITE]
            [FLOOR-SURFACE = WOOD])

(FORM APT1
      AN    APT-AT-100-YORK
      WITH  [NO-OF-ROOMS = 3])
```

FIG. 15.2. Having ISA links for inheritance of properties.

such requests; in fact, in our example we did not include this one. On the other hand, often it is possible to decide on street noise given the address. In the case of APT-1 we might know that any place on York has high street noise, and if the number is less than 200, it is really bad. To accommodate this we have the structures given in Fig. 15.3.

```
(FORM APARTMENT
       A DWELLING)

(FORM DWELLING
       A THING
  WITH   [STREET-NOISE IF-NEEDED
              (COND((NOT (EQ (SLOT-VAL *FORM* 'STREET-NAME) 'YORK)) NIL)
                    ((GREATERP (SLOT-VAL *FORM* 'STREET-NO) 200) 'BAD)
                    (T 'VERY-BAD))  ]   )
```

FIG. 15.3.   An example of an IF-NEEDED slot attachment.

In Fig. 15.3 we first define an apartment as a dwelling, but one without any specific properties of its own. We then define dwelling. In particular we say that we have a LISP program to calculate street noise for dwellings. We indicate this by attaching the program to STREET-NOISE and marking it as an IF-NEEDED method. This is a method to be used IF we NEED the street noise but do not have an explicitly stated value. In the literature this method of attaching programs to data structures is frequently called *procedural attachment*. The reader might also note the similarity to the backward chaining formulas of Chapter 13.

In the case at hand the LISP program sees if the street of the dwelling we are looking at is York, and, if so, it then sees if it is above or below 200 in its number. (The variable *FORM* is bound to the FORM about which we are making the inquiry, in this case APT-1.) The function

(SLOT-VAL *form slot-name*)

returns the value associated with *slot-name* in *form*. As we shall see later, SLOT-VAL is sensitive to the ISA hierarchy and uses default values from FORMs higher in the hierarchy if necessary.

The use of IF-NEEDEDs in slots in another way in which our FORMs differ from straight property lists. Each property list indicator has a value, and that is all. A slot in a FORM may have a value (indicated by =), an IF-NEEDED method, or both. As we shall see, it may have further aspects as well. In general, a slot in a FORM may have one or more *aspects,* of which the value of the slot (indicated by the = sign) is just one.

On the other hand, the = aspect is used more than the rest, so we will reserve certain words to describe it. In particular when we talk of a slot being *filled,* we mean that it has an = aspect. Similarly, the value of a slot is the value of its = aspect. Figure 15.4 shows the structure of a slot with its aspects.

(*slot-name*   *aspect-1*   *aspect-2*   ...   *aspect-n*)

(*aspect-name . aspect-val*)

FIG. 15.4. Slots, aspects, and values of aspects.

So far we have said nothing about how we will handle the ISA links. It seems reasonable to store them as slots (albeit ones with a special significance to XRL) so that an ISA link may have different aspects as well. When we say

```
(FORM APT-1
      AN APARTMENT WITH...)
```

we say that APARTMENT is the value of the = aspect of the ISA slot.

It should be pointed out that since aspects of slots only have one value, a FORM can only be an immediate member of a single class; that is, we will have an ISA tree rather than an ISA net. This restriction can be lifted without major complications, except for the fact that the value of a slot will no longer be well defined. It might inherit different values from competing superclasses.

The code to accomplish what has been described so far is in Fig. 15.5. The extra function ADDSPEC

```
(ADDSPEC form slot aspect value)
(ADDSPEC APT-1 RENT = 250)
```

adds a *value* to *form* under *aspect* of *slot*. It is used to add an aspect after we have already created the FORM. ADDSPEC is a FEXPR. The EXPR version is ADDSPEC-E.

Another feature that proves useful is the IF-ADDED feature. This feature allows us to perform an arbitrary computation when a slot in a FORM is filled in. [More accurately, we will run IF-ADDED routines whenever we add a new item to the = (or value) aspect of a slot.]

For example, suppose we wanted to fill in the STREET-NOISE slot immediately rather than waiting to be asked. To do this we want to add to our DWELLING FORM under the STREET-NOISE slot an IF-ADDED aspect, which is accomplished by

```
(ADDSPEC DWELLING STREET-NOISE IF-ADDED
 (COND((NOT (EQ (SLOT-VAL *FORM* 'STREET-NAME) 'YORK)))
      ((GREATERP (SLOT-VAL *FORM* 'STREET-NO) 200)
       (ADDSPEC-E *FORM* 'STREET-NOISE '= 'BAD))
      ((ADDSPEC-E *FORM* 'STREET-NOISE '= 'VERY-BAD]
```

Note that whenever we add a new value, we must go up the ISA chain looking for IF-ADDEDs all the way up. In this case we must trace up to DWELLING.

```
~The function responsible for creating FORMs.
(DF FORM (EXP)
  (LET (NAME (CAR EXP) ISA (CADDR EXP) SLOTS (CDDDDR EXP))
    (:= (GET NAME 'TYPE) 'FORM)      ~This marks NAME as being a FORM
    (ADDSPEC-E NAME 'ISA '= ISA)
    (FOR (SLOT IN SLOTS)
      (DO (LOOP [INITIAL SLOT-NAME (CAR SLOT) ASPECTS (CDR SLOT)]
              [WHILE ASPECTS]
              [DO (ADDSPEC-E NAME SLOT-NAME (CAR ASPECTS) (CADR ASPECTS
              [NEXT ASPECTS (CDDR ASPECTS)]   ]

~Adds a new aspect value to an already existing FORM.
(DF ADDSPEC (EXP) (APPLY 'ADDSPEC-E EXP]

(DE ADDSPEC-E (NAME SLOT ASPECT VAL)
    (:= (GET SLOT ' SLOT-NAME) T)
    ~This serves to label slot-names so that SLOT-NAME-P (below) can
    ~decide which properties are slots of a FORM and which (like
    ~PNAME) are put there by somebody else. Will be used later.
    (LET (ASPECT-VAL (ASSOC ASPECT (GET NAME SLOT)))
        (COND  (ASPECT-VAL (:= (CDR ASPECT-VAL) VAL))
               (T (ADDPROP NAME (CONS ASPECT VAL) SLOT]

(DE SLOT-NAME-P (NAME) (GET NAME 'SLOT-NAME]
(DE FORM-P (NAME) (EQ (GET NAME 'TYPE) 'FORM]

(DECLARE (SPECIAL *FORM*))

~Retrieves the SLOT of *FORM* using ISAs and IF-NEEDEDs. We separate SLOT-VAL
~from SLOT-VAL2 so *FORM* will be bound to the initial FORM we asked about.
(DE SLOT-VAL (*FORM* SLOT) (SLOT-VAL2 *FORM* SLOT]

(DE SLOT-VAL2 (NAME SLOT)
    (LOOP  (INITIAL ANSWER NIL AN-ISA NAME)
           (WHILE AN-ISA)
           (DO (:= ANSWER
              (COND ((GET-VAL AN-ISA SLOT))
                 ~Either there is an = aspect,
                   ((EVAL (GET-ASPECT AN-ISA SLOT 'IF NEEDED))))))
                 ~Or an IF-NEEDED aspect which evaluates non-NIL,
           (NEXT AN-ISA (GET-ISA AN-ISA))
           (UNTIL ANSWER)
           (RESULT ANSWER]

~Retrieves the ASPECT from SLOT on NAME, but does not use ISAs etc.
(DE GET-ASPECT (NAME SLOT ASPECT)
    (LET (VAL (ASSOC ASPECT (GET NAME SLOT)))
        (COND (VAL (CDR VAL]

(DE GET-VAL (NAME SLOT) (GET-ASPECT NAME SLOT '=]
(DE GET-ISA (NAME) (GET-VAL NAME 'ISA]
```

FIG. 15.5.   Initial code for creating and using FORMs.

182

Exercise 15.1   Add the ability to handle IF-ADDED aspects. This means that you must modify FORM and ADDSPEC to (1) make sure that *FORM* and *VALUE* (the new value for the slot) are defined (and special) during the process of adding a slot value; (2) see if the aspect is =; and (3) if so, execute all IF-ADDED aspects found on the same slot of all FORM above the current one in the ISA chain.

15.3 PATTERN MATCHING IN XRL

Pattern matching can be naturally combined with the ISA hierarchy as follows: FORM1 will be said to match FORM2 if we can establish that "FORM1 might be a FORM2." By "FORM1 might be a FORM2" we mean that none of the known properties of FORM1 conflict with the known properties of FORM2. (The "known properties" might, of course, be inherited from higher FORMs.)

As an example, suppose someone uses our system to find an apartment. He describes what he wants by giving us a FORM whose properties specify his desires rather than anything that actually exists. Perhaps he must have a four-room dwelling with wood floors and low street noise. This might be translated into the FORM in Fig. 15.6. (Our customer is named Fred.)

```
(FORM   FREDS-DREAM-APT
        AN APARTMENT
        WITH  [NUMBER-OF-ROOMS = 4]
              [FLOOR-SURFACE = WOOD]
              [STREET-NOISE = LOW])
```

FIG. 15.6.   A first guess at a FORM pattern.

Unfortunately, although Fig. 15.6 seems reasonable, it cannot be what we want. The reason is that according to our previous description of FORM Fig. 15.6 does not "mean" what we want to say. We stated that Fred "must have" certain features, including low street noise, but suppose we had an apartment with high street noise. Could it match FREDS-DREAM-APT? We want the answer to be no, but in fact it is yes because slot values on higher FORMs are only default conditions for lower FORMs. Hence the various = aspects of FREDS-DREAM-APT do not restrict at all what is allowed to match this FORM.

To rectify this situation we need a new aspect to a slot, which we call the ALWAYS aspect. Its use in correcting FREDS-DREAM-APT is shown in Fig. 15.7. Like =, the ALWAYS aspect may determine the default filler for lower FORMs in the ISA hierarchy. Unlike =, it cannot be "overwritten." Hence any time we add a value to a slot, we must check to see if the value is compatible with the ALWAYS aspect on that slot in any FORM above the

```
(FORM FREDS-DREAM-APT
ALWAYS   APARTMENT
  WITH   [NUMBER-OF-ROOMS ALWAYS 4]
         [FLOOR-SURFACE ALWAYS WOOD]
         [STREET-NOISE ALWAYS LOW])
```

FIG. 15.7.   A second guess at a FORM pattern.

current FORM in the ISA hierarchy. If not, that value must be rejected. Similarly, any time we wish to show that FORM1 ISA FORM2, we must check all values of FORM1, making sure there are no conflicts with the ALWAYS properties in FORM2.

Given this description of ALWAYS we can now write a matching procedure (Fig. 15.8). Since it is somewhat more complicated than one might expect, let us go over it to see why.

Looking at MATCH we see that any two things will match if they are EQUAL. If the two things are FORMs, then we can use more sophisticated tests. If we already know that FORM1 ISA FORM2, then we already know the two match. If we do not, then we must go through the two forms on a slot-by-slot basis.

Given the two forms, and the name of the slot, the function COMPATIBLE says whether the two forms are compatible with respect to that slot. It says that if FORM1 has a slot value for that slot, and if FORM2 has an ALWAYS aspect for the slot, then the = aspect of FORM1 must match the ALWAYS aspect of FORM 2. Anytime the = and ALWAYS aspects have not been filled in, we assume a match. This implies that whenever we make a successful match, we are really saying "these two match, given what I know about them now."

So far things are straightforward. It is the function SLOT-BY-SLOT-MATCH that is the problem. This function is in charge of finding the appropriate slots to use in the comparison of the two forms. Each time it finds

```
(DE MATCH (INST PAT)
  (COND((EQUAL INST PAT))               ~Anything matches itself.
       ((NOT (AND (FORM-P INST) (FORM-P PAT))) NIL)
                            ~Matching non EQUAL things must be FORMs.
       ((ISA-P INST PAT))    ~A form matches its superclasses. Else
       ((SLOT-BY-SLOT-MATCH INST PAT]  ~check it out slot by slot.

~Decide if INST is compatible with PAT only looking at SLOT.
(DE COMPATIBLE (INST PAT SLOT)
   (LET   (INST-VAL   (SLOT-VAL INST SLOT)
          PAT-ALWAYS (SLOT-ALWAYS PAT SLOT)  )
          (OR (NULL INST-VAL) (NULL PAT-ALWAYS)
                       (MATCH INST-VAL PAT-ALWAYS]
```

FIG. 15.8.   Code for a FORM matcher.

```
(DE SLOT-BY-SLOT-MATCH (INST PAT)
    (LET (MARKER (NEWSYM 'MARK))  ˜Create a unique marker.
    (EVERY                        ˜Go through all the ISAs of PAT
    '(LAMBDA (AN-ISA)
        (LOOP (INITIAL P-LIST            (GET-P-LIST AN-ISA)
                     PROP               NIL
                     MISMATCH-FLAG NIL              )
            (WHILE (:= PROP (POP P-LIST)))
                ˜We go down the property list of the pattern looking at
                ˜each PROP until we have done them all.
            (DO (POP P-LIST)
                ˜We must remove the property value from P-LIST also.
                (COND    ((NOT (SLOT-NAME-P PROP)))
                     ˜Ignore everything but slots.
                     ((EQ MARKER (GET PROP 'NEW-SLOT-MARK)))
                     ˜If it has current mark it has been checked.
                     ((COMPATIBLE INST PAT PROP)
                     ˜Are INST and PAT compatible as far as PROP
                     ˜slot is concerned? If so, then mark PROP.
                     (:= (GET PROP 'NEW-SLOT-MARK) MARKER))
                     ((:=MISMATCH-FLAG T))))
            (UNTIL MISMATCH-FLAG)
            ˜Once we have a mismatch, return NIL.
            (RESULT (NOT MISMATCH-FLAG))))
        (ISAS PAT]

(DE GET-P-LIST (ATM) (CDR ATM))

(DE ISA-P (FORM1 FORM2) (MEMBER FORM2 (ISAS FORM1]

(DE SLOT-ALWAYS (FORM SLOT)
    LET (ANS (SOME '(LAMBDA (AN-ISA) (GET-ASPECT AN-ISA SLOT 'ALWAYS))
                (ISAS FORM)))
        (COND (ANS (GET-ASPECT (CAR ANS) SLOT 'ALWAYS]

˜Creates a list of all ISAs of FORM (including FORM itself).
(DE ISAS (FORM)
    (LOOP   (INITIAL ANSWER NIL)
            (WHILE FORM)
            (DO (PUSH FORM ANSWER))
            (NEXT FORM (GET-ISA FORM))
            (RESULT (REVERSE ANSWER]
```
                                              FIG. 15.8.   Continued.

an appropriate slot, it uses COMPATIBLE to see if the two forms are compatible according to that slot, but the task of slot selection is not so simple.

Let us start by considering a simple solution to the slot selection problem. In this solution we simply look at every slot on FORM2. The trouble is that this may miss significant slots. To see how this could occur, consider the situation in Fig. 15.9. Here, if we simply compare all the slots in APT-B against the corresponding ones in APT-A, we will find they match. But APT-

A should not match APT-B because A inherits a high street noise from APT-A-SUPERSET, whereas APT-B must have low street noise, due to inheritance from APT-B-SUPERSET.

APT-A-SUPERSET
   [STREET-NOISE = HIGH]

  ISA

APT-A
   [WALL-COLOR = WHITE]
   [FLOOR-SURFACE = WOOD]

APT-B-SUPERSET
   [STREET-NOISE ALWAYS LOW]
   [WALL-COLOR = GREEN]

  ISA

APT-B
   [WALL-COLOR ALWAYS WHITE]

FIG. 15.9.   A difficult case for the matcher.

The solution to this problem is have SLOT-BY-SLOT-MATCH not only use the appropriate slots in APT-B (the pattern) but also the slots in all supersets of the pattern. In this way we are guaranteed that no potentially conflicting slot will go overlooked.

We may end up checking the COMPATIBILITY of a slot many times, however. In Fig. 15.9 we will check the WALL-COLOR slot twice. The way to avoid this is to mark each slot when we check it, and before checking a slot for compatibility we first see if it has been marked. If so, we need not check it again. This is what we do, using a variation of the fast intersection method discussed in Chapter 10. In particular we generate a new atom with NEWSYM to give us a new mark, so that we need not erase the marks after we are done.

Exercise 15.2 In order to introduce ALWAYS into our system we need to make several changes. (1) FORM should check to see if the ISA property is specified by A (or AN) or by ALWAYS and use the appropriate aspect. (2) GET-VAL should retrieve an ALWAYS aspects for that slot. (3) ADDSPEC should check the ALWAYS aspects of the FORM and its superclasses any time an = or ALWAYS aspect is added. (4) ADDSPEC should use matching to check for consistency when adding an ISA link. This in turn implies that when we say

(FORM FORM1 A FORM2 WITH . . .)

FORM2 should be a preexisting FORM and not simply an undefined atom such as we were using earlier (e.g., THING). But if we can't define a FORM without defining it in terms of a preexisting FORM, we have an obvious circularity. Break this loop by having the system define THING as a FORM with no slots.

15.4   FORM RETRIEVAL

Suppose someone comes into our housing service and asks for places that rent for somewhere between $200 and $250 per month, with wood floors and low street noise. How, short of going through every apartment known to the system, will we locate such a place? The answer is that at the moment we simply have no way to do it. Given a dwelling we can retrieve its properties, but given some properties we have no way to retrieve the dwelling. To do this we first need a method for indexing FORMs according to their properties and then a retrieval function that uses the resulting indexes to find potential matches for a given FORM.

An indexing mechanism sets up pointers from properties of objects to the objects themselves. Rather than provide a universal index, as we did in Chapter 14 with our discrimination net, we just use IF-ADDED methods to index each FORM in an appropriate way. So, we could keep track of places with wood floors with the code of Fig. 15.10. The result of this addition is that

```
(ADDSPEC DWELLING FLOOR-SURFACE IF-ADDED
  (INDEX 'FLOOR-SURFACE *VALUE* *FORM*))

(DE INDEX (SLOT FORM-NAME VAL)
  (LET (A-LST-ENTRY (ASSOC# VAL (GET SLOT 'INDEX)))
    (COND   (A-LST-ENTRY (:= (CDR A-LST-ENTRY) (CONS FORM-NAME *—*)))
            ((:= (GET SLOT 'INDEX) (CONS (LIST VAL FORM-NAME) *—*]
```

FIG. 15.10.   Adding an IF-ADDED method for indexing.

each time we learn of a floor surface of a dwelling (e.g., the floor surface of APT-2 is CARPET), we will call INDEX. This will put on the property list of the slot name (FLOOR-SURFACE) an INDEX property that will contain an a-list of the form

$$((slot\text{-}val\text{-}1\ form\text{-}1.1 \ldots form\text{-}1.n) \ldots (slot\text{-}val\text{-}n \ldots form\text{-}n.n))$$

Note the use of := and GET here rather than their XRL equivalents. The reason is that intuitively the indexes we create are not semantically relevant parts of FORMs. If we did not do this, two forms could fail to match because their indexes are different.

If this is how we intend to handle indexing in XRL, we will be using this sort of IF-ADDED aspect quite often. Rather than having to hand code it in each time we wish to index under a new property, it would be better to define a new function INDEX-PROPERTY. So to use this function for the example above we simply would have said

(INDEX-PROPERTY FLOOR-SURFACE DWELLING)

The execution of this command will cause the addition to DWELLING of the appropriate IF-ADDED expression.

Exercise 15.3 Define the function INDEX-PROPERTY. Also, write the function (GET-INDEX *slot val*) which will fetch the index of FORMS which have *slot* filled with *val*.

There are some problems with this indexing scheme, however. As we currently have things implemented, a FORM describing a customer's desires (e.g., FREDS-DREAM-APT) is manipulated just like any other FORM. Uniformity is a good thing (it makes the program easier to write) but in this case there are difficulties. In particular, when Fred comes in and states his preferences (FREDS-DREAM-APT), our indexing program will index this FORM along with everything else. This is a bit wasteful of space, but the real problem is that when George comes in and states his preferences, the retrieval mechanism (designed in Exercise 15.6) might retrieve FREDS-DREAM-APT. Needless to say, this is not exactly what George had in mind.

There are several ways we might try to fix this, but all of them depend on distinguishing different types of FORMs, something we currently do not do. Those FORMs that represent actual individual dwellings we might label as INDIVIDUAL FORMs. Those things like FREDS-DREAM-APT we can call PATTERN FORMs. It would then seem reasonable not to index PATTERN FORMs.

There are, however, other FORMs that fall between these two extremes. For example, APT-AT-100-YORK, or DWELLING. It is not completely clear how we want to handle these cases. In the case of DWELLING it is unlikely that we would want it to come back as a response to an apartment hunter. But APT-AT-100-YORK might be reasonable. It would tell the apartment hunter than 100 York Street is a place he might consider. What we will do is call things like APT-AT-100-YORK PROTOTYPES, whereas DWELLING will be called a CLASS and the former will be indexed but the latter will not. Each time we define a FORM we must specify its type, and our indexing functions must be made sensitive to types. The new input format is

```
(FORM FREDS-DREAM-APT PATTERN
         ALWAYS APARTMENT
         WITH [NUMBER-OF-ROOMS ALWAYS 4]   )
```

We continue to use the same ISA link to connect an INDIVIDUAL to a PROTOTYPE and one PROTOTYPE to another; that is, it is used to indicate both the "element of" relation and the "subset" relation.

Exercise 15.4 Redo FORM to accept the new input format and redo our indexing function to ignore PATTERN and CLASS FORMs.

Exercise 15.5 Modify MATCH so that it checks the type of the two FORMs. In particular, except for equality checking, nothing should match an INDIVIDUAL.

Now let us turn directly to the question of a retrieval function. The problem is a difficult one, and for much the same reasons that matching turned out to be more difficult than one might expect: the inheritance of properties makes it hard to decide which FORMs have which properties. Suppose we wanted to find an INDIVIDUAL with white walls and a high level of street noise. We might try intersecting the list of places with WALL-COLOR = WHITE with a list of places with STREET-NOISE = HIGH to obtain a list of places that satisfied both requirements. Unfortunately this does not work. To see why, look again at Fig. 15.9. Here APT-A is one of the FORMs we should end up with, but we will not, because it will not appear in the list of FORMs with STREET-NOISE = HIGH. APT-A-SUPERCLASS will appear there but not APT-A.

The solution is to redefine what we mean by intersection. Normally we say that the intersection of sets A and B is the set containing exactly those elements Ai from set A, and Bj from set B such that (EQUAL Ai Bj). We basically now want to replace EQUAL by ISA-P (ISA-P is defined in Fig. 15.9.) The exact definition, ISA-INTERSECTION, is given in Fig. 15.11.

```
(DE  ISA-INTERSECTION (L1 L2)
     (FOR   (E1 IN L1)
            (FILTER (LOOP  (INITIAL TEMP-L2 L2   E2 NIL   ANS NIL)
                           (WHILE (:= E2 (POP TEMP-L2)))
                           (UNTIL (:= ANS (COND  ((ISA-P E1 E2) E1)
                                                 ((ISA-P E2 E1) E2)))))
            (RESULT ANS]
```

FIG. 15.11. ISA-INTERSECTION.

Exercise 15.6 Write a retrieval function FORM-FIND, which given a FORM first finds potential candidates and then hands them off to the matcher. The potential candidate finder will look at each ALWAYS aspect and see if it is cross-indexed. If it is, the program will intersect it with the current list.

Exercise 15.7 Note that there is an interaction between our definition of CLASS FORMs and the method of FORM retrieval. In our scheme, APT-A (from Fig. 15.10) will be retrieved on the basis of

[WALL-COLOR ALWAYS WHITE]
[STREET-NOISE ALWAYS HIGH]

if APT-A-SUPERCLASS is a PROTOTYPE FORM but not if it is a CLASS FORM. Why is this the case?

15.5   MORE ON MATCHING FORMS

There are still many places for further refinement of our matcher. For example, at the moment we can only say that FORM1 matches or fails to match FORM2. Our apartment hunters will certainly need something more sophisticated. In particular they will want to say "the apartment *must* have white walls" (which we can handle with ALWAYS), and "I would *prefer* wood floors" (which we cannot handle). We need the ability to distinguish between better and worse matches in order to answer the question, given two individuals both of which are members of a certain class, which is the more typical member?

We have already noted that an = aspect of a FORM gives default values for those FORMs lower on the ISA hierarchy. Clearly the more a FORM corresponds to the default values of a CLASS, PROTOTYPE, or PATTERN, the more typical it is for that CLASS, etc. So to express the set of desires given in the last paragraph we could say

(FORM FREDS-DREAM-APT PATTERN
    ALWAYS APARTMENT
        WITH [WALL-COLOR ALWAYS WHITE]
              [FLOOR-SURFACE = WOOD]

Exercise 15.8   Redo MATCH so that it checks for = aspects of the pattern FORM and, in the case of a match, returns the number of = aspects in the pattern that match the value of the corresponding slots in the constant FORM. You might then redo the retrieval function so that it places the higher scoring FORMs at the front of the list.

There is another matching feature for which we already have most of the code but which has not been used in our examples so far. Up till now = and ALWAYS aspects have taken atoms as values, but it is a fairly easy change to allow them to also take FORMs as their values. In fact, we need not change MATCH at all to accommodate this generalization. The reader should check the definition of MATCH given in Fig. 15.9 to convince himself that this is the case.

Given this new-found freedom it would be convenient to extend the input format. For example, now rather than saying that the floor covering is CARPET, we might like to give the color and texture at the same time. A reasonable format might be that given in Fig. 15.12a. It will be translated as if it had been written as Fig. 15.12b.

Exercise 15.9   Redo FORM to accept embedded FORMs. Note that, as shown in Fig. 15.12, embedded FORMs will not have explicit names. One must be made up on the spot.

```
(FORM APT-5 INDIVIDUAL
    AN APARTMENT
    WITH [FLOOR-SURFACE = (INDIVIDUAL A CARPET
                                WITH [COLOR = GREY]
                                     [TEXTURE = FINE]
                                     [SIZE = WALL-TO-WALL])   ]
         [NUMBER-OF-ROOMS = 2]   )
```

FIG. 15.12a.   A FORM within a FORM.

```
    (FORM APT-5 INDIVIDUAL
        AN APARTMENT
        WITH [FLOOR-SURFACE = CARPET-1]
             [NUMBER-OF-ROOMS = 2]        )

    (FORM CARPET-1 INDIVIDUAL
        A CARPET
        WITH [COLOR = GREY]
             [TEXTURE = FINE]
             [SIZE = WALL-TO-WALL]   )
```

FIG. 15.12b.   Translation of Fig. 15.12a.

There are still a wide range of things which would be useful but which are beyond the expressive powers of our representation. For example, suppose we divide STREET-NOISE into five categories, VERY-LOW, LOW, AVERAGE, HIGH, VERY-HIGH, and suppose a customer comes in and says he wants the street noise to be either VERY-LOW or LOW. Well, he can say it, but there is no way to express his desire in a FORM. We would like to say things like Fig. 15.13. In the first expression in Fig. 15.13, we are restricting STREET-NOISE here not to a particular value but to satisfying a particular predicate.

There are several problems that must be overcome before we can do this. The easy ones are syntactic. Depending on your implementation of Exercise 15.9 the function FORM might interpret (OR LOW VERY-LOW) as an embedded FORM. But the major problem is semantic. In particular our

```
(FORM ALS-DREAM-APT PATTERN
    ALWAYS APARTMENT
    WITH [STREET-NOISE ALWAYS (OR LOW VERY-LOW)]
        ...)

(FORM DWELLING CLASS
    A THING
    WITH [FLOOR-SURFACE ALWAYS (OR CARPET WOOD TILE LINOLEUM)]
        ...)
```

FIG. 15.13.   Possible uses for the OR construct.

matcher must know what to do when it sees one of these things. In the normal cases this is not too difficult. If our matcher is asked to match some FORM against a predicate, it will use an evaluation function attached to the predicate (the MATCHING-FUNCTION). The difficult case is when the matcher is given two predicates to match. What should it do then? It can be shown that there is no general way to decide if two arbitrary predicates are compatible, so that route is out. One can check to see if the S-expressions are equal, but after that one must (1) assume the predicates are compatible; (2) assume they are not; or (3) consult the user (or some other convenient oracle). The reader may choose the solution he likes best.

Exercise 15.10   To implement this we need to make several changes to our code. FORM must check nonatomic aspect values to see if they are embedded FORMs or if they are predicates. (There are several ways to do this, the easiest being a check for the presence of a MATCHING-FUNCTION.) INDEX-PROPERTY must not attempt to index a FORM according to predicates therein. FORM-FIND must not try to retrieve an index list for a slot filled with a predicate. MATCH must check if its inputs are predicates and, if so, take the appropriate action. Finally we need MATCHING-FUNCTIONS for OR (and any other predicates you might like, such as AND).

16 Data Dependencies

16.1 THE NEED FOR DATA DEPENDENCIES

In Chapter 13 we developed functions for adding and retrieving formulas. We omitted functions for erasing formulas from the data base, although in Chapter 14 we described how to erase them from discrimination trees. The reason for this omission is that erasure may require bookkeeping in order to interact properly with forward chaining. For example, if the data base contains (→ (IS ?X DOG) (IS ?X MAMMAL)), then (IS FIDO MAMMAL) will be added as a side effect of adding (IS FIDO DOG). Simply deleting (IS FIDO DOG) leaves (IS FIDO MAMMAL) around with no visible means of support.

In this chapter, we will describe the mechanism of *data dependencies*, which solves this problem and is useful for other purposes besides. A data dependency is a note, attached to each element of a set of assertions, which records that one element of the set was derived from the others. In the example given, the note would say, "(IS FIDO MAMMAL) was deduced from (IS FIDO DOG) and (→ (IS ?X DOG) (IS ?X MAMMAL))." These notes allow the erase function to find subordinate data that must also be erased. They have several other uses that are making them increasingly popular among AI researchers (Davis, 1976; de Kleer et al., 1977a; 1977b; Doyle, 1978; McDermott, 1974; Stallman and Sussman, 1977). These uses include:

1. retrieving explanations of conclusions to clarify a system's actions to a user;

2. finding faulty assumptions that are responsible for the deduction of contradictions, by tracing data dependencies from conclusions back to axioms.

Data dependencies are of use in any system that builds data structures based on the existence of other data structures. But it is most convenient to describe how they work in a predicate-calculus system, so that is how we will proceed. [This chapter consists almost entirely of material from Doyle (1978), suitably simplified and cleaned up.]

16.2   ERASING FORMULAS FROM A DATA BASE

In order to attach notes to formulas in the data base, we must implement the suggestion we made in Chapter 11 to treat stored formulas as "superatoms" with "property lists." We will call such a superatom a *molecule.* Rather than store its properties as we would an atom's, we just define it thus:

```
(RECORD-TYPE MOLEC
    (PAT JUSTIFICATIONS JUSTIFICANDS))
```

For our first cut at implementing ERASE, the only properties a molecule will need to have are its justifications and justificands. Each justification is a list of molecules that together justify the presence of the given molecule. Each justificand is a molecule in one of whose justifications this molecule appears. The FIDO example would give rise to a structure of molecules like this:

```
M1 = (MOLEC (→ (IS ?X DOG) (IS ?X MAMMAL)) NIL (M3))
M2 = (MOLEC (IS FIDO DOG) NIL (M3))
M3 = (MOLEC (IS FIDO MAMMAL) ((M1 M2)) NIL)
```

(Inside the machine, this structure is actually a circular nest of pointers, which would have an infinite printed representation. For practical purposes, the data types should probably be more complex, to avoid the nuisance of infinite printouts during debugging. For example, a molecule could be implemented as an atom with the actual record on its property list.)

ADD must be redefined to create these structures, so ERASE can use them in propagating erasures. The code for doing this is shown in Fig. 16.1. We assume that INDEX, UNINDEX, FETCH, and FETCH-VARIANT all create or return molecules. The top node of the discrimination net is kept in the special variable *DATA-BASE*.

Exercise 16.1   Write versions of these functions that handle molecules.

```
(RECORD-TYPE MOLEC (PAT JUSTIFICATIONS JUSTIFICANDS))
˜Each justification is a list of molecules
˜Each justificand is a single molecule.

(DE ADD (PAT JUSTIFICATION)
   (LET (M (UNIQUIFY PAT) IMPLPAT NIL)
       (COND  ((NULL M)
               (:= M (INDEX PAT))
               (:= IMPLPAT  |"(→ @PAT ?RIGHT))
               (FOR (AX-MOLEC IN (FETCH IMPLPAT))
                   (DO (FOR (SUB IN
                                (UNIFY IMPLPAT
                                       (VARS-RENAME (PAT:MOLEC AX-MOLEC))))
                            (DO (ADD (PCVAR-VAL '?RIGHT SUB)
                                     (LIST M AX-MOLEC)))   ))))    )
      (DD-INSTALL JUSTIFICATION M)
      M ))

(DE ERASE (PAT)
   (LET (M (UNIQUIFY PAT))
       (COND (M
              (UNINDEX PAT)
              (FOR (S IN (JUSTIFICANDS:MOLEC M))
                  (DO (ERASE-DD-LINK M S)
                      (COND ((NULL (JUSTIFICATIONS:MOLEC S))
                             (ERASE (PAT:MOLEC S)))  ))  )    )
      M ))

(DE UNIQUIFY (PAT)
   (CAR (SOME '(LAMBDA (M) (VARIANTS PAT (PAT:MOLEC M))  )
             (FETCH-VARIANT PAT)))    )

(DE DD-INSTALL (J M)
   (FOR (S IN J)
       (DO (:= (JUSTIFICANDS:MOLEC S) (CONS M *—*)))  )
   (:= (JUSTIFICATIONS:MOLEC M)
       (CONS J *—*))  )

(DE ERASE-DD-LINK (M1 M2)
   (FOR (J IN (JUSTIFICATIONS:MOLEC M2))
      (WHEN (MEMQ M1 J))
      (DO (DD-ERASE J S))    ))

(DE DD-ERASE (J M)
   (FOR (S IN J)
       (DO (:= (JUSTIFICANDS:MOLEC S) (DREMOVE M *—*)))  )
   (:= (JUSTIFICATIONS:MOLEC M)
       (DREMOVE J *—*))  )
```

FIG. 16.1. Data-dependency manipulations by ADD and ERASE.

ADD now takes two arguments, a pattern and a justification. (Much later we will provide functions for creating justifications; for now, just assume the program doing the ADD has a list of molecules to use for this purpose.) ADD first does a FETCH-VARIANT (in the function UNIQUIFY) to see if the pattern has already been added. If so, it merely gives it another justification and returns. Otherwise, it does forward chaining as before, except that the formulas deduced are themselves justified by the added formula and the implication used in the deduction.

ERASE uses these justification links. It takes a pattern PAT and finds its molecule in the index. (If it isn't there, there's nothing to erase.) This molecule is UNINDEXed, and th link between it and each of its justificands is broken (with ERASE-DD-LINK). If this leaves a justificand with no remaining justifications, then it is erased, too.

Exercise 16.2 The purpose of this exercise is to coordinate data dependencies with the AI language features we developed in Chapter 13. We would like to have the code

```
(FOR-EACH-ANSWER (IS ?X DOG)
    (ADD '(IS ?X MAMMAL))  )
```

not just add (IS FIDO MAMMAL) when (IS FIDO DOG) is deducible, but support it appropriately. Here is a sketch of how to do this: In Exercise 13.5, the function RETRIEVE was revised to return proofs (i.e., lists of formulas). Revise it again to return lists of molecules. Then change FOR-EACH-ANSWER and ADD to use these lists; that is, introduce a new data type ANSWER, which contains both variable bindings and justifier lists, and replace the special variable *PCVARBDGS* with a variable *ANSWER* that contains the current result of the ongoing deduction. To use this variable, make ADD's second argument be optional, with default value (JUSTIFICATION:ANSWER *ANSWER*). (NOTE and SUCCEED should also use *ANSWER*.)

Exercise 16.3 In Chapter 13, we mentioned that the LISP code called during forward chaining could do anything, not just make further deductions; such a piece of code is called a "demon." We can also have demons that are called during erasure. Change ERASE so that it looks for formulas of the form (IF-ERASED *pat action*) when a formula is removed. One use for this is the smooth translation of data-base formulas to more specialized representations. For example, let us say we wished to maintain some data on property lists as well as in the data base. We could use the following three formulas:

```
(ADD '(← (QUADRUPED ?X)
         (LISP (COND ((EQUAL (GET ?X 'LEGS) 4) (SUCCEED]
(ADD '(→ (QUADRUPED ?X)
         (LISP (:= (GET ?X 'LEGS) 4))))
(ADD '(IF-ERASED  (QUADRUPED ?X)
                  (LISP (REMPROP ?X 'LEGS))))
```

16.3   HANDLING CIRCULARITIES

Unfortunately, the versions of ADD and ERASE we just gave do not always work. The problem is that ERASE occasionally leaves in justificands that should be erased. For example, if the following three axioms are in the data base,

(→ (IS ?X MAN) (IS ?X PERSON))
(→ (IS ?X PERSON) (IS ?X HUMAN))
(→ (IS ?X HUMAN) (IS ?X PERSON))

then adding (IS FRED MAN) will cause (IS FRED HUMAN) to be added, which will then add another justification to (IS FRED PERSON) (Fig. 16.2). Now erasing (IS FRED MAN) will leave (IS FRED HUMAN) and (IS FRED PERSON) in the data base, since each of them will have a remaining justification (i.e., the other one).

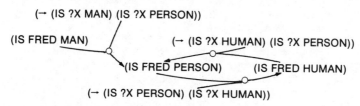

FIG. 16.2.   Circular data-dependency network.

If you are quite sure that this can never happen in your application, then you may use the original version of ERASE. But this is hard to guarantee, so we will describe how to get around this problem.

Notice that a molecule is to be present only if it has *well-founded support,* that is, if there is a chain of justifications back to *premises,* molecules justified by an empty justification. We will change the data structure and algorithms to maintain the well-founded support of each molecule, as well as all its possible justifications. Erasure of a molecule can only propagate through these well-founded support links.

The job of ERASE must change somewhat to handle this new structure. Not only must ERASE use the support links in pursuing further erasures, but it must make sure when it is done that every remaining molecule has well-founded support. The program must take special care to handle the case where the original support of a molecule is no longer satisfied, but a new justification has been ADDed. If an ERASE wipes out the well-founded support of a molecule, the system must look around for alternative support, and, if it isn't found, go ahead and erase the threatened molecule. Looking around for alternative support requires scanning through all the molecules

```
(RECORD-TYPE MOLEC (PAT STATUS SUPPORTERS JUSTIFICATIONS JUSTIFICANDS))
(DE MOLEC (PAT) (LIST 'MOLEC PAT 'IN NIL NIL NIL)   )

(DE SUPPORTEES:MOLEC (M)
  (FOR (S IN (JUSTIFICANDS:MOLEC M))
    (WHEN (MEMQ M (SUPPORTERS:MOLEC S)))
    (SAVE S)   ))

(DECLARE (SPECIAL *MOLECS-TO-BE-ERASED*))

(DE ERASE (PAT JUST)
  (LET   (M (UNIQUIFY PAT)
         *MOLECS-TO-BE-ERASED* NIL OLD-JUST NIL)
    (COND ((AND M
               (:= OLD-JUST
                   (CAR (SOME '(LAMBDA (J)
                                 (EQUIV-JUST JUST J)   )
                             (MOLEC:JUSTIFICATIONS M)))))
          (DD-ERASE OLD-JUST M)
          (MOLECS-CLOBBER-STATUS M 0)
          (MOLECS-ASSIGN-STATUS M 0)
          (FORM (M IN *MOLECS-TO-BE-ERASED*)
            (WHEN (EQ (STATUS:MOLEC M) 'OUT))
            (DO (FOR (S IN (JUSTIFICANDS:MOLEC M))
                  DO (ERASE-DD-LINK M S))   )
            (UNINDEX (PAT:MOLEC M))
            (:= (STATUS:MOLEC M) 'ERASED))   )   )
      M   ))

(DE MOLECS-CLOBBER-STATUS (M LEVEL)
  (COND   ((MEMQ (STATUS:MOLEC M) '(IN OUT))
           (:= (STATUS:MOLEC M) LEVEL)
           (:= (SUPPORTERS:MOLEC M) NIL)
           (FOR (S IN (SUPPORTEES:MOLEC M))
             (DO (MOLECS-CLOBBER-STATUS S LEVEL))   )   ))

(DE MOLECS-ASSIGN-STATUS (M LEVEL)
  (COND   ((EQUAL (STATUS:MOLEC M) LEVEL)
           (COND [(EQ (ASSIGN-TENTATIVE-STATUS M) 'IN)
                  (LET (SUPPORTEES (SUPPORTEES:MOLEC M))
                    (FOR (S IN SUPPORTEES)
                      (DO (MOLECS-CLOBBER-STATUS S (ADD1 LEVEL)))   )
                    (FOR (S IN SUPPORTEES)
                      (DO (MOLECS-ASSIGN-STATUS S (ADD1 LEVEL]
                  (T (:= *MOLECS-TO-BE-ERASED* (CONS M *—*)))   )
           (FOR (S IN (JUSTIFICANDS:MOLEC M))
             (DO (MOLECS-ASSIGN-STATUS S LEVEL))   )   ))
```

FIG. 16.3a.   "Garbage-collecting" ERASE to handle circularities.

198

```
(DE ASSIGN-TENTATIVE-STATUS (M)
    (LET (SUPPS (SOME 'JUSTIFICATION-SATISFIED (JUSTIFICATIONS:MOLEC M)))
        (COND  (SUPPS
                    (:= (SUPPORTERS:MOLEC M) (CAR SUPPS))
                    (:= (STATUS:MOLEC M) 'IN))
                (T (:= (STATUS: MOLEC M) 'OUT))  )))

(DE JUSTIFICATION-SATISFIED (J)
    (EVERY  '(LAMBDA (M) (EQ (STATUS:MOLEC M) 'IN)  )
            J)  )

(DE EQUIV-JUST (J1 J2)
    (AND (EVERY '(LAMBDA (M) (MEMQ M J2)    ) J1)
        (EVERY '(LAMBDA (M) (MEMQ M J1)    ) J2))    )
```

FIG. 16.3b.   Low-level functions for Fig. 16.3a.

that may be affected by the erasure, because an apparently valid justification may depend ultimately on the threatened molecule.

The presence of the well-founded support links between erasures is an important side effect of ERASE. These links enable the user to perform various scans through the data base and be guaranteed that he is not getting stuck in meaningless circularities. We will see examples of these scans in Section 16.5.

The process of finding and unindexing molecules that lack well-founded support resembles LISP garbage collection in some ways. Every time a LISP program does a CONS, a free cell is taken off an internal list of free cells to hold the new CAR and CDR. When there are no more free cells, LISP calls a program called the *garbage collector* to find more. The job of the garbage collector is to find all cells in the machine's memory that can never be referred to by user code and hence are free to be used again. These cells are all those that cannot be reached by any CAR-CDR chain from any variable value cell or stack location. To find them, the garbage collector uses a two-stage process. In the first stage, it marks all the nonfree cells, by marking all the variable value cells and stack locations and then continuing to mark all cells pointed to by a marked cell, until no more cells can be marked. In the second stage, it sweeps through the entire memory in consecutive order, linking together all unmarked cells into a new free-cell list.

The algorithm for ERASE is somewhat similar, but it has an additional "unmark" phase at the beginning, and it combines the mark and sweep phases. The code is shown in Fig. 16.3. We have added two fields to the MOLEC data type: the SUPPORTERS, which is the chosen well-founded justification; and a STATUS field, which is normally IN, but is set to a number during the search for well-founded support, and ultimately becomes OUT when a molecule is to be erased.

Another change we have made is to change the meaning of ERASE so that it is more symmetrical with ADD. ERASE now removes a justification from a molecule, not the molecule itself. (If the molecule has other justifications, it may not actually be unindexed.) ERASE's first action is to remove the given justification. Then it calls MOLECS-CLOBBER-STATUS to set to 0 the status of each molecule that could be affected by removing it. This function also wipes out the SUPPORTERS of each molecule.

Now ERASE calls MOLECS-ASSIGN-STATUS to scan through the affected molecules again, recomputing their STATUS and SUPPORTERS. This may take more than one pass because of circularities. For example, say the leftmost justification of Fig. 16.2 were erased. MOLECS-CLOBBER-STATUS would mark (IS FRED PERSON) and (IS FRED HUMAN) with STATUS = 0. Then MOLECS-ASSIGN-STATUS would see (IS FRED PERSON) justified by (IS FRED HUMAN). It might seem at first that it can confidently assign (IS FRED PERSON) STATUS = OUT, but although this is true in Fig. 16.2, there is no way for the algorithm to tell whether (IS FRED HUMAN) will turn out to have independent well-founded support, in which case (IS FRED PERSON) will be IN after all.

So MOLECS-ASSIGN-STATUS can only tentatively assign status to molecules, assuming that any non-IN justifier will eventually be labeled OUT. (This is done by the function ASSIGN-TENTATIVE-STATUS.) If this is correct, there is no problem. When a molecule is assigned STATUS IN, however, the program must check to see if any other molecule was assigned a status based on the assumption that it was going to end up OUT. These molecules, whose status is now suspect, will be just those that have the newly IN molecule as a supporter, that is, its SUPPORTEES. They and their supportees must be CLOBBERed, and the system must try again with them. This call to CLOBBER uses a different number to mark with, so that the corrective calls to MOLECS-ASSIGN-STATUS confine their effects to freshly clobbered parts of the data base. (See Section 16.7.)

Because of the tentative nature of status assignments, a molecule cannot be erased as soon as it is marked OUT. Instead, it is put on a list, *MOLECS-TO-BE-ERASED*, which ERASE goes through after the data base has been marked. It UNINDEXes all molecules that really did become OUT and unlinks them from their justificands; since a molecule might get on the list more than once, the loop must set an erased molecule's status to ERASED to save unindexing more than once.

This concludes our discussion of this version of ERASE. We should mention an alternative way to compute well-founded support, which resembes LISP garbage collection more closely. This would involve three phases: unmarking all the molecules, as the current algorithm does; scanning through the molecules to mark those with guaranteed well-founded support and then marking their justificands recursively; and finally sweeping through the original unmarked set collecting the molecules that never were marked. This algorithm would be a bit more efficient in some circumstances (since it never guesses wrong) and bit less efficient in others (since it never makes lucky guesses). The reason we presented the other algorithm instead is that it generalizes better to handle the problems we discuss next.

Exercise 16.4 Implement this alternative version of ERASE.

16.4 NON-MONOTONIC DEPENDENCIES

The system we have looked at so far is *monotonic*, in the sense that ADDing a molecule can only cause additions to, never erasures from, the data base, and ERASing can only cause erasures.

There are many applications where this is inadequate. For example, in Section 13.6 we presented a rule *Two things are unequal if they cannot be unified.* Let us present a slightly different version of this:

```
(ADD '(← (NOT ( = ?X ?Y))
          (LISP (COND) ((NOT (RETRIEVE   |"(= @?X @?Y)))
                        (SUCCEED)) ))))

(ADD '( = ?X ?X))
```

If we try (RETRIEVE '(NOT (= A B))), this rule enables us to succeed, if (= A B) is not in the data base. [The rule will block the success of (RETRIEVE '(NOT (= A A))).] Suppose, however that (= A B) is added to the data base later. Now the conclusion is no longer legitimate, but deductions may already have been made from it.

Exercise 16.5 Assuming the mechanisms of Exercise 16.2 have been implemented, what will the support for (NOT (= A B)) be after execution of (FOR-EACH-ANSWER (NOT (= A B)) (ADD '(NOT (= A B))))?

This kind of deduction of a formula from the inability to deduce something else is called *non-monotonic*. It is quite common in AI applications. It is often called "default reasoning," from the common case where something is true of almost all of a class of objects. For example, we have

```
(ADD '(← (CAN-FLY ?X)
          (LISP (FOR-EACH-ANSWER (IS ?X BIRD)
                  (COND ((NOT (RETRIEVE
                                '(NOT (CAN-FLY ?X))))
                         (NOTE)) )))))
```

which expresses the rule, *Every bird can fly, unless you can prove otherwise.*

In spite of its ubiquity, non-monotonic reasoning is somewhat suspect. For one thing, its theoretical foundations are still being elaborated (see McDermott & Doyle, 1978). But even from a practical point of view, programs that do this kind of reasoning tend not to be very robust, because they are so prone to timing errors of the kind we alluded to; a program's conclusions can be invalidated without the program ever realizing it.

In this section, we describe a system for avoiding this problem, a *non-monotonic data-dependency system*. The basic idea is to allow the *absence* of a molecule to justify the presence of another molecule. This means that ADDing a formula can cause formulas to be erased, and ERASing a formula can cause formulas to be added.

In order to do this, we have to undertake a significant departure from our practice so far. Up to now, a formula's being in the index has been equivalent to its being accepted by the program. But, if we are to attach data-dependency links to "absent" molecules, we must have molecules in the index that are not actually "believed;" that is, we must allow molecules with status OUT to remain in the index after garbage collection. (RETRIEVE must be changed to ignore OUT molecules.)

The format of justifications must also change. So far, they have been treated just as lists of molecules, but now we must give them the definition

(RECORD-TYPE JUST (IN-JUSTIFIERS OUT-JUSTIFIERS))

The intended meaning is that the justification is satisfied if all the in-justifiers are IN and all the out-justifiers are OUT. If a molecule P depends on another molecule Q being OUT, we will say P depends on OUT Q.

Thinking about non-monotonic dependency systems can be bewildering. The source of the confusion is, as before, the possibility of circularities, but now the circularities can involve "out" molecules. For example, we could have two conflicting items, such as (LIVING FRED) and (DEAD FRED), whose dependency markers indicate that the IN-ness of each depends on the OUT-ness of the other. With monotonic data dependencies, the proper response to an isolated circularity is always to toss every molecule involved OUT, but this is not possible for FRED: As soon as the system picks one of his formulas to be OUT, the other will come IN. This is intuitively correct, since it means the system will pick one of the formulas involved as an "assumption," at least until further evidence accumulates that gives independent support to one or the other. In general, an *assumption* is a formula that has at least one OUT supporter.

Amazingly enough, in spite of these new phenomena, we use almost exactly the same data-base maintenance algorithm as before. The heart of the algorithm is the same "tentative mark and sweep" procedure. The differences lie solely in the handling of justifications. The code is shown in Fig. 16.4. There are two changes in the MOLEC data type. The MOLEC constructor

```
(RECORD-TYPE MOLEC (PAT STATUS SUPPORTERS
                   JUSTIFICATIONS JUSTIFICANDS
                   PENDING-CHAINS))
(DE MOLEC (PAT) (LIST 'MOLEC PAT ' OUT NIL NIL NIL NIL)   )

(RECORD-TYPE PENDING-CHAIN NIL (JUSTIFICATION PAT)   )

(RECORD-TYPE JUST (IN-JUSTIFIERS OUT-JUSTIFIERS))

(DE ADD (PAT JUST)
   (LET (M (UNIQUIFY PAT))
       (DD-INSTALL JUST M)
       (COND ((JUSTIFICATION-SATISFIED JUST)
              (DBGC M))
             (T (ASSIGN-TENTATIVE-STATUS M))   )
       M  ))

(DE ERASE (PAT JUST)
   (LET (M (UNIQUIFY PAT) OLD-JUST NIL)
       (COND ((:= OLD-JUST
                (CAR (SOME '(LAMBDA (J)
                               (EQUIV-JUST JUST J)   )
                            (JUSTIFICATIONS:MOLEC M))))
              (DD-ERASE OLD-JUST M)
              (COND  ((JUSTIFICATION-SATISFIED JUST)
                      (DBGC M))
                     (T (ASSIGN-TENTATIVE-STATUS M))  )   )
       M  ))

(DE UNIQUIFY (PAT)
   (LET  (FOUND
            (SOME '(LAMBDA (M) (VARIANTS PAT (PAT:MOLEC M))   )
                   (FETCH-VARIANT PAT)))
       (COND  (FOUND (CAR FOUND))
              ((LET (NEW-MOLEC (INDEX PAT)
                     IMPLPAT  |"(→ @PAT ?RIGHT))
                 (FOR (IMPL IN (FETCH IMPLPAT))
                    (DO (FOR (SUB IN
                               (UNIFY IMPLPAT
                                    (VARS-RENAME (PAT:MOLEC IMPL))))
                       (DO (:= (PENDING-CHAINS:MOLEC NEW-MOLEC)
                               (CONS (PENDING-CHAIN
                                        (JUST  (LIST NEW-MOLEC IMPL)
                                           NIL)
                                        (PCVAR-VAL '?RIGHT SUB))
                                 *-*)))  )))
                 NEW-MOLEC))  )))
```

FIG. 16.4a. Non-monotonic ADD and ERASE.

203

```
(DECLARE (SPECIAL *POSSIBLE-CHAINS*))

(DE DBGC (M)
   (LET (*POSSIBLE-CHAINS* NIL)
      (MOLECS-CLOBBER-STATUS M 0)
      (MOLECS-ASSIGN-STATUS M 0)
      (FOR (M IN *POSSIBLE-CHAINS*)
         (WHEN (EQ (STATUS:MOLEC M) 'IN))
         (DO (LET (PCS (PENDING-CHAINS:MOLEC M))
            (:= (PENDING-CHAINS:MOLEC M) NIL)
            (FOR (PC IN PCS)
               (DO (TRY-PENDING-CHAIN PC]

(DE TRY-PENDING-CHAIN (PC)
   (LET (BLOCKED (SOME '(LAMBDA (J)
                     (EQ (STATUS:MOLEC J) 'OUT))
                  (JUSTIFICATION:PENDING-CHAIN PC)))
      (COND (BLOCKED
               (:= (PENDING-CHAINS:MOLEC (CAR BLOCKED))
                  (CONS PC *—*)))
            (T (ADD   (PAT:PENDING-CHAIN PC)
                  (JUSTIFICATION:PENDING-CHAIN PC)))   )))

(DE MOLECS-ASSIGN-STATUS (M LEVEL)
   (COND   ((EQUAL (STATUS:MOLEC M) LEVEL)
            [COND ((EQ (ASSIGN-TENTATIVE-STATUS M) 'IN)
                  (COND ((PENDING-CHAINS:MOLEC M)
                     (:= *POSSIBLE-CHAINS* (CONS M *—*)))   )
               (LET (SUPPORTEES (SUPPORTEES:MOLEC M))
                  (FOR (S IN SUPPORTEES)
                     (DO (MOLECS-CLOBBER-STATUS S (ADD1 LEVEL)))   )
                  (FOR (S IN SUPPORTEES)
                     (DO (MOLECS-ASSIGN-STATUS S (ADD1 LEVEL]
               (FOR (S IN (JUSTIFICANDS:MOLEC M))
                  (DO (MOLECS-ASSIGN-STATUS S LEVEL))   ))   ))
```

FIG. 16.4b.   Non-monotonic data-dependency system.

initially makes molecules OUT, since, as we will show, it is up to the data-dependency system to bring them IN. The other change is the addition of a "PENDING-CHAINS" slot; we will describe this shortly.

Now both ADD and ERASE must do data-dependency manipulations. In fact, they can call the same function, DBGC, for "data-base garbage collector." DBGC does just what ERASE used to do: mark possibly affected molecules and then reassign statuses. MOLECS-CLOBBER-STATUS is exactly the same as before. MOLECS-ASSIGN-STATUS is almost the same. (We will describe shortly the manipulations by DBGC and MOLECS-ASSIGN-STATUS of the list *POSSIBLE-CHAINS*.)

```
(DE ASSIGN-TENTATIVE-STATUS (M)
    (LET (SUPPS (SOME  'JUSTIFICATION-SATISFIED
                         (JUSTIFICATIONS:MOLEC M)))
       (COND  (SUPPS
                   (:= (SUPPORTERS:MOLEC M)
                       (APPEND (IN-JUSTIFIERS:JUST (CAR SUPPS))
                               (OUT-JUSTIFIERS:JUST (CAR SUPPS))))
                   (:= (STATUS:MOLEC M) 'IN)
                   'IN)
              (T
                   (:= (SUPPORTERS:MOLEC M)
                       (FOR (J IN (JUSTIFICATIONS:MOLEC M))
                          (SAVE
                             (OR (CAR (SOME  '(LAMBDA (IN-M)
                                                (NOT (EQ  (STATUS:MOLEC IN-M)
                                                          'IN))  )
                                              (IN-JUSTIFIERS:JUST J)))
                                 (CAR (SOME  '(LAMBDA (OUT-M)
                                                (EQ (STATUS:MOLEC OUT-M)
                                                    'IN)  )
                                              (OUT-JUSTIFIERS:JUST J)))))  ))
                   (:= (STATUS:MOLEC M) 'OUT)
                   'OUT)  )))
```

~New versions of
~DD-INSTALL, DD-ERASE, JUSTIFICATION-SATISFIED and EQUIV-JUST
~are not shown (see Exercise 16.7).

FIG. 16.4c.   Low-level functions for Fig. 16.4b.

The major change is in ASSIGN-TENTATIVE-STATUS; if the molecule is made OUT, its SUPPORTERS are set to an arbitrarily chosen set of molecules whose statuses are a sufficient reason for the molecule to be OUT. This list will include a non-IN molecule that should be IN or an IN molecule that should be OUT from each justification. So whether a molecule is IN or OUT, its SUPPORTERS will be a set of molecules that are responsible for its status. (Notice that ADD and ERASE check to see whether the justification they are given is satisfied. If it isn't, no molecule can change status as a result of installing or erasing the justification, so it is not necessary to call DBGC. But the SUPPORTERS of the affected molecule can change, if the molecule is OUT; the calls to ASSIGN-TENTATIVE-STATUS are necessary to keep the SUPPORTERS accurate in this case.)

Exercise 16.6   Explain why ASSIGN-TENTATIVE-STATUS, in selecting a SUPPORTER from each invalid justification, looks for an IN out-justifier but is satisfied with a non-IN in-justifier. (*Hint:* It doesn't make any difference except during data base garbage collection.)

Exercise 16.7 Write the new versions of DD-INSTALL, DD-ERASE, JUSTIFICATION-SATISFIED, and EQUIV-JUST to handle the new form of justification. (*Warning:* JUSTIFICATION-SATISFIED must check for IN-ness of in-justifiers but only non-IN-ness of out-justifiers. Do you see why?)

DBGC is rather unusual among the programs we give in this book, in that it is not obviously correct. The most suspicious code is the calls to MOLECS-ASSIGN-STATUS to correct molecule statuses base on the improper assumption of the OUTness of non-IN justifiers. It looks like these calls might wipe out everything that has been done so far and plunge the program into an infinite loop. You may take it on faith that this won't happen or check Section 16.7 for an informal proof that it happens only in pathological cases.

The data-dependency system proper is not very different from what we had before. What is quite different is the way chaining is done. Under the old regime, an ADD definitely added its argument to the data base and could chain from it immediately. Under the new regime, a molecule may not be made IN for some time after it is indexed, because its first justification may be unsatisfied. In fact, it can happen that some LISP program calls ERASE to remove a justification before a molecule has ever been indexed; this will cause it to be indexed, with no chance of its being IN. So chaining must be divorced from indexing. A little thought should convince you that a forward chain must wait to be carried out until the first time that all the molecules justifying it are IN.

This is implemented by code in UNIQUIFY, DBGC, and MOLECS-ASSIGN-STATUS. UNIQUIFY finds the → formulas that can be used for forward chaining but does not actually do the chaining. Instead, it saves what it finds in a new slot in the MOLEC data type: the PENDING-CHAINS slot. This slot points to a list of structures of type PENDING-CHAIN, which encode forward chainings that cannot be done until the MOLEC comes IN. This event is detected by DBGC, in cooperation wtih MOLECS-ASSIGN-STATUS. When MOLECS-ASSIGN-STATUS notices that a molecule with pending chains might be brought IN, it puts it on the list *POSSIBLE-CHAINS*. When DBGC is done with its status manipulations, it calls TRY-PENDING-CHAIN on each saved possible chain. If this function is given a pending chain whose justifiers are all IN, it (finally!) calls ADD to do the chaining. But it can happen that another justifier has gone OUT, so the chaining is not possible after all. In this case, TRY-PENDING-CHAIN picks one of the OUT justifiers that is blocking the chain and hangs the pending chain off this molecule; when it eventually comes in, the chain will be tried again.

An example will make this process clearer. Say that the data base contains the molecule M1 with pattern (→ *P Q*) and that the molecule M2 with pattern *P* is indexed (but not IN'ed). UNIQUIFY will add the PENDING-CHAIN

$((M1\ M2)\ Q)$

to M2's list. Now if M1 goes OUT, and M2 comes IN, DBGC will try to discharge M2's pending chains. It will fail on this one, because M1 is OUT. So it just transfers this PENDING-CHAIN to M1's list. If M1 comes IN again before M2 goes OUT, the conclusion Q will finally be ADDed. (It is conceivable, but unlikely, that this pending chain will be passed back and forth between M1 and M2 forever without ever getting done!)

A desirable property of a data-base system is that it be *order invariant*, in the sense that its contents and data dependencies depend only on the premises in effect at any time and not the sequence of ADDs and ERASEs responsible for them. The system we have shown so far is not order invariant, since Q will be derived as a consequence of P and $(\rightarrow P\ Q)$ only if the $\rightarrow$ formula comes in first. One way to get around this particular source of order dependence is to have UNIQUIFY treat $\rightarrow$ formulas specially; when it finds one, it could set up a possible chain for each indexed formula that unifies with the left-hand side.

Exercise 16.8 Implement this code. It should require a change only to UNIQUIFY.

Exercise 16.9 Notice that ERASE now never unindexes anything. The reason is because even an OUT molecule can be involved in dependencies. This is a bit too conservative, since under some circumstances a molecule and its justificands can be removed. What are they? Change ERASE (and MOLECS-ASSIGN-STATUS) to unindex when these circumstances arise. (*Hint:* At least order invariance is required.)

The flavor of our data-base management system has changed considerably. The new version reflects a commitment to view the data base as gradually converging on a correct model of some situation, as more dependency information comes into view. Alternative parts of the model shift in and out of favor as assumptions change. Since the system is order invariant, all the possible inferential consequences of a formula can be found once, when it becomes IN for the first time.

This interpretation makes sense for the code we have shown so far. But we haven't discussed how to implement "demons" of the sort we described in Chapter 13, programs of the form

$(\rightarrow\ pattern\ (\text{LISP}\ body))$

triggered during forward chaining. The problem with demons is that the LISP code may do more than set up a dependency structure. For example, a problem solver might require the predicate (SHOULD-DO *action*), which is interpreted by demons like

```
(→ (SHOULD-DO (GRASP ?OBJECT))
   (LISP  (MOVE-ROBOT-ARM (COORDS ?OBJECT))
          (GRASP)))
```

where MOVE-ROBOT-ARM and GRASP actually cause a physical arm to move. It is clear that it is insufficient to call this code just the first time (SHOULD-DO (GRASP BLOCK1)) is ADDed.

There are two approaches to this issue. One is to forbid demon code to do anything but set up new dependency structures, with the constraint that it set up the same dependency structures no matter when it is called; the fact that they might be OUT when set up is irrelevant. This is the tack taken by the AMORD group at MIT (de Kleer et al., 1977a, b). A little thought will show that this is a substantial commitment. For example, demons are no longer allowed to call RETRIEVE or FOR-EACH-ANSWER, because what is retrieved depends strongly on what is IN. (In fact, AMORD accomplishes retrieval in an ingenious way that involves constructing order-invariant dependency structures among requests.) Adopting this approach means that a formula like (SHOULD-DO *action*) must be interpreted by an outside module that reads the data base when it is in equilibrium.

The other approach is to separate demon calls from ordinary forward chaining, creating two kinds of "demons," (IF-ADDED *pat lisp-code*) and (IF-ERASED *pat lisp-code*), in addition to ordinary → formulas. These demons are called by DBGC whenever a molecule changes status.

Exercise 16.10 Implement this scheme. It will require having MOLECS-CLOBBER-STATUS return a list of all molecules whose status might change and having DBGC examine this list to decide what demons to run. You should also make TRY-PENDING-CHAIN handle conclusions of the form (LISP *code*), to allow the user to run order-invariant code in the usual way.

16.5   APPLICATIONS OF DATA DEPENDENCIES

In this section, we describe four things to do with data dependencies: finding proofs, generating explanations, tracking down wrong assumptions, and representing time.

16.5.1 Finding Proofs Of Things

In Chapter 13, we showed how to prove an implication by assuming the antecedent and proving the consequent. This idea is basically good, but there are two problems. First, we used a trick there that we can't use with an indexed data base; namely, rebinding *DATA-BASE* temporarily. (This won't work any more, because INDEX changes the structure of the index.)

Second, the simple version we gave does not return proofs of implications (see Exercise 16.2). At best, it would return a proof of the consequent, including the antecedent.

The problem is solved with data dependencies, if we make one little addition. We can no longer just rebind *DATA-BASE*, but we can now erase. The solution is shown in Fig. 16.5. The program (FINDINDEP *q 1*)

```
(← (IMPLIES ?P ?Q)
    (LISP  (ADD ?P (JUST NIL NIL))
           (FOR-EACH-ANSWER (RETRIEVE ?Q)
               (:= (JUSTIFICATION:ANSWER *ANSWER*)
                   (FINDINDEP ?Q (LIST ?P)))
               (NOTE)    )
           (ERASE ?P (JUST NIL NIL))  ))
```

FIG. 16.5. Implication prover.

returns a new justification, which consists of all the data that ultimately support *q* but are neither elements of *1* nor supported by any element of *1* (i.e., it "FINDs INDEPendent" support). For example, in trying to prove (IMPLIES (IS FRED PROFESSOR) (POOR FRED)) (see Chapter 13), the program would ADD (IS FRED PROFESSOR) and RETRIEVE (POOR FRED) with justifiers:

(PAY FRED LOW)
(← (POOR ?X) (PAY ?X LOW))

But the first of these justifiers itself depends on (IS FRED PROFESSOR) and (→ (IS ?X PROFESSOR) (PAY ?X LOW)). So FINDINDEP must return just the two implications.

Exercise 16.11 Write (FINDINDEP *q 1*). The best way to do this involves adding a MARK field to the MOLEC data type. Then mark from the elements of *1* (a la MOLECS-CLOBBER-STATUS), until all their supportees are marked. Now sweep backward from *q* (i.e., through the   SUPPORTERS:MOLEC links), collecting molecules whose marks indicate that they are not elements of *1* and are not supported by any element of *1*. Don't forget to clean up the marks. (*Hint:* You need only one mark field, but you will need several possible flags to encode how and when a molecule was marked.)

In the version of RETRIEVE we developed in Chapter 13 and modified in Exercise 16.2, no out-justifiers are ever set up. An elegant way to provide for out-justifiers is to implement the predicate CONSISTENT, such that (CONSISTENT *p*) is true only if (NOT *p*) is not provable. For example, we could then write

```
(ADD '(← (PHD ?X)
          (AND (IS ?X PROFESSOR)
               (CONSISTENT (PHD ?X)))))
```

The code for proving CONSISTENT formulas is as shown in Fig. 16.6. The program checks to see if (CONSISTENT ?P) has already been added to the data base; if so, it will already have been seen by RETRIEVE. Otherwise, it checks to see if (NOT ?P) can be proved; if not, it adds (CONSISTENT ?P), supported by (NOT ?P) being OUT. (We are assuming here that ADD's second argument defaults to the justification of *ANSWER*, as described in Exercise 16.2.)

```
(← (CONSISTENT ?P)
   (LISP (LET (CMOLEC (UNIQUIFY |"(CONSISTENT @?P)))
         (COND ((AND (NOT (EQ (STATUS:MOLEC CMOLEC) 'IN))
                     (NOT (RETRIEVE |"(NOT @?P))))
                (LET (NOT-MOLEC (UNIQUIFY |"(NOT @?P)))
                     (:= (OUT-JUSTIFIERS:JUST
                               (JUSTIFICATION:ANSWER *ANSWER*))
                         (LIST NOT-MOLEC))
                     (ADD |"(CONSISTENT @?P))
                     (SUCCEED)   ))   ))))
```

FIG. 16.6.   Proving (CONSISTENT p).

Exercise 16.12   Revise the code you developed for Exercise 16.2 so that it handles justifications with out-justifiers (This should be a very small change!)

Exercise 16.13   (Very difficult) Notice that the CONSISTENT code will do weird things if ?P contains variables. For example, the request (CONSISTENT (ON ?X TABLE)) presumably means, "Find things that could be on the table." But the given code will suceed only if it can't show that something is not on the table. So even if (ON A TABLE) is consistent, the presence of (NOT (ON B TABLE)) will prevent the binding ?X = A from being returned. (If you solve this problem, please mail the solution to the authors, since you will have helped prove the completeness of non-monotonic predicate calculus.)

16.5.2 Generating Explanations

People can find large AI programs baffling and intimidating if the programs are incapable of explaining their actions. For example, doctors would be reluctant to follow the unexplained advice of a program on what drugs to prescribe. (It might be different if the patient was willing to sue the machine for malpractice!) Often explanation capabilities are neglected in developing a program, since having to think about them is distracting. One advantage of a system organized around data dependencies is that the information needed for explanation is gathered in the normal course of events.

The idea is that an explanation is most naturally thought of as a "proof," the set of formulas whose presence or absence supports the presence of the datum to be explained. For example, if the rule

```
(← (HAS PATIENT APPENDICITIS)
    (AND (PAIN ?PATIENT RIGHT-SIDE)
         (CONSISTENT
           (NOT (HAS ?PATIENT INDIGESTION)))))
```

is known to the system, one explanation for why the system thinks Fred has appendicitis would be "Fred has pain in the right side and apparently does not have indigestion."

Exercise 16.14 Write a function (EXPLAIN *pat*) that prints out explanations like this. Supply a feature to allow the user to ask for further explanations of the things dumped out without having to type them. For example, we might have

```
~Person's inputs flagged by *
  *(EXPLAIN '(HAS FRED APPENDICITIS))
Explanation:
  (1) (PAIN FRED RIGHT-SIDE)
  (2) No evidence for (HAS FRED INDIGESTION)
  (3) (← (HAS ?PATIENT APPENDICITIS) ... )
Do you wish further explanation? *(1)
Explanation:
  (1 1) (SAYS WELBY (PAIN FRED RIGHT-SIDE))
  (1 2) (RELIABLE WELBY)
Do you wish further explanation? *(3)
Full text:
(← (HAS ?PATIENT APPENDICITIS)
   (AND (PAIN ?PATIENT RIGHT-SIDE)
        (CONSISTENT (NOT (HAS ?PATIENT INDIGESTION)))))
This is a premiss.
Do you wish further explanation? *NIL
DONE
```

Exercise 16.15 Augment the explanation program to explain outputs like "No evidence for (HAS FRED INDIGESTION)." This requires explaining why each possible justification of an OUT formula is invalid. It also requires finding rules in the data base that could have been used to infer (HAS FRED INDIGESTION) and printing out these rules, along with an explanation of why they failed.

The idea of using dependencies for explanation has been applied by Davis (1976) and Stallman and Sussman (1977).

16.5.3 Dependency-Directed Backtracking

One of the most important uses of data dependencies is to debug the data base when trouble is encountered. This can occur when the user makes an assumption that leads to a contradiction. The solution is to get rid of the assumptions that are causing the trouble. This requires tracing back through the dependencies from the contradiction to the assumptions supporting it and then taking action to remove them.

Recall that an *assumption* is a molecule supported by at least one OUT molecule. The intent is that the assumption will be believed until one of its OUT supporters comes IN. For example, in Subsection 16.5.2, the molecule (HAS FRED APPENDICITIS) was an assumption, based on the absence of evidence that FRED has indigestion.

So when a contradiction is found, we must pick a relevant assumption and shove it OUT by making one of its OUT supporters IN. The general problem of how to pick the right assumption to flush is unsolved. The decision might be based on such factors as a priori probabilities or the relative expense of data-base garbage collection. (For example, someone who believes in the Ptolemaic cosmology might be more willing to doubt a single experimental observation that contradicts his system than to throw away the entire system.) In some cases, it doesn't matter which assumption is eliminated. This happens when any consistent data-base configuration will do, a situation that could arise in solving logical puzzles, doing proof by contradiction, or analyzing nonlinear physical systems by assuming different states for the components (Stallman & Sussman, 1977). In cases like these, the worst that can happen from picking the wrong assumption to remove is that the program can take a little longer to arrive at a consistent state. We will assume that this is the situation.

The assumption picked to be flushed, called the *culprit*, is removed by bringing another molecule IN. The only way to make a molecule IN is to add a data dependency to it. We coud just make it a premiss by adding an empty justification to it, but this is too optimistic. It may later turn out (when another contradiction occurs) that we picked the wrong assumption, and we will have to change our mind. For example, consider the dependency network shown in Fig. 16.7. The contradiction depends on two assumptions: that Fred has appendicitis and that Fred has no appendix. If we pick (HAS FRED INDIGESTION) to support, it may be that other rules [such as (→ (INGESTED-A ?X TUMS) (NOT (HAS ?X INDIGESTION)))] will enable us to derive another contradiction later, and this one will be unremovable. So we must be more careful in our choice of justifications.

The solution is to justify the molecule with a data dependency that expresses the following idea: Any time the molecules that caused the contradiction are IN, and all the other OUT supporters of the culprit are

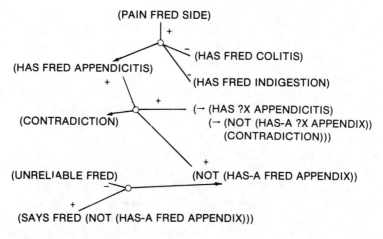

FIG. 16.7. Contradictory assumptions.

OUT, then the chosen OUT supporter must be IN. In Fig. 16.7, we can add a dependency that supports (HAS FRED INDIGESTION) based on (NOT (HAS-A FRED APPENDIX)) and

(→ (HAS ?X APPENDICITIS)
   (→ (NOT (HAS-A ?X APPENDIX)) (CONTRADICTION)))

being IN and (HAS FRED COLITIS) being OUT. This means that (HAS FRED INDIGESTION) is ultimately based on assumptions, which can be removed if we later deduce a contradiction from it. The result is shown in Fig. 16.8.

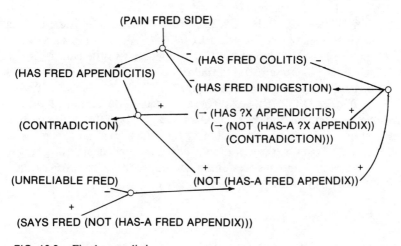

FIG. 16.8. Fixed contradiction.

Another way to look at this is to see it as a proof by contradiction of the newly IN formula. In this case, we have proved that (NOT (HAS-A FRED APPENDIX)) and OUT (HAS FRED COLITIS) imply (HAS FRED INDIGESTION), which a little reflection will show is a sound conclusion.

Exercise 16.16 Explain what should happen now if further dependencies are added that link (HAS FRED INDIGESTION) to a contradiction (i.e., what assumptions will be at fault, and what can be done to eliminate one of them?).

The code to handle contradictions is shown in Fig. 16.9. We have had to redefine MOLEC slightly to include a mark field for use in tracing dependencies. We have redefined DBGC to keep a special variable *CONTRADICTIONS* that is a list of contradictions that have come IN.

Exercise 16.17 Rewrite MOLECS-ASSIGN-STATUS to add potentially dangerous contradictions to the list *CONTRADICTIONS*.

If DBGC finds a contradiction, it calls FIX-CONTRA to get rid of it. FIX-CONTRA finds the assumptions that support the contradiction, by calling SUPPORTING-ASSUMPTIONS. This subroutine finds assumptions by marking backward from the contradiction through IN molecules until an assumption is found. The program MARK-ASSUMPTIONS that does this distinguishes between "recent" and "old" assumptions. A recent assumption is one that supports the contradiction without any intervening assumptions. The program returns only recent assumptions, to avoid making large changes in the data base unnecessarily. It does this by marking an assumption OLD if it has been reached through another assumption. (UNMARK-ASSUMPTIONS just cleans up the marks.)

SUPPORTING-ASSUMPTIONS returns all the RECENT assumptions found by MARK-ASSUMPTIONS. FIX-CONTRA then creates a new data dependency to bring IN one of the OUT supporters of the culprit. It calls FINDINDEP (see Exercise 16.11) to find the molecules that were responsible for making the assumptions contradictory. In Fig. 16.7, this would find (→ (HAS ?X APPENDICITIS) ...). These molecules are combined with the remaining assumptions and the other OUT supporters of the culprit to make a new justification. ADDing this will bring the culprit OUT and get rid of the contradiction. (Actually, the culprit may have independent support, or there may be unforeseen consequences of the new dependency, so further calls to FIX-CONTRA from ADD may be necessary.)

16.5.4 Representing Time

So far, our data bases have been used to represent only static facts. In many applications, it is necessary to represent several different situations and the

```
(RECORD-TYPE MOLEC
                (PAT STATUS MARK SUPPORTERS JUSTIFICATIONS JUSTIFICANDS))
(DE MOLEC (PAT)
   (LIST 'MOLEC PAT 'OUT NIL NIL NIL NIL)   )


(DECLARE (SPECIAL *CONTRADICTIONS* *POSSIBLE-CHAINS*))

(DE DBGC (M)
   (LET (*CONTRADICTIONS* NIL *POSSIBLE-CHAINS* NIL)
      (MOLECS-CLOBBER-STATUS M 0)
      (MOLECS-ASSIGN-STATUS M 0)
      (FOR (C IN *CONTRADICTIONS*)
         (WHEN (EQ (STATUS:MOLEC C) 'IN))
         (DO (FIX-CONTRA C))   )
      (FOR (M IN *POSSIBLE-CHAINS*)
         (WHEN (EQ (STATUS:MOLEC M) 'IN))
         (DO (LET (PCS (PENDING-CHAINS:MOLEC M))
               (:= (PENDING-CHAINS:MOLEC M) NIL)
               (FOR (PC IN PCS)
                  (DO (TRY-PENDING-CHAIN PC]

~MOLECS-ASSIGN-STATUS must be changed to set *CONTRADICTIONS*

~
(DE FIX-CONTRA (CONTRA)
   (LET (ASSUMPTIONS (SUPPORTING-ASSUMPTIONS CONTRA) CULPRIT NIL)
      (COND ((NULL ASSUMPTIONS)
               (ERROR '"Unfixable contradiction"))   )
      (:= CULPRIT (CAR ASSUMPTIONS))
      (LET    (J (FINDINDEP CONTRA ASSUMPTIONS)
               OUT-CULPRIT-SUPPORTERS
               (FOR (M IN (SUPPORTERS:MOLEC CULPRIT))
                  (WHEN (EQ (STATUS:MOLEC M) 'OUT))
                  (SAVE M)    ))
~The first assumption is picked to be the "culprit." Its first
~OUT supporter is made IN by the following ADD, supported by all the
~the other assumptions, the rules (in J) that made the assumptions
~contradictory, and the OUT-ness of the other OUT supporters of the
~culprit. This ADD will trigger a new data-base garbage collection,
~leading to harmony or recursive backtracking calls.
               (ADD (PAT:MOLEC (CAR OUT-CULPRIT-SUPPORTERS))
                  (JUST (APPEND (IN-JUSTIFIERS:JUST J)
                           (CDR ASSUMPTIONS))
                     (APPEND (OUT-JUSTIFIERS:JUST J)
                           (CDR OUT-CULPRIT-SUPPORTERS))))   )))
```

FIG. 16.9a.   Dependency-directed backtracker.

```
(DE SUPPORTING-ASSUMPTIONS (M)
   (PROG1 (FOR (A IN (MARK-ASSUMPTIONS M 'RECENT))
            (WHEN (EQ (MARK:MOLEC A) 'RECENT))
            (SAVE A)      )
      (UNMARK-ASSUMPTIONS M))   )

(DE MARK-ASSUMPTIONS (M MARK)
   (COND ((EQ (STATUS:MOLEC M) 'OUT) NIL)
         ((EQ (MARK:MOLEC M) 'OLD) NIL
         ((NOT (EQ (MARK:MOLEC M) MARK))
         (:= (MARK:MOLEC M) MARK)
         (LET (SUPPORTERS (SUPPORTERS:MOLEC M))
            (COND ((AND  (EQ MARK 'RECENT)
                     (SOME '(LAMBDA (S)
                              (EQ (STATUS:MOLEC S) 'OUT)   )
                        SUPPORTERS))
                  (CONS M (MARKEM SUPPORTERS 'OLD)))
                  (T (MARKEM SUPPORTERS MARK))  )))  ))

(DE MARKEM (MOLECS MARK)
   (FOR (M IN MOLECS)
      (SPLICE (MARK-ASSUMPTIONS M MARK))   ))

(DE UNMARK-ASSUMPTIONS (M)
   (COND ((MARK:MOLEC M)
         (:= (MARK:MOLEC M) NIL)
         (COND  ((EQ (STATUS:MOLEC M) 'IN)
               (FOR (S IN (SUPPORTERS:MOLEC M))
                  (DO (UNMARK-ASSUMPTIONS S))  ))  ))  ))
```

FIG. 16.9b.   Assumption finder for backtracker.

transitions among them. A complete solution to this problem has not been
found, but there are some techniques for solving it in special cases.

Data dependencies can provide one such technique. The idea is to represent
a sequence of situations by a set of terms *sit0, sit1,* .... There is one situation,
the current situation, for which the formula

(PRESENT *current-sit*)

is IN. For each situation, the formula (PAST *sit*) means the situation is in the
past. Situations fall into sequences through time. If a situation *I* precedes
situation *J*, then (PAST *sitI*) is IN if (PRESENT *sitJ*) or (PAST *sitJ*) is IN.
(This is done with two dependencies, of course.)

For each molecule whose pattern expresses a fact whose truth value varies
with time, we create two extra molecules representing the beginning and the
end of its period of validity. For example, the fact (IN BLOCK1 BOX1)
would depend on IN (BEGIN (IN BLOCK1 BOX1)) and OUT (END (IN
BLOCK1 BOX1)). To express the fact that (IN BLOCK1 BOX1) is true

from situation 2 through situation 7, we simply create two data dependencies, one to make (BEGIN (IN BLOCK1 BOX1)) depend on IN (PAST *sit1*) and one to make (END (IN BLOCK1 BOX1)) depend on IN (PAST *sit7*).

This notation allows us to talk about the effects of actions on the world model. For example, the action PUTIN moves a block from one box to another. Whenever someone does a PUTIN, a new situation is created. We can model this by a program that simulates a PUTIN (i.e., changes the PRESENT situation to a new situation that obtains after a PUTIN). The program is shown in Fig. 16.10. The first item in this figure are a set of macros for building justifications. (IN: *pat pat*... OUT: *pat*...) is the same as

$$\text{(JUST (LIST (UNIQUIFY } pat\text{) (UNIQUIFY } pat\text{)}...\text{)}$$
$$\text{(LIST (UNIQUIFY } pat\text{)}...\text{))}.$$

(PREMISS) is the same as (JUST NIL NIL). The function DO-PUTIN then sets up all the appropriate dependencies, and changes the current situation.

> *Exercise 16.18* Generalize DO-PUTIN to (DO-ACTION *act*). This function must find the side effects of *act* by RETRIEVing the patterns (ADDS *act* ?WHAT) and (DELETES *act* ?WHAT). For example, PUTIN's effects could be defined by
>
> (ADDS (PUTIN ?X ?Y) (IN ?X ?Y))
> (← (DELETES (PUTIN ?X ?Y) (IN ?X ?Z))
> (IN ?X ?Z))

```
(DM IN: (L) (MAKE-JUST L))
(DM OUT: (L) (MAKE-JUST L))
(DM PREMISS (L) '(JUST NIL NIL))

~Allows you to write justification in form (IN: -ins- OUT: -outs-)
~or (OUT: -outs-).
(DE MAKE-JUST (L)
    (LET (HASINS (MEMQ 'IN: L)
          HASOUTS (MEMQ 'OUT: L)
          INS NIL OUTS NIL)
      (:= INS (LOPOFF (CDR HASINS) HASOUTS))
      (:= OUTS (LOPOFF (CDR HASOUTS) HASINS))
      |~(JUST (LIST . @(UNIQUIFY-CALLS INS))
             (LIST . @(UNIQUIFY-CALLS OUTS)))  ))

~All elements of L1 up to beginning of L2.
(DE LOPOFF (L1 L2)
    (COND ((OR (NULL L1) (EQ L1 L2)) NIL)
          ((CONS (CAR L1) (LOPOFF (CDR L1) L2)))  ))
```

FIG. 16.10. Updating situation after an action.

```
(DE UNIQUIFY-CALLS (FORMULA-EXPS)
   (FOR (F IN FORMULA-EXPS)
      (SAVE  |"(UNIQUIFY @F))  ))

(DE DO-PUTIN (BLK NEWBOX)
   (LET   (NEWSIT (GENSYM)
         CURRENTSIT NIL)
      (FOR-EACH-ANSWER (PRESENT ?CURRENTSIT)
         (:= CURRENTSIT ?CURRENTSIT)  )
~NEWSIT follows CURRENTSIT
      (PUT-AFTER CURRENTSIT NEWSIT)
~Get rid of old location of BLK
      (FOR (ANS IN (RETRIEVE  |"(IN @BLK ?OLDBOX)))
         (DO (LET (OLDBOX (PCVAR-VAL '?OLDBOX ANS))
               (END-ASSERTION  |"(IN @BLK @OLDBOX) CURRENTSIT)  )))
~Set up new location
      (BEGIN-ASSERTION  |"(IN @BLK @NEWBOX) CURRENTSIT)
~Make move to new situation
      (SWITCH-SIT CURRENTSIT NEWSIT)
      NEWSIT  ))

~Put SIT2 after SIT1
(DE PUT-AFTER (SIT1 SIT2)
   (ADD  |"(PAST @SIT1) (IN:  |"(PRESENT @SIT2)))
   (ADD  |"(PAST @SIT1) (IN:  |"(PAST @SIT2)))  )

~Indicate that F is true starting after SIT
(DE BEGIN-ASSERTION (F SIT)
   (ADD F (IN:  |"(BEGIN @F) OUT:  |"(END @F)))
   (ADD  |"(BEGIN @F) (IN:  |"(PAST @SIT)))  )

~Indicate that F ceases after SIT
(DE END-ASSERTION (F SIT)
   (ADD  |"(END @F) (IN:  |"(PAST @SIT)))  )

~Move to new situation
(DE SWITCH-SIT (CURRENTSIT NEWSIT)
   (ADD  |"(PRESENT @NEWSIT) (PREMISS))
   (ERASE  |"(PRESENT @CURRENTSIT) (PREMISS))  )
```

FIG. 16.10.   Continued.

One thing a time representation should allow is answering questions about times other than the present (e.g., "Was the block in the box yesterday?"). In this system, such requests are answered by ERASing (PRESENT *current-sit*) and ADDing (PRESENT *target-sit*), doing the appropriate retrieval, and restoring the data base. This will temporarily reconfigure the data base so that just the set of facts true at the target situation will be IN.

This process is efficient for reasonable-sized data bases, since switching the situation usually just requires OUTing one bunch of facts and INing another.

Exercise 16.19   Complete the following retrieval formula:

(← (DURING ?SIT ?P) (LISP...))

according to the idea just outlined.

Of course, this is not a complete solution to the problem of representing time. One thing it doesn't allow is the retrieval of the situations when a formula was true (i.e., in Exercise 16.19, ?SIT must be unified only with a constant). However, it may be useful in some applications, such as problem solving and story understanding, where an important problem is to update the data base to reflect the results of an event.

16.6   ADVICE ON USING DATA BASES

We have spent a lot of time in this book talking about data bases. (Chapters 11, 13, 14, 15, and 16 are devoted mainly to this topic.) You may have the impression that no AI program is complete without one. Actually, there are substantial costs to be paid for using a data base, so you should think carefully before incurring them.

We have looked at predicate-calculus data bases and the slot-and-filler type, but in this section we are a bit more general. A data base is any collection of data structures representing a set of facts, used by some other program in a disciplined way. The modules of the program interact with the data base via a module called the data base *manager*. They ask the manager to file away or erase facts and to answer queries (Fig. 16.11). For example, in our predicate-calculus data base, the manager consists of the routines ADD, ERASE, and RETRIEVE.

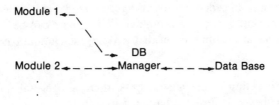

FIG. 16.11.   Program and data base.

There are substantial advantages to this method of writing programs:

1. If the data structures are robust enough, a wide variety of facts may be encoded in a single data base. This allows a certain freedom in planning the contents of the data base independently of the modules using it. (Of course, a

data base may use different data structures; sometimes a single fact may be encoded in more than one way to make different kinds of access efficient.)

2. The data base acts as a "blackboard" that all modules may write on and examine. This allows a wide communication channel (Lesser & Erman, 1977). In particular, routine inferences (i.e., those performed by the manager) may easily be made from facts "belonging" to different modules (McDermott 1977c).

3. Most important, it is very easy to change what the program knows by just adding or deleting facts from the data base. Such change can come about in several ways: Users can tell the system new things, the system can deduce new things, it can learn new things from experience, etc.

But there are real disadvantages as well:

1. It is inefficient to have to use a common data-structuring convention and transact all business through the manager. If a module wishes to record the single fact that it is a leap year, it takes less time and storage to have a Boolean variable LEAP-YEAR set to T than to keep

(= (CARDINALITY (DAYS THIS-YEAR)) 366)

or even

(LEAP-YEAR)

in the data base. In fact, every module will "cheat" on the data base to some extent and keep to itself all information that never has to be seen by another module.

2. If almost everything a program knows is kept in a single data base, then the data base can become very large. If your data base reaches a size where secondary storage is needed, then you have entered *terra incognita;* no one knows how efficient a large, random-access data base can be. On the other hand, few people are willing to bet that making such a data base efficient is impossible.

Even after deciding to use a data base, there are several further design considerations beyond those we have discussed:

1. Should the data base support simple retrieval or more complex deductions?
2. What should go into the data base?
3. Can everything be done in the data base, without bothering with external modules?

Allowing complex deductions has obvious and not so obvious costs. As we saw in Chapter 14 allowing variables slows down the tree searcher, and variables are needed in deductive rules. Above this level, the conjunctive request problem appears (as we discussed in Chapter 13). Of course, you get what you pay for; there is no way to do conjunctive requests cheaply. The problem is that the data-base users are shielded from the cost. Simple retrievals and all-day deductions are both calls to RETRIEVE. This can lead to hidden inefficiencies. On the other hand, in many cases there are general request optimizations that are better done once and for all in the manager.

A more subtle problem is that the possibility of deduction makes it harder to visualize the effects of data-base changes. For example, Sacerdoti's (1977) problem solver NOAH had to reason about goal conflicts to decide what order to do things in (see Chapter 18). It used a data base to represent the state of the world after each step of a plan. One type of goal conflict it looked for was a situation in which one plan step required the presence in the data base of a formula that some other step would delete. Of course, the complete contents of the data base after each step could not be calculated until the order of the plan steps was known, since the state of the world after an action can depend on what other actions have been taken. So NOAH had to rely on incomplete information about each step.

An example of the kind of goal conflict NOAH could resolve by reordering steps is the conflict that arises in planning to paint your ceiling and your ladder. In this case, the plan step "Paint ceiling" requires "Ladder available," and the step "Paint ladder" deletes "Ladder available." So the ceiling should be painted first.

Sacerdoti's program did not allow adds and deletes to cause further effects. This meant that it could, for each prerequisite, check for each plan step that might delete it; since all deletes had to be explicit, this could be done with a discrimination tree containing lists of the form (DELETES *step formula*).

In a data base with forward chaining and erasure propagation, this algorithm would not work. The problem is that the additions and deletions caused by a change in the status of an assertion depend on what else is in the data base. As we pointed out, what else is in the data base after a plan step depends on the (as yet unknown) order of all the plan steps. So Sacerdoti's simple look-ahead algorithm would miss some conflicts. (Unfortunately, the only known alternative is to try all possible orderings of steps.)

Issues like this come up repeatedly. For example, consider the use of "demons" to monitor some condition (see Charniak, 1972). A demon is a formula of the form

(IF-ADDED *pattern action*)

It is important to realize that such demons are practicable only for recognizing conditions that are explicitly added to the data base. If the *pattern* is merely deducible, there is no known efficient way to check for it. (Unless it happens that the rules for deducing it are all forward rules.) For example, the demon

   (IF-ADDED (MORTAL ?X) ...)

will not be triggered by

   (IS FRED MAN)

in the presence of the rule

   (← (MORTAL ?X) (IS ?X MAN))

The moral of these two examples is that two apparently independent features—deduction and efficient detection of assertions—interact strongly. If you implement deduction, you must make sure that every assertion to be detected will be deduced when it can be.

Our second issue, what should go into the data base?, may seem too obvious to need discussion. But there is a tendency to make hasty assumptions about the contents of a data base. For example, many people assume that the contents of a "predicate-calculus" data base must be at the level of Peano's axioms. In fact, the contents should reflect the theory the data base is implementing. If this is, say, a theory of how theorems are proved, the rules in the data base will be about proving theorems, in whatever formal notation and with whatever content the theory specifies. There might be a rule that says. "If you are trying to prove a theorem of the form so-and-so about all integers, you should consider an induction hypothesis of the form such-and-such." Of course, theories of this sort are not as familiar as Peano's, which is all the more reason to work on them.

This point of view sheds a little light on "production systems," an implementation mechanism advocated by many people (Davis & King, 1975; Newell, 1973a; Rychener & Newell, 1978). A production system is a set of rules called *productions,* of the form

   condition → action

The difference between a production and a forward inference rule is that the *action* is not restricted to inference but may perform other symbol manipulations or input/output. In fact, productions and demons are very similar, except for various details that add up to a difference in usage. Productions usually refer to and alter the contents of "working memory," a small data base sometimes identified with human short-term memory and usually distinguished from the data base containing the productions. The words "sometimes" and "usually" are necessary because the concept of production system has grown to include many very different kinds of program. [For example, Davis & King (1975) count all deduction systems as production systems.]

One way to understand productions is to interpret *"condition → action"* as saying, "If *condition,* then *action* is advisable." This is an ordinary deductive rule, which can be used by some program module to deduce what to do. (This requires a theory of "advisability.") However, production-system theorists resist seeing productions in this way. They dispense with any such external module and let the data base manager (now called the *production interpreter*) just do the *action* as soon as it appears. (It becomes an issue what to do when more than one appears.)

Some programs have been written that exhibit these two features (noninferential actions and autonomous data base). They tend to be used for psychological modeling (Moran, 1973; Young, 1977), by researchers who feel that this organization is likely to maximize novel interactions among behaviors and that learning in such a system might be facilitated by being able to change behavior just by adding or deleting productions.

It is hard to make a definite recommendation about this. The second supposed advantage ("additivity") is, as we have pointed out, a potential feature of any data-base system. (We emphasize that this idea about learning, like most ideas about learning, is an article of faith for everyone at this point.) The first supposed advantage ("novel interactions") is hard to evaluate. It comes down to whether you believe novel interactions are likely to be harmful or beneficial and whether you believe production systems are more likely to promote them. As Davis and King (1975) point out, in practice some production systems tend to evolve two components: a set of truly additive inferential rules and a set of control rules with special control conventions that defeat additivity. If this happens, then the system is reflecting the structure of Fig. 16.11 in spite of itself. Many production-system advocates (J. McDermott & Forgy, 1978) claim that a good production interpreter will not have this problem.

16.7 APPENDIX—CORRECTNESS OF DBGC

In this section, we sketch an informal proof that MOLECS-ASSIGN-STATUS will terminate. It should be obvious that it finds a well-founded and consistent labeling if it terminates. (Exercise: Prove this.)

However, it looks as if the algorithm might go into an infinite loop, if some call to MOLECS-CLOBBER-STATUS wipes out everything since the last call to MOLECS-CLOBBER-STATUS. In fact, this can happen. Consider the dependency shown in Fig. 16.12. If the algorithm starts with P, it will try

FIG. 16.12.   Unsatisfiable dependency.

setting it IN. When it discovers that it depends on itself, it will wipe out its status and try again, with unfortunate results.

This case is obviously pathological, in that there is no consistent assignment of labels to *P*. There are other cases in which there is a satisfactory label assignment, but the algorithm will never find it. Consider the graph shown in Fig. 16.13. If *C* is OUT, then *D* can be IN and everything else OUT with no trouble. But the algorithm, if it starts on *C*, will make it IN, and this will cause an infinite loop to develop around *A* and *B*.

The problem in both Fig. 16.12 and 16.13 is the presence of a loop of dependencies with an odd number of minus signs. By a *loop* we mean a sequence of dependencies

$$(<\!J0\ M0\!>\ <\ J1\ M1\!>\ \ldots\ <\!Jn\ Mn\!>)$$

where each Ji is a justification of molecule Mi, each Mi is an in-justifier or out-justifier of $Ji+1$, and $<\!Ji\ Mi\!> =<\!Jk\ Mk\!>$ iff $i = 0$ and $k = n$. Define the *precursor* of Mi to be Mi-1. The dependency $<\!Ji\ Mi\!>$ is negative if Mi-1 is an out-justifier of Ji and positive if Mi-1 is an in-justifier of Ji. The loop is *odd*

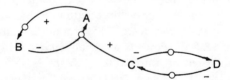

FIG. 16.13.   Pathological dependency network.

if the number of distinct negative dependencies is odd, otherwise, *even*. There is no reason an odd loop should ever occur in a normal network, since it means that some circumstances a molecule's being OUT implies that it is IN. What we will prove is the

THEOREM: MOLECS-ASSIGN-STATUS will terminate if the dependency network contains no odd loops.

It should be clear that MOLECS-ASSIGN-STATUS will terminate if the graph contains no loops at all. Define a *loop structure* to be a set of molecules such that every molecule in the set is connected by a chain of dependencies to every other molecule in the set. The algorithm will halt if it halts when started on a molecule of a loop structure.

The potential trouble spots arise when a molecule is labeled IN and it is the supporter of a supportee (see Fig. 16.4). At this point there must be a loop from the supportee back to the IN molecule. We will call this an *inconsistently labeled* loop. Call the IN molecule the *killer* and its supportee the *victim*. (There may be more than one such loop.) We have the following lemma:

LEMMA 1: If a dependency network has no odd loops, then an inconsistently labeled loop has at least one molecule whose precursor is not one of its supporters.

PROOF: Assume that all the molecules in the loop have supporters in the loop. The killer is by definition IN, but there are two cases for the victim: Either it is OUT and the dependency between them has a plus (+) sign or the victim is IN and the dependency has a minus (–) sign (see Fig. 16.14). But this

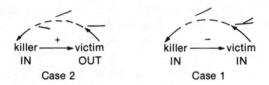

FIG. 16.14.   Inconsistent loop structure.

means that there must be a transition, from OUT to IN or IN to IN, as you go counterclockwise from the victim to the killer, that depends on no molecules outside the loop. Each component dependency link must be labeled—if the sign of a justifier differs from the sign of the justificand; otherwise, plus. (Show this.) This means that a transition from OUT to IN must have an odd number of minuses, and a transition from IN to IN must have an even number of minuses. But then, in either case, the loop will be odd. This contradicts the assumption that the network has no odd loops.   QED

Now we can prove our main lemma:

LEMMA 2: The program will halt when started on a molecule of a loop structure.

Proof: A loop structure contains a finite number of loops. We prove the lemma by induction on the number of loops in the structure. If the structure contains no loops, the lemma is obviously true. Now assume it is true for loop structures containing 0, 1, ..., or i loops. Consider its behavior on a structure of $i + 1$ loops. If there is no inconsistency, the algorithm obviously halts. Otherwise, when an inconsistency is detected, there will be one or more victims and one inconsistent loop per victim, all with the same killer (see Fig.

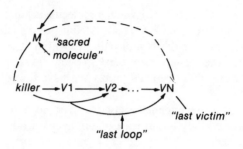

FIG. 16.15.   Inconsistent nest of loops.

16.15). All the victims must be on the same loop because MOLECS-ASSIGN-STATUS marks depth first. Let the "last victim" be the one such that no other victim appears between it and the killer, and let the "last loop" be the one containing only the last victim. Now by Lemma 1, the last loop has a molecule (perhaps the killer) that is not supported by its precursor. It can't be supported by any molecule between the killer and the last victim; if it were, a different inconsistent loop would have been found, since the algorithm is depth first. Call this the *sacred molecule*. So MOLECS-CLOBBER-STATUS, since it starts from victims and clobbers supportees, cannot affect this molecule. Furthermore, MOLECS-ASSIGN-STATUS will alter only molecules that it identifies (via level number) as having been clobbered by the most recent call to MOLECS-CLOBBER-STATUS. This will mean that the recursive calls to MOLECS-ASSIGN-STATUS will not affect the sacred molecule; it has been taken out of the loop structure, cutting it into one or more loop structures of i or fewer loops. By the induction hypothesis, MOLECS-ASSIGN-STATUS will halt on all these loops. The net effect will be that the original call of MOLECS-ASSIGN-STATUS must leave one more node assigned than it found unassigned, so DBGC will eventually run out of nodes and halt.   QED

The theorem follows straightforwardly from Lemma 2.

This theorem says nothing about the efficiency of data-base garbage collection. It is not hard to construct cases that require multiple passes through the data base, taking time proportional to the cube of the size of the data base. Whether this is the worst case is not known. In any event, in the "average" case, the cost should be approximately linear.

17

Alternative Control Structures

17.1 INTRODUCTION

In previous chapters, especially Chapter 12, we have implemented sophisticated control structures entirely within LISP, by exploiting LISP's natural representation of functions. For complicated applications, these methods can lead to awkward, hard-to-manage programs. If you want to exploit sophisticated control structures heavily, it may be worth your while to use LISP in a more indirect way, to implement a language of a higher level, in which these control structures are easy to use. This is the technique we will present in this chapter. The higher-level language we will talk about is called SCHUM; it is a variant of a language, called SCHEME, developed by Gerald J. Sussman and Guy Steele (1975, 1978).

Before we describe in detail how to do this, we will sketch the trade-offs involved in doing it. What we will implement is a SCHUM interpreter, a piece of code directly analogous to the LISP interpreter but written in LISP (and compiled for efficiency). Just as the LISP interpreter uses the machine's data structures (stacks and arrays) to implement representations of LISP's control states and data types, so the SCHUM interpreter uses LISP data structures to represent SCHUM's control states and data types. It turns out that LISP is well suited to the task of implementing interpreters for languages with syntax and data types like LISP's. So it is easy to get started with an interpreter and make changes in it to tailor the developing high-level language to your needs. (We urge you to understand our approach to interpreters and to write your own rather than mechanically copying our code.) The main drawback to this approach is that we lose the compiler. Writing a compiler for SCHUM is a major undertaking that is not much helped by having written an interpreter; in fact of all the higher-level languages implemented in LISP (Rulifson et al., 1972; Sussman et al., 1971; Sussman & McDermott, 1972; Sussman & Steele, 1978), only one, Sussman and Steele's SCHEME, has a compiler. (Steele, 1978)

This chapter is organized as follows: first we describe the language we implement; then we describe the basic trick of writing an interpreter for a language with those constructs; finally, we give an annotated listing of one such interpreter.

17.2   THE DESIGN OF SCHUM

In Chapter 12, you may recall, we were forced to implement coroutines by breaking the text of a coroutine into several chunks and implementing each chunk as a LISP function. What we would rather be able to do is write PROG-bodies with sequences like

```
-coroutine-set-up-
(LOOP
   (SUSPEND -message-to-monitor-)
   -coroutine-continues-
   (SUSPEND -another-message-)
   -coroutine-continues-again-)
```

In order to implement SUSPEND, there must be a way of saving the state of the interpreter at the point the SUSPEND is executed, and restarting the interpretation later from the saved state. We could hide all these details and make SUSPEND a primitive of the language. Rather than do this, we introduce the "LABEL" construct, which allows the user to access saved states directly.

The concept of saved interpreter state can be hard to grasp. We lead up to it by easy stages. Consider what must happen to make the following piece of LISP code work:

```
(PRINT
   (PROG (X Y)
      ...
      (COND (...(RETURN Z)))
      ...))
```

When the LISP interpreter starts to work on the PROG, it must save certain pieces of information. For example, it must keep the old bindings of X and Y somewhere, and it must remember what to do when the PROG is finished. (As it happens, it uses a pushdown stack for this.) It goes through a similar ritual for each statement in the PROG body, because after each statement it must be able to remember which statement is next. For example, when it sees the COND, it must save the statements that come after it. After each statement is executed, the information saved can be used and discarded.

When the RETURN is seen, something unusual must happen. The interpreter must be able to skip over all the information saved for the COND and go directly to the PROG call itself, restoring the original bindings of X and Y and passing the value Z to PRINT; that is, it must be able to restore the interpreter state that obtained just when the PROG was called.

We tend to take this ability for granted, but actually there is a lot going on here. In fact, in early versions of LISP, it was not understood how to restore the interpreter state from an arbitrary place, so RETURNs could not be put just anywhere.

The LABEL construct makes this concept of saved state a little more explicit. We can use it to mimic the PROG (and introduce a little of our SCHUM language) by writing

```
(PRINT
  (LABEL EXIT-LAB
    (BLOCK (X NIL Y NIL)
      ...
      (IF (...(EXIT-LAB Z)))
      ...)))
```

In SCHUM, we separate the variable-binding machinery of PROG from its interpreter-state-saving machinery. LABEL binds the variable EXIT-LAB to something called a *label function*, which corresponds exactly to the interpreter state saved by PROG in LISP. BLOCK binds variables; its syntax is the same as our LET. IF corresponds to COND in LISP.

Inside the IF, the label function EXIT-LAB is used by giving it the argument Z. Keep in mind that a label function is *exactly* analogous to the state saved by PROG; you can't restore such a state without returning a value (in this case, to PRINT), and Z is that value.

In general, (LABEL *variable -body-*) is evaluated by binding *variable* to the "label function" corresponding to the interpreter's state and then evaluating the statements in the *body*. If the label function is used, execution of the body ceases, and the call to LABEL returns whatever value was given to the label function.

If the label function is not used, the value of the LABEL is the value of the last expression in the body, *variable* is unbound (or restored to whatever value it had before), and that's the end of it.

Or is it? Since we are designing our very own language, we are free to make design decisions that violate ordinary LISP restrictions. There is no way in LISP to preserve the interpreter state of a PROG once the PROG has returned. But there is apparently a way to do this in SCHUM. Consider the following code:

```
(PRINT (LABEL F (ASN *WEIRD* F) NIL))
```

ASN is the SCHUM analog of SETQ in LISP. Here we use it to set the global variable *WEIRD* to the label function that is the value of the local variable F. After that, the call to LABEL returns NIL, which is printed. Now the variable F is unbound, but its value is still saved as the value of *WEIRD*. What if someone later executes (*WEIRD* 'HELLO)? It would be understandable to insist that the result of this be undefined, but there is an alternative. We can allow an interpreter state to survive as long as there is a label function designating it. Then using such a function will cause the state to be reestablished. So, in our example, the effect of (*WEIRD* 'HELLO) is to cause the original label call to return again, this time with value HELLO, which is printed.

This concept takes some getting used to. Until you have gained experience with it, you may not be entirely clear about what an interpreter state is. It is very helpful to return to the PROG-RETURN analogy for guidance. Consider the example in Fig. 17.1. Here there are two bindings of the variable

```
(BLOCK (X 'FOO GOBACK NIL)
  (BLOCK (X 2)
    (LABEL LF (ASN GOBACK LF))
    (PRINT X)
    (ASN X (TIMES 2 X)))
  (PRINT X)
  (GOBACK NIL))
```

FIG. 17.1.   Restoring variable bindings.

X. The outer X is always bound to the symbol FOO. The inner X is initialized to 2. The first time through the inner BLOCK, 2 is printed. Then X is doubled, the inner BLOCK returns, and the outer X (always FOO) is printed. Now GOBACK is used to make the LABEL return again. This restores the interpreter state, including the inner binding of X. This is slightly ambiguous; do we mean literally the value that X had when the LABEL was entered before (i.e., 2) or the last value X had in the inner BLOCK (i.e., 4)? In fact, we mean the latter; the new value, 4, is printed. This continues indefinitely, printing 2, FOO, 4, FOO, 8, FOO, 16, ...

You can understand why the ambiguity is resolved this way by contemplating what RETURN does in analogous circumstances. You know from experience that RETURN causes its PROG to return but does not undo side effects that occurred since the PROG was entered. It merely changes which values of each variable are "visible."

As promised, we can implement SUSPEND with LABEL, as shown in Fig. 17.2. A process is just a data type consisting of a label function and a priority. The label function encodes the saved state of the process; using the label function restarts the process. SUSPEND builds such a structure and sends it to *MONITOR*, a label function that encodes the saved state of the executive. The executive is supposed to decide which process to run next, using the transmitted priority level. When (and if) this process is chosen again, the monitor can restart it by using the label function in the transmitted PROC. Since this label function was obtained as the value of RESUMER, using it causes this call to SUSPEND to return and the process to resume.

The executive for this simple multiprocess mechanism would look like MULTI-PROC in Fig. 17.2. Take a minute to decipher this code. The initial process INITIAL-PROC is a process that, if started, will call FUN. (By

```
~A PROC is a suspended process. It consists of a label function
~and information for the executive's use. In this simple version,
~we just keep a priority for each process.

(RECORD-TYPE PROC NIL (LABEL-FUN PRIORITY))

~DEF is used to define SCHUM functions (like DE in LISP).

(DEF SUSPEND (PRIORITY)
     (LABEL RESUMER
        (*MONITOR* (PROC RESUMER PRIORITY))  ))

~Executive for a set of processes. Initially, the set is
~to consist of just one process, begun by calling FUN.
(DEF MULTI-PROC (FUN)
     (BLOCK (INITIAL-PROC NIL SUSPENDED-PROCESSES NIL NEXT-PROC-LABEL NIL)
        (ASN INITIAL-PROC
           (PROC (IF ((LABEL START-LAB START-LAB))
                     (T
                      (FUN)
                      (ERROR '"Processes should not return"))  )
                 0))

        (ASN SUSPENDED-PROCESSES
           (PROC-LIST-SORT
              (CONS (LABEL MONITOR-LABEL-OBJ
                       (ASN *MONITOR* MONITOR-LABEL-OBJ)
                    INITIAL-PROC)
                 SUSPENDED-PROCESSES)))
        (ASN NEXT-PROC-LABEL
           (LABEL-FUN:PROC (POP SUSPENDED-PROCESSES)))
        (NEXT-PROC-LABEL NIL)  ))
```

FIG. 17.2. Sketch of a multiprocess executive.

convention, processes are restarted with the value NIL. The IF in the argument to PROC will call FUN when this happens. Notice that FUN is not supposed ever to return but to use SUSPEND to get back to the monitor.) The executive maintains a list SUSPENDED-PROCESSES of PROCs that are waiting to run. It initializes this list to just the element INITIAL-PROC. A side effect of the initialization is to bind *MONITOR* to a label function that saves the interpreter state just before the call to CONS. So every time *MONITOR* is called, its argument is CONSed onto SUSPENDED-PROCESSES.

So the CONS will be executed many times over (not always with the same arguments, of course). Each time, the same thing happens. MULTI-PROC calls PROC-LIST-SORT (a mythical process sorter) to order the alternative; then POPs the most attractive one off the SUSPENDED-PROCESSES list, and restarts it by calling its LABEL-FUN.

This schema is rather incomplete, since it doesn't say how more than one process comes to exist. We will deal with this later, after we have seen more about the use of SCHUM.

SCHUM's syntax is like LISP's, but its semantics are rather different. One difference, the existence of LABEL, we have already described. There are other major differences as well. Most languages, including LISP, do not treat functions as a data type in the same way that they treat ordinary types like integers or lists (although LISP is fairer than most). These ordinary types may be created and manipulated in the course of a computation with a freedom denied to functions. For example, in Algol, a function may be created only by explicit declaration when a block is entered. A function may be passed as an argument to subfunctions but may not be returned from the block in which it is declared.

In SCHUM, these restrictions are removed. Functions may be created anywhere and passed to any destination without regard to their origin. This extra freedom allows functions to perform many surprising roles.

Of course, functions are not the only data type in SCHUM. Although from a mathematical point of view functions can be shown to be the only data type you need, for practical purposes we require other data types and primitive operations. In SCHUM, we supply these by including all of LISP in SCHUM. So SCHUM's data types are S-expressions, manipulated by the usual functions. (We have already used functions like CONS and PRINT in SCHUM code.)

We illustrate the use of a powerful notion of function with an example. Let's say we need a predicate to test the approximate equality of two floating-point numbers. We can write

```
(DEF = (X Y)
    (LESSP (ABS (DIFFERENCE X Y)) 0.5)   )
```

that is, X is approximately equal to Y if their difference is between –0.5 and 0.5.

Now, say we want to generalize this to allow variation of the tolerance. We could write in EPSILON for 0.5, but where would EPSILON come from? We could let it be an argument to A=, so we would have to write (A= Z FOO 0.5). But SCHUM allows you to write a function that takes EPSILON as an argument and returns the function A=.

```
(DEF A=GEN (EPSILON)
      (\ (X Y) (LESSP (ABS (DIFFERENCE X Y)) EPSILON)   ))
```

The caller of A=GEN might write

```
(ASN A= (A=GEN 0.5))
```

and later

```
(A= Z FOO)
```

would use 0.5 as EPSILON.

A=GEN is returning the value of
```
(\ (X Y) (LESSP (ABS (DIFFERENCE X Y)) EPILSON)   )
```

This is called a \\-*expression*. ("\\" is pronounced "*lambda*," but our character set doesn't include Greek letters.) Its value is a function of two arguments, X and Y. When this function is used, its body, (LESSP (ABS (DIFFERENCE X Y)) EPSILON), will be evaluated. X and Y will be bound to the two argument values. EPSILON, on the other hand, will have the value it had when A=GEN was called. So the object returned by A=GEN must include the values of the variables mentioned in the \\-expression but not in the argument list. (These are called the *free variables* of the \\-expression.) The object is called a \\-*closure* and is one of the two main types of function definable in SCHUM. (The other is, of course, the label function.)

There are lots of things you can do with \\-closures. For example, we can define CMP, which composes two functions, thus:

```
(DEF CMP (F1 F2) (\ (F1 (F2 X))   ))
```

and NEG, which forms the negation of a predicate, as

```
(DEF NEG (PRED) (CMP NOT PRED)   )
```

For example, "non-atomic" might be defined by

```
(ASN NON-ATOMIC (NEG ATOM)).
```

Notice that SCHUM's evaluation rules are different from LISP's. The main difference is in the handling of

```
(function -args-)
```

In SCHUM, this is evaluated by applying the *value* of *function* to the values of the *args*. DEF, unlike DE, actually sets the value of the symbol being defined. So there is no difference (except readability) between the previous definitions of NEG and CMP and

```
(ASN NEG (\ (PRED) (CMP NOT PRED)  ))
(ASN CMP (\ (F1 F2) (\ (X) (F1 (F2 X))  )))
```

Another difference is that in SCHUM \-expressions have values; in LISP, we had to pass quoted LAMBDA-expressions around, but in SCHUM a quoted \-expression is just a data structure; only the values of \-expressions are used by the interpreter.

Finally, for convenience, LISP functions evaluate to themselves. Otherwise, we would have had to write ('LESSP ('ABS ('DIFFERENCE X Y)) 0.5) and (CMP 'NOT PRED).

Exercise 17.1 Write a function (CMP2 *f1 f2*), where *f1* is a function of one argument and *f2* is a function of two, such that ((CMP2 *f1 f2*) *x y*) = (*f1* (*f2 x y*)). Use CMP2 to define *not equal* in terms of NOT and EQUAL.

All of these features of SCHUM revolve around its scoping rule for variable bindings, which is called *static scoping*. When a function is applied in LISP, any free variables in it obtain their values from the *environment* in existence at that time. In SCHUM, as we have seen, functions carry around their environment with them. A function is a closure of a \-expression, and the free variables of a closure are bound to the values they had when the closure was created. For example, the value of a call to (CMP *f g*) is the closure of (\ (X) (F1 (F2 X))), with F1 bound to the value of *f* and F2 bound to the value of *g*.

This rule for where free variable values come from is called *static scoping*, because you can tell by looking at a function definition where its variables come from, without having to run the whole program to see where the function is used. LISP's rule is called *dynamic scoping*, because free variables' locations are determined only at run time.

The word *scope* appears in these phrases because which binding scheme you use determines where a variable binding is known. Any time you have a \ expression

$$(\backslash\ (\dots X \dots)\dots)$$

the scope of this binding of X is the body of the \-expression (not counting embedded \'s with their own bindings of X). This is true of both SCHUM and LISP (modulo their different spellings of lambda). The difference lies in whether this binding of X is known in functions called from the \-expression.

For example, consider

> (LAMBDA (X) (CAR (FOO X)))   [LISP]

vs.

> (\ (X) (CAR (FOO X)))   [SCHUM]

In LISP, the scope of X is the LAMBDA-expression, plus the call of FOO and any functions ultimately called in the call to FOO, provided they don't rebind X. In SCHUM, what you see is what you get; the scope of X can only be just this \-expression, because FOO carries along its own free variables. A reference to X within FOO is an error if those free variables do not include X.

Static scoping is also called *lexical scoping*, because the scope of a variable corresponds exactly to the printed representation of the expression in which it is bound.

Static scoping has been used mainly by compiled languages like Algol and PL/I. Dynamic scoping has been used by interpreted languages, including LISP, APL, and SNOBOL. The reason for this is that static scoping makes it possible to find variable locations (relative to the stack) at compile time. Dynamic scoping requires associating values with symbol-table entries, which are usually available only in interpreted languages.

Pure static scoping would be inconvenient in an interactive language like SCHUM, because, after every top-level evaluation, all variables would become unbound. So the SCHUM interpreter keeps a set of permanent global bindings. Variables not bound in a closure are assumed to be bound globally. DEF actually adds a binding to this global environment. *MONITOR* (Fig. 17.2) is another example of a global variable.

We should point out here that the two features we have examined, label functions and closures with static free variables, are independent. We could have implemented a language with either feature alone. We chose to be somewhat radical for two reasons. First, the power LABEL gives you to save control states is more valuable if you can save variable bindings as well, and closures are a natural way to do this. Second, we want to make you aware of alternatives to the way LISP does things; the more people are educated about things like closures, the more they may demand them in "real" languages.

The presence of both these features makes SCHUM programming rather different from LISP programming. For example, in Fig. 17.2, we had to make *MONITOR* a global variable; there is no way to bind a variable in one function to be accessed as a free variable by functions it calls. This means that there is no way to create new processes by resetting SUSPENDED-PROCESSES in a subfunction (but see Exercise 17.11).

Exercise 17.2 Change MULTI-PROC so that *MONITOR* expects a list of PROCs. Rewrite SUSPEND to interact with this new MULTI-PROC. Then write a function (FORK *priority funs*), which is like SUSPEND, but sends to the monitor a list of processes, one for each given function and one to continue from the FORK; and a function (DIE), which causes the process that evaluates it to disappear.

17.3   PROGRAMMING IN SCHUM

We have already introduced BLOCK, defined as follows: the expression

(BLOCK (*v1 val1 v2 val2 ... vN valN*)
  exp1 exp2 ... expK)

binds all the variables to the corresponding values and then evaluates the expressions in order, returning the value of the last. BLOCK is not exactly analogous to LET. LET is equivalent (via macro expansion) to a LISP LAMBDA call, so you might expect the BLOCK expression above to be equivalent to the following call of a \-expression:

((\(*v1 v2 ... vN*) *exp1 exp2 ... expK*)
  val1 val2 ... valN)

However, the *vals* in the BLOCK expression may be \-expressions, in which case BLOCK interprets them differently from the way \ would. As we described above, \-expressions evaluate to closures of themselves in the current environment. In the \ call, this rule means that there is no way in *val1* to access any of the *vJ*. In particular, if one *val* wants to call another, or even itself, it can't. BLOCK avoids this problem by closing the *vals* in an environment containing the new bindings of *v1, v2,* etc. So BLOCK can be used to write local recursive functions.

Here is an example. The function shown in Fig. 17.3 prints out the property list of a symbol. P1 is a recursive function, defined only inside PLIST-PRINT, in which it is bound to a \-closure using BLOCK.

```
(DEF PLIST-PRINT (SYM)
     (BLOCK (P1 (\ (L) (IF (L  (PRINT (CAR L))
                              (PRINT (CADR L))
                              (P1 (CDDR L)))
                          (T 'DONE)  )))
          (P1 (CDR SYM))  ))
```

FIG. 17.3.   A local function defined with BLOCK.

If we had instead written

```
(DEF PLIST-PRINT (SYM)
   ((\ (P1) (P1 (CDR SYM))  )
    (\ (L) (IF (L ... (P1 (CDDR L))) ...)))  )
```

the second occurrence of P1 would have referred to the global value of P1. Since P1 probably has no global value, or the wrong value, this would not do what we want. We could have defined P1 globally using DEF (which would be standard procedure in LISP), but that would conceal the fact that only PLIST-PRINT uses it.

It might appear that PLIST-PRINT would choke on very long property lists, since it calls a recursive function. In many languages, including LISP, the control stack would overflow before a recursive function reached the end of a long list. The reason a control stack is necessary is that the interpreter must unbind local variables when a function's work is done. In SCHUM, however, the function's variable bindings are not accessible during calls to subroutines, so there is nothing to do when the last subroutine returns.

An example will make this clearer. Say function FOO calls function BAR, and the very last thing BAR does is called ZOT (Fig. 17.4). When ZOT returns, there is nothing for BAR to do but pass the result back to FOO. The local variables of BAR are invisible from ZOT, so the interpreter can unbind BAR's variables *before* calling ZOT. In addition, BAR does not have to do any control manipulations before branching to ZOT, since ZOT can use directly the return address (to FOO) that BAR would have used. There is no point in having BAR play any further part in what has become a transaction between FOO and ZOT. Furthermore, ZOT can call other functions in the same way, ad infinitum, without ever growing a stack.

```
(DEF FOO (...)
    ...(BAR...)...)
DEF BAR (...)
    ....(ZOT...))
(DEF ZOT (...)...)
```

FIG. 17.4. Passing control from function to function.

The only time a control stack is needed is when a calling function plans to do something after the called function returns. In (H (F...) (G...)), the calls to F and G require saving a return address, since H will be called when they are done.

What all this amounts to is that, in a lexically scoped language, a procedure call is just a generalized GOTO that allows values to be transmitted. The use of a stack is associated with argument evaluation, not procedure calling. For example, here is how you would do an iterative factorial in SCHUM:

```
(DEF FACT (N)
    (BLOCK (MULTLOOP
(\ (I PRODUCT)
    (IF ((GREATERP I N) PRODUCT)
        (T (MULTLOOP (PLUS I 1) (TIMES I PRODUCT))) )))
(MULTLOOP 1 1)  ))
```

Since the last thing MULTLOOP does is call itself, this call acts just like a GOTO. Furthermore, since MULTLOOP has arguments, the GOTO is combined with simultaneous assignment to I and PRODUCT. This code is equivalent to the following in a LISP with simultaneous assignment:

```
(DE FACT (N)
    (PROG (I PRODUCT)
        (:=  <I PRODUCT> <1 1> )
MULTLOOP
        (COND ((GREATERP I N) (RETURN PRODUCT))  )
        (:= <I PRODUCT> <(PLUS I 1) (TIMES I PRODUCT)>)
        (GO MULTLOOP)  ))
```

This use of loops with arguments replaces most assignments in SCHUM.

By now it should be clear that a SCHUM function is not the same as a mathematical function. A SCHUM function is a kind of generalized statement label, a packaged piece of behavior that can be started by sending arguments to it. Since SCHUM functions can themselves be sent to any destination, a function with local functions like those of FACT and PLIST-PRINT can pass these functions to another function to be used as it pleases. If the receiver does use it, it in essence jumps back into the function that created it. Functions that communicate such "statement labels" back and forth may be thought of as coroutines.

As an example, we show two coroutines, READER and WRITER. READER is to read objects from the teletype and pass them to another coroutine, which it knows only as COROU. The input stream is uninterpreted, except for asterisks and exclamation points. An asterisk is a signal that all nonnumeric objects until the next asterisk are to be ignored. An exclamation point is a signal that the input stream is empty. WRITER is to accept S-expressions from some coroutine (possibly READER) and print them out. When it receives the symbol <, it is to treat it as a signal to make a list of what it receives from then on, until it receives a >, when it is to output the list and resume its normal printing loop. When it receives the object $DONE$, it is to terminate output and return DONE.

The code is shown in Fig. 17.5. READER and WRITER each take one argument: the coroutine to communicate with. A coroutine is, of course, represented as a function to send results to. If we wish to send N results, the function must take $N+1$ arguments, the extra one being reserved for the "return address;" that is, to resume a coroutine C and do X when C resumes you, just execute

$$(C \text{ -things-passed-to-him- } (\backslash \text{ (-things-I-expect-back-) } X))$$

This is the way READER and WRITER always use COROU. WRITER sends only a return address to its interlocutor, whereas READER must send the

```
(DEF READER (COROU)
  (BLOCK (MAINLOOP
            (\ (OBJ COROU)
              (IF ((EQ OBJ '*) (NUMLOOP (READ) COROU))
                  ((EQ OBJ '!)
                   (COROU '$DONE$ (\ (C) (ERROR '"Input Exhausted")  )))
                  (T (COROU OBJ (\ (C) (MAINLOOP (READ) C)  )))  ))
          NUMLOOP
            (\ (OBJ COROU)
              (IF ((EQ OBJ '*) (MAINLOOP (READ) COROU))
                  ((NUMBERP OBJ)
                   (COROU OBJ (\ (C) (NUMLOOP (READ) C)  )))
                  (T (NUMLOOP (READ) COROU))  )))
    (MAINLOOP (READ) COROU)  ))

(DEF WRITER (COROU)
  (BLOCK (WRITELOOP
            (\ (THING COROU)
              (IF ((EQ THING '$DONE$) 'DONE)
                  ((EQ THING '<)
                   (LISTLOOP NIL COROU))
                  (T (PRINT THING)
                     (COROU WRITELOOP))  ))

          LISTLOOP
            (\ (L COROU)
              (COROU (\ (THING C)
                      (IF  ((EQ THING '>)
                            (PRINT (REVERSE L))
                            (C WRITELOOP))
                           (T (LISTLOOP (CONS THING L) C))  )))  ))
    (COROU WRITELOOP)  ))
```

FIG. 17.5.   READER and WRITER coroutines.

object read as well. A useful programming convention is to transmit the "return address" function as the last argument to a coroutine function. Functions used as "return addresses" are called *continuations*. In the diagram above, $(\ (-things\text{-}I\text{-}expect\text{-}back\text{-}) X)$ is the continuation.

READER and WRITER consist of two loops each, of the kind that should be familiar to you by now. READER loops through MAINLOOP until it sees an asterisk. On each iteration, it sends the object read to COROU, by executing

```
(COROU OBJ (\ (C) (MAINLOOP (READ) C)  ))
```

The continuation is not simply MAINLOOP, since we must read a new object before going to MAINLOOP. We could have given this continuation a name, but there is no reason to; the code we used may naturally be read as, "Send the atom to COROU, and, when you come back, READ another object for MAINLOOP."

Once an asterisk has been seen in MAINLOOP, READER switches to NUMLOOP, which is very similar but ignores nonnumbers.

For simplicity, we assume asterisks are balanced, so that an exclamation point is seen only in MAINLOOP. When this happens, READER sends $DONE$ to COROU. Since this event means that the input stream is exhausted, the continuation passed will cause an error if it is ever used.

WRITER also has two loops, but it cannot start them immediately. It must go to COROU first to get an object (THING). It always sends to COROU a single argument, itself a function of two arguments, as in

(COROU (\ (THING C)...))

WRITELOOP prints out the things it receives from COROU. When a < is received, WRITER shifts to the LISTLOOP, which accumulates elements until a > is seen.

To start these coroutines talking to each other, we just execute

(WRITER READER)

We should emphasize that READER and WRITER can be plugged into other combinations. WRITER can talk to any coroutine that expects one argument and sends back two.

You might be wondering why we chose such a contrived example. The reason is that a simpler example would not have demonstrated the usefulness of coroutines so well. Consider how you would write this code without using coroutines. You would have to make one of the routines be a subroutine of the other. This introduces a misleading asymmetry into the two programs. Not only that, but each routine in its current version goes to the other from two different places. This is no problem for the calling routine, in the new version; it can just call the subroutine twice. But then we must introduce some state information somewhere to allow the subroutine to do different things depending on what its state was when it was last called. This would be awkward. In this simple case, the awkwardness would be bearable. In realistic applications, each coroutine might have many possible states, and it would be out of the question to implement them with subroutines.

More complicated coroutine structures are possible. There can be cycles of more than two coroutines. A coroutine can be given more than one continuation, and use only one of them, depending on some test. For example, READER could have been written to take two continuations, one to send atoms to and one to use when nothing is left. Let us call a coroutine of this sort a *generator*. Figure 17.6 shows a function, GEN-PRINT, which prints out everything a generator generates, and a function, NUMBERS, which takes an S-expression and returns a generator of all the numbers that

```
~This prints everything a generator can generate
(DEF GEN-PRINT (G)
   (G (\ ( ) '$DONE$)   (\ (X RES) (PRINT X) (GEN-PRINT RES)))))


~(NUMBERS x) generates all the numbers in S-expression x.
(DEF NUMBERS (S-EXP)
   (BLOCK (NUMS1
                  (\ (X POP-TREE NOMORE-C MORE-C)
                     (IF ((NUMBERP X)
                          (MORE-C X POP-TREE))
                         ((ATOM X) (POP-TREE NOMORE-C MORE-C))
                         ((NUMS1
                           (CAR X)
                           (\ (NC MC) (NUMS1 (CDR X) POP-TREE NC MC)  )
                           NOMORE-C
                           MORE-C))  )))
          (\ (NOMORE-C MORE-C)
             (NUMS1 S-EXP (\ (NC MC) (NC)  ) NOMORE-C MORE-C)  )))


~Returns T if X and Y have the same numbers in the same order.
(DEF SAMENUMS (X Y)
   (BLOCK (BUMP
            (\ (NXC NYC)
               (NXC (\ ( ) (NYC  (\ ( ) T)
                               (\ (NUM C) NIL)))
                    (\ (XNUM NEW-NXC)
                       (NYC (\ ( ) NIL)
                            (\ (YNUM NEW-NYC)
                               (IF  ((EQUAL XNUM YNUM)
                                     (BUMP NEW-NXC NEW-NYC))  )))  ))  ))
          (BUMP (NUMBERS X) (NUMBERS Y))  ))
```

FIG. 17.6. Using generator coroutines.

occur in it. Examine NUMBERS carefully until you understand it. Notice that NUMBERS takes one argument and returns a function of two arguments. It is this returned function that is a generator. All the work of this generator is done by the local function NUMS1, which takes a piece of the original S-expression, and three continuations: one to go to when there are no more numbers in that piece (NOMORE-C), one to send a number to when it's found (MORE-C), and one to go to when all the numbers have been found in this piece of the expression (POP-TREE). If X is a number, NUMS1 sends it to MORE-C. It must also send MORE-C a continuation, telling what to do to generate more numbers; since X was a number, it's trivially the last number in X, so the only way to generate more is by using POP-TREE to look elsewhere in the expression. If X is some other atom, we have nothing at this level to send to the caller, so we POP-TREE immediately. (Notice that we must send POP-TREE the other two continuations so that when a number is finally found, there will be someone to send it to.) Finally, if X is nonatomic, we call NUMS1 on its CAR, giving it a POP-TREE continuation that says to work on the CDR when the CAR is exhausted.

The functions GEN-PRINT and SAMENUMS operate on generators. (GEN-PRINT (NUMBERS '(((3 FOO) 8 (6)) . 8))) would print out 3, 8, 6, and 8. SAMENUMs test whether two S-expressions have the same numbers in the same order, by setting up two NUMBERS generators and tweaking them alternately. The advantage of doing this, in principle, is that we can detect a difference in the two expressions without having to generate all the numbers of either of them. Of course, in this toy example, this advantage is nullified by the overhead of using an extra interpreter; but in a sophisticated AI application (such as matching two large structures), this might mean a considerable saving.

> *Exercise 17.3*   Write a generator ATOMS to generate all the atoms in an S-expression, omitting terminal NILs.

> *Exercise 17.4*   Define streams (Chapter 12) in SCHUM. A $GEN will now mark a data type with just one field, a function (which will carry its own local variables, of course). Notice that the *REST* feature cannot be implemented, since SCHUM lacks dynamic free variables (but see Exercise 17.11).

This concludes our discussion of coroutines in SCHUM. We hope it is clear that we haven't exhausted the possibilities. You can probably think of applications of your own in which the control structure of some function is most naturally thought of as involving suspension of execution while some other function runs for awhile. Try writing these in SCHUM. (We use SCHUM some more in Chapter 18.)

17.4   IMPLEMENTING SCHUM

Now we turn our attention to implementation techniques for the language we have defined. It ought to be obvious that we cannot define SCHUM's reserved words as LISP functions or even macros. That would be the technique of choice if we had it. In a sense we have been implementing our own language (with LOOP and := for instance) throughout this book. But LABEL and \ are too much for us.

Instead, we will have to use LISP as a "machine language" for an interpreter for SCHUM. Just as the real machine has blocks of words that the LISP interpreter uses to represent the LISP stack and variable bindings, so the "virtual SCHUM machine" will use list structures for the analogous purposes in SCHUM. We will have a variable to hold the SCHUM stack and other variables to play the roles of other "registers."

Next, we have to decide how to get things done. Let's take the case of evaluating the body of a function or BLOCK. Such a body will be a list of expressions, to be evaluated one after the other. In machine language, this is accomplished by code like that in Fig. 17.7. In this hypothetical machine, the register STACK points to a block of words used to save return addresses. The subroutine calling convention is to load the argument into the register ACCUM, push the return address, and jump to the subroutine. The subroutine returns by popping the return address and going to it.

```
NEXT:   LOAD ACCUM, form-to-eval
        PUSH STACK, literal RET
        JUMP EVL
RET:    get-next-form
        JUMP NEXT
        . . .
EVL:    do-the-evaluation
        POP STACK,ACCUM
        JUMP indirect-thru ACCUM
```

FIG. 17.7.   Machine language for statement sequence evaluation.

We need to do something similar with LISP. One way would be to define the SCHUM interpreter as an enormous PROG, sketched in Fig. 17.8. But this is obviously very clumsy. Just to execute sequences of statements we needed the labels NEXT and RET. In a full interpreter, every internal function would require one or more labels. To add capabilities to the interpreter, we would have to recompile the whole thing. And most compilers will not compile (GO (POP STACK)) efficiently, since it requires translating symbolic statement labels into instruction addresses at run time.

The solution is a coding trick due to Gerry Sussman and originally used in the Conniver interpreter (McDermott & Sussman, 1973). We break the

```
(DE SCHUMINT ( )
    (PROG (STACK ACCUM -other-registers-)
        . . .
NEXT    (:= ACCUM form-to-eval)
        (PUSH 'RET STACK)
        (GO EVL)
RET     get-next-form
        (GO NEXT)
        . . .
EVL     do-the-evaluation
        (GO (POP STACK))
        . . .
))
```

FIG. 17.8.   LISP code for statement sequence evaluation.

enormous PROG of Fig. 17.8 into pieces, one per labeled segment of statements. We make each of these pieces into a function of no arguments, called a *code chunk*. Instead of using the LISP interpeter to sequence through the statements, we write a little function to call one code chunk after another. Variables like STACK and ACCUM are made into special variables (called *registers*, for obvious reasons). By convention, one such register, **PC**, is set by each code chunk to the next code chunk so the "virtual cpu" of the SCHUM machine can find it.

If you feel comfortable with the methods of Chapter 12, this technique should look familiar. By using these methods in the interpreter, we are forcing the SCHUM implementer to live with the awkwardness they entail, so the SCHUM user won't have to. At least we do not have to carry arguments around with each code chunk, saying what to do next, since the state of the machine is kept in the global registers. This will save some CONSing.

The stack register **STACK** is used to call a subroutine as shown in Fig. 17.9, which should be compared with the two previous figures. This is highly schematic (since EVL must actually itself consist of several code chunks), but

```
˜This is the "cpu" for the virtual machine.
˜**PC** is set to the next code chunk (by the last code chunk)
(DE MLOOP ( )
    (LOOP (DO (APPLY **PC** NIL))  ))

˜To call a subroutine, we use code chunks as return addresses
˜NEXT, RET, and EVL are all code chunks
(DE NEXT ( )
    (:= **ACCUM** FORM)
    (PUSH 'RET **STACK**)
    (:= **PC** 'EVL)  )
(DE RET ( )
    get-next-form
    (:= **PC** 'NEXT)  )
(DE EVL ( )
    do-the-evaluation
    (:= **PC** (POP **STACK**))  )
```

FIG. 17.9. Code chunks for statement sequence evaluation.

the structure should be clear. Each code chunk sets **PC** to be the next code chunk. Usually this is just a constant, but returning from a subroutine is done by popping a saved code chunk off the stack.

In the next section, we present the actual interpreter, which differs from this crude sketch in several ways.

17.5 AN INTERPRETER

The interpreter consists of several registers, the virtual cpu MLOOP, and several code chunks for doing evaluation and implementing reserved words. In what follows, we first define the global LISP variables and data types the interpreter needs. Then we give the interface between LISP and SCHUM and the code chunks.

This interpreter is a first-generation descendant of the SCHEME interpreter of Sussman and Steele (1975). The major differences are that it is somewhat cleaner (and somewhat less efficient), and it implements a slightly different language (lacking some of SCHEME's theoretical purity).

In Fig. 17.10, we define the special variables and data types needed by the interpreter. Figure 17.10a gives the definitions of straightforward types like \-

```
(DECLARE (SPECIAL
~There are seven registers
                **EXP**        ~Expression being evaluated
                **ENV**        ~Environment in which to do it
                **PC**         ~The program counter
                **VAL**        ~For passing values back
                **ARGS**       ~Args left to evaluate
                **ARGVALS**    ~Values of evaluated arguments
                **STACK**      ~Frame (saved state) of calling computation
~The mnemonic names summarize the standard use of each register, but ·
~registers can be used for other purposes. In particular,
~**ARGS** and **ARGVALS** are occasionally used to save temporary data.
                ))

~Now the data-type definitions

~A LAMBDA-EXP is a list (\ vars -body-).
(RECORD-TYPE LAMBDA-EXP \ (VARS . BODY))

~An APPL is a form of the form (fun -args-)
(RECORD-TYPE APPL NIL (FUN . ARGS))

~A CLOSURE is a pair (function environment)
(RECORD-TYPE CLOSURE (FUN ENV))

~A LABEL-FUNCTION is a saved control state
(RECORD-TYPE LABEL-FUNCTION (FRAME))

~A PRIMOP is a primitive function,
~i.e., a LISP function which evaluates its arguments
(DE IS-PRIMOP (F) (GETL F '(EXPR SUBR LSUBR))   )

~CODE-CHUNK flags functions of no arguments used as code chunks
(DM CODE-CHUNK (L)
   |"(DE @(CADR L) ( ) . @(CDDR L))   )
```

FIG. 17.10a.   Interpreter data-type definitions.

```
˜A FRAME is a saved interpreter state
˜Of the form (exp env pc args argvals super-frame)
(RECORD-TYPE FRAME NIL (EXP ENV PC ARGS ARGVALS . SUPER))

˜The next two functions are the real versions of the stack
˜manipulations shown in Fig. 17.9.

˜This routine saves a state, which, when restored, will cause the
˜interpreter to resume execution at code chunk TAG.
(DE SPUSH (TAG)
    (:= **STACK** (FRAME **EXP** **ENV** TAG **ARGS** **ARGVALS** **STACK**)))

˜This routine restores the saved state **STACK**.
(DE SPOP ( )
    (COND (**STACK**
            (:= **EXP** (POP **STACK**))
            (:= **ENV** (POP **STACK**))
            (:= **PC** (POP **STACK**))
            (:= **ARGS** (POP **STACK**))
            (:= **ARGVALS** (POP **STACK**)))
          (T (ERROR '"BLEW STACK"))  ))
```

FIG. 17.10b.   Data-type FRAME.

expression, \-closure, and label function. It also defines the CODE-CHUNK macro, which is essentially just DE. Figure 17.10b defines the FRAME data type, which is used to encode control information. Two functions, SPUSH and SPOP, are used by code chunks to perform the actual frame manipulations. Notice that they save and restore all the interpreter registers except **VAL**. **VAL** is used to return values from subroutine calls, so its contents must not be disturbed by SPOP.

Figure 17.10c defines the ENV ("environment") data type, which encodes variable bindings. We use a-lists to represent bindings; the variable v is bound to value x when the association $(v\ x)$ appears in the current environment **ENV**.

[This design decision might appear inefficient to those of you who are familiar with the trend in LISP implementations away from the use of a-lists. In SCHUM, however, a-lists work better than in LISP. The reason a-lists get long in LISP is that the current-bindings list must be lengthened every time a function is called; this is necessary because the called function might refer to the variables of its caller. Global variables suffer especially, since they get further and further from the front of the list as the stack gets deeper. But in SCHUM a function can only refer to the variables of the function that created it. This means that the number of "layers" of a-list depends only on the nesting of function *definitions,* not calls. For example, the maximum a-list length during the evaluation of any expression in NUMBERS (Fig. 17.6) is 8. When

˜Variable bindings are kept in ENVs (environments), which are
˜implemented as a-lists
˜A BDG is an element of such a list
(RECORD-TYPE BDG NIL (VAR VAL))

˜An ENV is a list of BDGS
(DE ENV (BDGS) BDGS)
(DE EMPTY-ENV ( ) NIL)
(DE VARS:ENV (E) (MAPCAR 'CAR E))
(DE BDGS: ENV (E) E)

˜This function looks bindings up
(DE VARBDG (V E) (ASSOC V E))

˜This function adds new bindings
(DE VARSBIND (VARS VALS ENV)
    (COND ((EQUAL (LENGTH VARS) (LENGTH VALS))
           (NCONC (MAPCAR 'BDG VARS VALS) ENV))
          (T (ERROR '"Wrong number of arguments"))))

FIG. 17.10c. Data-type ENV.

the body of (\ (NC MC) ...) is evaluated, the variables NC, MC, X, POP-
TREE, NOMORE-C, MORE-C, NUMS1, and S-EXP will be bound.]

This still leaves a design decision: how to store the bindings of global
variables. We could just keep them as the top-level value of the register
ENV. This would be a little more uniform but would involve some
inefficiency, since the set of global variables can get arbitrarily large. Instead,
we let the global value of the variable just be the LISP value. This has the side
effect that all LISP global values (such as flags to the pretty-printer) are easily
accessible from SCHUM.

These are all the data types we need. Figure 17.11 gives the heart of the
interpreter. Figure 17.11a is the real version of the schema of Fig. 17.9. One
improvement we have made is to provide an interface (SCHUMVAL)
between LISP and SCHUM, and a convention for leaving MLOOP to get
back to LISP. Another modification, of great importance, is that EVSEQ,
the code chunk for evaluating sequences of statements, does not push any
control stack for the last statement. It should be clear by now why this is
possible and desirable.

In Fig. 17.11b, we define the code chunk SEVAL, which is the workhorse of
the interpreter. When any chunk (including EVSEQ) has an expression to
evaluate, it sets **EXP** to that expression and sets **PC** to SEVAL.
SEVAL just decodes the type of the expression and performs the appropriate
actions to evaluate. For example, variables are looked upon in **ENV**, and
numbers evaluate to themselves.

```
˜This function, called from LISP, runs the SCHUM interpreter
˜to evaluate its argument in environment **ENV**
(DE SCHUMVAL (**EXP**)
   (LET (**ENV** **ENV**        **PC** 'SEVAL
         **ARGS** NIL           **ARGVALS** NIL
         **STACK** (FRAME NIL NIL NIL NIL NIL NIL))
      (MLOOP) ))


(:= **ENV** (EMPTY-ENV))


˜This function defines the "CPU" for the SCHUM virtual machine.
˜The register **PC** always holds the next code chunk to be executed.
˜Each code chunk sets **PC** to the next one to run.
˜By convention, a code chunk of NIL causes SCHUM to cease interpretation
˜and return **VAL** to LISP.
(DE MLOOP ( )
   (LOOP (DO (APPLY **PC** NIL))
         (WHILE **PC**)
         (RESULT **VAL**) ))


˜The following code chunk evaluates statement sequences—
˜\-bodies, IF-clauses, and BLOCK-bodies. (Compare with Fig. 17.9.)
˜EVSEQ expects to find the body in the register **ARGS**. The variable
˜**EXP** is used to pass arguments to SEVAL.


(CODE-CHUNK EVSEQ
   (COND (**ARGS**
˜In evaluating the last thing in a body, don't bother to push a
˜return address; just return the last value to whoever did the EVSEQ.
          (COND ((CDR **ARGS**) (SPUSH 'EVSEQ1)) )
          (:= **EXP** (CAR **ARGS**))
          (:= **PC** 'SEVAL))
         ((SPOP)) ))


˜SEVAL will leave its value in **VAL**, but we can ignore it. Just
˜CDR the **ARGS** and go back to EVSEQ (by setting **PC**, of course).
(CODE-CHUNK EVSEQ1
   (:= **ARGS** (CDR *—*))
   (:= **PC** 'EVSEQ) )
```

FIG. 17.11a.   The basic interpreter.

There are several cases if **EXP** is an APPL ("application"). If the object in functional position is not a special symbol, it must evaluate to a function, which will be applied to the argument values. But three classes of symbols are treated differently: SCHUM reserved words, LISP macros, and LISP reserved words (FEXPRs and FSUBRs).

```
˜SEVAL is the main function of the interpreter.
˜Other functions evaluate **EXP** by setting **PC** to SEVAL.
(CODE-CHUNK SEVAL
    (LET (TEMP NIL)
        (COND ((ATOM **EXP**)
                            ˜Numbers and LISP functions evaluate to themselves
                    (COND ((OR NUMBERP **EXP**) (IS-PRIMOP **EXP**))
                            (:= **VAL** **EXP**))
                            ˜Other symbols are looked up in **ENV**
                        ((:= TEMP (VARBDG **EXP** **ENV**))
                            (:= **VAL** (VAL:BDG TEMP)))
                            ˜ . . . or in global bindings (implemented as LISP bindings)
                        ((ERRSET (:= **VAL** (EVAL **EXP**)) T))
                        ((ERROR '"UNBOUND VARIABLE"))  )
                ˜Get pc from stack to return
                (SPOP))
                ˜Check for special symbol
            ((AND  (ATOM (FUN:APPL **EXP**))
                    (GETL (FUN:APPL **EXP**)
                            '(SCHUMRES MACRO FEXPR FSUBR)))
                            ˜SCHUM reserved words are defined by a code
                            ˜chunk under the SCHUMRES property
                (COND ((:= TEMP (GET (FUN:APPL **EXP**) 'SCHUMRES))
                        (:= **PC** TEMP))
                        ˜For convenience, LISP macros and reserved
                        ˜words are allowed:
                    ((:= TEMP (GET (FUN:APPL **EXP**) 'MACRO))
                        (:= **EXP** (TEMP **EXP**)))
                    ((GETL (FUN:APPL **EXP**) '(FSUBR FEXPR))
                        (:= **VAL** (EVAL **EXP**))
                        (SPOP))  ))
                ˜Once special cases are out of the way,
                ˜do the normal thing, namely, evaluate all elements
                ˜of **EXP** and apply the first to the others
                ˜This is done by EVLIS.
            (T
                (:= **ARGVALS** NIL)
                (:= **ARGS** **EXP**)
                (:= **PC** 'EVLIS))  )))
```

FIG. 17.11b. SEVAL.

1. A SCHUM reserved word is defined by a code chunk. The interpreter gives control to the designated code chunk. We will show examples of such code chunks shortly.
2. A LISP macro is applied to the form. The transformed version is then re-SEVAL-ed. (Do you see how this happens?) Allowing LISP macros

```
˜EVLIS and EVLIS1 together form a loop through arguments, evaluating them
˜Note: unlike LISP, SCHUM treats the function of an APPL as just another
˜argument during evaluation.
(CODE-CHUNK EVLIS
    (COND (**ARGS**
            (SPUSH 'EVLIS1)
            (:= **EXP** (CAR **ARGS**))
            (:= **PC** 'SEVAL))
          (T
˜The evaluated arguments are accumulated in **ARGVALS**, in reverse
˜order. When EVLIS reaches the end of the arguments, it rearranges
˜them and goes to SCHAPPLY.
            (:= **ARGVALS** (REVERSE **ARGVALS**))
            (:= **ARGS** (POP **ARGVALS**))
            (:= **PC** 'SCHAPPLY)) ))

(CODE-CHUNK EVLIS1
    (:= **ARGVALS** (CONS **VAL** **ARGVALS**))
    (:= **ARGS** (CDR **ARGS**))
    (:= **PC** 'EVLIS)  )


˜Applies a function to **ARGVALS**. Note: **ARGS** is used to hold
˜the function for SCHAPPLY
(CODE-CHUNK SCHAPPLY
            ˜An atomic function must be a LISP function
    (COND ((ATOM **ARGS**)
            (:= **VAL** (APPLY **ARGS** **ARGVALS**))
            (SPOP))
            ˜Closures are done by adding new bindings to old and
            ˜evaluating body
          ((IS-CLOSURE **ARGS**)
            (:= **ENV**
                (VARSBIND  (VARS:LAMBDA-EXP (FUN:CLOSURE **ARGS**))
                            **ARGVALS**
                            (ENV:CLOSURE **ARGS**)))
            (:= **ARGS** (BODY:LAMBDA-EXP (FUN:CLOSURE **ARGS**)))
            (:= **PC** 'EVSEQ))
            ˜Label functions are handled by restoring saved stack
          ((IS-LABEL-FUNCTION **ARGS**)
            (:= **VAL** (CAR **ARGVALS**))
            (:= **STACK** (FRAME:LABEL-FUNCTION **ARGS**))
            (SPOP))
          ((ERROR '"BAD FUNCTION")) ))
```

FIG. 17.11c.   Evaluating function applications.

saves us the trouble of implementing SCHUM macros and writing
SCHUM versions of macros like RECORD-TYPE.

3. A LISP FSUBR or FEXPR is just evaluated (using LISP's EVAL). This
   is to allow innocuous forms like (DE . . .). Reserved words like SETQ
   or COND, that can evaluate their arguments, are of limited usefulness,

since the evaluated arguments can't refer to SCHUM variables or use SCHUM constructs.

Exercise 17.5 Change SEVAL to handle SCHUM macros in addition to these three cases. These should be analogous to LISP macros. (Use a new symbol, say, SMACRO, to flag a SCHUM macro, so LISP macros can continue to be used.) Make sure you put the check for SMACRO in the right place. Try implementing our LOOP construct as an SMACRO.

SEVAL goes to EVLIS (by setting **PC**, of course) to evaluate a function and its arguments and then apply one to the other (Fig. 17.11c). EVLIS and EVLIS1 work together as EVSEQ and EVSEQ1 do. EVLIS calls SEVAL repeatedly, specifying EVLIS1 as a return address. EVLIS1 just accumulates argument values in **ARGVALS**, then goes back to EVLIS. Notice that, in contrast to EVSEQ, EVLIS does an SPUSH even on the last argument, since it must call the function after the arguments are evaluated.

This is done by SCHAPPLY, which applies the function held in register **ARGS** to the argument values held in **ARGVALS**. There are three cases. The function is either a LISP function (PRIMOP), a \-closure, or a label function.

1. LISP functions are handled with LISP's APPLY.
2. A closure is handled by adding bindings of its arguments to the bindings of its free variables and using the result as **ENV**. (The old **ENV** is discarded, although the caller of this function may have a copy saved on the stack. This is where SCHUM differs from LISP; LISP would add the new bindings to the current **ENV**.)
3. A label function is handled by throwing away the current **STACK** and replacing it with the stack saved in the label fucntion. Then an SPOP suffices to send the interpreter back to that state, a new **VAL** in hand. What could be simpler?

All that's left to define are the reserved words. Each reserved word (with a couple of exceptions) is defined by a set of code chunks, the first being stored under the SCHUMRES indicator on its property list. When the first code chunk is entered, **EXP** has been set to the expression whose first element is the reserved word. This code chunk typically does some manipulation on **EXP**, then goes to SEVAL, pushing a return tag corresponding to the next code chunk in the set.

The code for ASN (Fig. 17.12a) is instructive. It calls SEVAL to evaluate its second argument. When SEVAL returns (with the value in **VAL**), control is passed to ASN1. This checks two cases. If the variable is bound in **ENV**, its value is changed to **VAL**. Otherwise, the variable is global, so LISP's SET is used to change it.

```
~Reserved word ASN
(CODE-CHUNK ASN
   (SPUSH 'ASN1)
   (:= **EXP** (CADDR **EXP**))
   (:= **PC** SEVAL))

(CODE-CHUNK ASN1
   (LET (B (VARBDG (CADR **EXP**) **ENV**))
      (COND (B (:= (VAL:BDG B) **VAL**))
            ((SET (CADR **EXP**) **VAL**))   )
      (SPOP)   ))

(DEFPROP ASN ASN SCHUMRES)

~This reserved word does not evaluate its arguments, so it can
~be defined as a FEXPR.
(DF DEF (L)
   (SET (CAR L) (CLOSURE (LAMBDA-EXP (CADR L) (CDDR L)) (EMPTY-ENV)))
   (CAR L)   )

~\ is similar.
(DF \ (L) (CLOSURE (LAMBDA-EXP (CAR L) (CDR L)) **ENV**)   )

~Reserved word IF
(CODE-CHUNK IF
   (:= **ARGS** (CDR **EXP**))
   (:= **PC** 'IF1))

(CODE-CHUNK IF1
   (COND   (**ARGS**
               ~If you are evaluating the last thing in an IF, there is
               ~no need to return to this chunk set; just return whatever
               ~value you get
               (COND   ((OR (CDR **ARGS**) (CDAR **ARGS**))
                        (SPUSH 'IF2))   )
               (:= **EXP** (CAAR **ARGS**))
               (:= **PC** 'SEVAL))
            (T (:= **VAL** NIL) (SPOP))   ))

(CODE-CHUNK IF2
   (COND (**VAL**
               (:= **ARGS** (CDAR **ARGS**))
               (:= **PC** 'EVSEQ))
         (T
               (:= **ARGS** (CDR **ARGS**))
               (:= **PC** 'IF1))   ))

DEFPROP IF IF SCHUMRES)
```

FIG. 17.12a.   Reserved words ASN, DEF, \, and IF.

```
~Reserved word BLOCK
(CODE-CHUNK BLOCK
   (LET (BVARS (CADR **EXP**) VARS NIL VALS NIL)
      (LOOP (WHILE BVARS)
            (DO (PUSH (POP BVARS) VARS) (PUSH (POP BVARS) VALS)))
      (:= VARS (REVERSE *—*))  (:= VALS (REVERSE *—*))
      (:= **ENV**
         (VARSBIND  VARS
                    (MAPCAR '(LAMBDA (X) NIL) VALS)
                    **ENV**))
      (:= **ARGS** VALS)
      (:= **ARGVALS** (BDGS:ENV **ENV**))
      (:= **PC** 'REC-EVLIS)  ))

(CODE-CHUNK REC-EVLIS
   (COND (**ARGS**
          (SPUSH 'REC-EVLIS1)
          (:= **EXP** (CAR **ARGS**))
          (:= **PC** 'SEVAL))
         (T
          (:= **ARGS** (CDDR **EXP**))
          (:= **PC** 'EVSEQ))  ))

(CODE-CHUNK REC-EVLIS1
   (:= (VAL:BDG (POP **ARGVALS**)) **VAL**)
   (:= **ARGS** (CDR *—*))
   (:= **PC** 'REC-EVLIS)  )

(DEFPROP BLOCK BLOCK SCHUMRES)

~Reserved word LABEL
(CODE-CHUNK SLABEL
   (:= **ENV** (VARSBIND (LIST (CARD **EXP**))
                         (LIST (LABEL-FUNCTION **STACK**))
                         **ENV**))
   (:= **ARGS** (CDDR **EXP**))
   (:= **PC** 'EVSEQ)  )

(DEFPROP LABEL SLABEL SCHUMRES)
```

FIG. 17.12b. Reserved words BLOCK and LABEL.

Exercise 17.6 Notice that the := macro does the right thing in (:= (CAR . . .) . . .); i.e., SCHUM can handle the resulting RPLACA. Explain why (:= *var*. . .) will not be handled correctly by SCHUM. Change the interpreter so it will. (*HINT:* This requires one DEFPROP. There is no need to implement SCHUM macros.)

The next two reserved words in Fig. 17.12a, DEF and \, are peculiar in that they never evaluate any of their "arguments." So they can just be FEXPRs.

(We could have made them code chunks, but this would have been clumsier.) DEF sets the global value (i.e., the LISP value) of the function it defines to the appropriate closure. \ returns a closure (in the current environment) of the expression it appears in.

IF is a little more complex than ASN. It calls SEVAL to evaluate the test of each IF-clause in turn. If a non-NIL value is found, control passes to EVSEQ to evaluate the corresponding IF-clause elements. (Notice what happens if the test is the only element of a clause.) IF obeys the usual SCHUM rule never to push the control stack unnecessarily. So if the last clause consists only of a test, as in

> (IF (*test1 action1*)
>   (*test2*)   )

IF transfers control to SEVAL to evaluate it, without pushing a return tag.

Figure 17.12b shows the definitions of BLOCK and LABEL. BLOCK is a bit complicated, because it is trying to do an impossible task: evaluate its bound-variable values in the environment it is building! It approximates this by building an initial environment in which each variable is bound to NIL. Then it enters the REC-EVLIS/REC-EVLIS1 loop to calculate the argument values and enter them in this environment. (REC-EVLIS means "RECursive EVLIS," since this is used to define recursive local functions.) In this loop, **ARGVALS** is bound to a list of the bindings that have not been filled yet.

We end with LABEL, where we came in. Given the structure of our interpreter, it is simplicity itself. It binds its label variable to a label function for the current **STACK**, then calls EVSEQ to evaluate its body. We have already seen (in SCHAPPLY) how such a label function is used. Notice that SCHAPPLY does not have to concern itself with whether this EVSEQ has finished or not.

Finally, in Fig. 17.13, we demonstrate the harmful consequences of the use of trickery in programming. Somewhere in the family tree of our LISP, some black sheep noticed that LIST could be defined as a FEXPR:

> (DF LIST (L) (MAPCAR 'EVAL L))

This is unnatural but concise. The LISP compiler doesn't care, because it open-compiles calls to LIST. But the person who did this should have known that somebody, sometime, would care; as it happens, that somebody is us. SCHUM cannot tolerate LIST evaluating its own arguments, since it wants them SEVAL'ed. So we must either define LIST to be a reserved word (which just perpetuates the same mistake) or redefine it to be a LEXPR (and, when compiled, an LSUBR) as most LISPs do. (Notice that we can't use our LOOP or := macros to redefine LIST. It should be obvious why.)

This concludes our description of the interpreter. Just to make sure you understand it, here are some exercises.

~Incredibly enough, in Rutgers LISP, LIST is an FSUBR!!
~Since we want its arguments SEVAL'ed, we must make it a LEXPR.

```
(DE LIST N
   (PROG (RESULT)
LOOP  (COND (ZEROP N) (RETURN RESULT))  )
        (SETQ RESULT (CONS (ARG N) RESULT))
        (SETQ N (SUB1 N))
        (GO LOOP)  ))

(REMPROP 'LIST 'FSUBR)
```

FIG. 17.13. Redefinition of LIST for SCHUM.

Exercise 17.7 Add the reserved word (VALOF *exp*) to SCHUM. This should be analogous to EVAL in LISP. Further, let (VALOF *exp closure*) be the value of *exp* using the variable bindings in *closure*.

Exercise 17.8 Define the function (V *var clo*), which gets the value of *var* in the variable bindings of the given closure *clo*. Extend ASN to take an optional closure argument: (ASN *var clo val*) sets the value of *var* in *clo*; then make (:= (V *var clo*) *val*) expand into a call to ASN. [These changes will allow you to use closures as record structures (cf. Dahl et al., 1972).]

Exercise 17.9 Add the reserved words AND and OR to SCHUM. These should be defined, as in LISP, to return the value of the last argument that is evaluated. In keeping with the SCHUM philosophy, if the interpreter gets to the very last argument of one of these forms, it should not push any stack to evaluate it (since its value will become the value of the AND or OR). (You can do these as SCHUM macros, if you have done Exercise 17.5.)

Exercise 17.10 The only way the interpreter can currently be called is from LISP via SCHUMVAL. Define a READ-SCHUMVAL-PRINT loop function, so that the user can type forms at his terminal and have SCHUM evaluate them. (You might want to change calls to ERROR in the interpreter to create such a loop.) Then define (DSKUM *-file-specs-*) to read in a file of SCHUM forms and evaluate them.

Exercise 17.11 (Difficult) Add dynamic bindings to SCHUM; that is, define three reserved words *BLOCK, *V, and *ASN, which do for dynamic bindings what BLOCK, V, and ASN do for static ones. For example, in MULTI-PROC, we could actually make *MONITOR* be a local variable by surrounding the body of MULTI-PROC with (*BLOCK (*MONITOR* NIL)...), having MULTI-PROC do (*ASN *MONITOR* ...), and having SUSPEND use (*V *MONITOR*). (Notice that the same symbol could be used as a static and a dynamic variable.) *V and *ASN must look up variable bindings by searching up through the control stack rather than through **ENV**. Rather than add a new slot to the data type FRAME, it is enough to have *BLOCK rebind a (hidden) static variable DYNABDGS in **ENV** and have *V and *ASN look for this binding in **ENV**, (ENV:FRAME **STACK**), (ENV:FRAME

(SUPER:FRAME **STACK**)), etc. So nothing else in the interpreter has to change. (Notice that the optional argument to *V and *ASN should be a label function rather than a closure. Meditate on the elegant inevitability of this.) *BLOCK cannot, of course, use EVSEQ to evaluate its body, since the last form, like the others, must be evaluated with **STACK** holding the appropriate dynamic bindings.

Exercise 17.12   (1) Using the results of Exercise 17.11, redo Exercise 17.4, this time implementing *REST* as a dynamic free variable.
(2) Implement YIELD (Exercise 12.8) using dynamic variables. This will require adding to NORMALIZE a place for YIELD to send its argument.

We close with some remarks on efficiency. Using an interpreter implemented in LISP inevitably costs something, but there are ways to reduce the costs. The most obvious is to compile the SCHUM interpreter if you plan to use it for any real application. There are other techniques you can use to make it almost as efficient as the LISP interpreter itself:

Notice that the call to APPLY in MLOOP does a search down the property list of the symbol that is the value of **PC**. A better technique, once the interpreter has been compiled, is to have **PC** hold a SUBR pointer directly, instead of a symbol with a SUBR property. This will require replacing APPLY with a function that applies such SUBR pointers. If your LISP doesn't have one, you can write one in LAP.

In the current version, every time a function wants to SEVAL something, it must SPUSH. For example, in evaluating (PLUS 2 2), evaluating each 2 causes a stack frame to be CONSed and almost immediately discarded. A better approach is to write a function (CHEAP-SEVAL *exp return-tag*), which sets **VAL** to the value of *exp* and goes to *return-tag* immediately if *exp* is a symbol, number, or FEXPR or FSUBR call. In the trickier cases it does an (SPUSH *return-tag*) and does what the old SEVAL does.

It is not really necessary to have a uniform SPUSH that is used by everyone, although it makes the interpreter simpler. We could instead have each code chunk push just what it needs and let the return tag restore the state; that is, we could define

(RECORD-TYPE FRAME (PC . OTHER-STUFF))

where the "other stuff" is the responsibility of individual code chunks. That would mean that a function that didn't need to save some register wouldn't have to.

Experience has shown that the use of all possible tricks will make SCHUM run about twice as slow as LISP itself, which isn't at all bad.

18 Chronological Backtracking

At one time AI researchers believed that the problem of search was the central problem of AI. A parser would search through the possible syntactic structures of a sentence; a game player, through the possible legal moves in a game, etc. (cf. Nilsson, 1971). People now tend to emphasize the fact that programs with sufficient knowledge of their domains can avoid searching large spaces, but it is recognized that in some cases one will still have to resort to search.

There are, of course, many kinds of search. In this chapter we concentrate on one particular variety, *backtracking*. In this scheme, any time there is more than one way to go in the search (a *decision point*), only one will be followed. Should this lead to problems (a *failure*), the program returns to that decision point and tries another of the possibilities. To do this requires the ability to "undo" any side effects of the first trial or, in effect, to "backup" over everything done during this first attempt. (Compare this with the "best-first" searches in Chapter 12.)

There are two ways to justify the selection of backtracking for special consideration. The first is simply to note that of all the possible search techniques used in AI this has been by far the most common. It is used in the PLANNER-like problem-solving languages (Bobrow & Raphael, 1974), in theorem provers (Moore, 1975), and in grammatical parsing (Woods, 1972), to name a few.

The second way to justify our emphasis on backtracking is to ask why so many AI programs have used it. The reason is to be found in the aforementioned stress on using domain specific knowledge to reduce search. If this research program can be completely carried out in a domain, it means that every time we encounter a choice point we can pick the "best" possibility without search. But what happens if our domain is not quite so simple, and sometimes the initial estimates on the "best" continuation are wrong? The obvious answer is to stick to the approach of following only the perceived "best" approach but retain the ability to go back and "change our mind" should we later have a failure. That is to say, backtracking is the obvious way to go when you believe you have sound (but not perfect) goodness estimates for alternatives at a choice point. It is for this reason that backtracking assumes the importance it has in AI today.

There are, however, several different kinds of backtracking. What distinguishes them is the method used to select the choice point to which we will return. In Chapter 16 we discussed "dependency-directed backtracking." There the program keeps track of the reasons for each decision, and when a decision goes wrong (failed), it returns to one of the choice points (assumptions) that figured in the failure. But often such dependencies are not available. In such cases we are reduced to *chronological* backtracking, in which the program simply returns to the last decision point (the one chronologically closest). It is this chronological backtracking that is discussed in this chapter. (A synonymous phrase is *depth first search*. This name refers to the fact that a chronological backtracker may be thought of as exploring just one branch of a search tree at a time.)

18.1   A BASIC TRANSITION NETWORK GRAMMAR WITHOUT BACKUP

We illustrate backtracking through the concrete example of Augmented Transition Network (ATN) parsing. This is a method of syntactic parsing first developed in Thorn et al. (1968) and Bobrow and Fraser (1969). Its codification and current popularity are due to Woods (1972), and the formulation given here is similar but not identical to that of Woods. The basic idea is that one represents a grammar as a *transition network*. This is a set of *nodes* (or states) with *arcs* between them. The arcs are labeled with *tests,* and an arc may be traversed only if the test is true. The nodes are grouped into *subnets,* each subnet being responsible for parsing one kind of construction. These subnets can be called by tests on the arcs. Figure 18.1 gives a transition network with two subnets, one for sentences and one for noun phrases. The network is given first in net notation and then in a corresponding LISP notation. (DEF-NODES is defined later.)

Such grammars break sentences up into components. The net above will, in effect, break the sentence "The boy saw a box" into the tree structure given in Fig. 18.2. These tree structures are called *phrase markers.* (NP Stands for Noun Phrase, S for Sentence, and DET for DETerminer.)

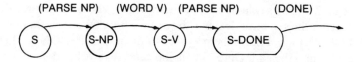

(PARSE NP)   (WORD V)   (PARSE NP)   (DONE)

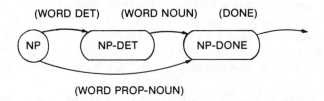

(WORD DET)   (WORD NOUN)   (DONE)

(WORD PROP-NOUN)

FIG. 18.1a.   A basic transition net grammar—graphic version.

```
(DEF-NODES  (S           ((PARSE NP)       S-NP  ))
            (S-NP        ((WORD VERB)  S-V  ))
            (S-V         ((PARSE NP)    S-DONE))
            (S-DONE      ((DONE)           NIL  )))

(DEF-NODES  (NP          ((WORD DET)            NP-DET)
                         ((WORD PROP-NOUN)  NP-DONE))
            (NP-DET      ((WORD NOUN)         NP-DONE))
            (NP-DONE  ((DONE)                 NIL    )))
```

FIG. 18.1b.   A basic transition net grammar—LISP version.

The transition net of Fig. 18.1 analyses (or *parses*) the sentence into the phrase marker of Fig. 18.2 in the following fashion. Starting at the node labeled S the net tries to follow an arc to the next node. It may only do so if the test indicated on the arc is true. For the first arc the test says (**PARSE NP**). This means that the net must first find an instance of an NP in the sentence. To do this it goes to the node labeled **NP** and starts the process again. It first tries to follow an arc out, but in this case there are two possibilities. Assume that it tries the upper one, (**WORD DET**), first. This means that to traverse the arc the first word in the unparsed portion of the sentence must be a determiner, as

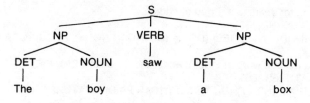

FIG. 18.2.   Phrase marker for "The boy saw a box."

is the case in "The boy saw a box." The first word now accounted for, we may remove it from the sentence, leaving "boy saw a box." We then traverse the **(WORD NOUN)** arc, taking the program to the node **NP-DONE**. There is only one arc out, labeled **DONE**, which indicates that we are done parsing a noun phrase, so we may return to whoever asked for an **NP**. This takes us back to the arc from S to **S-NP**. Having successfully parsed an **NP** we arrive at **S-NP**. We now want to find a **VERB** in the input, which will take care of "saw" and brings us to **S-V**. Again we need an **NP**. The process will be as before, and when we are done with the **NP**, we will arrive at node **S-DONE**. From there we traverse another **DONE** node. But the S network was not called as a subnet from anyplace else, so this **DONE** indicates that we are completely finished.

A network will encounter a failure if it reaches a node for which none of the arcs may be followed. For example, the sentence "The boy saw box the" will not make it through the net because after parsing the verb there is no way to parse an **NP**. Although handling failure is the theme of this chapter, we will start with an ATN interpreter that simply gives up at the first hint of trouble. (By an *ATN interpreter* we mean a program that takes an ATN and a sentence and parses the sentence using the ATN.)

˜***************************Data Types for a Simple ATN***************************

```
(DECLARE SPECIAL *S* *W*))
    ˜*S* is the remainder of the sentence, and *W* is the current word.

(RECORD-TYPE ARC NIL (TEST NODE))
    ˜An arc consists of a test and a node.

(RECORD-TYPE PARSE-TEST PARSE (NODE))
    ˜The PARSE test has the form (PARSE node)
(RECORD-TYPE WORD-TEST WORD (FEATURE))
    ˜A WORD test has the form (WORD feature).
(DE IS-DONE-TEST (X) (AND (CONSP X) (EQ (CAR X) 'DONE]
    ˜A DONE test has the form (DONE). We cannot use RECORD-TYPE to de-
    ˜fine DONE since RECORD-TYPE will not accept a record with no slots.

    ˜A node is an atom with a list of arcs on the indicator ARCS.
(DE ARCS:NODE (X) (AND X (GET X 'ARCS]

    ˜A function for defining a group of nodes.
(DF DEF-NODES (NODES)
        (FOR (NODE IN NODES) (DO (:= (GET (CAR NODE) 'ARCS) (CDR NODE]

    ˜The features of a word are found under the indicator FEATURES.
(DF DEF-FEATURES (LST)
        (FOR (PAIR IN LST) (DO (:= (GET (CAR PAIR) 'FEATURES) (CADR PAIR]
```

FIG. 18.3. Code for a nonbacktracking basic transition net grammar.

```
~*****************************Simple ATN Interpreter*****************************

    ~The top level parsing function.
(DE ATN1 (*S*) (DO-NODES1 (ARCS:NODE 'S]

    ~This is the function that really does the work. It takes as its
    ~argument the node where it is to start (for reasons which will
    ~become clear when we consider backtracking, it actually takes
    ~the arcs of the node rather than the name of the node) and it
    ~parses *S* until it sees a DONE test.
(DE DO-NODES1 (NODE-ARCS)
        ~The LOOP takes us from node to node until we either have no
        ~next node to try, or we have completed the parse successfully.
    (LOOP
    (INITIAL SUCCESS NIL)              ~SUCCESS indicates success.
    (WHILE NODE-ARCS)
    (NEXT NODE-ARCS
        ~To find the next node, pick an arc out of the current node,
        ~see if its test is true, and if so, follow it to the next node.
      (LET (AN-ARC (PICK1 NODE-ARCS) *W* (CAR *S*))
        (LET (ARC-TEST (TEST:ARC AN-ARC) NXT-NODE (NODE:ARC AN-ARC))
        (ARCS:NODE
          (COND ((IS-PARSE-TEST ARC-TEST)
                    ~E.g., to parse an NP, just call DO-NODES1 on NP
                  (AND  (DO-NODES1 (ARCS:NODE (NODE:PARSE-TEST ARC-TEST)))
                        NXT-NODE))
                ((IS-DONE-TEST ARC-TEST) (:= SUCCESS T) NIL)
                    ~If the test is a DONE, Then set the SUCCESS flag to
                    ~tell the LOOP that we have finished.
                ((IS-WORD-TEST ARC-TEST)
                  (COND ((MEMBER (FEATURE:WORD-TEST ARC-TEST)
                                  (GET *W* 'FEATURES))
                          (POP *S*)
                          NXT-NODE)))
                    ~If we have a WORD test succeed we must remove the
                    ~first word from *S*.
                ((EVAL ARC-TEST) NXT-NODE) )))))
    (UNTIL SUCCESS)
    (RESULT SUCCESS]

    ~In this version, we pick an arc by just taking the first one.
(DM PICK1 (LST)  |"(POP @(CADR LST]
```

Figure 18.3 gives code for a very simple ATN interpreter. This version is
deficient in several ways. First, it has no backtracking ability (if any test fails,
the entire parse fails). Second, the interpreter does not actually construct the
phrase marker. Figure 18.2 is simply a graphical representation of the arcs
followed in the course of parsing the sentence. We shall repair these
deficiencies in subsequent sections.

18.2 AN AUGMENTED TRANSITION NETWORK GRAMMAR

What we have just described is a *basic* transition net. To obtain an *augmented* transition net we augment the basic net with the ability to use *registers*. A register is simply a place where the net can store an intermediate result. A value is put into a register with the function SETR and retrieved with GETR.

> (SETR *register-name value*)
> (GETR *register-name*)

There is no limit on the number of registers a net may use.

To accommodate the addition of registers we extend the concept of an arc. Previously an arc consisted of a test and the next node to visit. Now we define an arc as consisting of a test, an action, and a next node. Typically the action will be a SETR, but it may be any LISP program. The action will only be performed if the test on the arc succeeds.

In Fig. 18.4 we repeat the net of Fig. 18.1, but now we add register commands that will explicitly create the tree structure of Fig. 18.2. By convention, "***" is always bound to the result of the arc test. By further convention the result of a WORD test is the word which passed the test and the result of a PARSE test is the value of the action on the DONE arc which caused us to return to the PARSE arc. DONE has no result.

Extending the code of Fig. 18.3 to handle registers is straightforward, except for one detail. The obvious way to implement registers, as LISP variables, does not work. The trouble is that since there are no constraints on the names of registers, the same register may be used by two different subnets. We did this in Fig., 18.4, where both the S subnet and the NP subnet use a register named NP. In such cases we do not want the two uses to be confused should the one subnet have a PARSE test calling on the second subnet, again the case in Fig. 18.4.

```
(DEF-NODES
 (S         ((PARSE NP)   (SETR NP ***)                                  S-NP    ))
 (S-NP      ((WORD VERB)  (SETR V |"(VERB @***))                         S-V     ))
 (S-V       ((PARSE NP)   (SETR NP2 ***)                                 S-DONE))
 (S-DONE    ((DONE)       |"(S @(GETR NP) @(GETR V) @(GETR NP2))  NIL    )))

(DEF-NODES
 (NP        ((WORD DET)        (SETR DET |"(DET @***))               NP-DET)
            ((WORD PROP-NOUN)  (SETR NP |"(NP (PROP-NOUN @***))) NP-DONE))
 (NP-DET    ((WORD NOUN)       (SETR NP
                               |"(NP @(GETR DET) (NOUN @***)))     NP-DONE))
 (NP-DONE   ((DONE)            (GETR NP)                              NIL    )))
```

FIG. 18.4. An augmented transition network grammar.

To handle this problem, as well as others that come up when we introduce backtracking, we will store register values in an a-list (cf. Chapter 17). The variable *REGS* is a special variable pointing to the current register a-list. GETR and SETR can then be defined:

```
(DM GETR (EXP)   |"(LET (ANS (ASSOC '@(CADR EXP) *REGS*))
                     (COND (ANS (CADR ANS]
(DM SETR (EXP)   |"(PUSH (LIST '@CADR EXP) @(CADDR EXP))
                     *REGS*]
```

DO-NODES1 (Fig. 18.3) then becomes a function of two variables, the second variable being *REGS*. To see how this will work, consider the situation when we use the net of Fig. 18.4 on the sentence of Fig. 18.2. In particular, consider the case after we have parsed "The boy saw," and we are about to do the (PARSE NP) test to find the final noun phrase. At this point *REGS* is as shown in Fig. 18.5a. We now call DO-NODES1 to parse an

```
(   (V (VERB SAW))
    (NP (NP (DET THE) (NOUN BOY))) )
```

FIG. 18.5a.   *REGS* as bound in the initial call to the S net.

```
(   (NP   (NP (DET A) (NOUN BOX)))
    (DET  (DET A))
    (V    (VERB SAW))
    (NP   (NP (DET THE) (NOUN BOY))) )
```

FIG. 18.5b.   *REGS* as bound in the recursive call to the NP net.

NP, and in the course of doing so we rebind *REGS*, hence saving the current value to be used when we return from the recursive call to DO-NODES1. When we have finished with the NP, but before we do the (DONE) command to return us to the S subnet, the situation is as shown in Fig. 18.5b. At this point we will have two pointers into the register a-list. The one used by the call to DO-NODES1 parsing the NP points to the front of the a-list; the one saved for our return to the S subnet points to the interior portion of the a-list corresponding to the value of *REGS* at the time we did the recursive call to DO-NODES1. When we return from the recursive call, *REGS* will be restored to the value in Fig. 18.5a, and any modifications to the NP register that occurred during the recursive call will have no effect.

Exercise 18.1   Redo the code of Fig. 18.3 to include actions on nodes, the *** convention for the value of tests, and the a-list implementation of registers.

18.3   BACKTRACKING IN ATNS—
A STATE-SAVING APPROACH

The version of ATNs we have implemented so far has one major drawback. Although we have allowed for more than one arc to leave a node, as in the two ways we may parse an NP in Fig. 18.1, the code we have written (in particular the function PICK1) only looks at the first arc. If that arc does not succeed, our ATN interpreter will simply fail to parse the sentence, even if the choice of a second arc would have worked. For example, ATN1 (Fig. 18.3) cannot parse the sentence "Fred saw the box", even though the second arc in NP checks for proper nouns.

Exercise 18.2   Improve PICK1 as follows: PICK1A will look at the first arc. If it is a DONE or a PARSE arc, it will return that arc as its value. If it is a WORD arc, it will evaluate the test. If the test comes out true, then it will return that arc; if it comes out false, PICK1A will then consider the next arc in exactly the same fashion.

There are still, however, cases that PICK1A (exercise 18.2) cannot handle. Consider the two sentences given in Fig. 18.6. An ATN that should be able to

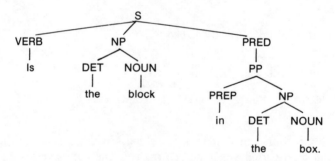

FIG. 18.6a.   A sentence that can require extensive ATN backup.

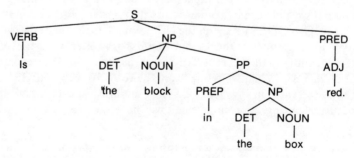

FIG. 18.6b.   A sentence that can require extensive ATN backup.

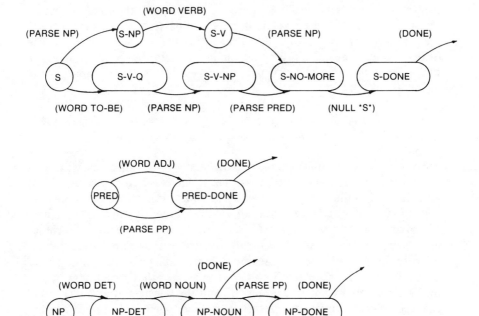

FIG. 18.7. An ATN requiring full backtracking.

parse them (given a backtracking ATN interpreter) is given in Fig. 18.7. (PP stands for Prepositional Phrase, ADJ for ADJective, and PRED for PREDicate.)

The problem for an ATN parsing the two sentences of Fig. 18.6 occurs after parsing "the block." The NP subnet has two possibilities after finding the noun (at NP-NOUN): return with the results so far or continue on to parse a PP. The former is required in Fig. 18.6a; the latter, for Fig. 18.6b. Since at this point in the sentence there is no way to know which is correct, our ATN must be able to recover from a wrong guess. The trouble is, the ATN will not realize that it has made a wrong guess until after it has finished with the NP subnet. If the NP net just parses "the block," the S-net will parse "in the box," but in Fig. 18.6b the (NULL *S*) test will fail. If the NP net parses "the block in the box," then the S-net will fail on Fig. 18.6a because no predicate will be present. The reader should convince himself that the modification suggested in Exercise 18.2 will not work, no matter which order the ATN uses for the arcs coming off of NP-NOUN.

Exercise 18.3   Show why the ATN of Fig. 18.7 will parse "Is Fred in the box?" but not "Is Fred in the box red?".

To ensure that our ATN interpreter can handle any contingency, we want it to note any occasion where more than one arc comes off a node. Later, should we encounter a failure, we look to see the last place where there was more than one arc off a node and try the next alternative. If there is still more than one, the program again notes that fact. That is to say, every time there is a choice point, the interpreter should record the choices that were not tried.

To do this properly the program must record more than just the alternative arcs. If the ATN interpreter follows the wrong arc, by the time it finds this out, the "state of the world" (including *S* and the registers, if any) may have changed. When the interpreter returns to a choice point, it must restore things to the way they were when the original incorrect decision was made. This requires saving the state of the world as well as the alternative choices.

Figure 18.8 gives the code for ATN2, a backtracking ATN interpreter using an agenda control structure. It makes use of many of the auxiliary functions in Fig. 18.3. To understand this code, let us concentrate on the four parts of the code that differ from the simple ATN interpreter of Fig. 18.3: ATN2, PICK2, and the portions of DO-NODES2 labeled 1 and 2. We first consider what these sections do in the processing of "Fred saw a box."

ATN2 initializes the agenda of choice points to indicate that the only thing to try is starting from the S node, with *S* bound to the complete sentence, and STACK set to NIL. STACK tells the interpreter how to reset the state of the world upon returning after a DONE. (As opposed to *AGENDA*, which indicates how to reset the world after a failure.) At this point *AGENDA* looks like Fig. 18.9a. ATN2 then takes the most recent choice point off *AGENDA* and applies DO-NODES2 to it. DO-NODES2 then PICK2s an arc, the first one in the list. Since there are further arcs, however, PICK2 adds a choice point to *AGENDA*. The resulting *AGENDA* is shown in Fig. 18.9b. Applying the test (WORD TO-BE) to "Fred" returns false. Thus DO-NODES2 returns NIL to ATN2, which therefore tries the next choice point on the agenda; that is, ATN2 applies DO-NODES2 to the second arc out of the first node and at the same time sets *AGENDA* to NIL. In trying to do a (PARSE NP), DO-NODES2 will reset STACK to (S-NP), indicating that when the program is done with the NP, it should return to the node S-NP.

```
~A CHOICE-PT requires saving the remaining ARCs, the rest of the
~sentence, S, and the STACK. The latter tells the program where
~to go when a (DONE) is encountered.
(RECORD-TYPE CHOICE-PT NIL (ARCS S STACK)]

   ~ATN2 keeps track of the choice points on an *AGENDA*.
(DECLARE (SPECIAL *AGENDA*))

    ~DO-NODES2 returns NIL to indicate that it failed, in which case
    ~the next choice point is tried.
(DE ATN2 (*S*)
       (LOOP (INITIAL *AGENDA* (LIST (CHOICE-PT (ARCS: NODE 'S) *S* NIL))
                      ANSWER   NIL)
             (WHILE *AGENDA*)
             (NEXT ANSWER (APPLY 'DO-NODES2 (POP *AGENDA*)))
             (UNTIL ANSWER)
             (RESULT ANSWER]


(DE DO-NODES2 (NODE-ARCS *S* STACK)
 (LOOP
  (INITIAL SUCCESS NIL)
  (WHILE NODE-ARCS)
  (NEXT NODE-ARCS
   (LET (AN-ARC (PICK2 NODE-ARCS) *W* (CAR *S*))
   (LET (ARC-TEST (TEST:ARC AN-ARC) NXT-NODE (NODE:ARC AN-ARC))
    (ARCS:NODE
     (COND ((IS-PARSE-TEST ARC-TEST)

              (PUSH NXT-NODE STACK)                               ~1
              (NODE:PARSE-TEST ARC-TEST))                         ~1
               ~To do a PARSE, go to the indicated node, recording
               ~on STACK the node to return to upon seeing a DONE

           ((IS-DONE-TEST ARC-TEST) (COND ((POP STACK))          ~2
                                          ((:= SUCCESS T) NIL)))  ~2
               ~So upon seeing a DONE, go to the top node on the
               ~STACK. A NIL STACK indicates a finished parse.

           ((IS-WORD-TEST ARC-TEST)
             (COND ((MEMBER (FEATURE:WORD-TEST ARC-TEST)
                            (GET *W* 'FEATURES))
                   (POP *S*)
                   NXT-NODE)))
           ((EVAL ARC-TEST) NXT-NODE)  )))))
  (UNTIL SUCCESS)
  (RESULT SUCCESS]

(DM PICK2 (EXP)
 |"(PROG1 (POP @(CADR EXP))
       (COND (@(CADR EXP)
               (PUSH (CHOICE—PT @(CADR EXP) *S* STACK) *AGENDA*)))
       ~If more than one arc leaves the node, record a CHOICE-PT.

FIG. 18.8.   A backtracking ATN interpreter.
```

```
(
 ( ( ((WORD TO-BE) S-V-Q)   ˜ | Arcs off       | The
        ((PARSE NP) S-NP) )  ˜ | the S node     | first
                             ˜                  | entry
       (FRED SAW THE BOX)    ˜ | Value of *S*   | on
                             ˜                  | the
       NIL)                  ˜ | The STACK      | *AGENDA*
 )
)
```

FIG. 18.9a.   The agenda at the start of "Fred saw the box."

```
(( ((PARSE NP) S-NP))    ˜ | Untried S arc
   (FRED SAW THE BOX)    ˜ | Value of *S*
   NIL ))                ˜ | The STACK
```

FIG. 18.9b.   The agenda after trying (WORD TO-BE) in S.

```
(( ((WORD DET) NP-DET))  ˜ | Untried NP arc
   (FRED SAW THE BOX)    ˜ | Value of *S*
   (S-NP) ))             ˜ | The STACK
```

FIG. 18.9c.   The agenda after trying of (WORD PROP-NOUN) in NP.

In the nonbacktracking version we did not need STACK to record return locations since the LISP stack automatically saved the necessary information. Here we do not use LISP recursion to implement PARSE tests. Rather we store the return information on STACK, and the program goes to the node NP (part 1 of the code in Fig. 18.8).

There are two arcs out of NP, so the program picks one of them (let's assume it is the one for proper nouns) and records the other on the agenda, which now looks like Fig. 18.9c. Since STACK now has a non-NIL value, if the interpreter ever fails back to this choice point, the saved stack will tell it that after redoing the NP it should go to S-NP. (Of course, should it ever fail back to this point, there is no way that the ATN of Fig. 18.7 could complete the NP. But the interpreter has no way of knowing this.)

Next DO-NODES2 will successfully follow the arc:

((WORD PROP-NOUN) NP-DONE)

At NP-DONE there is only one node out, labeled (DONE), so the program pops the STACK to reach the next node, S-NP. The *AGENDA*, however, remains the same. In this way should a failure later occur, the program may fail back into the NP arc and fix things there. This is what must happen in the example used to open this section "Is the block in the box (red)?". It should be noted that, although in the example so far the *AGENDA* only contained at most one choice point at a time, in general it may contain arbitrarily many.

Exercise 18.4 Redo the code of Fig. 18.8 to allow for actions on arcs and registers. You can save the contents of the registers by adding *REGS* to the information saved on *AGENDA*. Also, when you have a PARSE test, you must save several things on the STACK besides the next node: the action to be done upon returning from the PARSE and the *REGS* to be used after the return. The action will be performed when the STACK is popped.

18.4 BACKTRACKING WITH A TRANSITION-SAVING APPROACH

In Section 18.3 we implemented backtracking by saving on *AGENDA* a record of the choice points passed while processing the sentence. Since the processing of these choice points requires the reestablishment of the context that prevailed at the time, the values of variables (such as *S*, STACK and *REGS*) are saved as well.

There is a second basic method of backtracking that does not save the state of the computation but rather information about how the state was changed. For example, if *S* is changed, then this method keeps around information that will allow it to undo that change. This is called a *transition-saving* approach because it remembers the changes to the environment rather than the environment itself.

More concretely, if we remove FRED from *S* with a (POP *S*),

(PUSH 'FRED *S*)

is put on *AGENDA* to undo it. By doing this for all changes to *S*, STACK, and *REGS* (if used), we no longer need to store the state of the world at the time of a choice point.

For ATNs this approach does not make a great deal of sense, since saving the world state only means saving the value of three variables. There are cases, however, where saving the state of the world can be virtually impossible. An especially difficult case is having to back up over destructive LISP commands, like RPLACA. If the program may destroy any CONS-cell between one choice point and the next, the only way to save the state of the world is to copy the entire list storage area, a rather daunting prospect.

To give an idea of how the transition-saving approach works, let us see how we can use it on our ATN.

We already have a state-saving version, so all we need do, basically, is (1) undo the ability to save the state of *S* and STACK; and (2) replace all functions that change *S* and STACK with backtracking versions of the same functions. Looking at Fig. 18.8 we see that the only functions used for changing these variables are PUSH and POP. So we need backtracking versions, PUSH-BT and POP-BT. These will do the same thing as PUSH

```
(DM PUSH-BT (EXP)
    |"(CAR (SETQ-BT @(CADDR EXP) (CONS @(CADR EXP) @(CADDR EXP]

(DM POP-BT (EXP)
    |"(PROG1 (CAR @(CADR EXP)) (SETQ-BT @(CADR EXP) (CDR @(CADR EXP]

(DM SETQ-BT (EXP)
    |"(PROG2 (PUSH (LIST 'SETQ '@(CADR EXP) (LIST 'QUOTE @(CADR EXP)))
        *AGENDA*)
      (SETQ @(CADR EXP) @(CADDR EXP]
```

FIG. 18.10.   Backtracking versions of push and pop.

and POP except that rather than expand into SETQs our backtracking versions expand into SETQ-BT. SETQ-BT does a SETQ, but it also stores the reverse action on *AGENDA*. The code for all three is given in Fig. 18.10.

Also, when we store a choice point, we now store a call to DO-NODES with the remaining arcs as its argument. Thus *AGENDA* will have two conceptually different types of programs on it: the "undoer," put there by SETQ-BT, and the "fail catchers," put there when we encounter a choice point.

Exercise 18.5   Write the transition-saving version of our ATN interpreter. There will be several small changes besides the main one discussed in the text. For example, now *AGENDA* will contain programs to run, not arguments to DO-NODES2. Some of these programs (e.g., SETQ) will return non-NIL values. These do not indicate success, so DO-NODES2 must return a special symbol to flag success.

18.5   BACKTRACKING USING SCHUM

Chapter 17 introduced the language SCHUM. One of the features of this language is the ability to implement odd control structures easily. In this chapter we have been implementing an odd control structure, backtracking, but in LISP and with quite a bit of thinking. The backtracking ATN differs substantially from the nonbacktracking one, though we tried to keep them similar. Implementing backtracking in LISP is not a straightforward process. straightforward process.

The situation is quite different in SCHUM. In this section we implement a SCHUM version of an ATN interpreter. We do this in two steps. Since certain LISP constructs are not available in SCHUM, we first rewrite ATN1 (our nonbacktracking ATN) avoiding these constructs. Then we turn this into a backtracking SCHUM ATN interpreter. The second step is very simple.

```
(DE ATN3 (SNT) (:= *S* SNT)
               (DO-NODES3 (ARCS:NODE 'S]

(DE DO-NODES3 (NODES-ARCS)
    (LET (AN-ARC (PICK1 NODE-ARCS))
    (:= *W* (CAR *S*))
    (LET (ARC-TEST (TEST:ARC AN-ARC)) NXT-NODE (NODE:ARC AN-ARC))
    (COND ((IS-PARSE-TEST ARC-TEST)
                (AND (DO-NODES3 (ARCS:NODE (NODE:PARSE-TEST ARC-TEST)))
                (DO-NODES3 (ARCS:NODE NXT-NODE))))
          ((IS-DONE-TEST ARC-TEST))
          ((IS-WORD-TEST ARC-TEST)
            (COND ((MEMBER (FEATURE:WORD-TEST ARC-TEST)
                        (GET *W* 'FEATURES))
                (POP *S*)
                (DO-NODES3 (ARCS:NODE NXT-NODE))  )))
          ((EVAL ARC-TEST) (DO-NODES3 (ARCS:NODE NXT-NODE]
```

FIG. 18.11.   A recursive version of ATN1.

The LISP code for ATN3 (ATN1 made compatible with SCHUM) is given in Fig. 18. 11. ATN3 differs in three ways from ATN1. The two unimportant differences are the replacement of (POP *S*) with (:= *S* (CDR *S*)) and making *S* and *W* global variables. This latter is needed because SCHUM does not have dynamic bindings. The big difference is the substitution of recursion for looping. However, this change makes the ATN3, if anything, clearer than ATN1. We did not use this in ATN1 since the recursion might cause LISP stack overflow for large ATNs. In SCHUM this would not be a problem since, in situations like the above, SCHUM will not use the stack to save bindings.

Adding backtracking to ATN3 (yielding ATN4) requires only three changes. The simplest is replacing DE with DEF, COND with IF, and LET with BLOCK. Then there are two small changes needed to ATN4 and DO-NODES4 to allow for backtracking. In ATN4 we initialize the globally bound *FAIL-STATES*, and in DO-NODES4 we introduce the function FAIL. Lastly, we need a new definition for PICK (PICK4) and a definition for FAIL. The resulting code is given in Fig. 18.12.

The key to ATN4 is the function FAIL-POINT.

(FAIL-POINT *do-first do-if-fail*)

(FAIL-POINT is really a LISP macro, but we will talk about it initially as if it were a regular function.) FAIL-POINT takes two arguments. When FAIL-POINT is called, *do-first* is evaluated and its value returned as the value of FAIL-POINT. Should there be a failure, however, FAIL-POINT returns a

```
(DEF ATN4 (SNT)  (:= *FAIL-STATES* NIL) ~This := is specific to backup.
                 (:= *S* SNT)
                 (DO-NODES4 (ARCS:NODE 'S]

(DEF DO-NODES4 (NODE-ARCS)
 (BLOCK (AN-ARC (PICK4 NODE-ARCS))
   (:= *W* (CAR *S*))
   (BLOCK (ARC-TEST (TEST:ARC AN-ARC) NXT-NODE (NODE:ARC AN-ARC))
     (IF  ((IS-PARSE-TEST ARC-TEST)
           (AND (DO-NODES4 (ARCS:NODE (NODE:PARSE-TEST ARC-TEST)))
                (DO-NODES4 (ARCS:NODE NXT-NODE))))
          ((IS-DONE-TEST ARC-TEST))
          ((IS-WORD-TEST ARC-TEST)
           (IF ((MEMBER (FEATURE:WORD-TEST ARC-TEST)
                        (GET *W* 'FEATURES))
               (:= *S*    (CDR *S*))
               (DO-NODES4 (ARCS:NODE NXT-NODE)))
              ((FAIL))  ))
          ((EVAL ARC-TEST) (DO-NODES4 (ARCS:NODE NXT-NODE)))
          ((FAIL]        ~The explicit (FAIL)s are specific to backup.

(RECORD-TYPE FAIL-STATE NIL (FAIL-LABEL S]

(DEF PICK4 (L) (IF ((NULL L) (FAIL))
                   (T (FAIL-POINT (CAR L) (PICK4 (CDR L]

(DEF FAIL ( )
 (IF ((NULL *FAIL-STATES*) NIL)
     (T (BLOCK  (TOP-STATE (CAR *FAIL-STATES*))
                (:= *FAIL-STATES* (CDR *FAIL-STATES*))
                (:= *S* (S:FAIL-STATE TOP-STATE))
                ((FAIL-LABEL:FAIL-STATE TOP-STATE) NIL]

(DM FAIL-POINT (EXP)
  |"(IF ((LABEL FAIL-LABEL
            (:= *FAIL-STATES* (CONS  (FAIL-STATE FAIL-LABEL *S*)
                                     *FAIL-STATES*)))
        @(CADR EXP))
       (T @(CADDR EXP]
```

FIG. 18.12.   A backtracking ATN interpreter in SCHUM.

second time, only this time *do-if-fail* is evaluated and its value is returned. This is done with the SCHUM LABEL function. FAIL-POINT expands into

```
(IF ((LABEL FAIL-LABEL
        (:= *FAIL-STATES* (CONS (FAIL-STATE   FAIL-LABEL *S*)
                                *FAIL-STATES*)))
     do-first))
    (T do-if-fail]
```

FAIL-POINT saves the state of the world on the stack *FAIL-STATES*. It then returns the value of *do-first*. Included in the state of the world is a label function allowing the program to return from the LABEL a second time. When we fail, we will use this label function to return NIL from the LABEL function and hence the program will evaluate the second IF clause, returning the value of *do-if-fail*. PICK4 is simply a call to FAIL-POINT. Initially FAIL-POINT will take the first arc. If we fail back to this point, it will call PICK4 to pick among the rest of the arcs.

FAIL first checks if there are places to fail back to. If so, it resets the state of the world (in our case this is just resetting *S*) and causes the label function to return NIL to FAIL-POINT. This, in turn, causes FAIL-POINT to try the alternative.

Exercise 18.6   ATN4 is the SCHUM equivalent of a state-saving approach to backtracking. Write a transition-saving version of ATN4. In this version it will not be necessary to save anything on *FAIL-STATES* other than the label functions. However, it will be necessary to replace all modifications to *S* (and *REGS* if you want to add registers) so that information will be saved about how to undo the modification. To do this, define a function :=? that calls FAIL-POINT so that the first time through the variable is set to a new value and the second time through it is reset to its old value.

These versions of a SCHUM backtracker used LABEL to save the interpreter state. This approach had the advantage that it enabled us to change an existing program to do backtracking with little rewriting. If you are willing to rethink a program from scratch, you can often use coroutines to give it a very elegant structure. One way to do this is shown in Fig. 18.13. In this approach, each node or arc is modeled as a closure that expects three arguments. The first is the remainder of the sentence to be parsed. The closure is supposed to extract some piece of the sentence and pass the remainder to its second argument, which is a success continuation. If it cannot parse what it wants, it should instead go to its third argument, a failure continuation. The success continuation should expect two arguments: the remainder of the sentence and a resume continuation in case the rest of the parse goes wrong and a different decision needs to be made by this coroutine. The fail continuation needs no arguments.

Figure 18.13 shows a coroutine version of the ATN of Fig. 18.1. PARSE takes a sentence and attempts to parse it as a SENT. SENT looks for a noun phrase (NP), followed by a verb and another noun phrase. NP can find two kinds of structure, either a proper noun or a determiner-noun sequence. Both SENT and NP use (WORD *feature*) to look for a word of the proper class. WORD takes a feature to look for and returns a closure that succeeds if a word with that feature starts the sentence. NP calls (WORD 'PROPER-

```
(DEF PARSE (S)
   (SENT S
      (\ (END-OF-S RES)
         (IF ((NULL END-OF-S) 'SUCCESS)
             (T (RES))  ))
      (\ ( ) 'FAILURE))  )

(DEF SENT (S SUCC FAILC)
   (NP S
      (\ (AFTER-NP NEXT-NP)
         ((WORD 'VERB) AFTER-NP
            (\ (AFTER-VB NEXT-VB) (NP AFTER-VB SUCC NEXT-VB)  )
         NEXT-NP)  )
      FAILC)  )

(DEF NP (S SUCC FAILC)
   ((WORD 'PROP-NOUN) S SUCC
      (\ ( )    ((WORD 'DET) S
                   (\ (REST RES) ((WORD 'NOUN) REST SUCC RES)  )
                   FAILC) )))

(DEF WORD (FEATURE)
   (\ (S SUCC FAILC)
      (IF ((NULL S) (FAILC))
          ((MEMBER FEATURE (GET (CAR S) 'FEATURES))
           (SUCC (CDR S) FAILC))
          (T (FAILC))  )))
```

FIG. 18.13.   Coroutine version of an ATN.

NOUN) in such a way that if the call fails, it tries for a DET and NOUN instead. If this fails, NP fails completely, using FAILC.

Exercise 18.7   One thing this implementation of ATNs lacks is registers. Implement registers by giving each closure two extra arguments, one for the current REGS and one for the result of the last test, and writing SETR and GETR so that they use these values.

18.6   USING PROBLEM-SOLVING TECHNIQUES

In several chapters, notably Chapters 12, 13, 16, and 18, we looked at programming techniques for problem solving and deduction. In this section, we try to survey these techniques and make recommendations about their use.

For our purposes, a *problem* is a state of affairs to be brought about starting from a given initial state. This is a broad enough definition so that almost any computing activity may be thought of as directed toward solving some problem. There is a narrow class of "problem-solving" techniques, however, that are frequently of value in the sort of problems that come up in AI applications.

Consider the problem of implementing "abstract algorithms" (see Barstow, 1979); that is, starting from an algorithm described in terms of operations on abstract collections, find data representations and an efficient LISP program that implement it. There is (apparently) no straightforward method for performing this derivation. So we must fall back on weaker, but more general techniques (Newell, 1973b).

We discuss two such techniques: heuristic search and problem reduction. *Heuristic search* is applicable when the problem has available a set of *operators*, each an action that might take the program closer to its goal. In our example, one such operator might be "Implement a collection as a list." The search consists of trying operators in sequence until the goal is reached. The search is called *heuristic* because it is guided by an algorithm for estimating the value of different operators or sequences of them. One such algorithm uses a *distance estimator,* which estimates the remaining distance to the goal after an operator is applied (Nilsson, 1971). Another useful algorithm is *means-ends analysis,* which rates on operator valuable if it reduces the difference between the current state and the desired one or if it helps make another valuable operator applicable (Newell & Simon, 1972). Sometimes the estimator is very weak. For example, in our ATN examples, the choice of what to look for first at a given node was determined purely by the order of arcs from it.

Heuristic search was considered very important during the early years of AI. Currently, heuristic search is not often used as the top-level control structure of a program, because of the realization that tasks (such as puzzle solving) that succumb only to weak, general methods are not good areas for AI research. Heuristic search is still important, however, for solving subproblems generated by more powerful methods. For example, "macro" pattern matching (see Chapter 13) may be thought of as a search for a match, where an operator application consists of positing a correspondence between two pieces of the structures to be matched. Deductive information retrieval may be thought of as a search for a proof. Other examples are not hard to find.

For this reason, it is worth your while to understand these design issues that come up in writing searchers:

1. Should the search be deterministic or nondeterministic?
2. Is the object of the search the achieved state of affairs or the path (operator sequence) to it?
3. Is the program looking for one result, all results, or an optimal result?

The first issue arises because there is in general more than one operator applicable to each situation along the way to the goal. (Otherwise, there wouldn't be any search.) There are two responses to this uncertainty: try all the operators (nondeterministic), or commit the program to one operator (deterministic). The second alternative means discarding the old state in moving to the new. The first involves keeping track of each old state and its alternative operators. Keeping track of one sequence of states in case of trouble is just chronological backtracking. We discussed in Chapter 12 how to use agendas to manage a whole tree of states.

There are advantages and disadvantages to both the deterministic and nondeterministic approaches. Both procedures require some method of avoiding exploration from the same state twice. (If repeated states occur and are not noticed, the result will be severe inefficiency at best and infinite looping at worst.) With the nondeterministic approach, state descriptions may be stored ir a discrimination tree, to allow efficient detection and discarding of repeated states. You can do this with the deterministic approach, too, but that would require keeping history information that is not needed for any other purpose. It is more in keeping with the spirit of the deterministic method to design the search algorithm so that it never generates the same state twice. This is not always easy.

A nondeterministic program has the luxury of being able to switch to another branch of its search tree at any time. It uses the heuristic estimator to decide which branch to work on. If the heuristic estimator is not completely accurate, some branches will be pursued that lead to inferior subtrees, but as soon as the program realizes this, it can switch to a more promising branch. The deterministic searcher, by contrast, must decide once and for all which operator to apply—and this decision had better be clever or the program will have to introduce steps later just to get back on the track. In a sense, the nondeterministic approach is able to "look ahead" to see how a move will work out and, as it were, refine its estimates.

These considerations would seem to rule decisively in favor of the nondeterministic approach, but they don't, for three reasons. First, in some cases you have no choice. A robot finding its way out of a forest cannot split into two copies when it has a decision point; it must pick one way and live with the consequences if it picks wrong. Likewise, a chess player cannot take back its moves.

Second, a roundabout path is not necessarily a disadvantage if it is the end state rather than the path that is of interest. (This was the second design issue in our list.) If you care only about the final state, then the fact that the nondeterministic method could in principle take you there quickly is of no interest if finding the quick path is difficult. For example, consider the problem, discussed in Chapter 16, of finding a consistent set of assumptions in a data base. Here the operators are of the form "Assume P." At each stage, the system has two applicable operators, "Assume P" and "Assume (NOT P)." If the correct set of assumptions is $\{Q1, Q2, \ldots, Qn\}$, where $Qi = Pi$ or (NOT Pi), then there is a path of length n to the correct state. Unfortunately, there are 2^n possible paths, so finding this path is difficult (unless there is a very accurate heuristic estimator of, say, a priori probability). The dependency-directed backtracker we discussed in Chapter 16 is a deterministic searcher through the same space. This program picks Pi or (NOT Pi), depending on whatever heuristics it has, and sticks to it until an inconsistency arises. Then, rather than abandon a branch of the search tree (as the nondeterministic program would do), it changes its mind about whatever assumptions are causing the difficulty. Under favorable circumstances, this procedure can take much less time.

Sometimes, however, the path is more important than the state achieved. This is especially common when the result of the heuristic search is to be used as a plan of action. For example, if you are plotting to become President of the United States, you must first find a path to this goal and then actually carry it out. So it is important that the path be as reliable and inexpensive as possible. In a case like this, it is usually better to think of the problem as a search through a space of plans, in which each operator adds to the plan. This gives you the added flexibility of being able to delete or to rearrange steps as well. This search through a space of plans is an important part of problem reduction and merits a separate discussion that follows below.

There is a third reason for preferring determinism, perhaps the most important. The main advantage of nondeterminism is that it can tolerate a poor heuristic estimator. But a poor estimator is often a symptom that the program is searching in the wrong space or is not taking advantage of enough cues. Very often changing the search space leads to a dramatic improvement in search efficiency, to the point where the program becomes deterministic. It is always wise to look for a deterministic approach to a problem, especially when it is known that humans can solve it so fast that they must not be doing a lot of tree searching.

Historically, there has been a trend toward deterministic AI programs. In fact, parsing programs such as those we have examined in this chapter are an example. Although ATNs have proved to be a popular method of syntactic parsing, they have come under attack on a variety of grounds. In some cases the primary criticism is the division, implicit in ATNs, between syntax and semantics (Riesbeck, 1974). In our terms, the criticism made is that an ATN does not take nonsyntactic cues into account in deciding how to parse a sentence; this makes its search tree bigger than it has to be. Other researchers (notably Marcus, 1979) argue that ATNs are not sensitive enough even to purely syntactic cues. If a parser made its decisions based on a more complete view of its job, according to these critics, it would never have to backtrack, except in pathological cases called *garden path sentences* (e.g., "John told the boy the dog bit Sue was coming"). However, the difficulty people experience in parsing such sentences argues against automatic backtracking even in these cases.

Another example is the replacement of deductive retrieval with more domain-specific methods. In Chapter 13, we pointed out how inefficient a deductive retriever could be in finding plans. Notice that the algorithm we developed there for handling conjunctive goals can be looked at as a form of chronological backtracking. The operators in this application are data base assertions, which yield variable bindings when unified with requests. The search has failed when the values assigned to one conjunct yield no answers on the other conjuncts. The program's response to a failure is to backtrack to the most recent conjunct to find a new set of bindings. As we saw, this algorithm is not a very good way to construct plans. It has been supplanted by the problem-reduction methods we discuss shortly.

We see in all these cases an initial use of chronological backtracking for the solution of a search problem and the subsequent replacement of this technique by other methods that reflect a more sophisticated view of the domain.

Finally, the third design issue we listed was how many results to look for. In deductive retrieval, we generally want all answers to a query; so we keep exploring operator sequences until we are satisfied. In most applications, though, just one result is satisfactory.

The hard case is when we want an optimal result, better than all the others (as measured in some way). The problem here is that it is hard to be sure a solution is optimal without finding all the others, only to verify their inferiority and throw them away. This commits the program to an (almost) exhaustive nondeterministic search (see Hart, Nilsson, & Raphael, 1968, for an algorithm that isn't quite exhaustive). If you have a case where a deterministic algorithm is guaranteed to give an optimal answer, you are very lucky.

In the past few years, *problem reduction* has gained popularity over heuristic search. The technique is applicable when a program has available a set of plans, a *plan* for a *goal* being a set of *subgoals* whose achievement will achieve the goal. (The subgoals are supposed to be simpler, hence the name of the technique.) For example, to go to work, you have a standard plan, such as "Get in the car, drive to work, park, and walk to the office." The important feature is that the plan is "guaranteed" to work. Of course, life is not that simple; the guarantee applies only if each subgoal can be achieved and (most important) if the plan for one subgoal does not conflict with other goals. For example, the plan for parking must not leave you miles from the office. Notice that subgoals are not always goals in our original sense of "state of affairs to bring about." They can also be actions to be executed. The neutral term "task" can be used to cover both cases.

Given a problem, a problem reducer first finds a plan to solve it and then executes the plan. Finding a plan may be thought of as a heuristic search in which the operators add more detail (by attaching plans for goals and subgoals) and coordinate steps. Coordinating is done in two ways: by choosing harmonious plans for simultaneous subgoals and by choosing the order in which to execute subplans. An example from Sacerdoti (1977) is the problem of painting your ceiling and your ladder; the obvious plans will clash if you paint the ladder first. The final result of planning is a plan in which every goal has been reduced to a set of *primitive actions*, which can be taken without further planning.

Executing a plan means actually performing the primitive actions specified in a fully detailed plan. Planning and execution may be interleaved. For example, a chess-playing program might have a plan with steps "Protect king" and "Attack center." The first step may be elaborated down to "Castle" and this move taken before the second is examined very carefully.

The main advantage of problem reduction is that it trades the old problem of finding an operator sequence for the new problem of coordinating canned operator sequences. The main disadvantage of problem reduction is that a program using it requires much more knowledge of the problem domain. Instead of a small set of operators and a heuristic estimator, such a program requires a set of guaranteed plans. A plan can be a large structure, and there may be one for each of a large set of familiar situations, so a large set of plans may be required. There are just too many situations where maintaining such a set is out of the question; in these situations, heuristic search is unavoidable.

The trend in problem reduction is to make the plan-finding phase an efficient, mostly deterministic search. (See Nilsson, 1971, for the older, nondeterministic approach.) This trend, of course, puts even more of a burden on the programmer, since it requires him to supply methods for selecting a single plan for each problem.

Problem reduction *is* a good candidate for the top level of a program, since it combines general plan-coordination techniques with efficient, specific plans, and since the maintenance of a large set of plans is a price we are willing to pay if we only have to maintain one such set for the whole program. Problem reduction has been applied to advising human apprentices (Sacerdoti, 1977), designing electronic circuits (McDermott, 1977a), playing go (Brown, 1978), and other tasks. It might be applied profitably to proving theorems, playing other games, and getting from place to place. Finding and, especially, executing plans are still open research topics (so it is harder to make a list of concrete issues, as we did for heuristic search).

In the next two chapters, we present the outline of a "large" AI program for telling stories. The program's top level is a problem-reduction system, which retrieves plans for tasks of the form "Tell about character so-and-so's efforts to solve problem such-and-such." The result is a nondeterministic problem reducer, which searches for a plan structure that fits together coherently. Execution of the plan is relatively trivial, since it consists of just outputting the story after it has been constructed.

Keep in mind as you read our chapters that we might have done things differently. For example, it would probably mimic human casual story telling better to make the plan finder deterministic and to interleave telling the story with creating it. But, as usual in AI programming, you can buy determinism only with information—in the absence of knowledge about coordinating stories, you must just try things until one works.

SAMPLE PROJECT

19
The Idea of Tale-Spin

This chapter and the next outline the development of a story generator. The basic idea, though not the code, is based on James Meehan's program called TALE-SPIN (Meehan, 1976). That program generated stories by giving a set of characters some goals and then tracing a reasonable sequence of actions (called *plans*) that these characters might follow in attempting to reach their goals.

An example of a story that Meehan's program generated follows:

> JOHN BEAR IS SOMEWHAT HUNGRY. JOHN BEAR WANTS TO GET SOME BERRIES. JOHN BEAR WANTS TO GET NEAR THE BLUEBERRIES. JOHN BEAR WALKS FROM A CAVE ENTRANCE TO THE BUSH BY GOING THROUGH A PASS THROUGH A VALLEY THROUGH A MEADOW. JOHN BEAR TAKES THE BLUEBERRIES. JOHN BEAR EATS THE BLUEBERRIES. THE BLUEBERRIES ARE GONE. JOHN BEAR IS NOT VERY HUNGRY. THE END.

This is the simplest story in Meehan's thesis and is not intended to indicate what his system could do. It is only supposed to show the nature of the stories we are interested in handling.

The domain of Meehan's TALE-SPIN program was the "bear" world. Just like the "blocks" world (Winograd, 1972), the bear world is a microworld containing certain features of the real world that we want to treat but omitting as many other aspects as possible.

In particular, the bear world is concerned with intrapersonal and interpersonal behavior. This behavior is at about the level of complexity of very simple children's stories about talking animals, such as those found in some of Aesop's fables. The characters have simple needs (e.g., they get hungry) and simple plans for satisfying those needs (e.g., ask someone else for food).

The advantage of the bear world is that we don't have to worry about all the complex, stereotypical, standardized options that are open to people in similar situations. It sounds funny to say "John Smith was hungry. He asked Mary Jones if she knew where some food was." We wonder why John doesn't go into the kitchen or to the grocery store or to a restaurant, and we wonder what relationship he has with Mary Jones.

If we substitute Joe Bear for John Smith and Irving Bird for Mary Jones, the story seems more natural. We expect simplifications in stories about talking animals. Certain complications are still available, however, which is why the bear world is still of interest. For example, deceit, a very complex phenomenon, can be part of this domain:

JOE BEAR WAS HUNGRY. HE ASKED IRVING BIRD IF HE KNEW WHERE SOME FOOD WAS. IRVING DIDN'T BUT HE DECIDED TO TRICK JOE. HE SAID HE WOULD TELL JOE WHERE SOME BEES LIVED IF JOE BROUGHT IRVING A WORM. JOE DID AND IRVING ATE IT AND THEN FLEW OFF LAUGHING AT JOE. JOE NEVER TRUSTED IRVING AGAIN.

You influence the stories that TALE-SPIN generates by manipulating two kinds of data:

1. The rule base—this contains plausible sequences of events, plus preconditions specifying the situations when these sequences might occur. These rules are called *story fragments*.
2. The initial data base—this contains a description of some initial setting; that is, it gives the characters and their goals and other relevant facts, such as where they are, what they eat, and so on.

The story generator takes the initial data base and starts applying those story fragments that have preconditions satisfied by the data base. In tracing out the sequences of events, new goals are set up, new facts are added to the data base, old facts are deleted, and so on, until eventually no more can be said.

Your task is to build such a story generator, along with a reasonable rule base, capable of having several characters interacting in their attempts to reach their goals. As we shall see, in order to do this, many of the techniques from the previous chapters are necessary—especially those involving the maintenance of data bases and backtrack flow of control.

19.1 THE TASK OF STORY GENERATION

The story-generating program we are talking about here is not a piece of trickery that picks canned sentence fragments at random and sticks them together. Although such programs can be fun, they have nothing to do with Artificial Intelligence. TALE-SPIN has a real (if small) data base about objects, actions, goals, and plans. TALE-SPIN generates conceptual descriptions of a plausible sequence of events first, and then it translates these descriptions into English.

In order to do this, the story generator must know what the characters will do in certain situations. For example, if we initialize the data base with "John Bear is hungry," then it would be inappropriate for our generator to continue with "He went to sleep." That violates the rule that "If a character is hungry, then he will look for food."

The generator must be smart about what kinds of goals characters can have and how characters attain goals. If a character is hungry, he will try to find some food. If he knows another character has what he wants, he can ask that character for it. If one character lies to another, then the second character will no longer trust the first one. These are rules about planning. Meehan's program was based on a theory of plans and goals developed by Roger Schank and Robert Abelson (Schank & Abelson, 1977).

We can, of course, bias our rule base so that only plans with interesting consequences are tried. If we think that stories should start off with one character lying to another, then we make sure that the rule "If a character is asked something, he will lie" is in the rule base.

19.2 HOW TO REPRESENT EVENTS

The TALE-SPIN generator is concerned primarily with generating a plausible sequence of events for a set of characters with certain goals and traits. We need an internal, non-English language to represent the event descriptions so that TALE-SPIN can manipulate them without regard to the vagaries of syntax, ambiguity, and so on.

You can pick any one you want for your own project. We base our discussion on a simplified version of the Conceptual Dependency system (Schank, 1975).

In the Conceptual Dependency system (hereafter called CD), there are only 11 basic actions that actors can do. Of these, we refer only to the following in our discussion of TALE-SPIN:

1. PTRANS—physical transfer: used to represent a change of location; underlies the meanings of verbs like *come, go, send,* and *travel.*

2. MTRANS—mental transfer: used to represent a transfer of information; underlies the meanings of verbs like learn, teach, find out, and tell.
3. INGEST—ingest object: used to represent the eating of food or drink; underlies the meanings of verbs like eat, drink, swallow.

To represent an event, we specify an act plus the objects involved. For example, the CD form for "John ate an apple," in a simple LISP format, is

(INGEST JOHN APPLE)

Our syntax of CD forms for acts is

(*act -arguments-*)

where the number of arguments is different but fixed for each act. All of them take at least two (i.e., the actor and the object).

For physical motion (PTRANS) there are four arguments: actor, object, to, and from, in that order. For example, to represent the CD for "John went from Boston to New York," we write

(PTRANS JOHN JOHN NEW-YORK BOSTON)

Note that to represent someone going somewhere we say that he physically transferred himself to someplace.

For eating (INGEST), there are two arguments: actor and object, in that order. For example, "Joe ate the honey" is

(INGEST JOE HONEY)

For communication (MTRANS), there are three arguments: actor, to, and object, in that order. The object is itself another CD form, since what you tell someone is a conceptualization; that is, you can't say "John told Mary Bill," but you can say to represent "John told Mary Bill ate an apple," we write

(MTRANS JOHN MARY (INGEST BILL APPLE))

that is, John mentally transferred to Mary the information that Bill ate an apple. Note that there is an embedded CD, specifying what event John told Mary about.

There is a lot more to Conceptual Dependency than we are using, and the interested reader is referred to the articles on it listed in the references.

We also need some states to represent static situations. The states that we need in our discussion are

1. HAS—to indicate that a character owns something.
2. AT—to indicate where a character is.
3. GOAL—to indicate the goal of a character.

4. KNOW—to indicate that a character knows something.
5. HOME-OF—to indicate where a character lives.

For example, to represent "John is next to Mary," we write

(AT JOHN MARY)

Our syntax of CD forms for states is

(*state -arguments-*)

To represent "John knows that Bill has an apple," we write

(KNOW JOHN (HAS BILL APPLE))

Note that what John knows is itself a conceptualization, namely the state of Bill having an apple. Similarly, to represent that John wants to have an apple, we write

(GOAL JOHN (HAS JOHN APPLE))

which says that John has the goal of having an apple.

19.3   AN EXAMPLE OF GENERATION

Our stories are going to consist of events that are stored as parts of plan sequences. These sequences are themselves stored as being in the service (perhaps unsuccessfully) of goals. These goals can be events that are parts of even higher-level plans and so on.

We will follow the generation of this story:

JOE BEAR WANTED SOME HONEY. HE WENT TO HIS CAVE BUT THERE WASN'T ANY THERE. THEN HE ASKED IRVING BIRD FOR SOME. IRVING ASKED JOE FOR A WORM. JOE WENT TO HIS CAVE AND GOT A WORM. HE GAVE IT TO IRVING, AND IRVING GAVE JOE SOME HONEY. THE END.

We initialize the generation by saying that Joe wants some honey

(GOAL JOE (HAS JOE HONEY))

and that Irving wants a worm

(GOAL IRVING (HAS IRVING WORM))

and that Irving has some honey

(HAS IRVING HONEY)

and that Irving's home is a tree

   (HOME-OF IRVING TREE)

and that Joe's home is a cave

   (HOME-OF JOE CAVE)

and that a worm is in the cave

   (AT WORM CAVE)

and that Joe is by a rock

   (AT JOE ROCK)

The rule base has a story fragment called LOOK-FOR that says "If someone wants something, he will go to his home. If the thing is there, he takes it and the goal succeeds. If the thing is not there, then the goal of getting it fails."

Since Joe wants something and the cave is his home, the generator says the Joe went to his cave:

   (PTRANS JOE JOE CAVE ROCK)

Since the data base says that the honey is elsewhere (namely, it is with Irving Bird), Joe's plan for finding some honey fails and another plan must be tried.

The generator next chooses the rule TRADE, which says "If character W wants object X, and there is a character Y who wants object Z, then W will go to the home of Y and ask Y for an X. Y will offer an X in return for a Z. Y will then get an X and give it to W and W will get a Z and give it to Y."

Since the data base says Irving wants a worm, the generator decides that Joe (= W) will offer to trade a worm (= Z) for honey (= X) with Irving (= Y). This means that Joe has to ask Irving for some honey.

The fragment for asking somebody for something is called ASK-FOR. ASK-FOR has a precondition that says "If W is asking something of X, find the home of X." Then ASK-FOR says that W will go to the home of X. In this case, our data base says that Irving's home is a tree. Hence, TALE-SPIN generates

   (PTRANS JOE JOE TREE CAVE)

Then Joe asks Irving Bird for some honey.

(MTRANS JOE IRVING (PTRANS IRVING HONEY JOE IRVING))

Irving asks Joe for a worm.

   (MTRANS IRVING JOE (PTRANS JOE WORM IRVING JOE))

Now Joe is going to give Irving a worm and Irving is going to give Joe some honey. There is a fragment called GIVE for a character W giving an object X to another character Y. GIVE has a precondition that makes sure that the object X is either with W or where W can find it (i.e., at his home, since that is where LOOK-FOR says to go). The precondition for Joe giving Irving a worm is satisfied since there is a worm at Joe's cave.

The body of the GIVE fragment says that first you must have something and then you give it away. Since Joe doesn't have a worm with him, he has the goal of getting it. When the generator sees that Joe wants a worm, it uses the LOOK-FOR rule again. This means that Joe goes to his cave,

(PTRANS JOE JOE CAVE TREE)

gets the worm,

(PTRANS JOE WORM JOE CAVE)

goes back to Irving,

(PTRANS JOE JOE TREE CAVE)

and gives Irving the worm.

(PTRANS JOE WORM IRVING JOE)

Now Irving has the goal of giving Joe the honey. The precondition of GIVE is satisfied because Irving already has the honey. Therefore, he can give it to Joe directly.

(PTRANS IRVING HONEY JOE IRVING)

Note that there were two instances of the LOOK-FOR plan in this story: when Joe looked for honey in his cave and when he looked for a worm in his cave. The first instance failed, and the second succeeded.

19.4   STORY TELLING FAILURE

The story we generated was a successful one for both characters in that both achieved their goals. It is possible however to generate stories where one or more characters do not succeed. For example, if there had been no Irving Bird in the data base, then the TRADE rule would not have been applicable. Therefore the story would have been much shorter.

JOE BEAR WANTED SOME HONEY. HE WENT TO HIS CAVE BUT THERE WASN'T ANY THERE. THE END.

The failure of a character to achieve a goal is perfectly reasonable. What is unreasonable is to have a character and a goal and have no story at all to tell about it. This is called a *story telling failure* and is due to inadequacies and/or inconsistencies in the rule or data bases.

A trivial example of inadequacy in the story teller would be if we had the goal "Joe wanted to smoke a cigarette," and there were no fragments about smoking in the fragment base. The story generator obviously could not tell a story from this goal. Without some knowledge, it could not even make a reasonable assumption about whether Joe would succeed or fail.

A less trivial example of inadequacy would be if we failed to say what the homes of Joe Bear and Irving Bird were. Both the LOOK-FOR and the TRADE rules depend on this information. If they were absent, we would have goals for both characters but no rules that could be applied to tell a story about them. In this case no story at all would result.

Story telling failures become important when some rule fails after part of a story has been generated. The story teller has to backtrack, undoing the effects that the bad rule has had on the data base, so that some other rule can be tried instead.

For example, suppose our data base did not say that Irving has some honey. The fragment GIVE, which was used to generate "Irving gave Joe some honey," has a precondition that says that the object given must be either in the donor's possession or in his home. Neither of these conditions are true if Irving has no honey.

The flow of generation will be the same as before until we reach the part in TRADE where Irving is supposed to give Joe some honey. At this point, the GIVE fragment cannot be applied because its precondition is not met. The story generation cannot continue any further. Since GIVE cannot be told, the generator has to abort the execution of the TRADE rule.

The data base has already been changed several times, however, in the execution of the earlier parts of the TRADE rule. Joe was at the cave after his unsuccessful search for honey. The TRADE rule sent him to Irving Bird's tree, then back to the cave, and then back to the tree. This is where he is, according to the data base, when the story teller runs into trouble.

All this activity must be removed from the story because it leads to a dead end. The generator has to be able to backtrack to the point in the generation where Joe looked for the honey in his cave. If no other rule besides TRADE is applicable, then the story generation is finished. Joe looked for some honey and didn't find any and that is all that happened.

Note that as programmers of TALE-SPIN we could fix things in two ways: We can change the data base or we can change the fragment base. We can add to the data base the fact that Irving has some honey. Then we will obtain the story we generated before.

Alternatively, we can remove the filter from the GIVE fragment that said that a character couldn't give something if he didn't have it on him or at home. Then the story generator could apply GIVE to Irving giving Joe some honey. As we see in Chapter 20, the fact that Irving has no honey means GIVE will say that Irving can't give any honey, which in turn will cause TRADE to say that Joe didn't receive any honey. The story would look like this:

JOE BEAR WANTED SOME HONEY. HE WENT TO HIS CAVE BUT THERE WASN'T ANY THERE. HE WENT TO TREE WHERE IRVING BIRD LIVED AND ASKED IRVING BIRD FOR SOME. IRVING ASKED JOE FOR A WORM. JOE WENT TO HIS CAVE AND GOT A WORM AND BROUGHT IT TO IRVING. IRVING COULDN'T GET ANY HONEY SO HE DIDN'T GIVE ANY TO JOE. THE END.

The original filter on GIVE prevented the generation of stories like this. If we had more fragments available, we would use filters like GIVE's to prune out the generation of an excessive number of goal failure sequences.

20

The Specifics of Tale-Spin

20.1 REPRESENTING STORY FRAGMENTS

In Chapter 19 we described the CD representation of facts. Now we need to describe how our story fragments are defined. A set of story-generating fragments are given in Fig. 20.1. Things are left in a pseudo-English since part of your project is to develop a LISP data structure for fragments. The syntax for these fragments, in a simple Backus-Naur Form (BNF) format, is given in Fig. 20.2.

The syntax and semantics of these elements in English follow:

1. A fragment has a pattern (a CD form with variables), a filter (an S-expression that usually does FETCHes and binds variables), and a tree of subgoals indicating what the characters will do in this situation.
2. The pattern says what kinds of CD forms in the data base will trigger the fragment. For example, the TRADE has the pattern "A character wants something."
3. The filter says what special conditions must be met before the fragment can be applied. For example, the TRADE fragment has a filter that says that "Another character wants something else."
4. The body consists of a change-list and an event-tree:
   (a) The change-list specifies deletions and additions to the data base. In general, deletions should be done first.
   (b) An event-tree is either a terminal indicating that the fragment is finished and either success or failure should be returned or it is a triple, consisting of a new subgoal for a character, plus a branch to

TRADE

> Pattern: Goal of W: W have X
> Filter: Find Goal of Y: Y have Z
>   where Y is not equal W and Z is not equal to X
> Event-tree:
> > Goal of W: W asks Y for X
> > SUCCESS
> > > Goal of Y; Y asks W for Z
> > > SUCCESS
> > > > Goal of W: W gives Z to Y
> > > > SUCCESS
> > > > > Goal of Y: Y gives X to W
> > > > > > SUCCESS RETURN-SUCCESS
> > > > > > FAILURE RETURN-FAILURE
> > > > > FAILURE RETURN-FAILURE
> > > > FAILURE RETURN-FAILURE
> > > FAILURE RETURN-FAILURE

ASK-FOR

> Pattern: Goal of W: W asks X for Y
> Filter: Find Z such that Z is the home of X
> Event-tree:
> > Goal of W: W PTRANS to Z
> > SUCCESS ADD W MTRANS W wants Y to X
> > > RETURN-SUCCESS
> > FAILURE RETURN-FAILURE

GIVE

> Pattern: Goal of W: W gives X to Y
> Filter: Either W has X
>   Or X is at Z which is the home of W
> Event-tree:
> > Goal of W: W has X
> > SUCCESS
> > > Goal of W: W ATRANS X to Y
> > > > SUCCESS RETURN-SUCCESS
> > > > FAILURE RETURN-FAILURE
> > > FAILURE RETURN-FAILURE

LOOK-FOR

> Pattern: Goal of W: W have X
> Filter: Find Y Such That Y is the home of W
> Event-tree:
> > Goal of W: W PTRANS to Y
> > SUCCESS
> > > Goal of W: W takes X
> > > > SUCCESS RETURN-SUCCESS
> > > > FAILURE RETURN-FAILURE
> > > FAILURE RETURN-FAILURE

FIG. 20.1. Sample story fragments (part 1 of 2 parts).

TAKE-SUCCEED
 Pattern: Goal of W: W takes X
 Filter: W is at X
 Event-tree:
  ADD W has X
  RETURN-SUCCESS
TAKE-FAIL
 Pattern: Goal of W: W takes X
 Filter: W is not at X
 Event-tree:
  RETURN-FAILURE
PTRANS
 Pattern: Goal of W: W PTRANS to X from Y
 Event-tree:
  DELETE W is at Y
  ADD W is at X
  RETURN-SUCCESS
ATRANS
 Pattern: Goal of W: W ATRANS X to Y
 Event-tree:
  DELETE W has Y
  ADD Y has X
  RETURN-SUCCESS
MTRANS
 Pattern: Goal of W: W MTRANS X to Y
 Event-tree:
  ADD Y knows X
  RETURN-SUCCESS

FIG. 20.1.   Sample story fragments (part 2 of 2 parts).

Items within braces ("{","}") are optional.
Items within double quotes (") are English descriptions.

<fragment> ::= <pattern> { <filter> } <body>
<pattern> ::= "a CD form with zero or more variables"
<filter> ::= <an arbitrary S-expression>
<body> ::= { <change-list> } <event-tree>
<change-list> ::= <empty-list> ::=
  | DELETE <pattern> <change-list>
  |ADD <pattern> <change-list>
<event-tree > ::= RETURN-SUCCESS
  | RETURN-FAILURE
  | <pattern> <success-branch> <failure-branch>
<success-branch> ::= SUCCESS <body>
<failure-branch> ::= FAILURE <body>
<empty list> ::=

FIG. 20.2.   Syntax of story fragments.

294

a new body, if the subgoal is achieved, plus a branch to a different body, if the subgoal is not achieved.

The pattern of a fragment is used to index the set of fragments in the fragment base. The generator takes a CD and finds all the fragments with a pattern that matches it. For example, there are two story fragments whose patterns match CD forms describing someone with the goal of having something: LOOK-FOR and TRADE.

The filter of a fragment checks the data base to see if it contains information necessary to the execution of the fragment. For example, if the data base says that Joe Bear wants some honey, but there is no other character who wants something, then the TRADE fragment will be filtered out. Filters extend the power of the pattern matcher, allowing us to say things like "find *another* character who wants something."

The body of a fragment implements the actual story telling knowledge, specifying what characters do when they have goals. The body first says how to update the data base. For example, the PTRANS story fragment deletes the moved object's previous location predication from the data base and adds the new location predication.

The second part of the body is the event-tree that specifies what happens next. The alternative sequences of events are organized into a tree, with branches to the proper branch to take if the story is to say that a character succeeded or failed in achieving a goal.

Note that there are two fragments for taking something. One, which is applied if the character is at the object, generates a piece of story that says that the character succeeded in getting the object. The other, which is applied if the character is not at the object, generates a piece of story saying that he didn't get it.

20.2 THE BASIC LOOPS

The story generator has two central looping functions: the goal monitor and the story fragment monitor. They call each other recursively. They are responsible for keeping track of what goal is being worked on and what plan is being tried.

20.2.1 The Goal Monitor

The goal monitor is given a CD form that says some character has a goal. The goal monitor takes those story fragments with a pattern that matches the CD form. The monitor passes each fragment to the story fragment monitor until one of them generates a sequence of events that achieves the goal. If none of the fragments lead to success, then the goal is marked as failed. If no fragment can be applied, then NIL is returned, to indicate that inconsistencies in the data base or the fragment base prevented the telling of a story.

The algorithm for the goal monitor is as follows:

> IF   the object of the goal is in the data base
> THEN   mark the goal as achieved and return it
> ELSE
> IF   the goal itself is in the data base
> THEN   return NIL
> ELSE   Add the goal to the data base.
>   Make a list of the story fragments with trigger patterns
>   matching the goal.
>   LOOP WHILE   there are fragments left in the list
>   DO   remove one and pass it to the fragment
>   monitor
>   UNTIL   the goal is marked as achieved.
> IF   the goal is marked either achieved or not achieved
> THEN   return the goal
> ELSE   return NIL

Some comments: Remember that NIL indicates story telling failure. Note, however, that fragment failures (where NIL is returned by the fragment monitor) are ignored by the goal monitor, as long as at least one fragment does not return NIL. Note also that there is a check to see if the goal is already in the data base (which would say that it is already being pursued). Without this check we might end up with a story like

TO GET IRVING BIRD TO TELL HIM WHERE SOME HONEY WAS, JOE BEAR WANTED TO GET SOME HONEY TO GIVE IRVING BIRD. TO GET SOME HONEY TO GIVE IRVING BIRD, JOE BEAR WANTED TO GET IRVING BIRD TO TELL HIM WHERE SOME HONEY WAS. TO GET IRVING BIRD TO TELL HIM WHERE SOME HONEY WAS, JOE BEAR WANTED TO GET SOME HONEY TO GIVE IRVING BIRD....

20.2.2 The Story Fragment Monitor

The story fragment monitor takes a story fragment and the CD form (the object of the goal) that was used to index that fragment. The heart of a fragment is a binary tree structure of the body. Each node of the tree is a goal. One branch of the tree is taken if the goal succeeds and the other is taken if the goal fails. The terminal elements of the fragment trees are primitive nodes indicating either success or failure for the fragment as a whole.

The algorithm for the story fragment monitor is

IF   the input goal does not match the pattern or the filter returns NIL

THEN   return NIL

ELSE   get the event tree

        LOOP UNTIL the event tree is primitive

             DO   pass its goal to the goal monitor

                 IF   its goal is marked achieved.

                 THEN   set the event-tree to its success-branch

                 ELSE

                 IF   its goal is marked not achieved

                 THEN   set the event-tree to its failure-branch

                 ELSE   undo the goals done so far and return NIL

        IF   the event-tree is RETURN-SUCCESS

        THEN   mark the input goal as achieved

        ELSE

        IF   the event-tree is RETURN-FAILURE

        THEN   mark the input goal as not achieved

        return the input goal.

The above leaves out two important steps. First, before checking the event-tree, the fragment monitor has to check to see if the body has a change-list. If so, the monitor should first change the data base as specified.

Second, the fragment monitor has to keep track of variable bindings. The pattern of a fragment is generally a CD form wtih variables. For example, the TRADE fragment has the pattern "Goal of W: W has X," where both W and X are variables. When a fragment with this pattern is applied to the data base item "Goal of Joe: Joe has honey," then clearly W should be bound to Joe and X should be bound to honey.

Furthermore, the filter expression may bind some more variables. For example, the TRADE fragment has the filter "Find Goal of Y: Y have Z where Y is not equal W and Z is not equal to X." If this filter succeeds, then Y and Z will be bound to some particular values.

These variables bindings are used during the execution of the story fragment body in two places. First, they are used in the change-lists. A change-list contains forms to be added or removed from the data base. These forms contain fragment variables that need to be instantiated. For example, the TAKE-SUCCEED fragment change-list says "ADD W has X." The W and X must be replaced with the appropriate bindings before we add the predication about possession to the data base.

Second, variable bindings are used when executing the subgoals. For example, the first event in the TRADE fragment is "Goal of W: W asks Y for

X." Before this can be passed to the goal monitor, the variables W, X, and Y need to be replaced with their vlaues.

20.3 STORY FAILURE

The two loops given above account for the flow of control in TALE-SPIN. Starting with some top-level goal, the goal monitor finds story fragments that split the top goal into subgoals. These goals are handed to the goal monitor. Eventually primitive story fragments are reached that only change the data base and return success or failure. Assuming that story telling failure does not occur, the eventual result is a tree of goals and subgoals that can then be fed into an English generator to tell a story.

Note that story fragments are not quite the same as plans for achieving a goal. One would not expect a plan to have an explicit recipe for how to fail! But a good story telling data base would have many fragments about goal failure, since such failures make for interesting stories. Our data base does not, but in doing the exercise, you should add some.

Goal failure however is very different from story telling failure, which is indicated whenever either the goal monitor or the fragment monitor returns NIL. Story telling failure occurs when there is no consistent way to tell a story, given the data base and the set of fragments available.

Story telling failure can arise for several reasons:

1. A fragment asks for a goal to be set up that is already being pursued. Goals are put in the data base when they are initially begun and removed as soon as they are accomplished. Therefore finding a goal already in the data base means that we have a case of the same goal appearing as a subgoal of itself.
2. No fragments are found to fit the goal. This is because there are no fragments that have patterns that match the goal and filters that are true when evaluated in the current context for that goal. This means that we have a goal and no sequence of events that can be applied to that goal.
3. If any goal node in a story fragment returns NIL, then there is a story teller failure, because we have no way getting from that node to the next node in the fragment.
4. If every fragment node tried for a goal returns NIL, then there is a story teller failure, because every fragment had some subgoal that could not be told.

If we did not trap the first kind of failure, then we obtain stories like "In order to find Irving Bird, Joe Bear decided to ask Irving Bird where Irving Bird was. In order to ask Irving Bird, Joe Bear had to find Irving Bird. In order to find Irvind Bird, Joe Bear decided to ask Irving Bird where Irving Bird was...."

If we did not trap the second kind of failure, then we would obtain stories like "Joe Bear needed some honey. He decided to ask Joe Bear for some honey. Joe Bear didn't have any honey so he decided to trick Joe Bear...." The purpose of the patterns and filters is to avoid such problems.

The last two kinds of story failures arise from the simple observation that you can't tell a story if you can't tell how the subgoals are accomplished.

20.4 BACKTRACKING

When story telling failure occurs, TALE-SPIN has to backtrack (i.e., it has to undo the effects of those goals and fragments that have been made obsolete by the failure). Undoing goals and fragments is a recursive process:

1. To undo a goal, undo all the fragments that were applied to the goal, in reverse order; that is, first undo the fragment that led to the achievement of the goal, if any; then undo the fragment done previously that did not lead to success; then undo the fragment before that; and so on.

2. To undo a story fragment, go back up in the event-tree, undoing the change-list actions and the subgoal.

A change-list must be undone in reverse order; that is, if a change-list deleted some fact and then added another, then the added fact must be deleted before the deleted fact can be returned. Obviously this means that all additions and deletions to the data base must be remembered in case backtracking becomes necessary.

20.5 YOUR PROJECT

The exercises are concerned with implementing a TALE-SPIN event generator. We have not said anything about the English generation aspect of TALE-SPIN, primarily because, given a good meaning representation, it is easy to construct simple sentences.

You should try to apply as many of the techniques described in this book as possible. In particular we suggest the following:

1. Use your record package to define the data structures for the story fragments.

2. Use discrimination trees to store and fetch the fragments in the fragment base and the facts in the data base.
3. Use the flow of control functions to structure your implementation of the goal and story fragment monitors.
4. Use the chronological techniques for backtracking and debugging.
5. Use the data dependency techniques for managing the addition and removal of inferences.
6. Compile your TALE-SPIN when it seems debugged.

If your data structures for representing the goal and fragment interrelationships are reasonable, you should find that it is not hard to add backtracking to your program. An easy way to test it is to take a story that your program can generate and then change the initial data base so that a story teller failure will occur at the very end of the last fragment used. If your backtracking algorithm works, then no story should result and the data base should be unchanged.

Exercise 20.1 Define TALE-SPIN so that it can handle story fragments like those in Fig. 20.1.

Exercise 20.2 None of the fragments do anything when a character does not achieve a goal except return failure. Add some alternatives. For example, in GIVE, if a character can't give another an object, have him "trick" the other by giving a fake object or by promising to give the object.

Exercise 20.3 Add backtracking to TALE-SPIN.

Exercise 20.4 Make TALE—SPIN capable of generating a story of the following level of complexity: "Joe Bear was hungry. He looked in his cave for some honey but there was none there. He went to Irving Bird and asked him for some honey. Irving said he would give Joe some honey if Joe would give Irving a worm. Joe went to his cave and got a worm and brought it to Irving. Irving gave Joe some honey."

Exercise 20.5 Add a simple English generator to TALE-SPIN, using simple fragments such as "Goal of X . . . " becomes "X wanted . . . " and "X PTRANS X . . ." becomes 'X went . . ."

Appendix:
LISP Functions and
Reserved Words

This is a very brief run-through of the more important LISP functions and reserved words. Our notation uses the following conventions:

1. Any word in lowercase italics stands for an arbitrary LISP expression that can be substituted where the word appears.
2. An "atom," "number," "function," "list," or "a-list" indicates that the argument should be an atom, number, function name (or LAMBDA body), list, or a-list, respectively. An "exp" indicates that any S-expression can be used. Numbers may be concatenated to distinguish arguments of the same type (e.g., "atom1").
3. Any form or sequence of forms that begins and ends with a hyphen (-) stands for zero or more occurrences of that form or sequence, separated by spaces. An "s" is appended to the form type (e.g., "-atoms-").
4. Anything else is exactly what should appear in the LISP expression.
5. Arguments to reserved words are surrounded by double quotes (") to indicate that they may or may not be evaluated.
6. Vertical bars ("|") are used to separate alternatives (e.g., "A | B | C" means either A, B, or C is possible).

(ABS *number*)
    ABS returns the absolute value of *number*.
(ADD1 *number*)
    ADD1 returns *number* plus 1.

(ADDPROP *atom1 exp atom2*)

 This is the same as

 (PUTPROP *atom1*

 (CONS *exp* (GET *atom1 atom2*))

 atom2)

 except that nothing is changed if *exp* is already an element of (GET *atom1 atom2*).

(AND -*"exps"*-)

 AND evaluates each argument, from left to right, until one returns NIL (if any). AND returns the value of the last expression evaluated.

(APPEND -*lists*-)

 APPEND returns the list formed by joining the lists together. For example,

 (APPEND '(A B) '(C D) '(E F)) ⇒ (A B C D E F)

(APPLY *function list*)

 APPLY calls *function* with the arguments given in *list*. For example,

 (APPLY 'CONS '(A B)) ⇒ (A . B)

(ASSOC *exp a-list*)

 ASSOC returns the first pair in *a-list* whose first element is EQ to *exp* or NIL if there isn't one.

(ASSOC# *exp a-list*)

 ASSOC# is like ASSOC but EQUAL is used instead of EQ.

(ATOM *exp*)

 ATOM returns T if *exp* is a symbol or a number; otherwise it returns NIL.

(CAR *list*)

 CAR returns the first element of *list*.

(CDR *list*)

 CDR returns *list* minus its first element.

(CADR *list*)...(CDDDDR *list*)

 (CADR *list*) is equivalent to (CAR (CDR *list*)) (i.e., it returns the second element of *list*). (CDDDDR *list*) is equivalent to (CDR (CDR (CDR (CDR *list*)))), etc. Our LISP recognizes this short notation for all combinations of As and Ds, up to four long.

(CHARCT)

 CHARCT returns how many more characters can be printed on the current line.

(COND -(*test -exps-*)-)

 COND is the branching function. The tests are evaluated in order until one returns a non-NIL value. If such a one is found, then the expressions following that test are evaluated and the value of the last is returned. If no test returns a non-NIL value, then NIL is returned.

(CONS *exp list*)

 CONS returns a list whose CAR is *exp* and whose CDR is *list*.

(CONSP *exp*)

    CONSP returns T if *exp* is a list; otherwise, NIL.

(CURRCOL)

    CURRCOL returns the number of the column where the next output character will go.

(DE *"function"* (-*"atom"*-) -*"exps"*-)

(DE *"function"* *"atom"* -*"exps"*-)

    The first form of DE defines *function* to be an EXPR with the atoms as local variables and the expressions as the function body. The second form defines *function* to be a LEXPR with the local variable *atom*.

(DECLARE -*"declarations"*-)

    where a declaration is one of the following:

(SPECIAL -*"atoms"*-) (UNSPECIAL -*"atoms"*-) (*FEXPR -*"atoms"*-) (*LEXPR -*"atoms"*-)

    DECLARE tells the compiler that the atoms listed are special variables, not special variables, FEXPRs, or LEXPRs.

(DEFPROP *"atom1"* *"exp"* *"atom2"*)

    The same as (PUTPROP *'atom1* *'exp* *'atom2*) except that *atom1* is returned.

(DF *"function"* (*"atom"*) -*"exps"*-)

    DF defines *function* to be a FEXPR with *atom* as the local variable and the expressions as the function body.

(DIFFERENCE -*numbers*-)

    DIFFERENCE returns the first number minus the sum of the rest.

(DM *"function"* (*"atom"*) -*"exps"*-)

    DM defines *function* to be a MACRO with *atom* as the local variable and the expressions as the function body.

(DRM *"character"* *"function"*)

    DRM *character* to be a read macro that calls *function* when the character is read. *Function* should be a function that takes no arguments. The value returned by *function* is returned to READ in place of the character.

(DSKIN -*"atom"*-)

    DSKIN reads and evaluates all the S-expressions on each of the files named by the atoms.

(DSKOUT *"atom"* -*"exps"*-)

    DSKOUT evaluates all the expressions, and any printing they do is placed on the file *atom*, overwriting whatever was there before.

(DSM *"character"* *"function"*)

    DSM *character* to be a read macro that calls *function* when the character is read. *Function* should be a function that takes no arguments. The value returned by *function* is appended into the expression READ is building in place of the character.

(EQ *exp1 exp2*)

EQ returns T if *exp1* and *exp2* are the same word in memory; otherwise, NIL.

(EQUAL *exp1 exp2*)

EQUAL returns T if *exp1* has the same form as *exp2*; otherwise, NIL.

(ERROR *exp*)

ERROR prints *exp* (without the double quotes if it is a string) and then causes a LISP error. Depending on the LISP being used, this might mean that control returns to the top-level READ-EVAL-PRINT loop of the interpreter or that an error handling package is called.

(ERRSET *"exp"*T)

ERRSET evaluates *exp*. If a LISP error occurs during this evaluation, then ERRSET returns an atomic value, usually NIL. If no error occurs, then ERRSET returns a list of the result of evaluating *exp*.

(EVAL *exp*)

EVAL evaluates *exp* and returns the result. For example.

(EVAL '(PLUS 1 2)) ⇒ 3

Notice that two evaluations occur—first *exp* is evaluated because it is an argument to a function and then the value of *exp* is explicitly evaluated by EVAL.

(EVERY *function list*)

EVERY applies *function* to successive elements of *list*, returning NIL, as soon as one of these applications returns NIL. If all applications return a non-NIL value, then T is returned.

(EXPANDMACROS *exp*)

EXPANDMACROS expands all the macro calls in *exp* (see Chapter 3).

(EXPLODE *list*)

EXPLODE returns a list of the characters that would be needed to print *list*. For example,

(EXPLODE 'ATOM) ⇒ (A T O M)

(FILEIN *function atom*)

FILEIN applies *function* to every expression in the file *atom* (see Chapter 6).

(FILEOUT *atom -list-*)

FILEOUT evaluates the elements of *list* and sends all output to the file *atom* (see Chapter 6).

(FOR -(*"variable"* IN *list*)-
        (WHEN *"exp1"*)
        (DO| SAVE| FILTER| SPLICE *"exp2"*))

FOR is used to implement iterative loops (see Chapter 5).

(GET *atom 1 atom2*)

GET returns the value attached to *atom1* under the property name *atom2*. If none is found, NIL is returned. Note that NIL is also returned if NIL is the value stored.

(GETL *atom list*)

    GETL finds the first property in the property list of *atom* that is a member of *list* and returns the property list from that point on. If none is found, NIL is returned.

(GO *"atom"*)

    This is legal only inside a PROG. GO causes the evaluation of the PROG to jump to the step following the label *atom*. GO cannot be used to jump into or out of a PROG. (*Note:* If GO is given a nonatomic argument, it is evaluated repeatedly until an atomic value is returned.

(GREATERP *number1 number2*)

    GREATERP returns T if *number1* is greater than *number2;* otherwise it returns NIL.

(INC *atom exp*)

    INC switches input to the channel *atom*. If *exp* is not NIL, then the previous channel is closed.

(INCHAN *atom*)

    INCHAN opens the file *atom* for input, returning the name generated for the channel (see Chapter 6).

(INPUT *"atom1" "atom2"*)

    INPUT opens the file *atom2* for input, with the channel *atom1*. The channel NIL is reserved for the user's terminal.

(LAST *list*)

    LAST returns the last cell (i.e., the last nonatomic CDR) of *list*.

(LENGTH *list*)

    LENGTH returns the number of top-level elements in *list*. For example, (LENGTH '((A B) (C D))) $\Rightarrow$ 2

(LESSP *number1 number2*)

    LESSP returns T if *number1* is less than *number2*; otherwise, NIL.

(LET (-*"atom exp"*-) -*"exps"*-)

    LET evaluates the expressions with local bindings (see Chapter 3).

(LINELENGTH *exp*)

    LINELENGTH sets the length of the output lines. If *exp* is NIL, then LINELENGTH returns the current line length.

(LINES -*number*-)

    LINES prints *number* blank lines.

(LIST -*exps*-)

    LIST returns a list of the expressions.

(LOOP (INITIAL -*"var" "exp"*-)

           (WHILE *"exp"*)

           (DO -*"exps"*-)

           (NEXT -*"var" "exp"*-)

           (UNTIL *"exp"*)

           (RESULT *"exp"*))

    LOOP is used to implement iterative loops (see Chapter 5).

(MAPC *function -lists-*)

MAPC applies *function* to successive elements of *list* and returns NIL. For example, to print every element in the list L, we would write

(MAPC 'PRINT L)

(MAPCAN *function -lists-*)

MAPCAN applies *function* to successive elements of *list* and returns a new list obtained by NCONC'ing the results together.

(MAPCAR *function -lists-*)

MAPCAR applies *function* to successive elements of *list* and returns a list of the results.

(MEMBER *exp list*)

MEMBER returns the tail of *list* starting with the first element EQUAL to *exp*.

(MEMQ *exp list*).

MEMQ is like MEMBER, but uses EQ instead of EQUAL.

(MINUS *number*)

MINUS returns the negative of *number*.

(NCONC *-lists-*)

NCONC is like APPEND, but it actually RPLACD's the last CDR of each list but the last to make the appended list. This makes it more efficient but also means that the effects are global and lasting. Use with care.

(NCONC1 *list exp*)

This is the same as (NCONC *list* (LIST *exp*)). The effects are global and lasting. Use with care.

(NEWSYM *atom*)

Makes a new atomic symbol by adding a number to the end of *atom* (see Chapter 6).

(NOT *exp*)

NOT returns T if *exp* is NIL; otherwise it returns NIL. This is just the function NULL with a different name.

(NULL *exp*)

This is the same as (EQUAL *exp* NIL).

(NUMBERP *exp*)

NUMBERP returns T if *exp* is a number; otherwise, NIL.

(OR *-"exps"-*)

OR evaluates each argument, from left to right, until one returns a non-NIL value (if any). OR returns the value of the last expression evaluated.

(OUTC *atom exp*)

OUTC switches output to the channel *atom*. If *exp* is not NIL, then the previous channel is closed.

(OUTCHAN *atom*)

OUTCHAN opens the file *atom* for output, returning the name generated for the channel (see Chapter 6).

(OUTPUT *"atom1" "atom2"*)

OUTPUT opens the file *atom2* for output, with the channel *atom1*. The channel NIL is reserved for the user's terminal.

(PEEKC)

This returns the ASCII code for the next character in the input buffer. It does not cause the character to be read, however, which means that the character will still be seen by the next READ.

(PLUS -*numbers*-)

PLUS returns the sum of the numbers.

(POP *atom*)

POP sets *atom* to the CDR of itself and returns the old CAR (see Chapter 3).

(PP -*"atoms"*-)

PP prints in indented format the function definition and/or value (if any) attached to each atom.

(PRELIST *list number*)

PRELIST returns the a new list consisting of the first *number* elements of *list*. If *list* has less than *number* elements, then *list* is returned.

(PRIN1 *exp*)

PRIN1 prints and returns *exp*.

(PRINC *exp*)

Like PRIN1 except that string quotes are omitted and special characters are not preceded by a slash (/).

(PRINT *exp*)

PRINT starts a new line, PRIN1s and returns *exp*.

(PRINTSTR *exp*)

Like PRINT but using PRINC.

(PROG (-*"atoms"*-) -*"exps"*-)

PROG makes the atoms local variables and binds them to NIL and then evaluates each expression from left to right (unless GO or RETURN is executed). Atomic expressions are labels for the expressions following and are not evaluated. NIL is returned unless a RETURN is evaluated.

(PROG1 -*exps*-)

PROG1 takes at most five expressions and returns the value of the first one.

(PROG2 -*exps*-)

PROG2 takes at most five expressions and returns the value of the second one.

(PROGN *-exps-*)

> PROGN takes any number of expressions and returns the value of the last one.

(PUSH *exp atom*)

> PUSH sets *atom* to (CONS *exp atom*) and returns *exp* (see Chapter 3).

(PUTPROP *atom1 exp atom2*)

> PUTPROP attaches *exp* to *atom1* under the property name *atom2* and returns *exp*.

(QUOTE *"exp"*)

> QUOTE returns *exp* unevaluated. Can also be written '*exp*.

(QUOTIENT *number1 number2*)

> QUOTIENT returns the integer part of *number1* divided by *number2*.

(READ)

> READ reads and returns one S-expression.

(READCH)

> READCH reads and returns one character.

(READLIST *list*)

> *List* should be a list of characters. READLIST returns the S-expression formed by putting these characters together. It is the opposite of EXPLODE. For example,
> (READLIST '(A T O M)) ⇒ ATOM

(RECORD-TYPE *"atom1" "atom2" "exp"*)

> *Atom2* is optional. RECORD-TYPE is used to construct data types (see Chapter 4).

(REMAINDER *number1 number2*)

> REMAINDER returns the integer remainder after dividing *number1* by *number2*.

(REMPROP *atom1 atom2*)

> REMPROP removes the property name *atom2* and any value stored under it from *atom1*. REMPROP returns T if there was such a property; otherwise, NIL.

(RETURN *exp*)

> This is legal only inside a PROG. RETURN causes the evaluation of the PROG to stop and the PROG returns with the value of *exp*.

(REVERSE *list*)

> REVERSE returns a list with the elements of *list* in reverse order. For example,
> (REVERSE '((A B) (C D))) ⇒ ((C D) (A B))

(RPLACA *exp1 exp2*)

> RPLACA makes *exp2* the CAR of *exp1* and returns *exp1*. It actually changes the first CONS cell of *exp1*, which makes its effect global and lasting. Use with care.

(RPLACD *exp1 exp2*)

RPLACD makes *exp2* the CDR of *exp1* and returns *exp1*. It actually changes the first CONS cell of *exp1*, which makes its effect global and lasting. Use with care.

(SELECTQ *"exp"* -*("test"* -*"exps"*-*)* *"else-exp"*)

SELECTQ evaluates *exp* and then looks at each *test*. If a test is an atom and *exp2* is equal to it, or if a test is a list and *exp* is a member of it, then the remaining expressions in the clause containing the test are evaluated, and the value of the last is returned. If no test can be found for *exp*, then *else-exp* is evaluated and returned.

(SET *atom exp*)

SET makes *exp* the value of *atom. Exp* is returned. For example,

    (SET (CAR '(A B C)) (PLUS 2 2)) ⇒ 4

binds A to 4.

(SETQ *"atom" "exp"*)

This is the same as (SET *'atom exp*).

(SOME *function list*)

SOME applies *function* to successive elements of *list,* until one of them returns a non-NIL value. If this happens, then SOME returns the elements of *list* from that point on. Otherwise it returns NIL. For example,

    (SOME '(LAMBDA (X) (GREATERP X 0)) '(-1 1 0 2))
      ⇒ (1 0 2).

(SPACES -*number*-)

SPACES prints *number* blank spaces.

(SPRINT *exp number*)

SPRINT pretty-prints *exp*, with the left margin set at *number.*

(STRINGP *exp*)

STRINGP returns T if *exp* is a string; otherwise, NIL.

(SUB1 *number*)

SUB1 returns *number* minus 1.

(SUBSET *function list*)

SUBSET applies *function* to successive elements of *list* and returns a list of the elements that returned non-NIL values. For example,

    (SUBSET '(LAMBDA (X) (GREATERP X 0)) '(-1 1 0 2))
      ⇒ (1 2)

(SUBST *exp1 exp2 exp3*)

SUBST returns a copy of *exp3* formed by substituting *exp1* for all EQUAL occurrences of *exp2* in *exp3*. For example,

    (SUBST 'Y 'X '(DE FN (X) (CAR X))) ⇒ (DE FN (Y) (CAR Y))

(SUFLIST *list number*)

SUFLIST takes *number* CDRs of *list*. If *list* has less than *number* + 1 elements, SUFLIST returns NIL.

(TAB *-number-*)

TAB outputs enough spaces so that the next character printed will be in column *number*.

(TERPRI *exp*)

TERPRI starts a new line and returns *exp*.

(TIMES *-numbers-*)

TIMES returns the product of the numbers.

(TYI)

TYI reads one character and returns the ASCII code for it.

(TYO *number*)

TYO writes the character with the ASCII code *number*.

(ZEROP *exp*)

This is the same as (EQUAL *exp* 0).

(:= *"exp1" exp2*)

:= uses *exp1* to store *exp2* (see Chapter 9).

Bibliography

Barstow, D. R. *Knowledge-Based Program Construction.* New York: American Elsevier, 1979.

Bobrow, D. G., & Fraser, J. B. An augmented state transition network analysis procedure. *Proc. Int. Joint Conf. on AI,* 1969, *1,* 557.

Bobrow, D. G., & Raphael, B. New programming languages for artificial intelligence. *Computing Surveys,* 1974, *6,* No. 3, 155.

Bobrow, D. G., & Winograd, T. An overview of KRL, a knowledge representation language. *Cognitive Science,* 1977, *1,* No. 1, 3.

Boyer, R. S., & Moore, J. S. The sharing of structure in theorem-proving programs. In B. Meltzer, & D. Michie, (Eds.), *Machine Intelligence* (Vol. 7). New York: John Wiley, 1972.

Brown, D. J. *A computational model of understanding.* Paper presented at AISB/GI Conf. on AI, Hamburg, 1978.

Chang, C., & Lee, R. C. *Symbolic Logic and Mechanical Theorem Proving.* New York: Academic Press, 1973.

Charniak, E. *Toward a model of children's story comprehension.* Cambridge: MIT AI Laboratory Technical Report 266, 1972.

Charniak, E. A framed PAINTING: The representation of a common sense knowledge fragment. *Cognitive Science,* 1977, *1,* No. 4, 355.

Cullingford, R. *Script application: Computer understanding of newspaper stories.* New Haven: Yale Computer Science Research Report 116, 1978.

Dahl, O.-J., Dijkstra, E. W., & Hoare, C. A. R. *Structured Programming.* New York: Academic Press, 1972.

Davis, R. Applications of meta level knowledge to the construction, maintenance, and use of large knowledge bases. Stanford: AI Laboratory Memo 283, 1976.

Davis, R., & King, J. *An overview of production systems.* Stanford: AI Laboratory Memo 271, 1975.

de Kleer, J., Doyle, J., Steele, G. L., & Sussman, G. J. AMORD: Explicit control of reasoning. *Proc. Symp. on AI and Programming Languages,* Rochester (*SIGART Newsletter* No. 64), 1977, 116. (a)

de Kleer, J., Doyle, J., Steele, G. L., & Sussman, G. J. *AMORD, a deductive procedure system.* Cambridge: MIT AI Laboratory Working Paper 151, 1977. (b) de Kleer, J., Doyle, J., Steele, G. L., & Sussman, G. J. AMORD, a deductive procedure system. Cambridge: MIT AI Laboratory Memo 435, 1978.

Dijkstra, E. W. The humble programmer. *Comm. ACM,* 1972, *15,* No. 10, 859.

Doyle, J. *Truth maintenance systems for problem solving.* Cambridge: MIT AI Laboratory Technical Report 419, 1978.

Ernst, G., & Newell, A. *GPS: A Case Study in Generality and Problem Solving.* New York: Academic Press, 1969.

Fikes, R., & Nilsson, N. J. *STRIPS: A new approach to the application of theorem proving to problem solving.* Proc. Int. Joint Conf. on AI, 1971, *2,* 608.

Goldman, N. Conceptual generation. In R. C. Schank (Ed.), *Conceptual information processing.* New York: American Elsevier, 1975.

Griswold, R., Poage, J. F., & Polonsky, I. P. *The SNOBOL4 Programming Language.* Englewood Cliffs, N.J.: Prentice-Hall, 1971.

Hart, P., Nilsson, N. J., & Raphael, B. A formal basis for the heuristic determination of minimum cost paths. *IEEE Trans. Sys. Sci. Cybernetics SSC-4,* 1968, No. 2, 100.

Hayes-Roth, F. The role of partial and best matches in knowledge systems. In D. A. Waterman & F. Hayes-Roth (Eds.) *Pattern-directed inference systems.* New York: Academic Press, 1978.

Hewitt, C. Procedural embedding of knowledge in PLANNER. *Proc. Int. Joint Conf. on AI,* 1971, *2,* 167.

Knuth, D. E. *The art of computer programming* (Vol. 1): *Fundamental Algorithms* (2nd ed.). Reading, Mass.: Addison-Wesley, 1973. (a)

Knuth, D. E. *The art of computer programming* (Vol. 3): *Sorting and Searching.* Reading, Mass.: Addison-Wesley, 1973. (b)

Lesser, V. R., & Erman, L. D. A retrospective view of the Hearsay-II architecture. *Proc. Int. Joint Conf. on AI,* 1977, *5,* 790.

Marcus, M. *Wait-and-see strategies for parsing natural language.* Cambridge: MIT AI Laboratory Working Paper 75, 1974.

Marcus, M. *A theory of syntactic recognition for natural language.* Cambridge: MIT Press, 1979.

McDermott, D. V. *Assimilation of new information by a natural language-understanding system.* Cambridge: MIT AI Laboratory Technical Report 291, 1974.

McDermott, D. V. *Flexibility and efficiency in a computer program for designing circuits.* Cambridge: MIT AI Laboratory Technical Report 402, 1977. (a)

McDermott, D. V. *DUCK reference manual.* Unpublished manuscript, 1977. (b)

McDermott, D. V. Vocabularies for problem-solver state descriptions. *Proc. Int. Joint Conf. on AI,* 1977, *5,* 229. (c)

McDermott, D. V. Planning and acting. *Cognitive Science,* 1978, *2,* No. 2, 71.

McDermott, D. V., & Doyle, J. *Non-monotonic logic I.* Cambridge: MIT AI Laboratory Memo 486, 1978.

McDermott, D. V., & Sussman, G. J. *The Conniver reference manual.* Cambridge: MIT AI Laboratory Memo 259a, 1973.

McDermott, J., & Forgy, C. Production system conflict resolution strategies. In D. A. Waterman & F. Hayes-Roth (Eds.), *Pattern-directed inference systems.* New York: Academic Press, 1978.

Meehan, J. R. *The metanovel: Writing stories by computer.* New Haven: Yale Computer Science Research Report 74, 1976.

Meehan, J. R. *The New UCI Lisp Manual.* Irvine, CA: Dept. of Information and Computer Science, University of California, Irvine, 1978.

Minsky, M. A framework for representing knowledge. In P. H. Winston (Ed.), *The psychology of computer vision.* New York: McGraw-Hill, 1975.

Moore, R. C. *Reasoning from incomplete knowledge in a procedural deductive system.* Cambridge: MIT AI Laboratory Technical Report 347, 1975.

Moran, T. P. The symbolic nature of visual imagery. *Proc. Int. Joint Conf. on AI,* 1973, *3,* 472.

Newell, A. Production systems: models of control structures. In W. C. Chase (Ed.), *Visual Information Processing.* New York: Academic Press, 1973. (a)

Newell, A. Artificial intelligence and the concept of mind. In R. C. Schank & K. M. Colby (Eds.), *Computer Models of Thought and Language,* San Francisco: Freeman, 1973. (b)

Newell, A., & Simon, H. A. *Human problem solving.* Englewood Cliffs, N.J.: Prentice-Hall, 1972.

Newell, A., Tonge, F. M., Feigenbaum, E. A., Green, B. F., Kelley, H. A., & Mealy, G. *Information processing language V manual* (2nd ed.). Englewood Cliffs, N. J.: 1964.

Nilsson, N. *Problem-solving methods in artificial intelligence.* New York: McGraw-Hill, 1971.

Patterson, M. S., & Wegman, M. N. Linear unification. *Proc. Symp. on Theory of Complexity,* 1976, *8,* Hershey, Pa., 181.

Rieger, C. Spontaneous computation in cognitive models. *Cognitive Science,* 1977, *1,* No. 3, 315.

Riesbeck, C. K. *Computational understanding: Analysis of sentences and context.* Stanford: AI Laboratory Memo 238, 1974.

Roberts, R. B., & Goldstein, I. P. *The FRL manual.* Cambridge: MIT AI Laboratory Memo 409, 1977.

Robinson, J. A. A machine-oriented logic based on the resolution principle. *J. ACM,* 1965, *12,* No. 1, 23.

Rulifson, J. F. *QA4 programming concepts.* Menlo Park, Calif.: SRI AI Technical Note 60, 1971.

Rulifson, J. F., Derksen, J. A., & Waldinger, R. J. *QA4: A procedural calculus for intuitive reasoning.* Menlo Park, Calif.: SRI AI Technical Note 73, 1972.

Rychener, M. D., & Newell, A. An instructable production system: basic design issues. In D. A. Waterman & F. Hayes–Roth (Eds.), *Pattern-directed inference systems.* New York: Academic Press, 1978.

Sacerdoti, E. D. *A structure for plans and behavior.* New York: American Elsevier, 1977.

Sandewall, E. *Ideas about management of LISP data bases.* Cambridge: MIT AI Laboratory Memo 332, 1975.

Schank, R. C. *Conceptual information processing.* New York: American Elsevier, 1975.

Schank, R. C., & Abelson, R. P. *Scripts, plans, goals and understanding.* Hillsdale, N.J.: Lawrence Erlbaum Associates, 1977.

Shortliffe, E. H. *Computer-based medical consultations: MYCIN.* New York: American Elsevier, 1976.

Smith, D. C., & Enea, H. J. Backtracking in MLISP2. *Proc. Int. Joint Conf. on AI,* 1973, *3,* 677.

Stallman, R., & Sussman, G. J. Forward reasoning and dependency-directed backtracking in a system for computer-aided circuit analysis. *Artificial Intelligence,* 1977, *9,* No. 2, 135.

Steele, G. L. RABBIT: A compiler for SCHEME (a study in compiler optimization). Cambridge: MIT AI Laboratory Technical Report 474, 1978.

Sussman, G. J., & McDermott, D. V. From PLANNER to Conniver—A genetic approach. *Proc. FJCC,* 1972, *41,* 1171.

Sussman, G. J., & Steele, G. L. *SCHEME: An interpreter for extended lambda calculus.* Cambridge: MIT AI Laboratory Memo 349, 1975.

Sussman, G. J., & Steele, G. L. The revised report on SCHEME. Cambridge: MIT AI Laboratory Memo 452, 1978.

Sussman, G. J., Winograd T., & Charniak, E. *MICRO-PLANNER reference manual.* Cambridge: MIT AI Laboratory Memo 203a, 1971.

Teitelman, W. *Interlisp reference manual.* Palo Alto, Calif.: Xerox Corporation, 1975.

Thorne, J., Bratley, P., & Dewar, H. The syntactic analysis of English by machine. In D. Michie (Ed.), *Machine Intelligence* (Vol. 3). New York: American Elsevier, 1968.

Waterman, D. A., & Hayes-Roth, F. (Eds.). *Pattern-directed inference systems*. New York: Academic Press, 1978.

Winograd, T. *Understanding natural language*. New York: Academic Press, 1972.

Winston, P. H. Learning structural descriptions from examples. In P. H. Winston (Ed.), *The psychology of computer vision*. New York: McGraw-Hill, 1975.

Winston, P. H. (Ed.). *The psychology of computer vision*. New York: McGraw-Hill, 1975.

Woods, W. A. An experimental parsing system for transition network grammars. In R. Rustin (Ed.), *Natural language processing*. New York: Algorithmics Press, 1972.

Young, R. M. Mixtures of strategies in structurally adaptive production systems: Examples from seriation and subtraction. *Proc. Workshop on Pattern-Directed Inference Systems. SIGART Newsletter,* 1977, No. 63, 65.

Author Index

Numbers in italic indicate the page on which the complete reference appears.

Subject Index

317